The Far Western Frontier

The Far Western Frontier

Advisory Editor

RAY A. BILLINGTON

Senior Research Associate
at the Henry E. Huntington Library
and Art Gallery

Colorado

ITS

Gold and Silver Mines

Farms and Stock Ranges,

AND

Health and Pleasure Resorts

BY FRANK FOSSETT

ARNO PRESS

A NEW YORK TIMES COMPANY

New York • 1973

Reprint Edition 1973 by Arno Press Inc.

Reprinted from a copy in The State
Historical Society of Wisconsin Library

The Far Western Frontier
ISBN for complete set: 0-405-04955-2
See last pages of this volume for titles.

Manufactured in the United States of America

Publisher's Note: This volume was reprinted
from the best available copy.

Library of Congress Cataloging in Publication Data

Fossett, Frank.
    Colorado; its gold and silver mines, farms and stock
ranges, and health and pleasure resorts.

    (The Far Western frontier)
    Reprint of the 1879 ed.
    1. Colorado. 2. Mines and mineral resources--
Colorado. I. Series.
F776.F76 1973   917.88   72-9444
ISBN 0-405-04973-0

Colorado

LEADVILLE.

Colorado

ITS

GOLD AND SILVER MINES,

FARMS AND STOCK RANGES,

AND

HEALTH AND PLEASURE RESORTS.

Tourist's Guide

TO THE

ROCKY MOUNTAINS.

BY FRANK FOSSETT.

New York:
C. G. CRAWFORD, PRINTER AND STATIONER, 49 and 51 PARK PLACE.
1879.

PREFACE.

THIS volume, as its name implies. is devoted to Colorado. Its contents are descriptive, statistical, and historical, and embrace a detailed account of the State's resources, productions, and progress. For general convenience it has been divided into four parts. The first of these will answer for a traveler's guide, and relates to routes of travel, health and pleasure resorts, scenic attractions, and climate. The second part is historical, and the third contains much information concerning the State at large and the farming and live stock interests. Part fourth is devoted to the mines. As mining is Colorado's main industry and source of wealth, it receives the space and attention its merits deserve. The statistics in this department are of the most elaborate character, and are as accurate as time, labor, and research could make them. The narrative of gold and silver mining possesses enough of romance and adventure to interest the general reader, and the descriptions of mines, and of mining and milling, together with statements of requisite outlays from beginning to end, will prove especially serviceable to investors or capitalists. The author has endeavored to furnish a compendium of useful and general information concerning Colorado, and trusts this book will meet the present requirements of the public in that respect.

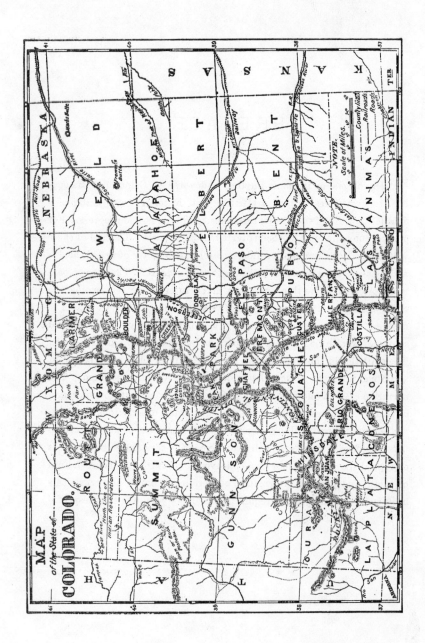

CONTENTS.

————◆————

PART FIRST.

PART SECOND.

PART THIRD.

PART FOURTH.

PART FIRST.

CHAPTER I.

THE GENERAL RECORD OF THE CENTENNIAL STATE—HER REMARK-
ABLE PROGRESS AND PROSPERITY—GEOGRAPHICAL FEATURES
AND NATURAL ADVANTAGES.

At the present time Colorado is attracting more attention than
any other one section of the country. This is true as regards moneyed
men as well as with the masses. The tide of emigration that ·is
setting so strongly in that direction, and a growing disposition
for mining investments, indicate a general belief in Colorado's superior prospects for labor and capital. So widely prevalent an opinion
can only be caused by continuous prosperity and great natural wealth.
That Colorado deserves the reputation and renown she is securing,
her present rapid advancement and growing productions attest.
Brilliant as her recent record has been, it is evident that it can bear
no comparison with that of the future.

It is generally admitted that Colorado is the most prosperous
division of the West, or of the whole country. This is due to her
varied and extensive resources, developed and taken advantage of by
an enterprising and intelligent population. It is fast being demonstrated as an established fact that Colorado's mineral resources exceed
those of any other western state or territory. These will soon be
developed so that she will surpass all other sections in production. Added to mountain locked treasure vaults of gold and
silver, and endless deposits of coal and many valuable minerals, are
agricultural and stock-growing lands of an extensive and most
productive character. To crown the whole are climatic advantages
that have made the State famous far and wide, and an empire of
scenic attractions, such as no other region in either hemisphere
can boast of. Thus, while her gold and silver veins are astonishing
the world and enriching her people as well as outside investors, and
her farms and stock ranges are extremely remunerative, her fine

climate and grand scenery attract as many health and pleasure seekers as her mines do settlers and investors.

Colorado is situated in the centre of that part of the United
States lying between the Mississippi river and the Pacific ocean and
British America and Mexico. The eastern section of the State embraces a portion of the great plains, while the central and western
divisions are mainly composed of mountain ranges and their
offshoots, with occasional valleys and plateaus of great extent. The
Rocky mountains here attain their greatest elevation, and from their
summits and slopes rivers flow to either ocean. Colorado has
an area of 104,500 square miles, or more than any other state,
excepting Texas and California. It lies between the thirty-seventh
and forty-first parallels of north latitude, and extends from the
one hundred and second to the one hundred and ninth meridians of
longitude. It is almost square or rectangular in shape, having a
width from north to south of very nearly two hundred and eighty
miles and an average length of about three hundred and seventy
miles from east to west. It is west of Kansas, north of New
Mexico, east of Utah, and south of Wyoming.

The great plains rise gradually from the Missouri westward for
six hundred miles to the base of the foot hills and spurs of the
great mountain system. The elevation of the western limit of these
plains is usually about one mile above sea level. This broad and
level expanse is destitute of timber, except along the river bottoms,
but is covered with nutritious grasses that afford excellent grazing
for cattle and buffalo. What are known as the "foot hills" are
the less elevated portions of the mountains. These gradually increase in altitude for a distance westward of from twenty to fifty
miles, where they merge into the main or "snowy range." Some
are smooth and rolling and others rugged masses of rock and earth,
but all more or less heavily timbered. The "Continental Divide,"
or higher portion of the mountains, is usually from forty to sixty
miles beyond the base of the hills first mentioned. The elevation of this divide is generally from 12,000 to 14,400 feet above tide
water and several thousand feet above the line where timber and
nearly all vegetation ceases. This has been termed the backbone
of the American continent. From its eternal snows, crystal lakes,
and sparkling rivulets, streams are formed that eventually unite
and make great rivers. Here the Arkansas, Platte, Grande, and

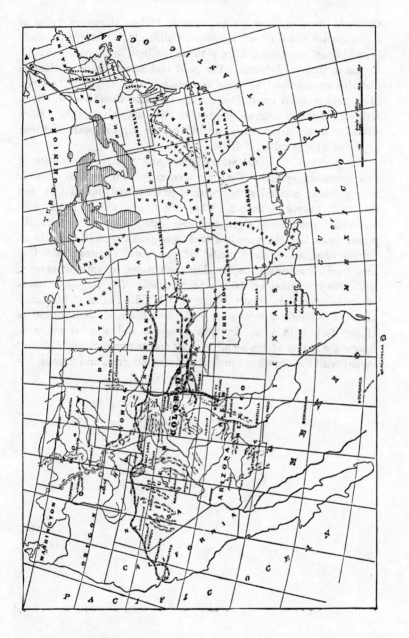

Colorado start on their long journeys of two thousand miles or
more toward the Gulf of Mexico or California. Western Colorado
is made up of mountains, hills, plateaus, valleys, and ravines, extending on to Utah or Arizona. The gold and silver bearing belts and
districts are confined to these mountain chains, hills, and ravines.
Most gold sections are of less average elevation than those of silver,
although there is no great degree of regularity about this. Many
silver lodes and deposits are situated on the highest peaks and near
or above what is called "timber line."

The parks of Colorado are a distinct and remarkable feature of
this mountain system. They are generally composed of level or
rolling lands, covered with luxuriant grasses, and dotted here and
there with groves of timber. They are firmly walled about with
mountains grand and high, and are watered by streams of the
purest character. It is evident that these parks were the basins of
former lakes at an early period of the world's history, and that
they were subsequently deprived of their water by volcanic agency,
while their original outlines were retained. The largest of these
are called San Luis, South, North, and Middle Parks. The mountains of Colorado are covered, up to elevations of from 10,800 to
11,800 feet, with pine, fir, spruce, aspen, and other forest trees.
Above the region of timber all is bleak and barren rock and "slide,"
varied with the occasional presence of stunted grass and flowers.

CHAPTER II.

INFORMATION FOR THE TOURIST, TRAVELER, AND IMMIGRANT—WAYS
OF REACHING COLORADO AND POINTS OF INTEREST, DISTANCES
AND ELEVATIONS, CLIMATE AND SCENERY—HUNTING AND FISHING
GROUNDS, AND MINERAL SPRINGS.

A trip to Colorado during the summer months is at once pleasant,
interesting, and instructive in the highest degree. To all wishing to
escape the confinement of city life, the heat of summer or the re-
curring monotony of eastern watering-places, or who would see
something of life on the western prairies and among the gold and
silver mines, the advice is tendered, Go to Colorado. It requires
less time and money than to visit Europe, and will prove far more
satisfactory than to remain at home. Take the western train,
breathe the pure air of the mountains, feast your eyes on the picturesque features, the golden ores and silver bullion of this wonder-
land, and in a few weeks you can return, feeling better than you
ever could do in the damp heavy atmosphere of a lower clime.

While the foundations of enduring wealth are secured by the
mining, farming, and pastoral resources, Colorado offers a world of
attractions and advantages, as beneficial to those who reside within
her borders as to sojourners from abroad. Possessing a climate any
land might envy, and surpassing all others in extent and beauty of
her mountain ranges, one cannot do otherwise than admit that Nature
has dealt with a lavish hand in this new land of the West. Thus it
is that her balmy air, exhilarating atmosphere, health-restoring
mineral waters, picturesque scenery, and unrivaled fishing and
hunting grounds are bringing visitors or residents from almost the
wide world over.

So vast is this land of mountain, park, and plain, that Switzer-
land is insignificant in comparison, and far behind in variety and
attractiveness. Pen fails to do justice to the massive grandeur of
the "Snowy Range," the majesty of its cloud-capped towers, the
awful depths of its mysterious cañons, or to the beauties of vale
and stream that everywhere abound from the Platte to the Colorado.

MU-AV CAÑON—WESTERN COLORADO.

But all of these subjects have been dwelt upon so often that even most Eastern readers have become more or less familiar with them.

For the convenience of the traveler, a collection of facts and information which may serve as a tourist's guide is presented here rather than in the closing portion of the book. Beginning with this chapter, routes of travel into and through Colorado are given, together with descriptions of towns, pleasure resorts, points of interest, and such other matter as is mostly likely to be called for. In this connection are tables of distances, elevations, and a variety of facts that will be found useful or instructive, if not especially interesting.

And by way of prefacing what is to follow, it may be well to say that, in going to Colorado, one does not necessarily bid farewell to civilization or to the comforts of ordinary life. There is as much culture, education, and refinement in Denver or many of the larger towns as in places of similar size at the East or West. There are as many well-stocked stores, as great a variety of goods of all descriptions, and as well-kept and comfortable hotels as anywhere else outside of the great cities. Everything one is likely to require can be purchased as cheaply or with but a trifling advance on New York prices. Owing to the scattered character of the population, and the difficulties attending their construction and operation, railway and stage fares are somewhat high, but this is so in all far Western regions. In some of the newer settlements up among the mountains time has not yet been given to secure all the accommodations desirable, nor do circumstances permit of low rates in all places—but this can hardly be expected. At the pleasure resorts are first-class hotels, and the charges compare favorably with those of like localities in other parts.

Those wishing to avoid to some extent the beaten track of the excursionist can enjoy a world of novelty by embarking on a "camping-out trip" through the mountains. And to do this but a very short distance need be traveled before one obtains all the solitude and necessary surroundings to enable him to "rough it" to his heart's content. To go on one of these camping-out tours in park or mountain glen, be it near or distant, all requisite equipments, tents, supplies, wagon teams, and saddle animals, can be obtained at reasonable figures at any of the prominent towns or cities.

All of the leading mining towns or health and pleasure resorts can be reached by railway or stage, and it is only the newer or smaller mining camps that still depend on the latter means of transportation, except in the case of remote localities. So, in going to Colorado, only about the same preparation is needed as in starting on a trip of a few weeks' duration to other sections. No laying in of stores or supplies is necessary, for everything that can be obtained in an ordinary Eastern town can be had there.

Schools and churches are as numerous and as liberally endowed as elsewhere, and the population will rank with that of any of the older commonwealths in all the requirements of life. The towns are well built, and most of them are being made attractive and beautiful as fast as circumstances will permit. Well-regulated railways extend to all thickly-settled parts of the plains, along the eastern base of the mountains, and several lines are being rapidly pushed up through the cañons and gorges of the Sierras. Some of these already connect the plains cities with their more elevated neighbors up among the gold and silver mines; beyond, first-class daily stage lines ply between all important points or mining districts.

Three great railways enter Colorado from the East, either one of which will land the traveler in Denver or some important objective point. These are the Atchison, Topeka & Santa Fe, the Kansas Pacific and the Union Pacific, or rather the Colorado Central, which diverges therefrom at Cheyenne. They are all supplied with Pullman palace cars and the usual comforts attending railway travel. Starting from the Missouri river, where connection is made with all leading Eastern lines, the great plains are gradually ascended until the summit of this inland plateau is reached, near the base of the mountains.

The cities of Denver and Pueblo are what may be termed the ports of entry for the country around about and beyond. While all points can be reached from either road, the more southern sections of the plains or mountains can be gained most advantageously by taking the Southern route. This extends up the Arkansas valley, with one line entering New Mexico and the others making connections with all important localities yet touched by rail facilities from the southern boundary up to Denver. At Pueblo the Denver & Rio Grande forks in four different directions, pointing towards the San Juan region and Leadville, and extending from El Moro on the south to Colorado Springs and Denver on the north. Some of the most desirable points to visit in the whole State—mines, mineral springs, and scenic attractions—can be reached by this route or its stage connections.

Denver is the natural halting-place for tourists and visitors, by reason of its extended connections with mining towns and pleasure resorts, its excellent hotel accommodations, and its size, prominence, and general attractions. It is the finest and most enterprising city of the New West. Few places can compare with it in beauty or in all that goes to make life desirable. While much will be found to interest the stranger, all parts of northern and central Colorado can be reached therefrom easily and quickly. Six railways centre here, radiating to all points of the compass. The great gold mines of Gilpin, or the productive silver mines of Clear Creek county, are all within a few hours' ride across the prairie and up the renowned mountain gorge and valley of Clear Creek. The Colorado Central railway conveys one there, or to the interesting towns of Golden and Boulder, whose smelting and reduction works are of great extent and capacity. Up the line of this same railway, nestling in its mountain retreat, is the famous watering-place and summer resort of Idaho Springs. In either direction are the great mining towns of Central, Georgetown, and Black Hawk, whose annual bullion product is counted by millions. All of these places have first-class hotels.

Southward, the Denver & Rio Grande road invites to those fashionable resorts, Colorado Springs and Manitou, the best patronized of all western watering-places. Near each and all of the localities above enumerated are points of rare beauty and attractiveness, well worth a visit to the Rocky mountains to look upon. Scenery, lovely and picturesque or grand and majestic, await inspection in all directions, and, to crown all, a climate of Italian mildness or Alpine purity.

To the southwest the Denver & South Park conveys the traveler to the weird beauties of Platte River Cañon, and up through the mountains to where the tide of humanity on its way to Leadville halts to take a fresh start, by stage or foot-path. North from this plains railway centre the Denver Pacific and the Boulder Valley take their respective courses to Cheyenne and Boulder.

After leaving the magnificent farming sections of eastern Kansas and Nebraska, the only available routes to the Rocky Mountains are up the courses of the streams which flow eastward to the Missouri or

Mississippi. Although lacking the moisture of more eastern localities, water is obtainable, agriculture practicable, and settlements are becoming numerous in the western uplands of the Arkansas and Platte valleys. While farming is successfully prosecuted with the assistance of irrigation in that comparatively rainless country, and stock growing is remarkably remunerative, the elevated tracts of country between these main watercourses are of little service.

The region known as the Great Plains rise to the westward from the Missouri river to the western basis of the Rocky Mountains, where they attain an elevation of a mile, more or less, above sea level. This rise is so gradual as to be imperceptible to the traveler, and yet it amounts to an average of nearly ten feet per mile. It is interesting to know how fast one is ascending in crossing the great inland plateau or among the mountains beyond, and no little diversion can be obtained from noting the variations of a pocket barometer. In the tables of elevations and distances on the great through lines and mountain roads given below, it will be seen that the upward tendency is slight until the "Rockies" themselves are reached, when it becomes much more rapid and manifest.

Distances between Eastern and Colorado cities vary with different routes. From New York to Denver the distance is 1,960 miles, more or less, by various railway systems. From Boston the distance is some 200 miles or more greater, and from Philadelphia 90 miles less. Different routes from Chicago run from 1,155 to 1,250 miles, and from St. Louis 916 miles and over. Pueblo is a little nearer from central and southern points, and about the same from Chicago and Boston. The railway jumping-off points at Central, Georgetown, and Cañon City are not far from 2,000 miles from New York, and Alamosa is over 2,100 miles distant.

The schedule railway time from Eastern points to Colorado is something as follows, in days of twenty-four hours and fractions thereof. To Denver, from New York, 3 days and 8 hours; Philadelphia, 3 days and 5 hours; Pittsburg, 2 days and 17 hours; Baltimore, 3 days and 3 hours; Saint Louis, 42 hours; Chicago, 50 hours; Kansas City, 32 hours. To Pueblo, 3 to 4 hours less; Cañon City, about the same time as to Denver.

ATCHISON, TOPEKA & SANTA FE RAILWAY.

The subjoined table contains nearly all the stations of the main lines of the Atchison, Topeka & Santa Fe railway, with their elevations in feet above the sea and distances in miles from Kansas City. Atchison, one of the eastern termini on the Missouri river, has an elevation above tide water of 803 feet.

Name of Station.	Miles from Kansas City.	Elevation.	Name of Station.	Miles from Kansas City.	Elevation.
Kansas City		763	Great Bend......	286	1,854
Lawrence	41	845	Larned..........	308	2,011
Topeka	66	904	Kinsley	332	2,200
Carbondale......	84	1,081	Dodge City......	369	2,492
Burlingame......	93	1,050	Lakin...........	440	3,013
Osage City.......	101	1,082	Colorado & Kan-		
Reading.........	112	1,072	sas State Line..	482	3,129
Emporia	128	1,161	Granada.........	497	3,296
Cottonwood	148	1,183	Las Animas......	538	3,952
Florence	173	1,277	*Arkansas Valley Line.*		
Peabody.........	194	1,256	La Junta........	571	4,137
Newton	201	1,433	Napiesta.........	....	4,395
Halstead........	210	1,320	Pueblo..........	635	4,713
Burrton.........	220	1,410	*New Mexico Line.*		
Hutchinson......	234	1,482	Trinidad........	651	6,005
Sterling.........	244	1,494	Raton Pass......	666	7,863
Raymond........	265	1,679	Las Vegas.......	786	6,397
Ellinwood	276	1,738			

Santa Fe is 30 miles beyond Las Vegas and 7,047 feet above sea level.

DENVER & RIO GRANDE RAILWAY.

(Western Division of A., T. & S. F.)

This line being operated in connection with the A., T. & S. F., and practically a part of the same concern, the distances of leading stations from Kansas City via that road are given here. Elsewhere is a more complete table of the D. & R. G.:

Name of Station.	Miles from Kansas City.	Elevation.	Name of Station.	Miles from Kansas City.	Elevation.
North from Pueblo.			*Southwest from Pueblo.*		
South Pueblo.....	635	* { 4,615 { 4,713	Cuchara.........	684	5,893
Colorado Springs.	680	5,985	Walsenburg......	691	6,134
Monument.......	699	6,931	La Veta.........	706	6,970
Divide.	703	7,186	Veta Pass........	720	9,339
Castle Rock......	723	6,173	Alamosa.........	765	7,492
Littleton.........	745	5,320			
Denver..........	755	5,143	*South from Cuchara.*		
West from Pueblo.			El Moro	721	5,825
Canon...........	675	5,287			

* Elevations taken by two different persons.

STAGE LINES FROM THE ABOVE RAILWAY SYSTEM.

In the San Juan Region, Lake City is 116 miles beyond Alamosa; altitude, 8,550.   Silverton, 146 miles; altitude, 9,400.   Summit gold mines, 49 miles; altitude, 11,500.

In Custer County, Silver Cliff is 30 miles from Cañon; altitude, 7,500.   Rosita, 32 miles; altitude, 8,500.

Leadville, 126 miles from Cañon, altitude, 10,025 feet.

RAILWAY CONNECTIONS.

Continuing on to the mountains from Denver *via* the Colorado Central, an elevation of 8,300 feet is attained at Central, 40 miles from Denver; one of 7,531 feet at Idaho Springs, 37½ miles, and 8,452 feet at Georgetown, 53½ miles.   Or, taking the Denver & South Park, an elevation of 10,139 feet is attained, the highest railroading in the United States, at the Kenosha Divide, about 75 miles from Denver.

KANSAS PACIFIC RAILWAY.

Names of leading stations, elevations, and distances from Kansas City.   The elevation of Leavenworth is 783 feet.

Name of Station.	Miles from Kansas City.	Elevation.	Name of Station.	Miles from Kansas City.	Elevation.
Kansas City.......	....	763	Solomon.........	172	1,193
Armstrong.......	1	773	Salina...........	185	1,243
Edouardsville....	13	801	Brookville.......	200	1,366
Lenape..........	22	799	Fort Harker.....	218	1,600
Lawrence........	38	845	Ellsworth........	223	1,556
Perryville.......	51	870	Bunker Hill.	252	1,882
Medina..........	52	871	Victoria	279	....
Grantville	60	895	Hays............	289	2,099
Topeka..........	67	904	Ellis.............	302	2,135
Rossville.........	83	951	Grinnell.........	364	2,922
St. Mary's.......	90	973	Sheridan........	405	3,121
Bellevue.........	97	....	Wallace	420	3,319
Wamego.........	104	1,018	Monotony........	440	3,792
St. George.......	110	1,018	Cheyenne Wells..	462	4,295
Manhattan.......	118	1,042	First View.......	472	4,595
Ogden...........	129	1,078	Kit Carson.......	487	4,307
Fort Riley.......	135	1,090	Hugo...........	534	5,068
Junction City....	138	1,100	Deer Trail	583	5,203
Detroit..........	157	1,153	Box Elder........	617	5,430
Abilene..........	163	1,173	Denver..........	639	5,196

COLORADO CENTRAL RAILROAD—MOUNTAIN DIVISION.

Name of Station.	Miles from Denver.	Elevation.	Name of Station.	Miles from Denver.	Elevation.
Denver............	....	5,197	Fall River.......	39.3	7,719
Golden..........	15.8	5,687	Mill City........	43.1	7,930
Forks Clear Creek	29.0	6,893	Lawson..........	48.2	8,120
Black Hawk.....	35.8	7,875	Empire Station...	49.5	8,286
Central..........	39.6	8,325	Georgetown......	53.5	8,514
Idaho Springs....	37.5	7,535			

DENVER & SOUTH PARK RAILROAD.

Name of Station.	Miles from Denver.	Elevation.	Name of Station.	Miles from Denver.	Elevation.
Denver............	....	5,197	Fairville.........	58	8,175
Platte Cañon.....	20	5,487	Geneva..........	68	8,514
South Platte.....	29	6,037	Webster.........	70	9,120
Deer Creek......	48	7,084	Kenosha Divide..		10,139
Bailey's..........	54	7,880	Jefferson........	80	9,754

The next important point to which this road will be constructed is Fairplay, with an elevation of 9,964 feet. Trout Creek Pass has an altitude of 9,620 feet.

UNION PACIFIC & COLORADO CENTRAL RAILROADS.

Below are leading stations, elevations, and distances from Omaha on Union Pacific to Cheyenne, and Colorado Central to Denver.

Name of Station.	Miles from Omaha.	Elevation.	Name of Station.	Miles from Omaha.	Elevation.
Omaha............	....	1,003	Big Spring.......	361	3,360
Gilmore.........	10	1,013	Julesburg........	377	3,535
Papillion.........	15	1,009	Sidney...	414	4,108
Elkhorn.........	29	1,187	Pine Bluffs......	473	5,061
Valley	35	1,157	Cheyenne........	516	6,075
Tremont.........	47	1,220	*Colorado Central R. R.*		
North Bend......	62	1,296	Colorado Junction.	522	6,357
Schuyler.........	76	1,372	Fort Collins......	564	4,815
Columbus........	92	1,469	Loveland........	576	....
Central City......	132	....	Longmont.......	595	2,957
Grand Island....	154	1,887	Boulder.........	605	5,278
Kearney Junction.	195	2,143	Ralston..........	628	5,579
Stevenson........	201	2,207	Golden..........	631	5,728
Plum Creek......	231	2,406	Denver..........	652	5,196
Brady Island.....	268	2,683	*C. C. R. R.—Mountain Division.*		
McPherson.......	278	2,731	Central	40	8,300
North Platte.....	291	2,825	Georgetown.......	53½	8,452
O'Fallon's.......	308	3,012			

TABLES OF COLORADO ELEVATIONS, TOWNS AND CITIES, MINES, MOUNTAINS, PASSES, AND LAKES.

The reports of Professor Hayden and Lieutenant Wheeler give, among much other valuable information, the average elevations of different portions of Colorado's area. The greatest elevation of any one point is 14,464 feet, and there are about one hundred peaks of a greater elevation than 14,000 feet. The lowest part of the State is on the eastern or Kansas border, where it varies from 3,047 to 3,500 feet above the sea. There are valleys in the extreme southwest, on the tributaries of the San Juan, that are but little over 4,000 feet. Colorado contains 104,500 square miles. The mean height above the sea is 7,000 feet, being much greater than that of any other state or territory. The following table shows the approximate number of square miles of area between various elevations :

Elevations.	Square Miles.
Between 3,000 and 4,000 feet	9,000
" 4,000 " 5,000 "	21,800
" 5,000 " 6,000 "	15,000
" 6,000 " 7,000 "	10,000
" 7,000 " 8,000 "	11,000
" 8,000 " 9,000 "	14,000
" 9,000 " 10,000 "	10,000
" 10,000 " 11,000 "	6,800
" 11,000 " 12,000 "	5,000
" 12,000 " 13,000 "	1,400
Area above 13,000 feet	500

TOWNS AND CITIES.

Below are the elevations in feet above sea level of important towns and localities of Colorado :

Alamosa	7,492	Caribou	9,905
Alma	10,254	Central	8,300
Animas City	6,622	Colorado Springs	6,023
Baker Mine	11,956	Conejos	7,880
Bakerville	9,753	Del Norte	7,750
Black Hawk	7,875	Denver	5,197
Boulder	5,536	El Moro	5,886
Breckenridge	9,674	Empire	8,583
Cañon	5,287	Evans	4,745

Fairplay...............	9,964	Longmont...............	4,957
Fall River............	7,719	Los Pinos..............	9,065
Fort Collins..........	4,815	Manitou...,...........	6,297
Fort Garland..........	7,945	Marshall...............	5,578
Fort Lupton...........	5,027	Montezuma (9,652)......10,295
Fort Lyon.............	3,725	Nederland..............	8,263
Frisco (about)........	9,500	Nevadaville............	8,800
Georgetown............	8,514	Oro....................10,704
Gold Hill.............	8,463	Ouray..................	7,640
Golden................	5,687	Pagosa Springs.........	7,108
Granite...............	8,883	Present Help Mine, on Mt.
Greeley...............	4,779	Lincoln.........14,000
Grenada...............	3,434	Platteville............	4,690
Gunnison..............	7,743	Pueblo, North..........	4,713
Hamilton..............	9,743	Pueblo, South..........	4,676
Hermesillo............	4,723	Quartz Hill (about)....	9,300
Hot Sulphur Springs....	7,725	Rollinsville...........	8,323
Howardville...........	9,527	Rosita.................	8,500
Idaho Springs.........	7,512	Saguache...............	7,723
Jamestown.............	7,123	Saints John............10,807
Jefferson.............	9,862	Salt Works in South Park . 8,917
Kit Carson............	4,307	Silverton..............	9,400
Kokomo (about).........10,200	Stevens Mine...........11,943
La Junta..............	4,137	Terrible Mine..........	9,243
Lake City.............	8,550	Trinidad...............	6,032
Las Animas............	3,952	Uncompahgre Agency.....	6,400
Leadville (R. R.)......10,025	White River Agency.....	6,491
Leadville (Hayden).....10,247		

ELEVATIONS OF THE ROCKY MOUNTAINS.

Below are elevations of most of the prominent peaks of Colorado, with others of less elevations, but noticeable from mines or from being near towns or railways. There are a large number of peaks, especially in the San Juan mountains, yet unnamed, whose elevations exceed 14,000 feet, and some two hundred that run from that height down to 13,000 feet. It is impossible to give in this statement all of the higher peaks elsewhere, or of the multitude that exceed 12,000 feet. As there are several spurs or connecting ranges of mountains, the name of the range appears with the name of peak and elevation.

Central Colorado—Front Range.

Mount Evans.............14,330	Mount Rosalie...........14,340
Pike's Peak.............14,147	Chief Mountain..........11,833

Northern Colorado—Main Range.

Arapahoe Peak...........13,520	James' Peak.............13,283
Gray's Peak.............14,341	Long's Peak.............14,271
Irwin's Peak............14,336	Bald Mountain (Gilpin Co.)..10,322
Mount Guyot.............13,565		

Central Colorado—Park Range.

Buckskin Mountain, . , ...	14,296	Quandary Peak.	14,269
Mount Cameron.	14,000	Sheep Mountain.	12,589
Horseshoe Mountain.	13,988	Silverheels.	13,897
Mount Lincoln.	14,297		

Central Colorado—Sawatch or Main Range.

Mount Antero.	14,245	La Plata.	14,311
Mount Elbert.	14,351	Massive Mountain†	14,298
Grizzley.	13,956	Mount Princeton.	14,196
Mount Harvard*.	14,375	Shavano	14,239
Holy Cross Mountain.	14,176	Mount Yale.	14,187

* By Hayden. Wheeler makes it 14,151 ; and another, 14,383.
† Another measurement gives 14,368.

Southern Colorado—Sangre de Christo Range.

Baldy Peak.	14,176	Hunt's Peak.	14,056
Blanca Peak*.	14,464	Spanish Peaks { W.	13,620
Culebra.	14,069	{ E.	12,720

* Highest in Colorado, and highest but one in United States.

Southern Colorado, San Juan Region—Main Range and Spurs.

Mount Æolus	14,054	Simpson's Peak.	14,055
Blaine's Peak.	13,905	Mount Sneffels.	14,158
Engineer Mountain.	13,076	Stewart's Peak.	14,032
Handie's Peak.	14,149	Uncompahgre Peak*.	14,235
Pyramid.	14,146	Wetterhorn	14,069
Pridgeon's.	14,054	Mount Wilson†	14,280
San Luis Peak	14,100		

* Wheeler makes this 14,408 feet.   † Wheeler, 14,309.

Western Colorado—Elk Range.

Capitol Mountain.	13,997	Snow Mass.	13,970
Castle Peak.	14,115	Teocalli.	13,113
Maroon.	14,003		

ELEVATIONS OF LAKES.

Chicago Lakes.	11,500	San Cristoval.	9,000
Grand.	8,153	San Luis.	7,592
Green.	10,000	San Miguel.	9,720
Mary, or Santa Maria.	9,324	Twin Lakes.	9,357
Osborn's.	8,821		

MOUNTAIN PASSES IN COLORADO.

The following gives the names and elevations of the more famous passes over the Rocky mountains and spurs:

Arkansas (about)............	11,100	Hoosier.....	11,500
Argentine.................	13,100	Lake Fork...............	12,540
Berthoud.................	11,349	Loveland	11,500
Boulder...................	11,670	Marshall.................	10,852
Cochetopa	10,032	Poncho...................	8,945
Cunningham..............	12,090	Raton...................	7,863
Georgia..................	11,811	Tarryall.................	12,176
Gore.....................	9,590	Trout Creek.............	9,346
Hamilton	12,370	Tennessee*	10,418
Hayden..................	10,780	Veta.....................	9,339

* Now estimated at 10,700.

The river cañons, or deeply cut ravines that are found in all of the more elevated portions of Colorado, constitute a peculiar and striking feature of the great Rocky Mountain system. In the countless ages of the past the waters of the streams have worn channels deep down into the hearts of the mountains, leaving the perpendicular granite or sandstone standing on either side for hundreds, and in some localities for thousands of feet. Nowhere are the grand and beautiful in Nature more effectually illustrated than in these mountain cañons. The glories of Boulder, Clear Creek, Cheyenne, and Platte cañons, and the Grand cañon of the Arkansas, all on the eastern slope of the Continental Divide, have already been noted. The walls of the Colorado, Gunnison, and Uncompahgre rivers, in the western part of the State, are still more massive and wonderful. In many sections they rise without a break or an incline to heights of thousands of feet, and along the Colorado continue in that way with hardly an outlet of any kind for hundreds of miles. The Grand cañon of the Gunnison is one of the world's wonders. Its walls on either side of the stream, and bordering it for miles, are usually not far from 300 feet in width, and are composed of stratified rock. In places these perpendicular sides, rising from the water for distances of from one to three thousand feet, terminate in level summits surmounted by a second wall of prodigious height, thus forming a cañon within a cañon. Through the chasm between these giant formations and huge bastions and turrets one above another, dashes the river, its surface white with foam. The heights of these perpendicular cañon walls, and their elevations with that of the river above sea level at several points, are as follows: Level of the Gunnison at mouth of Mountain creek above sea level, 7,200 feet; of top of wall or plateau on north side, 8,800 feet; height of wall, 1,600 feet; height of wall at point below on east side, 1,900 feet; on west side, 1,800 feet; height of wall in gneiss rock, 900 feet. Some distance below, the cañon wall rises directly from the river, 3,000 feet, of which the 1,800 feet nearest the water is gneiss rock; total elevation of top of wall or plateau above the sea, 9,800 feet.

CHAPTER III.

ROUTES OF TRAVEL—POINTS OF INTEREST AND HOW TO REACH THEM
—RAILWAY AND STAGE LINES—FARES, DISTANCES, AND ELEVA-
TIONS—DENVER, PUEBLO, COLORADO SPRINGS, BOULDER, CEN-
TRAL, GEORGETOWN, LEADVILLE, GOLDEN, CAÑON, AND THE SAN
JUAN.

For the benefit of the traveler, tourist, and emigrant this chapter
will give a detailed account of the manner in which important points
of Colorado can be reached. Persons taking either one of the three
through lines from the Missouri river, can be landed in Denver.
The Atchison, Topeka & Santa Fe railway connects with that place
by means of the Denver & Rio Grande north and south line. The
western terminus of the Kansas Pacific is in that city, and the Union
Pacific connects at Cheyenne with the Colorado Central. The great
gold and silver mining districts of Gilpin and Clear Creek counties
are reached by the mountain division of the Colorado Central, which
leaves the plains or Denver and Cheyenne division at Golden. Leadville and Fairplay are approached for a distance of eighty miles
from Denver by the Denver & South Park road. Much of the
Leadville travel goes in from Pueblo and Cañon via the Arkansas
Valley and Denver & Rio Grande. Silver Cliff and Rosita have the
same rail communication but a different route for stage travel. The
regular route to the San Juan and Del Norte, Silverton, Lake City,
and Ouray is via Pueblo and the Denver & Rio Grande road to
Alamosa in San Luis Park, thence by stage to the various points to
be reached. The Atchison, Topeka & Santa Fe lines are in the same
latitude, and naturally secure the east and west travel for the San
Juan mines. The Denver & Rio Grande is the only road that approaches these mines, and it is controlled at the present time by
the Atchison, Topeka & Santa Fe. The main line of the latter
road leaves the Arkansas river valley at La Junta, and thence takes
a southwesterly direction to El Moro and Trinidad, and then passes
southward of the Raton Mountains into New Mexico. It will
soon be completed to Las Vegas. The Arkansas Valley division of

this same road passes westward up the river from La Junta to Pueblo.
Here the Denver & Rio Grande line takes the inland travel, including scores of passengers daily, bound for Leadville via Cañon and
the southern overland stage.

There are three classes of accommodations for this western travel,
viz., first class, second class, and emigrant. Emigrant fare includes
the ordinary passenger coaches in use, and all classes ride together on
the mountain railways and stage lines. Each full ticket is allowed
one hundred pounds of baggage, and each half ticket fifty pounds
on the railways, while the allowance on the mountain stage lines is
usually fifty pounds. The railways charge at the rate of from ten
to fifteen per cent. of first-class fare on every hundred pounds of

SHOOTING BUFFALO.

extra baggage, while the stages charge express rates on the same.
This can be avoided by shipping extra baggage by freight. First-
class meals on the railways are usually seventy-five cents on express
trains, and from fifty to seventy-five cents on all others. Sleeping-
car or stop-over accommodations are not usually allowed on second
or third class tickets, and baggage must be checked to destination.

Denver and Pueblo may be regarded as the starting-points for
various parts of the mountains, although the former is considered
the main base of operations for a trip in almost any direction.
Eastern emigrants will find the time required to reach Leadville
from Cañon pretty near the same as from Denver on the northern
system. The railway construction now going on will alter distances

and time considerably before the summer is over, both for northern and southern routes to Leadville. Colorado Springs is on the D. & R. G. line. All the northern points among the mountain mines, such as Georgetown, Central, and Idaho, must be reached via the Colorado Central from Denver, or, as with Boulder, from Denver and Cheyenne. By a glance at the map of Colorado the reader will gain a still better idea of the situation and of the routes of the different railway systems. By this it will be seen that the Colorado Central railway, with its forks and branches, is the main artery of communication between Denver and the Union Pacific and Kansas Pacific, and for most of the farming and coal districts and the mountain mining sections of northern Colorado. The Denver & Rio Grande acts in pretty much the same capacity for central and southern Colorado, and has the A., T. & S. F. for its outlet and feeder. This road extends through farming, pastoral, and coal lands, in a north and south direction, east of the base of the mountains, forking at Pueblo for Cañon, and at Cucharas for El Moro, while the main line continues southwesterly over the mountains to Alamosa —the latter place being 250 miles from Denver, while El Moro is 206 miles. The Denver & South Park is building up through the Platte and South Park country, and like the other two lines, is bound for Leadville. Since the last section of new road was completed, it has drawn heavily on the business of that locality. How to reach important towns, cities, and resorts will be the next matter considered.

Leadville is in the mountains, and quite a long distance inland from the plains. Through tickets can be obtained for that place from all leading railway centres in the East or West—including first class, second class, and emigrant. The last rates fixed from the Missouri river are $41 for first-class tickets, $38.50 for second class, and $34 for emigrant. Leadville can be reached by rail and stage by any one of three routes.

From Denver and Pueblo to Cañon by rail, thence by stage to Leadville; distance from Denver, 160 miles by rail, and 126 miles by stage; fare $17, and $3.50 for hotels at Cañon and on the road; time, about two days of day travel. Through passengers from the East, via the A., T. & S. F., arrive at Cañon at night, and then have the same two days of stage travel up the Arkansas Valley. This, of course, is their natural route.

The Denver & South Park railway and stage lines is largely patronized. This railway is building rapidly, with a proportionate decrease of staging. Fare, $17, which will be reduced with reduction of staging in the summer. Time, nearly two days. Meals and lodging at Fairplay and elsewhere, $4. The stage line charges ten cents per pound for all baggage in excess of forty pounds to the passenger.

The Colorado Central extends from Denver to Georgetown, 54 miles, connecting with stage to Leadville, 56 miles. Total distance, 110 miles ; fare, $10.

All of the above roads are building towards Leadville. The A., T. & S. F. will have the grading of their roadbed completed to Leadville by the time they succeed in blasting a way through the Grand Cañon near the lower end of the route. It is asserted that this road will be running railway trains into Leadville in August or September. The other two roads are also building in the same direction as rapidly as possible, so that the amount of staging will soon be greatly reduced. Fairplay and the Park and Summit county mines are reached by the Denver & South Park railway and by stages from the end of track. Where no stages are in operation saddle animals can be obtained. In these counties are noted silver mines, and gold-bearing placers and gulches.

A., T. & S. F. AND D. & R. G. RAILROADS AND CONNECTING STAGE LINES.

The famous summer resort of Colorado Springs is situated on the line of the Denver & Rio Grande, 75 miles south of Denver and 45 miles north of Pueblo, and has no other rail communication. Parties coming west over the Atchison, Topeka & Santa Fe line can stop off there on their way to Denver, and it is but three and a half hours' ride from the latter place. Five miles from Colorado Springs is Manitou, famed for its mineral waters and as a great summer resort for health and pleasure seekers. Near by is some of the most beautiful mountain scenery in the country, and over all towers the majestic summit of Pike's Peak, where is located a United States signal service station.

Trinidad and El Moro, with their coal mines, coke manufactories, and excellent farming and pastoral country, can be reached from the East via the main line of the A., T. & S. F., without coming to

Pueblo. Passengers can also go to El Moro from Denver or Pueblo by the D. & R. G. road, whose southerly terminus is there. The first-named railway passes through both towns and beyond into New Mexico.

The Denver & Rio Grande railway is the only one approaching or entering what is termed the San Juan region. From Pueblo this

OVER THE SANGRE DE CHRISTO MOUNTAINS VIA THE D. & R. G. RAILWAY.

division of the road runs southwesterly up the Cucharas valley and by the Walsenburg coal mines to the Sangre de Christo range, which it crosses at Veta Pass. Its course is then westward through the great San Luis Park to Alamosa on the Rio Grande, 250 miles south-southwest of Denver. This is the jumping-off place for the south-west, and serves as the distributing point for a wide scope of country. Almost all merchandise and supplies going into the mountains to the west are freighted from this place, and all ore and bullion from the mines, and wool, hides, pelts, and other material from the farms and stock ranges are here started eastward by rail.

The Southern Overland Mail and Express of Barlow & Sanderson, bound for Del Norte, Wagon Wheel Gap, and Lake City, and to connect with Silverton lines, starts westward from Alamosa on the arrival of the train from Denver and Pueblo. Railway fare from Denver, $23, and from Pueblo, $13. Stage fare from Alamosa to Del Norte, $4; to Wagon Wheel Gap, $8.65; Antelope Springs, $11.65; Lake City, $19—distance, 116 miles. Connection is made with another conveyance at Antelope Springs or Junction, 35½ miles southeast of Lake City, for Silverton and neighboring towns. The trip to Ouray is usually made on horseback from either of these places. During the warmer months a conveyance plies between Lake City and Ouray, distance 80 miles by this route. Distance by trail over the range 30 miles. The Summit, or Little Annie gold mining district is 25 miles south of Del Norte, and off of the main line noted above; fare, $5. At Wagon Wheel Gap 30 miles west of Del Norte, are hot sulphur mineral springs of a very valuable character, which are beginning to attract people from abroad. South from Alamosa another line of Barlow & Sanderson's coaches leaves daily for Conejos and for Santa Fe, N. M., and way stations.

If the fare continues as it was not long ago, it is as follows from Denver, and $10 less from Pueblo: Denver to Alamosa, $23; to Del Norte, $27; Lake City, $42; Silverton, $55. Stage tickets are procured at the end of track. Meals at stage stations are 75 cents. Twenty-six hours' staging between Alamosa and Lake City.

One branch of the Denver & Rio Grande railroad extends up the Arkansas valley from Pueblo to Cañon, a distance of 40 miles. Here passengers for Leadville take Barlow & Sanderson's stages, as mentioned before. Passengers for Silver Cliff leave Cañon by way of Megrue & Smith's stage line.

All of the stage lines extending from the Denver & Rio Grande railway, except one, belong to Barlow & Sanderson's Southern Overland Mail and Express. These convey passengers to Leadville, the San Juan country, and New Mexico. Fifty pounds of baggage are allowed to each passenger, but all over that amount is charged express rates. These stage routes are as follows—distance from Cañon in miles and rates of fare given with names of stations :

Leadville Line.—Stations, distance from Cañon in miles, and fare : Copper Gulch, 14 miles, $1.75 ; Texas Creek, 28 miles, $3.50 ; Pleasant Valley, 39 miles, $4.90 ; South Arkansas or Cleora, 60 miles, $7.50 ; Centreville, 78 miles, $9.75 ; Lenhardy, 98 miles, $12.25 ; Granite, 108 miles, $13.50 ; Leadville, 126 miles, $14. Time from Cañon to Leadville, 26 hours, going day and night.

On arrival of the stage at Cleora, a conveyance starts southwesterly for Saguache and Ouray.

Saguache and Ouray.—Barlow & Sanderson run a regular buckboard or open wagon line from Saguache, in San Luis Park, westward over the mountains to Ouray. Connection is made at Saguache with the same company's conveyance that leaves Cleora on the arrival of the Leadville stage at night. Ninety miles east of Ouray, twenty-one miles east of Lake City, and seventy-one miles west of Saguache is Indian Creek, where the roads from those points intersect. New stage line from Cleora to Ouray, 130 miles.

Alamosa and San Juan Line.—Stations, distances in miles, and fare from Alamosa westward : Station No. 1, 10½ miles, $2.10 ; Venables, 21¼ miles, $4.30 ; Del Norte, 34½ miles, $4 ; Bunker Hill, 46 miles, $9.20 ; Riverside, 57¼ miles, $11.50 ; Rio Grande, 69 miles, $13.80 ; Junction, 80½ miles, $16.10 ; Clear Creek, 91½ miles, $18.30 ; Powder Horn, 103½ miles, $20.70 ; Lake City, 116 miles, $19. What is called through fare is charged to Del Norte ; Wagon Wheel Gap, 64½ miles, $8.65 ; Antelope Springs, 84½ miles, $11.65, and Lake City, $19 ; which accounts for less than local rates.

Silverton, Howardsville, and Animas Forks and vicinity are reached in the summer and fall months by conveyance connecting with the above stage line at Junction, and with another conveyance from Lake City. Distance from the latter point to Silverton, 32 miles.

There is a trail from Silverton to Ouray by way of Cement creek and the Uncompahgre river, distance 23 miles ; also a trail to Ouray

2

via Hensen creek, and over the mountains via Poughkeepsie Fork;
distance 28 miles or more.

Lake City to Ouray.—Conveyance plies between these points, following water courses, via Indian creek and Cevolla, distance 80
miles.

Alamosa and Santa Fe Line.—Distance from Alamosa to Santa
Fe, 141 miles, fare $28; Alamosa to Conejos, 30 miles, fare $6.
West from Conejos are the famous Pagosa Springs, so valuable that
the United States government retains possession of them, and has
set apart the locality as a reservation. Distance from Conejos 70
miles, and from Alamosa 100 miles.

A railway may some day be constructed from Alamosa westward, via Conejos, Pagosa Springs, and Animas river to Silverton,
the metropolis of the mines of San Juan county. A good wagon
road is already in operation that is open winter and summer. This
has no high and difficult mountains to pass, and is much used by
Silverton and La Plata freighters. The distances from Alamosa by
this road are 30 miles to Conejos, 100 to Pagosa Springs, 180 to
Animas City and 223 to Silverton.

Cañon to Silver Cliff and Rosita.—Megrue & Smith run a daily
stage line between Cañon and Silver Cliff, connecting with another
line to Rosita, 14 miles from Cañon, and 18 miles from Rosita.
Fare to either point, $4; round trip, $7. A hack also plies between
those two towns; fare, $1; distance, 7 miles; from Cañon to Silver
Cliff, 30 miles; to Rosita, 32 miles. These are prominent mining
towns, and are so beautifully located, with fine valley and mountain
scenery, as to be well worthy of a visit from the tourist.

COLORADO CENTRAL R. R.

The Colorado Central is the only railway leading up through the
mountains to the great gold district of Gilpin county, with its
flourishing towns, Central, Black Hawk, and Nevadaville, and to the
productive silver belt of Clear Creek county, in which Georgetown,
Idaho Springs, Lawson, Fall River, Freeland, Silver Plume, and
Brownville are located. The Colorado Central extends from
Denver to Golden (the headquarters of the road and the seat of
smelting works and various manufactories, where the mountain
division branches off to the westward), and then continues northward

through coal and farming districts to Cheyenne; distance to Golden, 16 miles; fare, 80cts.; distance to Cheyenne, 138 miles; fare, $5.00. Twenty-nine miles from Denver and 13 above Golden, North and South Clear Creeks unite, and here the railway forks, one branch taking up one cañon to Central, 13 miles, and the other up another through

CLEAR CREEK CAÑON, C. C. R. R.

Idaho and on to Georgetown, 25 miles. Any of these points are less than three hours' ride from Denver; fare to Central, $3.10; to Idaho Springs, $2.90; Georgetown, $4.30. Outside of the picturesque scenery en route, these cities are of rare interest, on account of their famous and productive mines and numerous quartz mills and reduction works. They were the main source of Colorado's bullion product up to the time of very recent developments at Leadville, and arc steadily increasing their yield. Black Hawk and Nevadaville adjoin Central, and are located in the same district. The Smith stage line makes tri-weekly trips to Caribou, leaving on Tuesdays, Thursdays, and Saturdays, and returning on alternate days. Surrounding and lying between Idaho Springs and Georgetown are many prosperous mining camps; also, such attractive resorts as Chicago Lakes, the highest body of water in North America; Green and Clear Lakes, Gray's and Irwin's peaks, Argentine pass, and other points of interest, all of which can be visited either by carriage or on horseback by a few hours' drive or ride. Livery charges in these towns are usually $3.00 per day for saddle horses and $10.00 per day, or less, for two-horse carriages. At Denver and Boulder livery charges are one-third less. Idaho Springs is famous for its mineral waters and as a fashionable summer resort. Here are fine hotels and bath-houses, hot and cold soda springs, fine drives, mines, and mills, and other attractions.

Boulder is located on the plains, at the gateway of that portion of the mountains where numerous mining camps are producing largely. It can be reached from Denver or Cheyenne by the Colorado Central railway; distance from Denver, 49 miles; fare, $3.75. W. & L. Smith's stage line leaves tri-weekly—on Mondays, Wednesdays, and Saturdays—for the silver districts of Caribou and Nederland; fare to the former point, $3.50. From Boulder to Cheyenne are numerous flourishing towns, such as Longmont, Loveland, and Fort Collins; fare and distance noted in table.

The Colorado Central railway runs morning and evening trains into and out of the mountains and to Boulder and Longmont and way stations, and a morning train to Cheyenne to connect with the Union Pacific. Omnibuses ply between hotels and other points and the railway stations at Denver, Boulder, Cheyenne, Golden, Central, Black Hawk, and Georgetown. The fare on these is usually fifty cents.

The towns on the plains division are: Denver, population, 27,000; elevation, 5,196 feet. Golden, population, 3,000; elevation, 5,687 feet. Boulder, 3,500; elevation, 5,536. Longmont, 600 inhabitants and 4,957 elevation. Loveland, population, 250; and Fort Collins, 800 inhabitants. Cheyenne is 6,075 feet above the sea, and has nearly 5,000 people. In the mountains are Black Hawk, with 2,000 people and an elevation of 7,775; Central, with 3,500 people and an elevation of 8,300. With Nevadaville they form a city of 6,500 people. Fares on the Colorado Central were reduced from one-fourth to one-third on the first of June. Fares from Denver to Golden, 80 cents; to Black Hawk, $2.85; to Central, $3.10; to Idaho Springs, $2.90; to Georgetown, $4.30; to Boulder, $1.75. Summer excursion rates much lower.

STAGE LINES.

Stages connect at Boulder for the mining camps of Caribou, Neder-land, Four-Mile, and hacks with Gold Hill, Ballarat, Jamestown. In the summer months stages connect with the railway at Loveland, to and from the beautiful summer resort of Estes Park, distant a few hours' drive, where a first-class hotel is located. On certain days conveyances ply between Fort Collins and Greeley. Fare from Denver to Golden is 80 cents; to Boulder, $1.75; Cheyenne, $5.

Stages make regular trips from Georgetown, via Empire and Berth-oud Pass, to Hot Sulphur Springs in Middle Park. This is a delight-ful trip and is made in either direction in a single day.

TO LEADVILLE, TEN MILE, GUNNISON AND SAN JUAN—NEW RAILROAD.

Since this book began to be printed the Leadville division of the Atchison, Topeka & Santa Fe railroad has passed beyond Cañon City and the Grand Cañon, and up the Arkansas river to Pleasant Valley and towards Cleora. The latter place will be the railway terminus for some weeks to come, and will be a great outfitting point for the San Juan and Gunnison regions, as well as Leadville. It is distant but sixty miles and eight hours' staging from the latter point up a water grade.

KANSAS PACIFIC RAILWAY.

The Kansas Pacific railway stations within the limits of Colorado and their distances from Denver are as follows : Denver; Schuyler, 10; Box Elder, 22; Kiowa, 31; Byers, 44; Deer Trail, 56; Agate, 67; Cedar Point, 77; River Bend, 83; Lake, 92; Hugo, 105; Mirage, 115; Aroya, 128; Wild Horse, 140; Kit Carson, 152; First View, 167; Cheyenne Wells, 177; Arapahoe, 187; Monotony, 202; Eagle Trail, 210. The distance to Kansas City is 639 miles.

DENVER & BOULDER VALLEY R. R.

The Denver & Boulder Valley railroad, extending from Denver to the Erie coal mines, thence to Boulder, uses the Denver Pacific track as far as Hughes, where it branches off to the westward. Stations and distances from Denver are as follows : Denver Junction, 2 miles; Hughes, 20; Erie, 34; Mitchell's, 35; Canfield, 36; White Rock Mills, 42; Valmont, 44; C. C. Junction, 46; Boulder, 47.

DENVER & SOUTH PARK R. R. AND LEADVILLE STAGES.

Denver, South Park & Pacific stations and distances from Denver: Denver; West Denver, 1; Bear Creek Junction, 7; Littleton, 11; Archer's, 17; Platte Cañon, 20; Deane's, 26; South Platte, 29; Dome Rock, 31; Buffalo Tank, 38; Buffalo, 39; Pine Grove, 42; Deer Creek, 48; Esterbrook Park, 51; Bailey's, 54; Fairville, 58; Geneva, 68; Webster, 70; Jefferson, 80. The elevation of Webster is 9,120 feet, and of the Kenosha Divide 10,139.

One of the main thoroughfares to Leadville is via the Denver & South Park railway and stage lines. This route has been heavily patronized since the last two advances of the railway. From January to the present month there was 70 miles of railroading from Denver to Webster, and 70 miles of staging via Fairplay and Weston Pass. Very recently ten miles more of road were completed, with Jefferson as the terminus, giving 80 miles of railroading and 60 of staging. Fare, —. The Mosquito Pass wagon road was to have been completed by June 1st, when the stage companies would transfer their lines to that route. This would cut off nearly 20 miles of staging, and reduce the fare. In June it is expected that the railway will reach Fairplay. Three meals and lodging at Fairplay, on this route, cost $3. The summer will open with 80 miles of railroading and over 40 of staging, and there will soon be 20 miles less of staging. The programme of the past winter and spring was as follows:

Stages connect at Webster for Fairplay, 30 miles, and Leadville, 70 miles. Fare to Webster, $7; to Leadville, $17. Eating station at Webster; dinner, $1. Stopping over night at Fairplay, $2; station east slope of range, dinner, 75 cents.

Quicker time is made to Leadville by the newly established Leadville Express train. This connects with all roads running into Denver. Leaving the latter place at 9.30 P. M. the passenger breakfasts in Fairplay and arrives in Leadville that afternoon.

The Ten Mile country has communication with Leadville and Georgetown by different stage lines. Distance from Leadville, 17 to 19 miles; fare, $4 or $7 for the round trip, and has been still higher during the spring.

DENVER PACIFIC R. R.

Denver Pacific Railroad.—The Denver Pacific extends from Denver to Cheyenne, 106 miles, fare $7, with Greeley and Evans on the route. The stations and distances from Denver are Denver Junction, 2 miles; Henderson's Island, 14; Hughes, 20; Fort Lupton, 27; Johnson, 33; Platteville, 35; Evans, 48; Greeley, 52 (fare, $3.75); Pierce, 67; Carr, 86; Summit, 96; Cheyenne, 106.

The Golden Boulder & Caribou Company has 5½ miles of road in operation between Boulder and Marshall, where the Marshall coal mines are situated.

DENVER & RIO GRANDE MAIN LINE.

Dist. in Miles.	Name.	Elevation.	Fare.	Dist. in Miles.	Name.	Elevation.	Fare.
.	Denver..........	5,143		105	Pinon..............	4,986	
2	Machine Shops....	5,189		117	North Pueblo......	4,657	
8	Petersburg........	5,270		120	South Pueblo......	4,615	
10	Littleton..........	5,320		129	San Carlos........	4,986	
17	Acequia........	5,479		133	Greenhorn........	5,045	
24	Plum	5,782		140	Salt Creek........	5,411	
29	Mill No. 2........	5,985		146	Graneros..........	5,750	
32	Castle Rock.......	6,173		156	Huerfano......	5,690	
35	Douglas..........	6,273		169	Cuchara..........	5,893	
38	Glade............	6,466		176	Walsenburg	6,134	
43	Larkspur.........	6,590		183	Wahatoya	6,512	
47	Greenland...	6,875		191	La Veta..........	6,970	
52	Divide............	7,186		199	Ojo..............	8,129	
56	Monument........	6,931		202	Mule Shoe........	8,724	
58	Borst's...........	6,759		205	Veta Pass.........	9,339	
62	Husted's.........	6,557		207	Sangre de Christo..	9,009	
67	Edgerton	6,303		212	Placer............	8,352	
75	Colorado Springs..	5,931		220	Fort Garland......	7,882	
84	Widefield........	5,660		238	Baldy.............	7,494	
88	Fountain.........	5,510		250	Alamosa..........	7,492	
94	Little Buttes......	5,318					

CAÑON OR ARKANSAS VALLEY BRANCH D. & R. G. R. R.

Distances from Denver.	Names.	Elevation.	Distances from Denver.	Names.	Elevation.
120	South Pueblo........	....	143	Beaver Creek........	4,947
124	Goodnight	4,677	152	Labrun	5,130
129	Meadows............	4,749	153	Coal Junction	5,145
134	Swallow............	4,808	155	Coal Banks........	5,330
140	Carlisle Springs.....	4,905	160	Cañon City.........	5,287

Fare from Denver to Cañon, $14; from Pueblo, $4. Stages westward and south from Cañon, as noted above.

El Moro Branch.—This leaves main line at Cucharas and continues to El Moro, the coal mining and coke manufacturing headquarters. Stations : Cucharas, distance in miles from Denver, 169.
Santa Clara, 180 ; elevation, 6,147. Apishapa, distance, 189 ; elevation, 6,106. Chicosa, distance, 198 ; elevation, 6,104. El Moro,
distance, 206 ; elevation, 5,825. Fare, $18.60 from Denver and
$8.60 from Pueblo to El Moro.

BUFFALO HUNTING ON THE PLAINS.

CHAPTER IV.

THE CITIES OF THE PLAINS—DENVER, COLORADO SPRINGS, MANITOU, AND SOUTH PUEBLO—FACTS AND FIGURES CONCERNING THE GREAT SUMMER RESORTS OF COLORADO—PIKE'S PEAK AND VICINITY—THE TWIN LAKES AND OTHER POINTS.

The beautiful and attractive city of Denver is doubly welcome to the traveler after the long journey across the plains, and the fascination attending first sight is increased rather than diminished on closer inspection. There is a dash and animation to the place, along with a finish and elegance that suggests prosperity, wealth, and Eastern stability, as well as the progressive and aggressive frontier. It is the healthy vigor of the thriving trade centre, the prodigality of the mining metropolis combined with the life and display of the great thoroughfare and pleasure resort that give the Queen City of the plains and mountains this doubly attractive appearance.

It is generally conceded that Denver is the best built city between Saint Louis and San Francisco, and there is no denying the fact that her growth at the present time is more rapid and her prospects more brilliant than any other place excepting that new-born wonder, Leadville. The city is situated at the junction of Cherry creek with the Platte river, and is mainly built on ground sloping slightly towards the mountains which rise so grandly along the entire western horizon. The line of vision takes in the "snowy range" and its outlying foot hills for a distance of one hundred and fifty miles, forming a landscape the eye can never grow weary of. The streets are broad, solid, and cleanly, and are lined in all directions with massive blocks, or elegant residences and pretty cottages in the midst of running waters, handsome shade trees, green lawns, and pleasant groves. Stately school and church edifices and fine parks and tree-lined boulevards are distinctive features of this young western emporium.

Great changes have been wrought within the past twenty years in this locality. When the pioneer gold hunters were just beginning to put in an appearance, a barren plain alone was visible where now are handsome avenues, bubbling fountains, and thronged and busy

LARIMER STREET, DENVER.

marts of trade. In place of the wilderness is a flourishing city of nearly thirty thousand people, with street-cars, gas and water works, telephonic, telegraphic, and railway facilities, an effective fire department, theatres, first-class newspapers and hotels, and all the seeming requirements of a great metropolis. Denver is a fast city, with appendages corresponding to the inclinations of her citizens and temporary residents.

Being the grand port of entry to the mountain mining regions and to the health and pleasure resorts, and the State capital, she is the temporary abiding place of multitudes of strangers and immigrants as well as Coloradans. The floating population is always large, especially in the summer months, and no other city of double its population does half the hotel business. In an almost equal degree is the mercantile and jobbing trade remarkable, for this is the supply point for almost a thousand miles of territory and of the most progressive mining regions in the world. Consequently Denver is the receiving and distributing point for an immense industry and population, while the half-dozen railways centering there are of no little service in carrying on the work.

Last year nearly 150,000 tons of freight were received at Denver and over 120,000 tons were forwarded. The sales of merchandise aggregated $16,630,125, of which $4,800,000 were groceries, $1,750,000 dry goods, and $1,350,000 flour, feed, and grain. The value of goods manufactured was $1,791,695. This year extensive smelting works and rolling mills began operations. Although transactions in real estate were much less per month than now, the warranty deeds represented a total of $809,689. The assessed valuation of Arapahoe County in 1878 was $11,093,990—probably a fourth less than for 1879. It is evident that the actual valuation of Denver real estate and personal property is over $18,000,000. The receipts of the Denver post office for the last year were $54,856.90, mainly for sales of stamps, and the expenses $21,105. There were 12,274 money orders issued, representing $197,451; total deposits from other offices, $549,729. This is the distributing office for a large population. Some idea of the extent of travel may be had from the fact that the four large hotels of Denver alone had 50,100 arrivals in 1878, and the score of smaller houses had as many more. The value of buildings erected in 1878 was $410,822. This year may double those figures. Denver is the great focal railroad point of the Rocky

Mountain region, and rapid transit or quick connection is afforded to and with all important points. Leaving Denver for the present, we will proceed to those most attractive of all Colorado resorts, Colorado Springs and Manitou.

The towns of Colorado Springs and Manitou—and one of these places cannot be mentioned without suggesting the other—have a greater number of wonders and attractions easily accessible and within a short distance than any other single locality. These and their own beautiful scenery and medicinal waters are the causes of their large summer population. Days of unmixed pleasure await those lovers of the beautiful in nature who have a few days to devote to the cañons, grottoes, mountains, and curiosities of this section. First of all there is that giant sentinel, Pike's Peak, towering over plain and foot hill, the view from whose summit is indescribably grand. Although this attains the enormous altitude of 14,147 feet, by following the trail it can be ascended on horseback. On the barren rocky mountain top is a government signal-service station. To witness sunrise from this elevated locality is an experience long to be remembered, and should certainly be set down on the programme of the tourist. The Garden of the Gods, so named from the grotesque and gigantic rocks of red and white sandstone thrown into all manner of fantastic shapes and worn by the elements, constitutes one of the State's greatest natural wonders. These rocks are scattered in picturesque confusion from the enormous portal of the enclosure to the lofty crags that rise on either hand. Some of these giant pillars and cathedral-shaped towers are hundreds of feet in height, and altogether form a scene at once weird and enchanting. Ute Pass is a romantic spot amid almost perpendicular walls of rock, and rich in glens, grottoes, streams and waterfalls. Once solitary and unfrequented except by the tourist, it has recently been the thoroughfare of much of the Leadville trade and traffic. Long wagon trains are constantly ascending and descending this mountain defile on their way to and from the carbonate metropolis. Cheyenne and Williams cañons, with their sparkling brooklets, foaming streams, beautiful waterfalls, and general massiveness and sublimity of scenery are equally important objective points. Some distance to the northward is the famous Monument Park, and not far from Manitou is the lovely dell of Glen Eyrie. But it is impossible to note at length all the points of interest or beauty which abound on every hand. They are plentiful, from the plains to the hunting and fishing grounds of South Park and of the great range beyond. There is almost no limit to their extent and attractiveness.

GARDEN OF THE GODS.

On the western rim of the basin of the upper Arkansas are those gems of the Sierras, the Twin Lakes. These beautiful bodies of water are almost mountain locked, being located among the eastern slopes of the great Sawatch Range. Around them are the Twin Peaks, Lake Mountain, La Plata, and Mount Elbert. Leadville is eighteen miles distant and Granite three miles. Always a favorite resort these lakes are doubly so since the influx of population among the carbonate fields. A good hotel has been erected and sailboats are at the disposal of guests. The pleasure-seeker can here enjoy the highest yachting in the world, while trout are abundant and game of all kinds plentiful. The lower lake is three and a half miles long by two and a half wide, and the upper one is somewhat smaller. The altitude is 9,357 feet.

COLORADO SPRINGS.—The City of Colorado Springs is beautifully situated on the Denver & Rio Grande Railway, seventy-five miles south of Denver, near the foot of Pike's Peak, and at the mouth of Ute Pass, through which an excellent wagon road runs to Fairplay, Leadville, Alma, Oro City, and other places in South Park and on the headwaters of the Arkansas river. Its present population (May 1, 1879,) is 5,000, and it is growing with great rapidity. The town site was purchased in 1871, and the first stake driven on the first day of August of that year. Since then the growth of the town has been rapid and its prosperity uninterrupted.

During the year 1878 there was about $1,500,000 worth of merchandise sold, of which nearly $500,000 was in groceries and produce. It is the centre of a large lumber trade. Upon the ranges in the immediate vicinity of the town are over 200,000 head of sheep and 30,000 head of cattle and horses.

Owing to its magnificent climate and its proximity to the celebrated soda and iron springs at Manitou, five miles distant, Colorado Springs has become one of the most popular resorts in the United States for seekers after pleasure and health. During the year 1878, over 13,000 visitors were registered at its hotels, while nearly as many more were quartered in private boarding-houses. The winters in this locality are usually mild, with but little snow, no rain, and the air is dry and exhilarating. In the summer the nights are always cool and pleasant. The livery establishments are numerous and their charges moderate. There are eight churches, representing all the principal religious denominations, a magnificent public school, attended by nearly five hundred pupils, several private schools, and a flourishing college, with well-endowed professorships. The streets of the town are level, never either dusty or muddy, and are lined with shade trees to the number of over 7,000. Within a few miles of Colorado Springs are to be found many of the finest pieces of scenery

COLORADO SPRINGS.

in the Rocky Mountain region. Cheyenne Cañon, Manitou, The
Garden of the Gods, Glen Eyrie, Monument Park, Ute Pass are all
within an hour's drive, and the summit of Pike's Peak can be
reached with ease, on horseback, in a few hours' ride. The city has
recently supplied itself with abundance of the purest water from
Ruxton's creek, which is conducted in pipes through every street in
the town.

MANITOU.—This delightful resort for health and pleasure seekers
is located at the renowned soda and iron springs, eight in number,
in a nook in the mountains, at the very foot of Pike's Peak, and
about five miles west of Colorado Springs. The road from the latter
place to South Park and Leadville passes immediately through it.
Here are five hotels, three of which are quite large, capable of
accommodating a thousand guests. In the summer season this resort
is thronged with fashionable tourists from all parts of the United
States and Europe. Owing to its thorough protection from the
winds, it is a favorite winter resort for invalids. A number of beautiful villas have been erected here. Its present population is about
400. All the scenery tributary to Colorado Springs is equally accessible from Manitou. The town is well supplied with pure mountain
water, in pipes, under heavy pressure. During the season of 1878,
which was unusually short, 5,651 visitors registered at the several
hotels.

SOUTH PUEBLO.—This thriving town is situated on the south side
of the Arkansas river, immediately opposite Pueblo. It was laid
out in 1872 by the Central Colorado Improvement Company, and
now has a population of about 1,500. The business portion of the
town is located on the first bottom of the Arkansas river, while the
residence portion occupies the mesa or elevated table-land adjoining.
The view from this part of the town is one of the finest in the country. To the west and southwest rise in full view some of the loftiest
peaks of the Rocky Mountains, while to the eastward the eye takes
in the almost illimitable sweep of rolling prairie, through which, as
far as the view extends, flows the Arkansas river, on its way to the
Father of Waters.

The climate of South Pueblo is peculiarly adapted to such invalids as require warm and dry winters, and there are but few days in
the year when such persons cannot safely remain in the open air

from morning until night. The winter temperature is many degrees higher than in any other locality in Colorado.

This is one of the principal railroad centres of the State. The Denver & Rio Grande railway, extending from Denver to the great coal mines of El Moro, and thence, via La Veta, to the gold and silver mines of the southwest, passes through it from north to south, with a branch running west to Cañon City, while the Atchison, Topeka & Santa Fe, coming in from the east, up the Arkansas river, gives a direct broad gauge communication with the Mississippi Valley. Large smelting works have been located here, and its cheap coal and fine water power, combined with its railroad communication with all parts of the State, will certainly make it an important manufacturing centre in the near future.

It is well supplied with water for irrigating purposes from a large lake near the town, the latter being connected by means of an aqueduct with the St. Charles river. Ten thousand shade trees have been planted on each side of the streets in the residence part of the town.

South Pueblo is located in the midst of one of the best stock ranges on the continent. To the southeast stretches a vast section of rolling plains that cannot be irrigated, covered with the richest grasses, which afford pasturage for countless herds of cattle, sheep, and horses, requiring no other food and shelter throughout the year than such as they can find on their ranges. Northeasterly another vast and excellent section for grazing rolls on to the Great Divide.

PUEBLO.—This city adjoins South Pueblo on the north, and is a point of considerable importance. This is the county seat of Pueblo county. The court-house and public school building are fine structures, the first costing $50,000 and the other $30,000. There are many large stores, several banks, and two daily newspapers. The place was founded in the winter of 1859-60, and soon absorbed the earlier settlement of Fontaine. Its growth was slow up to the advent of the railways, but business is now steadily improving and enlarging. With South Pueblo, this constitutes much the largest city in Southern Colorado.

CHAPTER V.

AMONG THE MAGNIFICENT MOUNTAINS, CAÑONS, AND PARKS OF SOUTH-
ERN COLORADO—WHAT THE TOURIST AND INVALID CAN SEE AND
ENJOY—OUTLINES OF DESIRABLE EXCURSIONS—HUNTING, FISH-
ING, AND PLEASURE RESORTS.

Some of the most widely known summer resorts in Colorado, as
well as others of equal attractiveness, though not so generally familiar
to the outside world, are easily reached by the Atchison, Topeka &
Santa Fe railroad and its various connections. At Pueblo, the western terminus of this great highway, the tourist who travels for health
or pleasure, or both, finds easy access to Colorado Springs, Cañon
City, and the San Juan country. Each of these sections possesses a
wealth of enjoyable features that render them well worth the time
and money which one must expend in order to give them due consideration. As to the former item, the advantages given by steam
transportation have placed the trip within the power of the most
hurried tourist. And as to the latter, competition has reduced it to
the minimum.

The nearest point from Pueblo is Cañon City, where one may look
upon a rare wealth of natural scenery, draw pleasure and benefit
from medicinal springs, and observe the active operation of some of
the leading industries of the State. The place takes its name from
the various picturesque cañons and gorges that have been cut into
the mountains on every side, but more particularly from the Grand
Cañon of the Arkansas, which is one of the most famous works of
nature in any part of the world. The ride from Pueblo to Cañon
City is of brief duration, but full of pleasure to the lovers of the
grand works of nature. The tracks of the Denver & Rio Grande
road pass through a section of country than which there is
nothing more beautiful in the land. At the terminus of this
branch of the road one finds himself in a scrupulously neat little city,
much frequented by tourists and invalids, the centre of the greatest
coal region in the State, the location of several important mining interests, and outfitting headquarters for most of the San Juan coun-

try, as well as of Chalk Creek and California Gulch districts. The rates for accommodation are from $2 to $3 per day; per week, from $8 to $12.50. That grandest of all experiences, a railway excursion through the Grand Cañon of the Arkansas, can now be made from Cañon City. Distance, 5 to 10 miles. Livery rates are quite reasonable, to wit: team and single buggy to Grand Cañon, one horse, $5; two horses, $6, this being with or without a driver; Temple Cañon or Curiosity Hill, $2 to $3; Marble Cave, Oil Creek, or Oak Creek Cañon, same as to Grand Cañon. Carriage for four, by the day, $6.

JOSEPH'S POOL & COLORED ROCKS.   GRAPE CREEK CAÑON.

For three or more passengers the tariff to the Grand Cañon is $7 to $8 for the party, and for five or more $1.50 to $2 each. The proprietors of the hotel, however, furnish transportation to all desirous of visiting the Grand Cañon at the uniform rate of $2, no matter what the number of the party.

The ride to Grape Creek Cañon and return may be made with ease in half a day, and may include a visit to Temple Cañon by the way. The road is smooth and hard, and is rapidly traversed by the excellent horses provided by the Cañon City livery stables.

Grape Creek Cañon takes its name from the wonderful profusion of grape-vines which deck its lofty walls. The defile is one of the most beautiful in all the State. Its sides are composed of many colored rocks, which rise to an enormous height and are piled in fantastic shapes, which hold the spectator spell-bound. Through the bottom of the gorge flows Grape creek, a brawling crystal stream, which lashes the boulders in its bed with seething fury. In the early autumn, when the thickly clustering grape-vines are heavy with their purple fruit, and when their leaves have been touched by the pencil of gay Jack Frost, the many rich colors displayed in this cañon are well worth traveling thousands of miles to see. At any time the scene presented here is weird and picturesque in the extreme.

One enters Temple Cañon, which is a kind of side door from the one just mentioned, through a luxuriant grove of trees. Its various features must be inspected on foot, as there is no roadway. In the midst of this little rift in the rocks Nature has carved a wondrous structure, which is an exact counterpart of what we mortals know as a theatre. Before a broad floor there stands an immense stage, fronted by a proscenium arch, and backed by a "flat" upon which is pictured the rugged outlines of some rustic scene. The "flies" and "wings" are also to be discerned, and on either side of the stage are spaces which we may almost imagine were employed as dressing-rooms for the mystic actors who played upon that stage to an audience of the gods. The broad plateau in front of the great stage makes an excellent "orchestra," and one may readily find room for the fancy that the ledges towering hundreds of feet above, may, in some distant age, have been used as galleries for impecunious or low-grade gods who wished to see the play.

In Oak Creek Cañon, fifteen miles distant from the city, one may also find food for gratification, and half a day may be spent there both with profit and enjoyment. And upon Curiosity Hill the tourist has an opportunity for research which is likely to fascinate him for an indefinite period. There, scattered over the ground, are all sorts of odd and beautiful little specimens of ribbon moss, linear agate crystals and the like. The surface of the hill is one vast field of curiosities. By blasting, large bodies of the most perfect crystals are obtained, invariably bedded in ribbon agate of the most beautiful colors and shapes, and polishing readily, they form beyond all compar-

ison the loveliest of cabinet attractions. Many very valuable specimens of blood agate have been found upon Curiosity Hill, and for
agates of all hues and forms it is possibly the most satisfactory field
for the specimen-seeker in southern Colorado.

Oil Creek, unlike many other streams in the vicinity, is heavily

TEMPLE CAÑON.

wooded. It takes its title from the more or less valuable discoveries of petroleum along its banks. Several wells have been sunk at various places, and the result, though not extremely profitable, gives rise to the hope that at some future day coal oil may be found in large quantities near at hand. The waters of Oil Creek are strongly impregnated with petroleum, and in some places the oil floats in thick offensive layers upon the water. Improved methods of boring are now adopted, and the prospects for the establishment here of a new industry are most promising. Oil Creek Cañon is a deep and resplendent chasm, cut through variegated sandstone. The many-hued walls are wrought into strange forms, many of them strongly suggestive of the various works of man. Fortifications of massive strength, sculptured heads, clear-cut figures—all go to make this locality a great natural art gallery. The piñon trees which crest the towering heights, bear heavy harvests of sweet and nutritious nuts, which are eaten by wandering tribes of Indians with great avidity.

Marble Cave, Talbott Hill, and some property from his Satanic Majesty's household, including his bower, punch-bowl, and arm-chair, all form interesting points to be visited from Cañon City. The coal mines, situated about a dozen miles to the southward, should not be overlooked by tourists. The veins of almost bituminous coal here found are of marvelous extent and richness. For miles one is permitted to ride through the gloomy shaft of the mine upon a small wooden car, which is also used to freight the coal from its bed to the open air.

There are eighty-six side-chambers, or rooms, as the miners know them, in the main entry, fifty-seven in another entry, and in all, four miles of track upon which the coal is carried to the outer world. The veins average five feet two inches, and run three and one-half miles east and west and ten miles north and south. A hundred miners are at work, and the yield averages four hundred tons per day. The gigantic solid lump of coal, eight feet nine inches long, six feet across, and four feet four inches high, that attracted such great attention at he Centennial, being beyond all comparison the greatest single piece of coal on exhibition, was taken from this mine. It weighed seven tons, and was cut and brought out of the mine in three days. Cañon City coal is unquestionably the finest lignite coal in the world, and is so extensively used throughout the West as to require the running of special trains for coal alone on the Denver & Rio Grande road, which has its own track to the mines. The supply is beyond all human calculation, for the valley of the Arkansas is one vast coal bed for mile upon mile.

The Grand Cañon of the Arkansas is at last penetrated by a railway. The Atchison, Topeka & Santa Fe Company completed several miles of track from Cañon City up through the Royal Gorge early in May, and the first passenger excursion train passed up and down on the 7th day of that month. Far down in the depths, beside the foaming waters of the river, steam cars will soon make their daily trips to the mountain metropolis of Leadville. No sunshine ever enters long sections of this massive defile, and but a narrow strip of the heavens is visible from the train. Many prefer the old way of seeing the cañon from above. This trip is made by carriage or on horseback.

The drive from the hotel to the Grand Cañon covers thirteen miles over a stretch of country which is almost bewildering in its wealth of startling features. It is possible to ride almost to the very edge of the tremendous cleft through which the foaming Arkansas roars with intense fury. And when one stands upon the brink of that vast precipice and gazes down thousands of feet, he is overcome by awe at the magnitude of Nature's handiwork. So far beneath as to be almost lost from sight, the river winds its way like a tiny thread of the purest white. Indeed, it is almost impossible to realize that what appears to be but an insignificant rivulet is in reality the mighty Arkansas.

Near at hand is the Royal Gorge—the greatest and most impressive chasm on the "Eastern Slope." It is in many ways different from the cañon, and excites the greatest enthusiasm among the lovers of grand scenery. At the first point of observation the walls, though frightfully steep, are nevertheless sloping to more or less extent; here at the Royal Gorge there are sheer precipices, as perpendicular as the tallest house, as straight as if built by line. So narrow is the gorge that one would think the throwing of a stone from side to side the easiest of accomplishments, yet no living man has ever done it, or succeeded in throwing any object so that it would fall into the water below. Many tourists are content with the appalling view from the main walls, but others more venturesome work their way six hundred to a thousand feet down the ragged edges of a mountain that has parted and actually slid into the chasm.

Few dare to look over the edge of the precipice more than once,

SPANISH PEAKS AND THE PLAINS FROM VETA PASS.

and one glance suffices for a comprehension of the meaning of the
word depth never before even dreamed of, and never afterward forgotten. The gorge is 2,008 feet sheer depth. The opposite wall
towers hundreds of feet above the one on which the tourist stands,
and if possible to imagine anything more terrifying than the position
on this side, that upon the other would be, were its brink safe to
approach. Overhanging crags, black and blasted at their summits
or bristling with stark and gnarled pines, reach up into profoundly
dizzy heights, while lower down monstrous rocks threaten to topple
and carry to destruction any fool-hardy climber who would venture
upon them. Among all the thousands who have visited the Grand
Cañon and the Royal Gorge harm has befallen none, for despite the
seeming horror of the situation, the appalling depth and rugged
paths, the fascination of the danger gives birth to the greatest cau-
tion. The cañon, except in the dead of winter, is approachable
only from the top, the walls below being so precipitous and the river
such a torrent as to defy all access. While the original railway
surveys could be made only when the stream was frozen over, the
Atchison, Topeka & Santa Fe Company is succeeding in blasting a
road bed from the rocky walls for its Leadville extension.

There are, in addition to all these easily accessible places of interest, many points in the vicinity which may easily be taken in.
Rosita, Poncha Springs, and other places may be visited, the trip
occupying from two to four days. These journeys are inexpensive
in the extreme, and the tourist may either camp out or put up at the
various ranches which are found from time to time on all the roads
leading out of Cañon City. The streams abound in magnificent
specimens of trout, and among the woods and crags of the mountains the most enthusiastic hunter can find game in plenty.

A very pleasant journey, which will cover pretty much all the
Southern portion of Colorado, may be made as follows, starting from
Pueblo:

Cross the Sangre de Cristo range, over Veta Pass, on the Denver
& Rio Grande Railway; thence by stage to Del Norte; thence up
the valley of the Rio Grande through Wagon Wheel Gap to Antelope
Park; thence to Silverton, the seat of the great silver district of the
San Juan; thence into the Uncompahgre Valley and Park, making
the circuit to Ouray; thence to Lake City; thence via the Los Pinos
Agency, crossing the Continental Divide to Saguache; thence down

3

the San Luis Valley over Poncho Pass to South Arkansas; thence
to Chalk Creek, Twin Lakes, California Gulch, and the Mount of
the Holy Cross, returning via South Park to Fairplay, thence
through Ute Pass to Manitou and Colorado Springs. This the main
line to be followed; numberless side jaunts are permitted, and

SCENE AT VETA PASS, D. & R. G. R. R.

nearly if not quite the entire tour can be made by stage. The most
agreeable manner of making the tour is, however, the commingling
of stage, wagon, horseback, and jaunts on foot, as in this way one is
entirely independent of time schedules, gauging his rambles only so
as to make connection with stage at such points as it is most desirable. It is not unfrequently the case that horses, mules, and equip-

ment complete are purchased before starting, and at the completion of
the trip sold readily for such prices as render the expense very small.
Others charter conveyances for indefinite periods, and pay at a speci-
fied reduced rate per day. In short, one may make his own choice
of preliminaries, and thus fix the cost according to the means at
command.

TWIN LAKES—THE HIGHEST YACHTING IN THE WORLD,

Wagon Wheel Gap is becoming famous for its hot springs, and
various other attractive features. It is an exceedingly romantic
locality, and the road which leads to it follows along the bank of
the river through scenery of the wildest description. The Gap is a
sharp cut through walls of solid rock. In this cut the river flows,
and there is just room for the stage road beside the stream.

From Wagon-Wheel Gap the road leads west up the Rio Grande,
the valley narrow and rocky of surface to Antelope Park, twenty miles,
where it widens out in broad opens, profusely and richly clothed with
grass. Here the stage road leaves the river as it turns to the right,

and passing over a series of picturesque, pine-covered hills, runs into the shadows of a long range of mountains presenting stupendous cliff faces of exceeding ruggedness. They rise vertically to dizzy heights, and are relieved by innumerable columns and strange rock figures that stand out from the wall or crown the summit. In the early summer, while the snow is still melting on the towering peaks, innumerable streams of water pour down over these cliff-faces, forming beautiful cascades hundreds of feet in depth. Midway of this tremendous and magnificent rock scenery, and immediately on the left of the road, is Lake Santa Maria, two miles in length, but quite narrow, and without visible outlet. It is dotted with little rocky islands, and from the farther shore rises a long, sloping, half-wooded mountain ridge. The water is perfectly clear, perfectly smooth, and all indentations in the rocks, every streak of brown upon the majestic mountain sides, every tuft of evergreen that has gained footing, every tree from base to timber line, the peaks, and everything animate or inanimate, are pictured in the cool shadows with undeviating fidelity.

A few miles from Lake Santa Maria, or Mirror Lake, as it is often termed, is Clear Creek, a fine, large stream wonderfully beautiful in cascades. Here the road turns to the northward to surmount the snowy range, and thence onward the slopes are easy and gentle, the country more park like, and we soon reach a point where Clear Creek plunges down hundreds of feet in one tumultuous leap. Half a dozen miles farther is the pass over the summit of the Rocky range, the approach to which is not steep or abrupt on either side. The first waters we come upon that flow toward the Pacific are the head streams of the Powderhorn, which unite with the Cebolla, a prominent branch of the Gunnison. The streams are skirted by narrow, open valleys, but the road soon climbs up a timbered ridge—a mountain spur which diverges to the north—and for nearly twenty miles it winds through the dusky shadows of a dense forest, coming out at last at the summit of Slumgullion Gulch, a precipitous, rocky, and stumpy descent, with the Lake fork of the Gunnison at its mouth, and four miles beyond the largest commercial centre of the San Juan country—Lake City. The site is decidedly romantic, surrounded as is the city by stupendous mountains, now bare and bald, and then finely zoned with prodigious forest growth. The altitude of Lake City is 8,550 feet, and from a mere cluster of cabins in 1875 it has grown into a thriving, busy centre of from 1,500 to 2,000 population, its mills and reduction works comprising the most extensive system of mining machinery in all the San Juan country. It has churches of almost every denomination, three or four hotels, good schools, several banks, five saw-mills, free reading-room and library, two excellent and energetic newspapers, and other evidences too numerous to mention of substantial and lasting prosperity. Hotel rates run from $2 to $3 per day, and from $10 to $12 per week. Returning to Del Norte it is sometimes pleasant to leave the San Juan country by way of the stage route to Cañon City, and to take the cars at that point for Pueblo, Colorado Springs, and the northern resorts.

U. S. SIGNAL STATION—SUMMIT OF PIKE'S PEAK

CHAPTER VI.

For many years the stage-driver and freighter have been steadily receding from an immense scope of country in which their services were once indispensable. The ever-encroaching extensions of the railways and the sharp competition of lower prices are ever and anon crowding them to the newer fields which the prospector and pioneer are continually proving worthy of occupation. The same history is being repeated in central and southern Colorado that the northern settlements have seen enacted; and here, as there, the lips that welcome the advance of the steam motor tender a heartfelt good-bye and God-speed to the friends of other days. Outside of local farming or mining residents, once famous locations like Guy Hill and Virginia Cañon live only in the recollections of other days. They are now off the lines of travel and the locomotive wakens the echoes where once sped the driver with his "six-in-hand." Let due honor be accorded these gallant knights of the ribbons, who have conducted themselves with equal credit whether in scenes of peril and danger or in the routine every day duties of the road. Although crowded from their former scenes of usefulness, they are yet the autocrats of travel over an empire of park and mountain as matchless for grandeur and beauty as it is boundless in extent. Here the tourist can still be treated to an exhilarating drive from mountain top to cañon depth, or whirled at break-neck speed around the brink of yawning chasms until his love of excitement is fully gratified. Indian bullets no longer greet the driver and his load of human freight, as before the days of plains railways and Pullman sleepers, but there is enough of the sensational about one of these mountain excursions to satisfy the ordinary traveler.

In the multitude of inviting localities that await the inspection of

the pleasure-seeker, all or half of which it is impossible to visit in a
few weeks' time, or in a single season, it is a difficult matter to make
a choice of routes, or to lay out a plan of travel and live up to it.
But this region of picturesque novelties and ever-changing beauty is
so vast in extent that one can hardly go amiss in making any one of
the plains cities a base of operations, and any part of the mountains

BEAVER BROOK, C. C. R. R.

an objective point. The lover of the beautiful will find a world of
enjoyment, whether viewing the handiwork of the Great Architect
from lofty peak, wooded dell, or sunless cañon. In the variety that
is offered one can go from forest of luxuriant splendor to mountains
of unutterable barrenness and magnitude, from still lake to roaring
cataract, from verdure and cultivation to galleries of nature's

strangest fantasies, without the slightest hint of what the next transition may be. On any one of the most traveled routes, or near any of the pleasure resorts or railway termini, it is but a short remove from the bustling activity of the mining camp or business centre to the solitude and desolation of the mountain top with all its impressiveness. In recalling the attractions of a summer's excursion among the "Rockies," it must be confessed that each picture has a hundred phases rivaling some other in beauty and interest, and that every exquisitely perfect feature in mountain, lake, or river scenery is somewhere garnered here. So whether we explore the wonders of the Royal Gorge, scale the "snowy range," or view the rugged walls and towers of Clear Creek, the Platte or Boulder, there is enough in each or all to repay many long miles of travel. All of these places can be reached within four days from New York, and in less time from Chicago or St. Louis.

No one coming to Colorado should fail to visit the mountains. Without that the entire excursion would be like the play of Hamlet with Hamlet left out. This can be done from any one of several towns, but best of all from Denver. The railway towns of Boulder, Golden, Colorado Springs, and Cañon are located at or near the entrances to beautiful mountain gorges, rich with scenery of wooded dell, castled wall, and dashing waterfall.

At present the most entertaining trip that can be made, and the quickest and cheapest, is that by way of the Colorado Central railway from Denver to the mining cities of Central, Black Hawk, Idaho, and Georgetown. In this the tourist gets the greatest variety for the least expenditure of money that any single excursion affords that actually enters the mountains any distance. While this cañon may not compare with the Royal Gorge in massive grandeur, the tourist can derive infinite pleasure from the many and varied sights that continually offer themselves *en route* and at adjacent points on either hand. There is no finer prospect than that offered from Gray's lofty summit, no more beautiful lakes than those near Georgetown, and nowhere in Colorado are mines so deep or mills so numerous as on the headwaters of Clear creek. There are excellent hotels at all of the towns named, and one of the most noted pleasure resorts, with fine drives and livery turnouts, can be found on this line at Idaho Springs.

The railway time between these points and Denver is but a few

hours, and the round trip can be made in a single day. The time
between the arrival and departure of trains is too short, however, to
permit of seeing the many interesting and instructive features of
such an excursion, and at least one or two days should be devoted
to each locality. The expense of the round trip should not exceed
thirty dollars, although the outlay can be increased or diminished

CLEAR CREEK CAÑON, C. C. R. R.

according to time and number and variety of places visited. A few
days enables one to take in some of the grandest scenery on the continent, and to learn much of the mountains and of mining and
mining life.

Picturesque Clear Creek Cañon has been portrayed too often to require a detailed description here, and must be seen to be appreciated.

A twenty-mile ride up the curves and windings of this rocky defile brings one first to the creek mines and then to the stamp mills of Black Hawk. The business point of Central, by the wagon road, along which portions of these cities are built, is but little over a mile distant, but the difference of nearly five hundred feet in elevation is too much for any railway grade. Consequently, Gregory Gulch could not be followed, but a detour is made along the mountains until the requisite elevation is gained for a nearly straight shoot for the destination. Central is twenty-six hundred feet higher than Golden and over three thousand feet above Denver. Still further up among the hills is Nevadaville.

The first sight of these cities of the hills is one not soon forgotten. There is a novelty to the scene that attracts in spite of the general barrenness of the landscape—the forest having long since been consumed in furnaces or mines. Thus it is that the numberless prospect holes, dump piles, shafts, cuts, and tunnels that scar the earth's surface are all the more plainly visible. Streets and houses are wedged in narrow ravines and gulches, and again crowded up their steep inclines. The towns centre where streams and gulches unite; for there a little more room can be obtained than elsewhere, and room is an important item here. A main thoroughfare, over three miles in length, winds through these granite hills and busy, bustling towns. Down this numerous quartz teams make their way from mine to mill, loaded with precious ore. Far up the giddy slopes on either side hang cottages and mine buildings, seemingly ready to topple one on another. Where business centres are stately blocks of brick and granite, handsome banks, hotels, and warehouses, whose tops hardly reach to the levels of the streets behind. Beside the turbid streams are huge quartz mills, whose ponderous iron stamps never cease to thunder and rattle. These are the bullion producers and the receptacle of the gold-bearing rock that is constantly being blasted and hoisted from the shafts, levels, and tunnels of the honeycombed hill sides. Here one can be inducted into the mysteries of "wet crushing and raw amalgamation"—of extracting the precious metals from the ore.

It is a strange sight to the new comer, these cities built at the tops of the shafts or mouths of the tunnels which lead to nature's treasure vaults below and on either hand. Down in the depths, hundreds of feet from the light of day, are other cities, less habit-

FROM BLACK HAWK TO CENTRAL, COLORADO CENTRAL RAILWAY

able, but equally active. Here, by the dim candle light, scores and
hundreds of miners wield the drill, pick, and shovel, delving for
the hidden wealth of centuries. Thus do they help to swell the
millions that steadily find their way into the channels of commerce.
A visit to these underground workings is a notable event to the
tourist or stranger.

A trip on the Black Hawk and Central extension of this narrow-
gauge railway is full of interest, and sensational in the extreme.
The grade is even steeper than in the cañon below, and averages
something like one hundred and thirty-five feet to the mile. But, as
the train keeps on ascending, one is brought more into the sun-
light than there, and the prospect becomes far more extensive and
exciting. At one place streets are crossed above the level of the
house tops, and at another, after circling the mountain sides for two
miles, the train makes its appearance hugging the mountain side
hundreds of feet above, and almost directly over the town. One
can almost look down into the fiery chimneys of the great smelters,
while streets rise above, and seemingly bottomless shafts and excavations yawn beneath in this thrilling ride among the gold mines.

At Central one can step into the banks and look upon the glitter-
ing gold retorts fresh from the mills, and ready for export. These
big lumps of the yellow metal, varying in value from one hundred to
fifteen or sixteen thousand dollars each, and in weight from a few
ounces up to a thousand, are continually arriving, as one mill after
another makes its "clean up," and consequently bank shipments
are made almost daily. "Specimens" of gold and silver-bearing
ore, of many colors and varieties, and often strikingly beautiful,
are collectable at the mines and purchasable elsewhere. Many
residents of these places have been diligent in gathering mineral
collections which they would not part with at almost any figure.
Magnificent views of the surrounding country can be obtained from
James' Peak or Bellevue Mountain.

Taking the same railway, with its zigzags, curves, and windings,
back again to the forks of the creeks, twelve miles below Central,
the down train is exchanged for that bound up the main branch of
Clear Creek for Idaho Springs and Georgetown; or if the delightful
experience of a mountain drive is preferred, the short cut of six
miles to Idaho by way of the Divide and down the famous Virginia
cañon can be chosen. This was once the old stage route, but the

railway around the line of the creek supplanted that some time ago.
Seated in a carriage behind a first-class livery team, the prospect
is well worthy of attention. All along the route are lode and gulch
mines, and far away the great range glistens with its mantle of snow
and disappears from sight as the rapid run down the cañon begins.
Nearly a thousand feet to the mile is the descent made on this steep
and rugged slope.

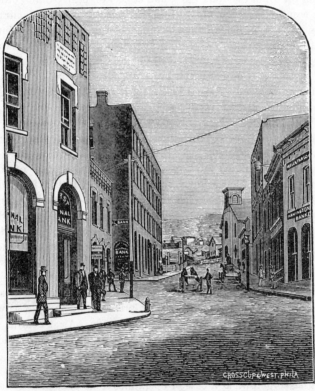

VIEW IN CENTRAL.

If a township several miles square, surrounding and including
Idaho Springs, could be transplanted, with all of its wealth of
mountains and dark cañons, whispering pines, bubbling springs,
leaping, splashing waterfalls, and heavenly atmosphere, to some
central location in the East, it would secure such a population and

fashionable assemblage as no seaside resort can boast of. Idaho stands unsurpassed in natural attractions for those seeking health, pleasure, or novelty. The hotels are spacious and good, the hot soda springs highly beneficial, and the bathing facilities first-class. In the overhanging hills are gold and silver mines, and along the bars and creeks gravel and pay dirt are still washed for gold, as in the earlier days of the country. There are mills for crushing or concentrating ore from the lode veins, and streets of neatly-built cottages, with a mingling of more pretentious structures. The contracted cañon up which the railroad makes its way here widens into a beautiful sunny valley, with green sloping hillsides. All the way to Georgetown numerous mines dot the mountains, with here and there a thriving mining camp. A few miles distant are those noted resorts, Chief Mountain and Chicago Lakes, the latter comprising the highest body of still water in North America.

Beyond Idaho Springs the silver region proper is entered, and quartz mills are succeeded by concentrating and reduction works and ore-buying and sampling establishments.

Inviting as may be the appearance and surroundings of Idaho Springs, those of Georgetown are still more so. Under the shadows of grand old mountains, the "Silver Queen" reigns prosperous, productive, and progressive. All around are silver veins, whose annual output has been gradually creeping up into the millions. Close at hand are the mills for the extraction of the precious metal, and yet other mills where ores are purchased and shipped to distant smelters. The success that has attended mining makes itself manifest in the character and appearance of this fair city. Few western places can boast of as good a class of private residences, of as well-built streets or better patronized marts of trade. As at Central, and most other Colorado towns, the finest and most noticeable building that arrests the attention of the stranger is one devoted to educational purposes.

With Georgetown as a base of operations some of the most charming resorts that the country affords can be reached in rides or drives of a few hours. There are mines and tunnels along the steep mountains almost without number, and well worth the climb necessary to reach them. A few miles away are the famous Gray and Irwin Peaks, domes of the continent, rising respectively to heights of 14,341 and 14,336 feet above sea level. From their summits, reached

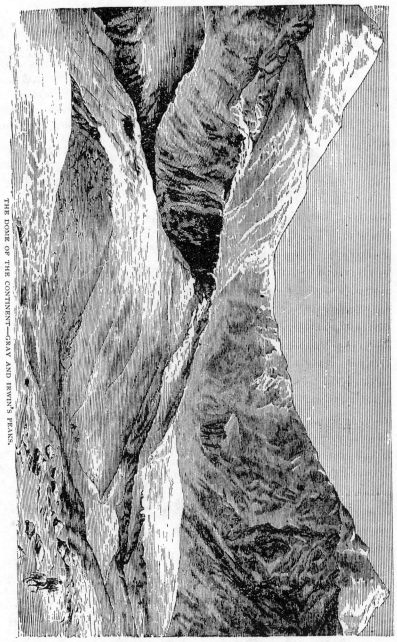

THE DOME OF THE CONTINENT—GRAY AND IRWIN'S PEAKS.

by well-worn trails and bridle-paths, views of surpassing grandeur
are afforded.   Far to the eastward extend the great plains, as level
and boundless as the ocean.   In all other directions countless peaks
and mountain ranges rear their billowy heads like storm-tossed sea
waves, while far below the western slopes are the green valleys of the
Snake, Blue and Grand and of Middle Park.   The range of vision
embraces objects one hundred and fifty miles distant in any direction.

DEVIL'S GATE, GEORGETOWN.

Within two miles of town are Green and Clear lakes, the most
beautiful of their kind that even Colorado has to offer.   Here one
can enjoy boating and fishing at an elevation of ten thousand feet
above the sea.   The Devil's Gate and Bridal Veil Fall are but a few
minutes' walk from the Barton House, and are objects of rare interest.

In the neighboring mountains are tunnels driven into the mountains for distances of from a quarter to nearly half a mile, and other mining enterprises whose deeper workings are hundreds of feet below the starting point.   Besides mines of great extent and richness, the tourist can view the silver mills, where the product is crushed, roasted, amalgamated, and converted into bright silver bullion.

From this same Colorado Central, a ramble up Boulder Cañon can be made in a single day from Boulder City.   This will prove a rare

IN THE PARK.

treat, for it is the most beautiful of all of the northern cañons.   If the trip can be lengthened to that extent, Boulder county should be included in the Georgetown and Central excursion.   The mountain sections must there be visited by stage or other conveyance, and these are at the traveler's disposal at either end of the route.   Pleasant summer retreats are afforded at Rollinsville and Fall River, both of which are unsurpassed for general attractiveness, and for hunting and fishing facilities.

An excursion to that delightful resort, Middle Park, should be by all means set down on the programme, if time and circumstances permit of it. This can be reached from Georgetown or Empire in a single day, by the regular stages of those localities. While stage and hotel accommodations are excellent, and such modes of travel simple and expeditious, many prefer to adopt the old Colorado style of summering in the wilderness by organizing "camping outfits" and to "rough it" in a more primitive and perhaps enjoyable manner. The saddle and pack animals, wagons, or materials and supplies for such an expedition, can be obtained at reasonable figures at Denver or the mountain cities of Central and Georgetown. Roads lead from either of the last-named places over mountain passes to the same destination.

It is difficult to convey a just idea of the world of beauty presented in this summer paradise of Middle Park. The broad expanse of mountain scenery unfolded from the passes of the Sierras or the valleys of the Park, and the rolling prairies and river bottoms, with their luxuriant carpeting of grasses and flowers diversified with groves of pine and aspen, form a picture at once lovely and enchanting. Here is everything that goes to make a mountain ramble enjoyable— cool, invigorating atmosphere, bright skies, unlimited hunting and fishing preserves, health-giving mineral waters, clear lakes, translucent streams and sparkling waterfalls; such are the attractions in store for the visitor. Once over the great Divide, whose lowest passage-way is more than two miles above the sea, and one can revel in the unrestricted freedom of mountain life in one of Nature's most favored localities. The mineral waters of Hot Sulphur Springs relieve all sorts of maladies, and are fast securing the invalid's attention. Distance and the intervening range alone have prevented as great a rush of visitors as at the railway watering-places. The groves and grassy slopes along and between the Frazer, Grand, Blue, and Troublesome abound in different varieties of the feathered species, and in deer, antelope, and elk. All of these and more dangerous game inhabit the timbered slopes of the surrounding mountains, while the streams referred to are alive with speckled beauties of the finny tribe. This variety and quantity is certainly sufficient to satisfy the most exacting disciple of the rod and gun, and the rewards that await his efforts are correspondingly liberal and satisfactory. To the pent-up denizens of the great cities nothing can furnish more rare enjoyment than a summer's jaunt among these far away solitudes of forest and stream beyond the "snowy range."

Less remote and difficult of access, but equally beautiful, is the lesser inland valley of Estes Park, reached by a few hours' staging from the Colorado Central railway towns of Loveland and Long- mont. This lovely and fashionable resort is close to the eastern base of that giant sentinel of the great range, Long's Peak, whose summit is 14,271 feet above sea level. This park has a first-class hotel and is frequented by large numbers of visitors every summer.

EMMA LAKE, ESTES PARK.

CHAPTER VII.

The construction of the Atchison, Topeka & Santa Fe railway over the prairies of Kansas and into the mountains and plateaus of Colorado and New Mexico is transforming an ocean of wilderness into a region of thrift and plenty. It affords a great through line of travel to or towards localities famous for their wealth and productiveness. It conveys multitudes of people to the new El Dorado of Leadville, to the health and pleasure resorts of Colorado, and yet other hundreds into the silver-ribbed mountains of the San Juan. The shrill notes of its locomotives waken the echoes among the hills of New Mexico and rouse the indolent descendants of the Spaniard and Aztec from their lethargic sleep.

The silver and gold veins of Southern Colorado and the traffic of the Mexicos shaped the course of this railway, whose location and objective points would be better understood if "Kansas, Colorado & New Mexico" was the title instead of that adopted. But its mission will not be complete with the construction of lines already contracted for. An outlet to and for the Pacific coast and its commerce is wanted, and the mines of Arizona are a strong incentive to further progress. Consequently, the road is to be pushed westward from Santa Fe to unite with the on-coming Southern Pacific or to secure through roads to California and Mexico of its own.

Already the Atchison, Topeka & Santa Fe, and its north, south, and west branches and leased lines, built and building, afford cheap and rapid transit and transportation to an ever-increasing area of immense proportions. What is termed the main line has already crossed the Raton mountains into New Mexico and will reach Las Vegas in July. The Arkansas Valley Division is being constructed from Cañon to Leadville as rapidly as possible, and is expected to reach the latter point early in the fall, if not sooner. The first-named line secures the traffic of New Mexico and the great southwest, and the latter will have all that one road can handle in the travel and transportation of the carbonate camps and the San Juan silver mines of the lower western slope. The corporation possesses ample means for carrying forward any and all of its construction projects, while its management evinces a degreee of enterprise commensurate with the magnitude of its operations. At the present time it is operating about 1,400 miles of railroad, which every week sees extending, and which will soon be increased to from 1,550 to 1,700. Connection is made at the eastern termini, Kansas City and Atchison, with the great routes leading through Missouri to Chicago, New York, St. Louis, and all leading eastern cities. It is the only direct route to New Mexico and San Juan, and is within twenty-six hours of Leadville by connecting stages.

After the two sections of the main line starting at the Missouri river unite at Topeka (the headquarters of the company), the road strikes off southwesterly to the fertile valley of the Arkansas, and follows up that stream on an ascending grade of not far from ten feet per mile to La Junta, Colorado. Here one division continues on up this valley to Pueblo, and the other passes southwesterly into New Mexico. Kansas has recently become the leading wheat-growing State in the Union, and ranks high in the production of other grains and of corn. This road passes through the entire length of this granary of the West, with its lands of unsurpassed fertility. The country is filling up with farmers all along the line of this road, a large portion of the settlers purchasing lands of this company at merely nominal figures. In Colorado the road intersects a splendid stock region, where cattle and sheep are raised at so trifling an outlay as to leave a wonderful margin of profit to those following the avocation. It crosses the great buffalo ranges of the plains, and for hundreds of miles follows the old Santa Fe trail, the natural highway of traffic adopted by the pioneers and Mexican traders of the last generation. Its travel and traffic is immense, especially into and for Colorado. Pullman palace cars are run on all through trains, and there is no better managed or equipped road in the country. The general officials of the company are

Thomas Nickerson, president; W. B. Strong, vice-president and general manager; George O. Manchester, assistant general manager; E. Wilder, secretary and treasurer; J. P. Whitehead, auditor; W. F. White, general passenger agent, and J. F. Goddard, general freight agent. W. W. Borst is superintendent of the Denver & Rio Grande division, and T. J. Anderson, general passenger agent.

The Colorado and New Mexico division of the Atchison, Topeka & Santa Fe railroad passes southwesterly up the valley of the Las Animas river through Trinidad and the Raton Mountains. From a recently published account of this section of the road by Henry Sturgis, the following is condensed :

The Raton Mountains reach out from the great Sangre de Christo range in a nearly easterly direction and almost on a line with the boundary of Colorado and New Mexico. Raton Peak, 9,400 feet high and seven miles south of Trinidad, is their culminating point. West of this peak begins Raton Cañon, crooked, savage, and picturesque, rising up to Raton Pass, 7,863 feet above the sea. Directly opposite, and on the southern or New Mexican slope, is Willow Cañon, which further down debouches upon the vast pastural plains beyond. The hollow thus scooped out by the finger of nature has long been a great viaduct of travel, the portal of New Mexico and the route of a vast traffic. This natural artery of trade, the Atchison, Topeka & Santa Fe Company has followed, and, after a successful contest with the Denver & Rio Grande Company for possession, had nothing to contend with save the great natural obstacles of the pathway.

The distance from Trinidad to the summit of the pass is a little over fifteen miles, and the average rise about 121 feet to the mile. This would not be excessive, even for a broad-gauge road, if it was equally distributed, but it is not. Before reaching the upper portion of the pass the gradient in places is 185 feet to the mile. Then comes the crest of the divide itself. To reach the foot of that hill enormous engineering obstacles had to be surmounted. The hill sides were dug into, rocks blasted away, streams diverted from their channels, rip-rap have been built to protect embankments, three iron bridges have been thrown across the cañon as the road changes from side to side seeking the least difficult path ; and, at last, the locomotive is brought face to face with a steep ascent no

CROSSING THE RATON MOUNTAINS INTO NEW MEXICO—A. T. AND S. F. R. R.

human machinery can climb. To surmount this two schemes were devised, one temporary and in present use, and the other permanent and to supersede the other.

The means now employed is called a switch-back. By it the cars leave what will be the direct line and are carried over a steep incline track, running diagonally up the hill; thence reversing their direction they shoot up another incline; then reversing again they climb to the summit, thus zigzagging up the steep they cannot directly scale. Even by this indirect route the enormous grade of 316.8 feet per mile is attained. Circling around the summit of the pass the road descends on the New Mexico side in a similar manner, and reaches the point where the direct line comes out of the tunnel, after having achieved the two thousand feet of what will hereafter be the tunneled distance by going nearly three miles around. To operate this portion of the road, over which trains now pass regularly, engines as comparatively great and powerful are used as the grade is heavy and difficult. These ponderous locomotives weigh from sixty-six to eighty tons each. Through the opening gaps of the Raton Mountains northward and southward broad expanses of level plains and fertile valleys are visible, while to the northwest the Spanish Peaks and the still more distant Pike lend additional beauty to the scene. The permanent line of this road will tunnel this pass or divide and thus overcome the heavier grade referred to. The tunnel is almost completed, and will be 2,011 feet long, 14.5 feet wide and 19 feet high. The cost of hauling through this will be only one-fourth what it is by way of the Switch-back.

Grand as was the accomplishment of this company in surmounting the Raton mountains, a still more stupendous undertaking is being pushed on to completion in the Grand Cañon of the Arkansas. Here is a defile of such gigantic proportions and of such seeming impassableness, that all projects looking towards the construction of a railway there were deemed chimerical and impracticable until the Atchison, Topeka & Santa Fe and the Denver & Rio Grande companies began operations last summer. This was before the consolidation of the latter road with the former, and as there was room for only one line, and that obtainable only by blasting a passage-way for miles from the sides of the cañon, these companies came into conflict one with another. Each company had an armed force on the coveted locality, and a contest for right of way began in the courts, which is yet hardly ended.   After the union of the roads the Atchison company continued work, and expects to have a road-bed in order

THE GRAND CAÑON.

4

this summer.   Leadville and the mountain mining districts are the objective points of this most difficult of all railway construction enterprises that has ever been prosecuted in the United States.   For long distances the cañon walls rise almost or quite perpendicularly to heights of from one to two thousand feet above the river that foams and dashes in its narrow bed.   There was no room for a railway in this narrow gorge, and consequently room had to be obtained by blasting a way in the solid rock.   This has been done, and the A., T. & S. F. railway will soon be in operation to the upper Arkansas and Leadville.

The Denver & Rio Grande railway forms the great north and south connection between the different railway systems and farming, stock and mining sections of Colorado.   Through it distant portions of the park and plains region are furnished with rapid transit and are afforded an opportunity to develop their resources.   Extensive coal measures are supplied with a market, and some of the great gold and silver bearing belts are brought nearer to the great centres of trade and reduction.   It was a grand conception, this idea of connecting with iron bands the outposts of the new and progressive American civilization with the land of the ancient Aztec and of the enervated descendants of his Spanish successors, yet great things have already been accomplished in the way of carrying out the original plans. General W. J. Palmer and associates, who projected this railway of the great inland plateau and mountain system of the continent, have been steadily extending the road from year to year as means and opportunity were afforded, until three hundred and twenty-seven miles of track are in operation and a point two hundred and fifty miles southwest of Denver has been attained.   The first construction began at Denver not long after the advent of the Kansas Pacific, and seventy-five miles of track were laid south of that city in 1871.   A town was then laid out, from which the beautiful city of Colorado Springs has resulted ; and Manitou has been an outgrowth of this same railway enterprise.   After a short stop, work was renewed, and Pueblo was reached in 1872.   The next objective point was Cañon City, at the base of the mountains, where the Arkansas river debouches on the plains.   The development of the excellent coal measures of that vicinity followed.   A year or two later another move southward was made, and the northern base of the Raton Mountains was attained.   Here were extensive coal fields, and the town of El Moro sprung into existence.   Then came the work of cross-

ing the great Sangre de Christo range, in order to reach the valley of
the Rio Grande, and thus have a comparatively level water grade
southward through New Mexico. Progress was sometimes slow and
occasionally interrupted for lack of capital, but the eastern base of
the range was reached in time, and then came the work that, in an
engineering point of view, has rarely been equaled in the history of
railway building. Onward and upward pressed the construction
force until the grade was completed and the iron laid to the summit;
and then began the descent of the western slope. Veta Pass is 9,339
feet above sea level, and this road was the first in the United States
to attain such an elevation.

No other railway in the world makes an ascent at all comparable
to this. In a distance of fourteen and three-tenths miles on the
eastern slope, an elevation of 2,369 feet is gained, or an average of
169 feet per mile, the grade for two miles of that distance being 211
feet to the mile. On the upper seven miles of the western slope the
average grade is 141 feet per mile, and three of these miles have an
average grade of 211 feet per mile. The elevation of the summit of
Veta Pass is very nearly one mile greater than that of Pueblo, and
Blanca Peak rises yet another mile into cloud land.

With the advent of the railway on the eastern rim of San Luis
Park, that magic town of the border, Garland, sprung into existence,
only to be put on wheels and moved on to Alamosa as soon as the
latter became the terminus. The bank of the Rio Grande was reached
in the summer of 1878, and here the extension of the road ceased.
Since last December, the Atchison, Topeka & Santa Fe company
has controlled the Denver & Rio Grande, and operate the same
in connection with that line. Connection is made at South Pueblo
with the broad and narrow gauge roads, and here freight and passengers are transferred from one to the other.

The scenery along the Denver & Rio Grande railway will well
repay a trip to Colorado. From Denver to El Moro, a distance of
206 miles, the road runs just east of and almost directly beneath the
Rocky Mountains. The eye can never grow weary of the glorious and
ever-changing landscape there presented. In crossing Veta Pass one
is brought in close proximity to some of the loftiest peaks in North
America. Among them is Mount Blanca, the highest of all Colorado
mountains, whose lofty summit rises 14,464 feet above sea level.
This magnificent range divides San Luis Park from the great plains
to the eastward.

CHAPTER VIII.

THE NORTHERN COLORADO RAILWAY SYSTEM—THE COLORADO CEN-
TRAL RAILWAY—ITS LOCATION, HISTORY, AND GENERAL BENEFITS
—PROGRESS OF RAILROAD BUILDING IN THE "ROCKIES"—OVER
THE SNOWY RANGE TO THE NEW LAND OF THE WEST—THE DEN-
VER & SOUTH PARK R. R.—THE HIGHEST RAILWAY IN THE UNITED
STATES AND THE HIGHEST STAGE LINE IN THE WORLD—ON TO
LEADVILLE.

The Colorado Central railway has been a very essential co-oper-
ator in developing and advancing the wealth and industries of
northern Colorado. It affords transportation and traveling facilities for some of the best mining and farming sections. The counties of Gilpin, Clear Creek, Boulder, Larimer, Jefferson, and Arapahoe are all traversed to a greater or less extent by this road. Until
Leadville came to the front, the two first-named districts supplied
two-thirds of the State's gold and silver export. The other counties
are equally conspicuous for their wheat and farming products, live
stock, or coal and other mines. Rapid transit, accessibility, and
cheaper freight and supplies are advantages of this railway system,
resulting in additional and enlarged mining, farming, and business
operations. A few years ago a tedious and somewhat disagreeable
mountain stage trip was necessary to reach the mines of Central or
Georgetown, and all machinery and supplies were freighted over
steep and difficult roads, and seemingly impassable hills and defiles.
Now the traveler is whirled along the enchanting cañon of Clear
Creek in luxurious railway cars, and ore and merchandise reach their
destinations speedily and cheaply by way of this iron trail of the
"Rockies."

This mountain division of the road is a marvel of engineering skill
and American enterprise, and much of it was constructed under more
than ordinary difficulties. There was lack of money, opposition from
rival schemes, and a belief that the project of building and operating a road up this wild and rugged cañon was impracticable. The
country had men, however, whose sagacity and public spirit led them

to conceive, and eventually to carry forward the undertaking to the present satisfactory condition. W. A. H. Loveland and Henry M. Teller, both prominently identified with building up the territory and State, were the leading original promoters, and eventually secured the construction of the road from Denver to Golden, and thence northward to Boulder and westward to Black Hawk. It was an auspicious event when the wild cañons of the "Rockies" first echoed to the scream of the locomotive, and the mines of Gilpin were afforded rail communication with the world. This was in 1873, and nearly three years after the first track-laying began from Denver westward.

Since then, President Loveland and associates have extended the road north and west until its mileage has more than doubled, and they are now engaged on a new project of still greater magnitude. Not content with halting among the gold and silver mines of the eastern slope, a construction force has been set at work to scale the snowy range and carry the line forward to Leadville and the mountains of the far southwest. While this is seemingly a stupendous undertaking, the effort is warranted by past achievements of this road. Nothing seems impossible in these days of steam and progress, and so we may look for railway traffic and travel over a still more elevated portion of the Rocky mountains even than has yet been surmounted. The surveyed route of this extension from Georgetown to Leadville is some fifty-six miles in length, and crosses the Continental Divide twice in that distance. In circling Gray's Peak, an elevation of between ten and eleven thousand feet will be attained, and Tennessee Pass will be crossed at an altitude nearly as great. The objective points are nevertheless sufficiently alluring for almost any effort and outlay, for a short route will thus be opened from Denver and Georgetown to the valleys of Leadville and Ten Mile and of the Eagle, the Snake, and the Blue.

The projected and surveyed railway lines to operate west of and in connection with the Colorado Central, and likely to be constructed in the ensuing year, are: first, the Gray's Peak, Snake River, and Leadville, from Georgetown via Silver Plume, Bakerville, Loveland Pass, Snake River, Ten Mile Creek, Frisco, Kokomo, and Carbonateville to Leadville; second, the Colorado Western Railroad Company line from Breckenridge down the Blue (crossing the other road) to Hot Sulphur Springs, and across the Middle Park to the

AT THE MOUTH OF THE LITTLE COLORADO.

Rabbit Ear Range mining district, and over Muddy Pass, and through North Park to the northern boundary of Colorado ; also westward from Hot Sulphur Springs to the White River Indian Agency, thence down the White River valley to the western boundary of Colorado ; also a branch from the main line at the junction of the Snake and Blue rivers, westerly down the valley of the Eagle river, and its new mining district, and down the Grand river to the White River Agency. Each of these railway companies have for incorporators and officials most of the present and past officers and directors of the Colorado Central line, including Messrs. Loveland, Welch, Nichols, Berthoud, Henry, Hummel, Thatcher, and Richman.

At the present time, the Colorado Central Company has 186 miles of railway in operation, of which 138 miles are of the standard broad gauge, and located on the plains or near the outlets of the foot hills, and 48 miles are of the narrow gauge of three feet, and extend up among the mountains and mining districts. The former passes through the most extensive, and what is considered the best farming section of the State. The mountain division presents rare attractions to the sight-seer, and is reached after crossing the fertile and culti-vated country between Denver and Golden. Far above the latter point are the headwaters of Clear Creek and the mountain-walled cities of Georgetown, Idaho Springs, Central and Black Hawk. That section of the railway extending around the lofty and precipitous hills overhanging the former place is the most interesting and impres-sive portion of even this remarkable road, but may yet be surpassed by localities on the Leadville extension. In and near these places, gold and silver ores are mined and milled and the bullion forwarded to its distant place of coinage. At intervals is scenery as grand, majestic, and beautiful as the world can offer. The distance from Golden to Central is twenty miles, and the average ascent per mile of track is considerably over one hundred feet. There are places where grades of one hundred and fifty and even two hundred and more feet are encountered, but these are only for short intervals. Central is about 2,600 feet higher than Golden, and about 500 feet higher than Black Hawk.

The towns along the narrow gauge divisions of the road are Cen-tral, Black Hawk, Idaho Springs, Lawson, Mill City, and George-town. Adjacent to the line of the road are Nevadaville, Freeland, Silver Plume, and Brownville. On the plains or broad gauge are

Boulder, Longmont, Loveland, and Fort Collins, with Golden at the junction, and Denver and Cheyenne at either terminus. Some of the most productive and valuable coal measures of the State are on the line of this road.

W. N. Babcock is General Western agent of the northern pooled lines at Denver, consisting of the Union Pacific, Kansas Pacific, and Colorado Central. A. A. Egbert is Superintendent of the last-named road, with headquarters at Golden.

The Denver, South Park & Pacific railway crosses the level territory from Denver to Morrison and the South Platte river, the main line following the latter up through the mountains to the mouth of Hall Valley. This road is still in course of construction and is expected to reach Fairplay during the coming season, and Leadville as soon thereafter as practicable. John Evans and other prominent Denver men were the projectors and are the leading stockholders and officials of the enterprise. In 1873, Arapahoe county voted bonds to the amount of $300,000, and in the following year sixteen miles of track were laid between Denver and Morrison, where the old South Park stage road enters the mountains. In 1877 the work of blasting and building a roadway through Platte cañon began. The next summer the road was completed and in operation as far as Bailey's ranch and soon after to Fairville. The mouth of Hall Valley was reached early in January, 1879, and the station at the end of the track was called Webster. This has since been a place of great activity.

The road is finely equipped and well supplied with rolling stock, and is of the narrow gauge of three feet. The scenery in Platte cañon is peculiarly grand and interesting. Gigantic walls of granite line the road and creek at intervals, broken by sloping hills and valleys covered more or less thickly with timber. The mining camps tributary to this road are those of Summit county, Geneva, Hall Valley, the placers of South Park, and the extended mineral belt of the Mosquito or Park range, together with so much of Leadville's trade and traffic as is not shipped to the Denver & Rio Grande railway. A good wagon road leads over the mountains to Summit county. The leading officials of the Denver & South Park are John Evans, president; Walter Cheesman, vice-president; C. W. Fisher, general superintendent; Charles Wheeler, auditor; and A. S. Hughes, general freight and passenger agent. The number of miles of track in operation is eighty-eight, of which all but eight are included in the main line.

All winter long hundreds of men have been employed, in storm or sunshine, up rugged ravines and steep mountain sides, in cutting out or building up a road-bed for what might be termed this aerial railway. From Webster the road, in order to gain the required elevation, makes a detour, first in one direction and then another, and finally, after a zigzag course of many curves and windings, succeeds in gaining the elevation necessary for crossing the great Kenosha divide. Once over this, and the descent into South Park commences. The altitude of Webster is 9,154 feet, and that of the divide referred to is over 10,100. For long distances the track hugs the mountain sides hundreds of feet above the creek almost immediately below it. Above and beneath are forests of lordly pines and cedars, and beyond rises the bald and blackened crest of the great range. Now that this difficult section of the road is in operation, progress in construction can be much more rapid, as the country yet to be traversed is much better adapted to a railway grade.

Since crossing the Kenosha Divide the Denver & South Park Company has had the proud pre-eminence of operating the most elevated section of railway in the United States, and the highest in the world, with but two exceptions—the Peruvian line over the Andes and the Gulf and City of Mexico road over the Cordilleras. The Kenosha Divide is surmounted at an elevation of 10,139 feet above sea level, according to the engineers' survey, and 9,928 feet according to Prof. Hayden's estimate. Jefferson, the new terminus of the road, on the northerly rim of South Park, has an elevation of 9,730 or of 9,519 feet. Beyond this the connecting stages for Leadville cross the Mosquito Pass at an elevation of over 12,000 feet, or over two and a quarter miles above sea-level. This is probably the highest stage route in the world.

CHAPTER IX.

THE UNION PACIFIC RAILROAD—FACTS AND INFORMATION ABOUT
THE GREAT TRANSCONTINENTAL LINE AND ITS COLORADO CON-
NECTIONS—THE KANSAS PACIFIC RAILWAY.

The Union Pacific and Kansas Pacific railways are the Eastern
connections of the Colorado Central, and of the Denver & South
Park roads. While not distinctively a Colorado institution, since but
a few miles are included within the borders of the State, yet in view
of its being, with the aid of its Colorado Central division, one of the
great Rocky Mountain through routes of travel, something concerning the Union Pacific will more or less interest the tourist and
traveler. The only present rail connection between the East and the
Pacific coast is that afforded by the great transcontinental line, 1,927
miles in length, whose divisions are known as the Union and Central
Pacific. The main line of the Union Pacific Company extends from
Council Bluffs, on the Missouri river, to Ogden, in Utah Territory, a
distance of 1,032 miles. But outside of this are a number of branches
and feeders, and of roads operated or being constructed by the same
great corporation. These include the Colorado Central, the Utah
Northern, and the Utah Southern, and some Nebraska and Kansas
roads. The Pacific roads with Eastern connections form, perhaps,
the strongest railway combination in existence.

The construction of the Union Pacific began late in 1865, and some
years after occurred the grandest exploits in the way of rapid railway building that the world has ever witnessed. The work was
completed on the 10th day of May, 1869, when the track-layers from
the East and West met on the northern border of Great Salt Lake.
Since then, crossing the continent has been a matter of a few days
only, instead of many months by wagon train, or of several weeks
by the overland stage, and more than a million square miles of territory have been afforded steam transit with the Mississippi Valley and
the Atlantic seaboard. The results are new settlements, new territories, and new mining districts, and a growth and development as

rapid as it is substantial. The route followed is pretty nearly the forty-first parallel of latitude, deviating slightly to the north or south as occasion demands, and the offshoots on either hand enter or approach the great gold and silver regions of the Sierras, and of either slope thereof.

This great overland ocean to ocean route offers peculiar advantages to the visitor of the "Rockies" and beyond. It is the only line leading to California, Nevada, and Utah, and towards the gold regions of Montana, the Black Hills, and the great Northwest. Through much of its course the scenery is grand in the extreme, while its management and equipments command universal admiration.

The Union Pacific follows the Platte river valley some four hundred miles west of Omaha. It leaves that stream at Julesburg, located just within the limits of Colorado, and then strikes up over the great inland plateau to Cheyenne. Here the Colorado Central diverges to the south, and to Denver, 138 miles distant. That city being the metropolis and the railway centre of Colorado, the traveler can determine, after sojourning a few days there, what portion of the State he desires to visit, provided his plans have not already been matured. This is the point where men congregate on business or pleasure from all of the mining camps, and in fact from all quarters of the State. A few days spent there will enable the stranger to learn enough of the surrounding country to move intelligently and to the best advantage. Further information, such as may be useful on arriving at this point, may be gleaned from the chapters and pages devoted to the Colorado Central and the Denver & South Park railways. Close connection is made with the latter road for Leadville, trains leaving immediately on the arrival of those from the East. The great gold mining city of Central, and the silver metropolis, Georgetown, can both be reached by the mountain division of the Pacific railway system. A grand combination excursion is offered the public at reduced rates over the Union Pacific and Kansas Pacific railways, with their connecting road, the Colorado Central. Excursion tickets good until October 31, 1879; are sold at Omaha, Kansas City, or other Missouri river cities, to Denver for $38 for the round trip, and proportionate rates at all points East. The traveler can pass westward over the Union Pacific, and southward over the Colorado Central, and return *via* the Kansas Pacific, or *vice versa* according to locality of starting-point or choice of the tourist. At Denver, excursion rates to the mountains and pleasure resorts will be furnished at reduced rates.

The Kansas Pacific extends from Kansas City westward up the Kansas and Smoky Hill valleys, and across the plains to Denver, making connection at the latter point with the Denver & South Park and Colorado Central. This road is controlled by pretty near the same management as the Union Pacific, and forms part of the great northern pooled railway system. The same rates of travel are afforded on this line as on the northern route, and the accommodations are substantially the same.

CHAPTER X.

TOWNS AND CITIES OF COLORADO ALPHABETICALLY ARRANGED—FACTS
AND FIGURES FOR THE TOURIST.

ADELAIDE CITY.—This is in reality a suburb of Leadville, although not included within the corporate limits. The location is along the hillsides, and in a beautiful park two miles above the centre of the latter place. Near by is the Adelaide smelter; also, many mines. Some months ago the population was said to be several hundred, and increasing rapidly.

ALAMOSA.—Population, 500; elevation, 7,492. Southwestern terminus of the Denver & Rio Grande railway. Distances: Del Norte, 40 miles; Lake City, 116; Pueblo, 130; Denver, 250; Santa Fe, 145; and Kansas City, 764. Daily coaches to the San Juan mines and Santa Fe. Large amount of freighting done to and from this place. At Alamosa and the previous railway terminus of Garland, the following was received by wagon train and forwarded East by rail in the year 1878: gold bullion, $15,190; refined silver, $141,396; base bullion, silver and lead, 683⅔ tons, worth $114,150; ore, 121 tons, $30,333. Wool, pelts, and hides, over 500,000 pounds. Merchandise and machinery received from the East by rail and sold or sent west and south by wagon train, 2,250 tons. Sales of merchandise in Alamosa in first six months of the town, up to January 1, 1879, over $600,000. The town was laid out in June, 1878, and the railway reached there and established a station on the 27th of that month. The place contains several large forwarding houses, a school, religious societies, and two weekly newspapers. Alamosa is situated on the westerly bank of the Rio Grande, and almost in the centre of San Luis Park. Looking beyond the treeless plain, the surroundings are remarkably grand and beautiful. No such panoramic view is afforded from any town in Colorado, as regards extent of mountain scenery. The place is entirely encircled with ranges of diversified appearance and varying elevations, with that distance requisite for the finest scenic effect. To the east is the lofty Sangre de Christo range, with the massive

Sierra Blanca or White Mountains, not twenty-five miles away, and westward, at an equal distance, the mountains of the San Juan region, with the Summit range, come into view.   San Luis Park has its greatest length in a northerly and southerly direction, and the two mountain systems referred to converge in the dim distance, with Poncho Pass as an outlet in one direction and the Rio Grande valley, in northern New Mexico, in the other.   Hotel, Perry House.

ANIMAS FORKS.—This place is situated in one of the valuable and extensive silver mining districts of San Juan county. Distance from Silverton, 13 miles; population, 300.

ANTELOPE SPRINGS.—Located in Hinsdale county, about 60 miles west of Del Norte, and nearly 50 east of Silverton, and near the junction of the stage road between those points and that leading to Lake City. It is surrounded by a beautiful park and mountain ranges with the Rio Grande river flowing between.

ALPINE.—This is a promising camp and district on Chalk creek, in Chaffee county, some sixty miles south-southwest of Leadville. During the past summer over 200 people had collected there. Some rich and valuable silver veins are being mined.

BIJOU BASIN.—Small village in El Paso county, 25 miles northeast of Colorado Springs, and in a good farming and stock country.

BLACK HAWK.—This is a busy, bustling city of over 2,000 people, located in the rich gold and silver bearing district of Gilpin county, at the junctions of Gregory and Chase gulches with North Clear creek. The business of the place consists in mining, milling, and shipping ores. Most of the quartz mills of Gilpin county are located here, on account of the water supply. Black Hawk unites with Central in Gregory gulch, forming a continuous city, and is the first place arrived at in entering this great district by rail. The Colorado Central railway passes through and over the city, and on around the hills to Central. Distance from Denver, 36 miles ; from Golden, 20 ; by rail to Georgetown, 32. The place contains many substantial brick blocks and business houses, several churches, a weekly newspaper and a graded school with five teachers, and not far from 280 pupils. Hotel, Teller House at Central.

BALLARAT.—A mining town in Boulder county, not far from Long's Peak and Jamestown. Here is the famous Smuggler mine. Fine summer resorts are afforded all through this section, and in Ward district, Jamestown, and Gold Hill.

BOULDER.—County seat of Boulder county, and a well-built city, beautifully located on the plains at the base of the mountains. Here Boulder creek leaves its rocky cañon to water the rich farm lands to the eastward, and several gulches open a roadway to distant mines. The situation is such that this is the natural gateway to the leading

THE FIFTEENTH OF AUGUST.

mining camps of Boulder county, while a market and trading point is here afforded for the adjacent productive farming districts. The town has been growing rapidly since the development of the Caribou silver mines and of the gold and telluride mines of Gold Hill, Ballarat, Sunshine, Magnolia, and other districts. Large stores and attractive private residences are seen on every hand. Boulder is a great summer resort, on account of its pleasant surroundings, equable climate, and general attractiveness. At all times of the year its hotels accommodate a very large number of guests, on account of the travel to and from the mines and other business points. Fine farms, superior stock, and excellent dairies can be seen all along the streams and intermediate country. There are two national banks, six churches, two weekly newspapers, and a graded school, with over 500 pupils and eight teachers. Here is the State University, with some eighty pupils in attendance. Boulder's location between the farms and mines has brought her two large flour mills, a foundry, Boyd's smelting works, one of the Boston and Colorado Company's ore buying and sampling mills, and other producing establishments. There is also an agricultural and industrial society that gives an annual exhibition of mining and farming products. The town is on the main line of the Colorado Central and is a terminus of the Denver & Boulder Valley railway. Another road (G. B. & C.) extends out to the productive Marshall coal banks, distant 5¼ miles. Stage for Caribou leaves on Mondays, Wednesdays, and Fridays. The sales of merchandise and other material in Boulder in 1878 exceeded $1,000,000. The population is not far from 4,000. Elevation 5,536. Distances : from Denver, 45½ miles ; Golden, 28 ; Erie, 12 ; Caribou, 22 ; Nederland, 18 ; Gold Hill, 10 ; Sunshine, 6 ; Sugar Loaf, 10 ; Valmont, 4 ; Ward, 19. Hotels, Brainard, Sale and Boulder.

BRECKINRIDGE.—County seat of Summit and business centre of the placer and creek gold diggings on the headwaters of the Blue river. Population during the summer season, 250. There is a prospect of a large increase this year, owing to new mineral discoveries. Elevation 9,674. This place is on the Pacific slope of the main range, and is 95 miles from Denver, 24 from Fairplay, 32 from Leadville, 7 from mouth of Ten Mile or Frisco, 20 from Montezuma, and 40 from Georgetown. Passengers from Denver to this place leave the South Park stages at Hamilton.

CAÑON CITY.—This is the present terminus of the Arkansas division of the Denver & Rio Grande and of the A., T. & S. F. railways, and is the county seat of Fremont county. It is located at the point where the Arkansas river leaves the mountains and on an arm of the plains that extends a short distance into the foot hills. There is an excellent farming country from this point down to Pueblo. Fine crops of wheat, corn, and other grains and vegetables are raised, and this is the only locality in Colorado where great success has yet been attained in raising fruit. The apple and peach orchards at and near Cañon are quite productive. Back from the river are fine stock ranges. Just above town are several mineral springs, hot and cold. Cañon has peculiar advantages as a health resort, and is fast becoming a place of refuge for invalids. Some of the most inviting points for the sight-seer that Colorado affords can be reached in a few hours drive from this place. The royal gorge of the Arkansas, the grandest of all the cañons on the eastern slope, can be inspected from above by following a wagon road for thirteen miles, and the tourist will soon have the thrilling pleasure of making the trip along the creek bed by rail. The perpendicular walls of this cañon are nearly 2,000 feet in height. Still nearer town, is the romantic locality known as Temple cañon, and not far distant are the singularly beautiful cañons of Grape, Oil, and Oak creeks. Stages leave this city for Leadville every morning, and stages for Silver Cliff and Rosita arrive and depart daily. Long trains of wagons, loaded with ore and bullion, are almost continually arriving from Leadville, and in lesser numbers from Silver Cliff and vicinity, and return laden with merchandise and supplies. All of this business and the grading forces of the Atchison, Topeka & Santa Fe railway in the neighboring cañon have tended to make matters lively in this growing city during the past year. The travel through the place is immense, and every hotel is crowded to its utmost capacity. Cañon is a well-built place of some 1,200 inhabitants, with bank, newspaper, public schools, and several churches. It is noticeable for the neat and attractive character of its private residences. Here is the State penitentiary, an imposing structure of granite quarried from the neighboring hills. The elevation of the railroad station above sea level is 5,287 feet. A 'bus line plies between the railway and the business centre and hotels. Cañon is 40 miles from Pueblo, 126 from Leadville, 160 from Denver, 32 from Rosita, and 30 from Silver Cliff. Leading hotel, McClure.

CARBONATEVILLE.—This is a new town in the Ten Mile district, near McNulty gulch, and 17 miles from Leadville. Last reports gave it several stores and a bank.

CARIBOU.—The leading mining town of Boulder county and of

the Grand Island silver district. It is located in a well timbered region, close up to the "snowy range," at an elevation of 9,995 feet above sea level. Population, 350. Distance from Boulder, 22 miles; Nederland, 4; Black Hawk, 19; Central, 20, and Denver, 56. Stages arrive and depart on alternate days for Boulder and Central, so that the traveler can lay over two nights and a day, and make a circuit between those points. Here are the Caribou, Native Silver, No Name, Boulder County, and other rich mines.

CENTRAL.—The centre of business for the great gold mines that underlie the hills and gulches of Gilpin county, of which it is the county seat. Adjoining, and just below, is the city of Black Hawk, and above is the town of Nevadaville. The three places have a combined population of 6,500, and contain the deepest and many of the most productive mines in Colorado. More gold has been shipped from here than from all the State beside, and the locality has played a very important part in the history of Colorado. Central has six churches, a daily newspaper, three banks, an elegant opera house, and a graded school of nearly 400 scholars, with a well-selected library of nearly 2,000 volumes. Beside this, the Catholic academy affords instruction to a large number of children. The Teller House is the finest and largest hotel in the State outside of Denver, and compares with the hostelries of that place. Distance from Denver, 40 miles; Golden, 26; New York, 2,000; Georgetown by rail, 36; by wagon road, 18 and 20 by different roads. Further particulars of Central will be found elsewhere.

COLORADO SPRINGS.—County seat of El Paso, located on plateau just east of Pike's Peak, and 75 miles from Denver, and 45 from Pueblo. See chapter on "Cities of the Plains." Hotels, Colorado Springs and Crawford, and the National.

COLORADO CITY.—Small village between Colorado Springs and Manitou, and two miles from the former. Population, 100. Daily mail, express and hacks from railway. In the early times was for a very short period designated as the capital of the territory.

DEL NORTE.—The capital of Rio Grande county, located on the river of the same name, at the eastern gateway of the San Juan Mountains and mining region. It grew to be a place of importance in 1873–4 on the early opening of the Summit Mountain gold mines and the silver mines further west. Here is an elegant school building, a bank, weekly newspaper, and many large stores and ware-

WATER BASIN IN GYPSUM CAÑON.

houses. The location is remarkably fine, the climate pleasant, and the town is substantial and prosperous. Across San Luis Park, which is here forty miles wide, the Sierra Blanca and connecting range presents a grand and majestic appearance. The population of Del Norte is nearly 1,500. Elevation, 7,750. Stages arrive from and depart for Alamosa and the mountains every day. Distance to Alamosa or the railway, 34½ miles; Lake City, 81½; Denver, 284½; Pueblo, 164½; Kansas City, 800; Santa Fe, 180. Hotel, Cuenin House.

EL MORO.—This is the terminus of the El Moro division of the Denver & Rio Grande railway, and the seat of the coke manufactories. It is situated five miles from Trinidad and not far north of the New Mexican boundary. The town attained its importance as the most southerly Colorado railway terminus, and as the supply point for the New Mexican trade. It has lost much of this advantage since the Atchison, Topeka & Santa Fe came in from the east and built southward toward Las Vegas and Santa Fe. Yet the coal mines and interests of the Southern Colorado Coal and Mining Company, local business, and the coke ovens will always make it a place of some importance. Heavy coke shipments are made to distant points. The coal of this section makes the best coke in the west, and the business has grown until 75 ovens are now engaged in the work. At El Moro, the immense mercantile and forwarding and commission houses of Otero, Sellars & Co., Browne & Manzanares, and of Bartels Brothers once handled millions of dollars' worth of goods annually and carried stocks of immense value. Some of this traffic is now carried on at more southerly points. Long trains of wagons, loaded with the products of New Mexico and Arizona, were constantly arriving, and after disembarking their goods would load up their requisite cargoes and depart on their long journeys to the points from whence they came. The north and east bound freights consisted of wool, pelts, hides, and tallow from the pastoral districts, and copper and silver bullion from the southern mines, while the south and west bound freights embraced general merchandise, dry goods, and machinery. El Moro has a population of from 300 to 400. Its elevation is 5,825 feet. Distance from Pueblo, 86 miles; Denver, 206.

EMPIRE.—A mining town in Clear Creek county, four miles from Georgetown. The Middle Park stage line passes through this place.

A few miles west is Berthoud Pass, leading over the "snowy range." The town is one mile above its railway station. Valuable gold placers and lode veins are worked in the vicinity, and from one to three quartz mills are always at work. Distance from Denver, 48 miles; Idaho, 11. Population, 250; elevation, 8,583.

ERIE.—This town has been built up by the coal measures among which it is located. Several mines are worked, and have usually been quite productive. The Denver & Boulder Valley railroad passes through the place. Population, 200. Distance from Denver, 34 miles; Boulder, 12. Location, in the southwestern part of Weld county.

EVANS.—This was first settled by a colony organization of Saint Louis and vicinity, and is located in the Platte valley, in Weld county. Around it is a productive farming section and good stock ranges, and a large flour mill does a heavy business. Population, 700; elevation, 4,745. Distance from Denver, 48 miles; Greeley, 4, and Cheyenne, 58. The Denver Pacific railway passes through this place. A weekly paper is published there.

FAIRPLAY.—This is located on the banks of the South Platte river in the South Park, and is the county seat of Park county. The place has been of more or less importance for nearly twenty years, and took a fresh growth after the Park Range silver discoveries of 1871-2. The Denver travel to Leadville passes through here by stages and other conveyances, and the hotels are always crowded. The Bergh House averaged forty arrivals per day last year, and at present it must greatly exceed that number. A large placer mine is operated at Fairplay by Chinese labor. Seven miles west is Alma, and just beyond are the silver mines of Lincoln, Bross, Buckskin, and other mountains. Population, 500; elevation, 9,964. Distance from Denver by stage and rail, 100 miles; Leadville, 40 by Weston Pass, and 21 by Mosquito Pass; Alma, 6; Montgomery, 12; Breckinridge, 23. Two lines of stages pass here.

FORT COLLINS.—This is a flourishing town on the Cache la Poudre river and Colorado Central railway, and is the county seat of Larimer. The State Agricultural College is located here, for which substantial buildings were recently erected. There are two newspapers, and schools and churches; semi-weekly stages to Greeley and La Porte; excellent farming and stock country. Population,

1,000. Distances: Cheyenne, 45 miles; La Porte, 4; Denver, 65. Elevation, 4,815.

GOLDEN.—County seat of Jefferson, and headquarters of Colorado Central railway. Here are located the shops, car works, and repair shops of the railway company. Also three sets of smelting works (two of them recently completed) and reduction works. These are now in operation. There are two pottery manufactories, fire-brick works, four large coal mines, two flour mills, and a paper mill. Splendid water power is afforded from Clear creek, which leaves the mountains here. A large amount of ground is irrigated from this stream, and a good farming district is the result. This is the junction of the broad and narrow gauge divisions of the Colorado Central, and freight for and from the mountains breaks bulk here. The State School of Mines is located at Golden. The public schools are attended by nearly 350 pupils, and there are seven churches. The Court-house is the best in the State. Distances: Denver, 16 miles; Cheyenne, 122 miles; Boulder, 29½; Central, 23½; Georgetown, 27½; Beaver Brook, 7. Population, 3,000; elevation, 5,690. On account of its manufacturing interests Golden is sometimes called the Lowell of Colorado. Years ago it was temporarily the capital of the territory.

GOLD HILL.—This is a small mining town on the hill of the same name in Boulder county. Near by are several prominent mines. Owing to the fine view and airy location, this makes a pleasant summer resort. Population, 200. Distance from Boulder, 10 miles. Tri-weekly stage to that city.

GREELEY.—This is situated between the Cache la Poudre and South Platte rivers, and near their points of union, and is the county seat of Weld county. It was laid out by a colony organization and settled in 1870. Since then the growth has been steady and uniform. The town charter provides that no property or land can be leased or sold for liquor selling purposes, and, like Colorado Springs, Greeley is called a temperance town. The public school building is one of the finest in the State. There are several churches, two weekly papers, two banks, two flour mills, and some well-stocked stores. Large amounts of wheat and other grains and vegetables are raised here, and vast herds of cattle roam over the plain and the valley of the Platte clear down to the Nebraska line. Tri-weekly stages to Fort Collins and La Porte. Distance to Denver by Denver

Pacific railroad, 52 miles ; Evans, 4 miles, and Cheyenne, 54 miles. Population, 2,500; elevation, 4,779 feet. The town is well laid out and watered from irrigating ditches, and the streets are lined with shade trees.

GEORGETOWN.—This is the county seat of Clear Creek county and the present southwestern terminus of the Colorado Central. Its appearance and surroundings are superior to those of any other mountain town. Around it are lofty mountains, ribbed with silver veins, which rise abruptly to heights of from twelve hundred to twenty-five hundred feet above the almost level valley in which the town is built. Here are silver reduction works, ore concentrating mills, and sampling and ore buying establishments, all of which do a large business. The mining operations of the district are very extensive, resulting in an annual export of silver bullion and ore to the value of over two millions per annum. The town has grown rapidly in the last ten years and now claims a population of 5,000. The town possesses an excellent system of water works, an effective fire department, five churches, an opera house and a graded school with some 360 scholars. There are two weekly newspapers, two banks, several hotels, and many business houses, some of which do a large trade. Three miles above are Silver Plume and Brownville. Elevation of Georgetown, 8,452 feet. Distance from Denver, 53½ miles; from Idaho, 14 miles ; Central, 18 and 20 miles ; Black Hawk, by rail, 36 miles ; Leadville, by Loveland Pass and Ten Mile, 56 miles; stages to Middle Park—46 miles ; Silver Plume, 2 miles; and to Leadville, 56 miles. There are many resorts near Georgetown that are unsurpassed in beauty and general attractions. Among them are Gray and Irwin's Peaks, among the very highest in the range, and from which magnificent views are obtained. Green lake is considered the most beautiful body of water in the State, and is supplied with boats and well filled with trout and salmon. There are good hotels and fine livery turnouts in Georgetown, with pleasant rides and drives above and below town. Hotel charges, $2.50 to $4 per day, and less by the week. Saddle horses, $3 per day, and double team and carriage, $10 or less. An easy bridle trail leads to the summit of Gray's Peak, 14 miles from town.

GRANITE.—County seat of Chaffee county and formerly of Lake.

Population, 100. Distances: Twin Lakes, 3 miles; Leadville, 18 miles; Alpine, 42 miles; Cottonwood Hot Springs, 20 miles; Cañon, 108 miles.

HOT SULPHUR SPRINGS.—Small town in the beautiful section known as Middle Park, and close beside the valuable mineral springs of the same name. This is getting to be more and more a great summer resort, and has been frequented by Colorado pleasure and camping-out parties for many years. There is a good hotel and a line of stages running over Berthoud Pass to Georgetown and Empire. Distance from Georgetown 46 miles; time of stages, one day. Middle Park has no superior for wild game and trout fishing, and the sportsman or angler will find it well worth his while to pass a week there, or in the same belt of country west of the range. Here are Grand lake and the head waters of Grand river.

IDAHO SPRINGS.—This is one of the most beautiful places in the country, and the only mountain town that has yet become a famous health and pleasure resort. This is mainly due to its hot soda springs and delightful surroundings. There are large and commodious hotels, extensive bath-houses, and fine livery turnouts here, and every summer sees a large influx of visitors from the East. Among the points well worth the attention of the tourist are Chief and Bellevue mountains, and Chicago lakes, said to be the highest body of fresh water in North America. The mineral springs of Idaho are highly beneficial to invalids. There are fine drives up and down the nearly level valley of South Clear Creek. Livery charges are from $2.50 to $3 per day for saddle-horses, and $10 for double team with carriage. The larger hotels charge $4 per day, with lower figures for permanent rates. Accommodations first-class. Good hunting and fishing in all directions. On the neighboring hills many lode mines are worked, and a quartz mill and two concentrating mills are employed along the creek. Here are also placer, creek, and bar mines that yield largely in gold. The air is cool and bracing in the summer months, and usually mild and pleasant in winter, and there are many features and sights about the place that recommend it to the tourist. Distance from Denver, 39 miles; fare, $4. Distance to Georgetown, 14 miles; Central, 6 miles; Golden, 22¼. Population, 500; elevation, 7,512.

JAMESTOWN.—A small mining camp with valuable lodes and

mines. It is situated in Boulder county, up among the mountains, twelve miles from Boulder. Near by are valuable mineral springs. Population, 100.

KOKOMO.—New town in the Ten Mile District, Summit county. Claims a population of fifteen hundred, and 2,000 was the latest figure estimated. This is a beautiful section of country, and is proving to be rich in mines. Distance from Leadville, 20 miles; from Georgetown, 36.

KIT CARSON.—A small town on the Kansas Pacific, and once famous as the end of track on that road. Distance from Kansas City, 487; from Denver, 152.

LAKE CITY.—This is the county seat of Hinsdale, and its main town. For some time it has been the most populous place in the San Juan country, although Silverton is gaining somewhat at present. This place grew rapidly in 1876-7, following the development of many silver veins. The Crooke Concentrating and Smelting Works, and those of the Ocean Wave Company are located here, and handle large amounts of ore in the summer and fall months. There is also a chlorination and lixiviation mill. Lake City contains a population of 1,500, with the usual newspaper, bank, and collection of business houses. The situation is wild and romantic, beside the Lake Fork of the Gunnison and Hensen creek, and surrounded by lofty mountains. Elevation, 8,550 feet. Distance to Alamosa, 116 miles, and daily stages thereto. Stages to Silverton, 32 miles, and to Ouray, 80 miles, in the warmer months. Ouray can be reached on horseback by a ride over the mountains of thirty miles. Denver is distant 366 miles by Alamosa and 335 miles by Saguache and Cañon.

LEADVILLE.—The capital of Lake county and the metropolis of the carbonate region. The wonderful growth and history of this magic city will be detailed in a later place in this volume. The town is situated on an almost level plain beside California gulch, and four miles from its junction with the Arkansas, but is gradually building up the gulches and hills among the mines. There are a multitude of stores, large and small, with saloons, hotels, restaurants, and like institutions at every hand. The town is building with marvelous rapidity, as is evidenced by fourteen or fifteen saw-mills in active operation. There are two great ore buying and shipping firms, with sampling mills, who do an immense business, and others about to begin work. There are also two large smelters in town, and more above and below, beside many new concerns building. The number of furnaces will soon be very large. The population of the town and suburbs is estimated at from 10,000 to 15,000, and each day sees the number increased by at least 100. Leadville is 10,025 feet above sea level, by the recent railway surveys. By others, 10,200 or more is given. Distance from Denver by stage line to Fairplay and Webster and D. & S. P. railway, 140 miles. By Mosquito Pass soon to be opened for summer travel, 120 or 121. Distance from Cañon, 126 miles; Granite, 18; Ten Mile, 18; Cottonwood Springs, 38; Alpine or Chalk Creek, 70; Chalk Bluff, 10. Stages leave daily for the ends of track at Cañon and Webster, and for Ten Mile. Fare to Webster, $12; to Denver, $17; fare to Cañon, $14; to Ten Mile, $4 to $5. Line of coaches to Georgetown is soon to be opened. Hotels, Clarendon, Tontine, and Grand.

LONGMONT.—This is the second town in population in Boulder county, and is situated on the Saint Vrain river, in the midst of a splendid farming district. On the arrival of the Chicago colony at this place the old village of Burlington was united with Longmont. The Colorado Central railway passes through the town, and stages arrive and depart for Estes Park during the summer months. Distance from latter place, 32 miles; from Greeley, 30; Erie, 10; Denver, 58. Two trains daily to and from Denver. Population, 1,000. Elevation, 4,957.

LAWSON.—Mining town at Red Elephant mountain, Clear Creek county, six miles below Georgetown and eight above Idaho Springs. Located on the line of the Colorado Central railway. Population, 400.

LA VETA.—Station on the D. & R. G. railway at foot of Veta Pass, on the eastern slope of the mountains. Not far away are the Spanish Peaks, where silver veins have been opened. Population, 200; elevation, 6,970.

LOVELAND.—A new town on the Colorado Central, in a fine farming section known as the Big and Little Thompson country. Population, 150. Distances: Denver, 76 miles; Boulder, 27; Longmont, 17; Fort Collins, 14; Cheyenne, 62. Stages to Estes Park, 28 miles distant.

MALTA.—This place is between three and four miles below Leadville, and near the junction of California gulch with the upper

Arkansas. A set of smelting works is in operation there. Population, 300.

MONUMENT.—In El Paso county, on the line of the D. & R. G. railway. A weekly newspaper is published here. Fine stock country and some farming. Population, 200. Distance to Colorado Springs, 20 miles ; to Denver, 55.

NEDERLAND.—This place is located on Middle Boulder creek, in Boulder county, four miles below Caribou, and eighteen above Boulder. Here is located the great Caribou silver mill and a gold quartz mill, several hotels and stores, and a saw-mill. Stages from Central, Caribou, and Boulder pass through the town. Population, 200. Distance from Central, 16 miles ; Black Hawk, 15.

NEVADAVILLE.—This is a flourishing mining town in the mountains, just above and adjoining Central. It is located in Nevada gulch, between Quartz and Gunnell hills. The mines on either side of it have been extremely productive and have been worked more or less ever since the country was first opened. There are several quartz mills here ; also churches, and a public school with 150 pupils. Population, nearly 1,000.

OURAY.—Few towns in the world are so beautifully located as Ouray, the county seat of the county of the same name. Grand and majestic scenery, health-giving mineral waters, and some of the best silver mines in the State are some of the attractions. The town is located on the banks of the Uncompahgre river, just above a series of fertile parks. It is situated far down on the western slope, with massive mountains all around it. The perpendicular walls of the stream rise to hundreds, and even thousands of feet. The place has been mainly built up within two years. Population, 700 ; elevation, 7,640. Distances: by trail to Silverton, 25 miles ; Lake City, 30 ; stage to Lake City, 80 ; to Saguache, 115 ; Cañon, 215; Denver, via Saguache and Alamosa, 429 ; via Cañon, 335.

PLATTEVILLE. — Station on Denver Pacific railway, thirty-five miles north of Denver and seventeen south of Greeley. Good coal and farming lands.

ROSITA.—The county seat of Custer county. Beauty of location and surroundings should make this a popular summer resort. The town is built in a lovely valley among the Wet mountains, near the valley of the same name and in full view of the great Sangre de Christo range just beyond. A little above the town are valuable silver

veins and productive mines, and below are reduction works. The
mineral belt continues northward for miles, embracing some of the
best mining properties in the country. Stages arrive and depart
daily, except Sundays, for Cañon and the railway, thirty-two miles
away, and every day for Silver Cliff, distant six miles. Population,
1,200 ; Elevation, 8,500. Distances: Denver, 192 ; Pueblo, 72.
Hotels, Melvin and Grand View.

SAGUACHE.—County seat of Saguache county. It is located in the
northwestern part of San Luis Park, and is the business centre for a
fine farming and stock growing district; has a weekly newspaper.
Stages to Cañon, Del Norte, Lake City, and Ouray. Population,
400 ; elevation, 7,723. Distances : Del Norte, 33 miles; Los Pinos
Indian Agency, 40 ; Lake City, 96 ; Ouray, 115 ; Cañon, 100 ;
Denver, 220.

SILVERTON.—This is a growing and prosperous mining town and
the county seat of San Juan county. In the lofty mountains that
overhang the beautiful park in which the town is built are numberless mineral veins, some of great size and many extremely rich in
silver. Here are Greene & Co.'s smelting works, which have been running successfully for several summers. A stage line connects with
Barlow & Sanderson's Lake City and Alamosa line, at Alden's
Junction, forty-nine miles east. In the winter months there are no
stages, on account of the snow, but the mail goes in on horseback or
with a pack animal. Snow falls to an immense depth during the
winter months, and avalanches occasionally sweep travelers on this
trail down the mountain sides. In the summer months a conveyance runs to Lake City. A weekly newspaper is published at
Silverton. Population, 1,000; elevation, 9,400. Distances: Alamosa, 131; Denver, 381 ; Ouray, 25 ; Lake City, 30 ; Howardsville,
4; Parrott City, 50.

SILVER CLIFF.—Although Silver Cliff is but little over eight
months old, it has become a very important point, and promises to
cut a still more prominent figure in the mining record of the State.
The wonderful discoveries made in that locality caused a town to
spring up as if by magic in a few weeks of last fall. The unusually
severe storms of December and January put an end to prospecting
and surface mining for a time, but the leading properties were soon
shipping ore again. During the past three months more discoveries
have been made, a sampling and ore-buying mill has been set in

operation, and two crushing and amalgamating mills are to be erected. The town is located on the eastern slope of Wet mountain valley. Population, 1,200; elevation, 7,500. Distances: Rosita, 6 miles; Cañon and the railway, 30; Pueblo, 40; Denver, via Cañon, 190. Daily stages to Cañon and Rosita. Hotel, Powell.

SILVER PLUME.—This is a lively mining camp, two miles above Georgetown, at the base of Sherman and Republican mountains, and near the Dives, Pelican, Pay Rock, Baxter, Frostburg, Silver Plume, and many other mines. Daily mails and conveyances run to Georgetown at intervals during the day and evening. Here are the Silver Plume Concentrating Works. Population, 600, and with Brownsville not far from twice that number.

SUNSHINE.—This place is located in the telluride belt of Boulder county, and but six miles from the base of the mountains in Boulder valley. Less mining is carried on there now than formerly, but some of the mines have been very productive. Population, 250; elevation, about 6,600. Distance from Boulder, 6 miles; Gold Hill, 4.

TRINIDAD.—This growing and prosperous town is situated in the valley of the Las Animas or Purgatoire, among the low hills that intervene between the plains and the Ratoñ mountains. This valley, while of no great width as far as farming purposes are concerned, extends from the New Mexican border over one hundred and fifty miles to the Arkansas river. It is quite fertile, and produces excellent crops of wheat, corn, oats, barley, and vegetables. Last year it yielded, with some tributary valleys, something like 250,000 bushels of wheat. Las Animas county, of which Trinidad is the county seat, is one of the leading stock districts of the State. Sheep are raised in large numbers all over these valleys and uplands. The main wealth of the locality surrounding the town lies in the coal measures, which are of immense extent, but iron and other materials bid fair to make an important showing hereafter. Some half a dozen coal mines are being worked on an extensive scale, and others are being developed. The production of coal is several hundreds of tons daily, and could be doubled from present workings alone. Two companies are engaged in converting this coal into coke. One of these, near El Moro, operates on a very large scale. This is the best coking coal in the West. Trinidad has long enjoyed a heavy trade with New Mexico, and has largely acted as a supply depot therefor.

Since the completion of the Atchison, Topeka & Santa Fe railway
to that place, last fall, its growth has been very rapid. Large
numbers of substantial stores, warehouses, and dwellings have been
erected, and the population is increasing rapidly. The leading hotel
is being doubled in size, and another of large dimensions is nearly
completed. Trinidad has resources at hand and a country to supply
that will insure a steady growth. There are two daily and weekly
newspapers, five churches, a catholic seminary, a private school,
well attended, and a public school with some 300 pupils. There
are three flour mills, planing and bucket shops, and several saw-
mills here and in the adjacent country. About two-thirds of the
population is American or European, and one-third Mexican. The
proportions are reversed in the county. The population of Trinidad
is over 3,000 ; elevation, 6,032. Distance north of boundary line of
Colorado and New Mexico, 14 miles; to head of Ratoñ Pass, by
Atchison, Topeka & Santa Fe railway, 15 ; to La Junta, 80 ;
Kansas City, 651 ; Pueblo, 91 ; El Moro, 5 ; Denver, 211. Elevation of Ratoñ Pass, the gateway to New Mexico for this part of
Colorado, 7,863. Hotel, United States.

WALSENBURG.—County seat of Huerfano. Has an extensive and
productive coal mine ; employs about 35 men. Population of the
settlement, 250. The D. &. R. G. railway has a station here. Distance from Pueblo, 49 miles ; Denver, 169.

WEST LAS ANIMAS.—County seat of Bent county and the business
point for the most prominent cattle section of the State. Elevation,
3,750. Distance from Pueblo, 86 miles ; Kansas City, 548 ; Fort
Lyon, 4 miles. Population, 600.

CHAPTER XI

SOMETHING ABOUT THE CLIMATE OF COLORADO—ITS BENEFICIAL
EFFECTS ON PULMONARY AND OTHER DISEASES—THE MINERAL
WATERS—THEIR EXTENT, VARIETY, AND STERLING QUALITIES—
FACTS AND FIGURES REGARDING THE ABOVE POINTS.

So beneficial have been found the climatic influences of Colorado
that her fame as a sanitarium is becoming world-wide, and the
influx of health-seekers is annually becoming greater. The dryness
and lightness of the air and its invigorating character, together
with the almost constant prevalence of sunshine, impart new energy
to the well, and a fresh lease of life for those whose constitutions
are impaired. Here on this elevated plateau, far removed from the
chilling winds and damp atmosphere of either ocean, all the con-
ditions of life to the new comer are fresh and inspiring.

This region possesses influences that arrest the tendency to pulmonary diseases. Consumptives who do not put off their coming
too long have been cured effectively, while others have had their
days prolonged by months or years. Many eastern people have
taken up a permanent abode in Colorado, because their health
would not permit of their living elsewhere. Others have found the
results of a sojourn so salutary that they return to stay. A variety
of diseases, chronic or otherwise, find a speedy or partial cure in
the pure air or in the health-giving mineral waters.

Investigation and long experience by the highest medical authority
have summed the advantages of this climate somewhat as follows :
To a person in the enjoyment of fair health, the sensations attending
a first entrance into this elevated region are always pleasant. The
dryness of the atmosphere, together with the electricity therein contained, combined with, perhaps, other peculiarities of climate, excites
the nervous system to a peculiar degree of tension. The physical
functions, which may have for some time been accomplished in a
sluggish, inefficient manner, at once assume a vigor of action to
which the system is a stranger. The appetite is keen, the digestion
is vigorous, and the sleep sound. The result of these innovations is

that all lurking ailments are swept away at once, and whatever there is in each individual to enjoy is called into the fullest action. He revels in what might be called intoxication of good health. An unclouded mind partakes of the elasticity of a healthy body, and a newly-aroused desire for activity is manifested, as well as an increased capacity to accomplish. This, in the beginning, is experienced to a greater or less degree by all who visit this section, and the pleasure attendant upon such a beginning will forever render the Rocky mountains a resort of unequaled attraction for the tourist.

But besides merely pleasure-seeking travelers who come westward every year, there are thousands of invalids, suffering from a wide range of chronic diseases, who come on a pilgrimage in search of health. In many cases the relief obtained is surprisingly rapid. The asthmatic forgets in the quiet of undisturbed slumber his nightly suffocation; the victim of chronic bronchitis discovers a new lease of life, and after the lapse of a very brief period he finds it hard to realize that he has been so recently afflicted with a cough so distressing, so violent, or so dangerous. The sufferer from malaria, in that most obnoxious form called fever and ague, is glad to have found a land where fever and ague never come.

While the climate is thus referred to in such seemingly flattering terms, the idea is not intended to be conveyed that there is no bad weather in Colorado. There are almost all kinds of climate, according to elevation and locality, from a warm temperate to that of the borders of the frigid zone, the latter being largely experienced on the lofty peaks of the main range of mountains. Under such circumstances, weather, good, bad, and indifferent must be expected. Still the belt of country skirting the eastern base of the mountains as well as a few other sections, enjoys an amount of sunshine and of delightful weather with a freedom from storms such as is but rarely encountered elsewhere, and in no section between Colorado and the seaboard. The temperature of a large portion of the foothills country, including such places as Central, Black Hawk, Idaho Springs, and Georgetown, is remarkably even for the entire year, there being less cold weather in winter and warm weather in summer than in any locality of less elevation. A record of three years at Denver shows the following temperature and rainfall : Highest range of thermometer for January of three years, 60°, 67°, and 58°; lowest, 5° above, 6 above, and 20° below zero;

mean, 29°, 34°, and 22.7° February, highest, 64°, 66°, and 64°; lowest, 1° and 13° above and 9° below; mean, 33°, 38°, and 34°. March, highest, 67°, 67°, and 78°; lowest, 8° below, and 10° and 4° above; mean, 32.7°, 46°, and 39°. April, highest, 80°, 80°, and 83°; lowest, 16°, 25°, and 25°; mean, 48°, 50.1°, and 49°. May, highest, 86°, 86°, and 89°; lowest, 40°, 42°, and 35°; mean, 56°, 65°, and 61°. June, highest, 94°, 97°, and 97°; lowest, 48°, 56°, and 49°; mean, 68.2°, 65.2°, and 69°. July, highest, 98°, 97°, and 93°; lowest, 53°, 58°, and 54°; mean, 74.2°, 78°, and 71°. August, highest, 97°, 95°, and 94°; lowest, 45°, 58°, and 52°;

BUTTES OF THE CROSS—WESTERN COLORADO.

mean, 64.8°, 75.2°, and 72°. September, highest, 89°, 86°, and 90; lowest, 40°, 45°, and 35°; mean, 60°, 66.5°, and 62°. October, highest, 83°, 85°, and 88°; lowest, 27°, 24°, and 19°; mean, 47.8°, 53.5°, and 53.6°. November, highest, 68°, 70° and 69°; lowest, 20°, 0°, and 5° below; mean, 41.8°, 36°, and 36°. December, highest, 60°, 55°, and 60°; lowest, 18° below, 2 below, and 8° below; mean, 23°, 31.3°, and 28°. Rain-fall, 12.65 inches for first year, 12.35 for second, and 18.77 for third.

The United States signal station at Denver made the following showing of climatology for the year 1878. Number of clear days during the year, 163; fair or partly clear days, 137; cloudy days on which no rain or snow fell, 13; stormy weather, 52 days. Total amount of precipitation, rain or melted snow, 15.51 inches. This amount accumulated from the rain or snow-fall which occurred on 127 days—the rain principally in the form of showers. With the exception of a short interval, the remainder of any day on which these occurred was bright and clear. The rain-fall of April was but 05 inches, while that of May was 2.90 inches. The mean barometer for the year was 29.973 inches. The greatest pressure occurred September 10, sustaining 30.447 inches, and the least April 8, when it was 29.299. The temperature has ranged from 12 degrees below zero to 100 above, while the mean annual temperature was 49.52. The prevalent rains were from the south, giving a total movement of 5,043 miles.

The United States signal office at Colorado Springs gave the mean temperature for one year at that place as follows: January, 27°; February, 29°; March, 42°; April, 40.61°; May, 52.84°; June, 67°; July, 69°; August, 67.31°; September, 58.65°; October, 45°; November, 40.76°; December, 26°. The year 1878 is not given, as it was not up to the average.

As the weather of April, 1879, is still somewhat fresh in the memory of all, Denver's record is given in order that Eastern people may see how far it excelled anything experienced along the seaboard or in the Mississippi Valley. The number of perfectly clear days in that month was 10; of fair days, 14; of cloudy days, 5; and the number on which rain fell (including slight showers on some of the days classed as fair), was 12. The mean humidity was 51.2; the pre-prevailing wind, "south;" monthly velocity of wind, 5,855; maximum temperature, 76 degrees; minimum temperature, 28 degrees; amount of precipitation, 2.62 inches; mean thermometer, at 5:43 A. M., 40.2 degrees; 2:43 P. M., 58.6; at 9:08 P. M., 50.2; mean thermometer, 50.4; mean barometer, 29.940. The least daily range of temperature, was 6 degrees; mean of maximum temperature, 62.3; of minimum temperature, 38.2; mean daily range of temperature, 24.1. Dates of frosts, April 2d, 3d, 7th, 14th, 17th, and 25th. It will be seen that changeable, disagreeable, cold, and stormy weather, such as prevailed during most of the month at the East, was rarely felt in the capital of Colorado.

"Infinite" is the term used by an old Coloradan to describe in brief the climate of this region. Infinite it certainly is in variety, purity, and sunshine. But the variety comes from difference in altitude, rather than in latitude. The Italian or Virginian warmth of the plains, and the frigidity of "timber line," or of the mountain tops, are experienced on the same parallel and within fifty miles one of another. It is but a short remove from a northern to a southern temperature, and from either to the eternal snows of the Sierras. Owing to the dry, bracing qualities of the atmosphere, heat or cold are not felt as severely or readily as where there is greater moisture and humidity.

The quantity of the snow-fall is not great, except on the great mountain ranges and higher elevations. It never entirely disappears from altitudes of from 12,000 to 14,400 feet. Elsewhere the sun's rays are too powerful to admit of snow laying on the ground a great while unless in case of unusually cold weather, and sleighing is of rare occurrence in many mountain towns.

The mineral springs of Colorado are an important feature and have come to be regarded as a specific for diseases of many kinds. They are more numerous than in any other State, and are found bubbling out of ravine, hill-side, and glen, from Pueblo and Manitou to Utah. Taking all varieties—hot and cold, sulphur, soda, iron, and so on, and the collection is too numerous to mention in detail. Some of them are said to have no superiors in curative qualities. The Pagosa stands at the head of American mineral waters, and the hot sulphur springs of Wagon-Wheel Gap, Middle Park, and other points, are said to be equally beneficial. Still better known to the general tourist are the soda and iron springs, hot and cold, of Manitou, Idaho, and Cañon.

Members of the Colorado State Board of Health have investigated and made excellent reports on the mineral springs of this region. Statements of analyses are given hereafter. Near Ouray, over the mountains, in the far southwestern part of the State, are nine springs, six hot, two cold, and one sulphur, all easy of access and undoubtedly capable of greatly benefiting chronic forms of gastric trouble. The hot springs vary in temperature from 120° to 138°. Two of them give off carbonic acid gas in small quantities. Another is impregnated with sulphur. The carbonates abound, with that of lime in excess. Bath-houses have been fitted up. Near by

is a hot sulphur spring, strong and clear, with carbonic and sulphu-
reted hydrogen gases; temperature 134°. Cañon Creek Springs in the
same district embrace a warm chalybeate spring, another hot spring
containing bitter salts, beside a hot soda and other springs. Ouray
is beautifully located on the Uncompahgre, in the midst of some of
the grandest scenery on the continent. There are other mineral
waters, including hot sulphur of a lower temperature than a similar
spring nearer town. Nine miles below Ouray, in the fertile Uncompahgre Park, are the famous Ouray Springs of the Ute Indians,
which they hold in great veneration. Near here is the government
Indian agency.

Iron Lake, near the mountain pass between Silverton and the San
Miguel country, and twelve miles from the former place, is a great
natural curiosity. It is circular in form and only seventy-five feet in
diameter and impregnated with iron. The waters taken internally
cause a fine appetizing and tonic effect.

That beautiful garden spot, beginning thirty miles south of Silverton, and known as the Animas Valley, is a most inviting locality for
invalids. Here are several springs. The waters of three of them are of
a red-brown color, containing carbonate of lime, magnesia, and iron;
temperature 90°; taste similar to the Iron Chief of Manitou. Another
flows a large stream and is of great value to those of debilitated constitutions. This spring is violently agitated, and the escaping carbonic acid gas issues with such force as to resemble escaping steam
from an engine, and can be heard for quite a distance. There are
also soda springs further down, near the banks of the Animas river.

The great Pagosa ranks first among mineral springs of this part of
the West, if not of the whole country. So important are they considered that the United States government has set them and the adjacent
grounds apart as a reservation. They are situated east from Animas, and west from Alamosa, and on the south side of San Juan
river, about twenty-five miles from its headwaters. The deposit surrounding the larger spring consists mainly of carbonate of lime, and
the principal outlet is underground, traceable by the steam rising
through seams in the deposit. The altitude is 7,084, and the location is most advantageous for climate and surroundings. The river
bottom is very productive; there are good grazing lands and the
streams abound in trout, as do the hills and mountains in wild game.
This will be a great resort in the near future.

The Parnassus Springs, near the foot hills of the Greenhorn range, and twelve miles from Pueblo, are found to be quite beneficial to invalids who frequent them. The Carlisle Springs, twenty miles from Pueblo, near the Cañon road, are also favorably regarded.

The springs at Wagon Wheel Gap are among the best in the State, and are visited quite extensively by the people of the San Juan region, as well as by strangers. In Chaffee county are several hot springs, whose waters are already beginning to be utilized. The hot spring in Puncha Pass is highly spoken of, and so are those of Cottonwood.

The Cottonwood hot springs, twelve in number, are situated at Mahonville, at the mouth of Cottonwood cañon, some distance south of Granite and near Yale and Princeton mountains. Patients from Leadville and elsewhere have obtained an entire or partial cure of rheumatism and other diseases. Bath-houses, a hotel, and other accommodations have been erected or secured, so that invalids can be properly cared for. The tests of several years show that these waters are highly beneficial for catarrh, rheumatism, dyspepsia, scrofulous affections, and for persons who have been "leaded" while at work at smelting furnaces.

The Hot Sulphur Springs of Middle Park have long been justly famous for their medicinal and healing virtues, and are beginning to be extensively visited now that stage lines are in operation to Georgetown. The surroundings are beautiful, and the fishing and hunting of Grand county cannot be surpassed. The Steamboat Springs in Routt county are also remarkable.

On the following page, in tabulated form, are statements of various analyses made of most of the prominent springs.

So far but two localities possessing valuable mineral waters have drawn large numbers of people from abroad. These are Manitou and Idaho Springs. The reason is mainly due to their proximity to railways, lines of travel, and centres of population, and to improvements made, liberal advertising effected, and excellent hotel accommodations. Other places can be made just as attractive, and possess equal merits, but their remoteness from railways and large towns has acted as a drawback so far. Time will see a great change in this particular as the country becomes settled up, and as health and pleasure seekers become better acquainted with what it has to offer for their advantage and amusement. This season large numbers of visitors may be expected at the Cottonwood, Middle Park, Wagon Wheel Gap, and Cañon City springs.

ANALYSES OF COLORADO MINERAL SPRINGS—CONSTITUENT PARTS IN ONE GALLON OF WATER.

Name of Spring	Pagosa	Parnassus	Carlisle	Hot Sulphur	Hot Springs.*	Hot Springs.‡	Tonic Iron	Navajoe	Shoshone	Iron Ute	Hot Springs	Little Ute	Hot Springs.§
Temperature	150° F.	72° F.	60° F.	121° F.	148° F.	140° F.	50° F.	50°.2 F.	48°.5 F.	44°.3 F.	102° F.	51° F.	110° F.
Location	San Juan.	Pueblo.	Pueblo.	Middle Park.	W. W. Gap.	Arkansas.	Estes Park.	Manitou.	Manitou.	Manitou.	Canon City.	Canon City.	Idaho.
Carbonate of Soda	2.74	69.10	8.99	76.43				72.74	51.81	34.62	73.20	76.40	30.80
Carbonate of Lithia	.42	1.04			†			.14	Trace.	Trace.	Trace.	Trace.	
Carbonate of Lime	34.42	31.82	22.40	18.86	18.09	2.40	2.08	75.49	63.30	34.44	33.50	22.50	9.52
Carbonate of Magnesia	2.83	13.09	11.39	11.26	2.98	.50	1.53	18.47		8.50	12.80	14.00	2.88
Carbonate of Iron		1.30	.30			Iron Oxide, .13	4.86			3.37		Trace.	4.12
Sulphate of Potassa	4.16	10.76	.70				.72	9.46	2.99	4.09			29.39
Sulphate of Soda	129.32	2.32	20.00					10.74	21.63	18.01	79.30	12.10	3.44
Sulphate of Lime	17.06	60.75		96.62	6.13	.35	.95	23.21	24.57	18.43	18.20		4.13
Chloride of Sodium			11.26		6.84	.21						118.00	
Silica	3.33	4.63	Trace.	.54	.62	1.40	.58	.86	Trace.	1.56			Sil. Soda, 4.08
Organic Matter	Trace.	Trace.	Trace.	Not determined.	Hydro. Sul., 7.00	1.16	1.31						
Total Solids	194.27	75.04	75.04	228.87	41.65	6.24	12.04	211.12	164.30	123.03	217.00	243.00	107.11
Gases	Carb. Acid. Hydro. Sul.			Hydro. Sul.	Hydro. Sul. 7.00 grains, 19.2 cub. in.			Carb. Acid.	Carb. Acid.	Carb. Acid.			

* Chloride of Potassium, 19.08; Sulphide of Sodium, 5.68; Alumina, 39.   ‡ Iodine, .05.

† Lithia could have been estimated, had there been sufficient water.   § Sulphate Magnesia, 18.72.

THE GRAND CAÑON OF THE ARKANSAS.

This cañon, and the first railway excursion therein, was thus described in the Denver Tribune:—The most stupendous achievement
of railway engineering over Nature's efforts to obstruct the pathway
of commerce, was triumphantly achieved on the seventh of May,
1879, by the Atchison, Topeka & Santa Fe Railway Company,
which on that day made the passage of the Grand Cañon of the
Arkansas, with a train of cars carrying an excursion party of ladies
and gentlemen, numbering over two hundred persons. This rock-
bound river pathway became known to the Spanish missionaries as
early as the year 1642. From that time it was not known that any
animal life had ever passed through it successfully until the winter
of 1870. The approach to the Cañon is gradual. The distant hills
draw nearer, and the valley of the Arkansas becomes narrower and narrower, until the river is shut in closely on both sides by high mountains, sloping gently away and covered with verdure. Then the
slope of the mountains becomes more perpendicular, and the hills
become higher, until suddenly the river is completely shut in by
mountains with mighty tops. The roar and rattle of the train
grows louder and echoes up and down. The train is fairly in the
Cañon. It moves slowly. The mountain walls are of a dizzy height,
and so close together that, looking ahead, they appear simply to form
a crevice, a huge, awful, crooked crevice, through which the miserable little train is timidly crawling. The curves of the Cañon are
superb. They constitute the finishing touch to its grandeur, and fill
the mind with a fuller appreciation of this great miracle of nature.
But the Royal Gorge! Imagine two almost perfectly perpendicular
walls rising to a height of 2,000 feet, those walls presenting jagged and
irregular masses of rock that on the railroad side hang over the train
all creviced and ready to fall in thousands of tons. The road-bed is
cut out of the solid rock, and masses of this hang over it stretching
out a hundred feet. One cannot look up to the top of this wall on
account of these projecting, irregular bluffs, but the height to the
top, even as measured by the eye, disturbs the faculties and brings on
vertigo. The cooped-up Arkansas rushes madly by, a narrow thread,
made still more so by the rocks thrown into it. There is not room to
step from the train without pitching into the river. Not a word is

uttered. The engineer whistles occasionally and timid folks look for
the rocks to fall.   It is really a strain on the mind to take it in; and
this can be only feebly done on a single trip.   Two thousand feet
above you are the tops of the mountain walls. You are imprisoned

BUENA VISTA GROTTO, NEAR MANITOU.

in a crack, thirty feet wide, and are partially under one mountain
wall. You can see on the opposite side the gradations of the
verdure, rich below, impoverished above.   And the curves become
more awful as you look ahead or back.

There was no sun in the Gorge, but it slanted down the opposite mountain wall as the party returned through the Cañon, increasing the surpassing beauty of the scene. The Cañon is eleven miles in length and the Gorge a mile and a half. The tourists had seen it all —seen the greatest natural wonder of the West, and the first train of

MANITOU.

passengers had passed through the Gorge. In cutting the road-bed in the Cañon the workmen would begin high up on the mountain wall and blast down to the level of the road. In this way masses of rock a hundred yards wide have been split from the mountain. In that narrow crevice it was difficult to dispose of this material.

Some was used for the road-bed, and the rest of necessity was thrown into the Arkansas. This made the already too much shut-in stream still more contracted. The bed of the road is some twelve feet above the river, perhaps more. There is no danger apprehended from the masses of rock overhanging the track. Every inch of this wall, the contractors say, has been examined and tested. Immediately at the entrance of the Royal Gorge is the grandest of its many scenes. The rock-bound sides of the cañon recede from each other with a gradual departure to the height of a thousand feet, when they commence curving inward until the summits of the two sides have approached each other within thirty-five feet, at an altitude of nearly two thousand feet.

It is stated that the first day of July will see this railway completed to Cleora. Then there will be less than ten hours' staging to Leadville. From that point, which will more or less command the trade of central, western and southwestern Colorado, the progress of the tracklayers will be rapid.

This volume gives the best possible account of routes of travel and of the mining, farming, and stock growing industries, that circumstances permit of, but the State is growing too fast to admit of any publication fully keeping pace with it. New mineral discoveries are constantly being made, new towns are springing up as if by magic, and stage lines and railways are being established where they were unthought of a few months or years before. The author has done his best to keep up with the march of events and here rests his case with the reader. For further information regarding routes of travel, lists of post offices, express offices, banks, newspapers, census and election returns, and other matters, see Appendix at the close of this volume.

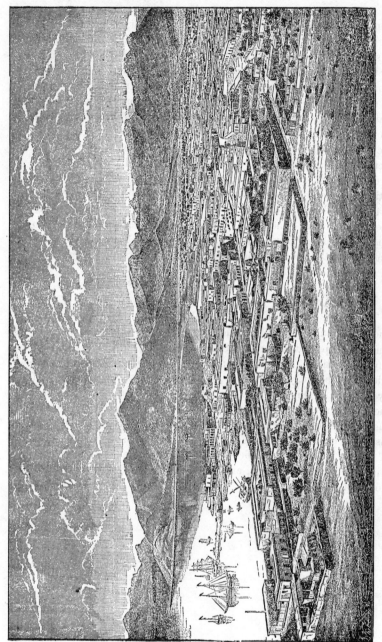

GUAYMAS, MEXICO, THE PACIFIC COAST TERMINUS OF THE ATCHISON, TOPEKA AND SANTA FE R. R.

PART SECOND.

CHAPTER I.

EARLY HISTORY OF COLORADO—AMERICAN ACQUISITION OF AN IN-
LAND EMPIRE — GOVERNMENT EXPLORING EXPEDITIONS — THE
FIRST DISCOVERIES AND THE MARCH TO THE LAND OF GOLD—
ANNALS OF THE FIFTY-NINERS.

France once claimed a large part of the vast region between the
Mississippi river and the Pacific ocean. In the same indefinite manner Spain asserted ownership northward of the Gulf of Mexico and
westward to the Pacific. In the year 1540, the Spanish viceroy of
Mexico sent Coronado and a force of troops and followers to explore the country toward the north for gold. The march was
unsuccessful, and, consequently, this portion of the country, that has
since added so largely to the world's store of the precious metals,
was left for centuries in the undisputed possession of the buffalo
and of the red man.

Soon after the United States purchased from France the immense
territory known as Louisiana the government took steps to ascertain
the value and resources of its newly acquired inland empire. In
1805, Lieut. Pike and twenty-three soldiers crossed the plains and
partly explored the mountains and headwaters of what has since
become Colorado. He and his command were captured near or on
the Rio Grande by the Spanish military forces stationed there, and
were afterwards released. The next expedition was that of Colonel
S.H. Long, in 1819. The two most prominent peaks of the Colorado
mountain range, as seen from the plains, take their names from these
men. In 1832 came Captain Bonneville of the American Fur Company. Fremont's expeditions of 1842 and of 1844 were the most
effective and serviceable of any sent out under the auspices of the
government.

In 1846 the Mexican war began, and the comparatively unsettled and unknown regions forming the northern half of our neighboring republic were taken possession of by the American forces under Doniphan, Fremont, and Stockton. Since then this valuable territory has been found to be enormously rich in the precious metals, and states and territories have been organized therefrom. California, Nevada, Utah, Arizona, New Mexico, and most of Colorado, yielding a gold and silver product greater than all the world beside, are the results of this acquisition. The California gold discoveries of thirty years ago caused such a tide of immigration westward as the world has seldom witnessed. The main overland route was just to the north of the wilderness of plain and mountain that, through its golden treasure, caused a similar excitement ten years later.

Before and after the Mexican war, fur traders visited the Rocky mountains, and some of them built small forts on the Arkansas and Platte rivers. During this same period an active trade was carried on by means of caravans between the western limits of American civilization and Santa Fé, the outpost and trade centre of northern Mexico. The town of Independence, in western Missouri, was the usual point from which the long wagon trains, or "fleets of prairie schooners," set out on their annual voyages toward the setting sun. Many were the battles these daring train men fought with hostile savages, and several expeditions were captured and destroyed. Yet this traffic was so remunerative that men were willing to brave any danger to engage in it.

Up to the close of the war of 1846–8, the Republic of Mexico claimed all of what is now Colorado south of the Arkansas river, and west of the mountains south of the forty-first parallel, and its authority was recognized from the time of Lieut. Pike's capture, in 1806, up to the conquests of Doniphan and Fremont. A few years before the war the Mexican government had donated a princely grant of land south of the Arkansas river to Colonels Vijil and Saint Vrain. This was known as the Las Animas land grant, the full extent of which has not yet been recognized by the United States government, although some other land grants of the old Mexican times have been.

Before or about the time of the Mexican war, Colonel Bent established a trading post or fort on the Arkansas river. This served as a place of refuge and defense from the Indians in after years. Previous to the Colorado gold discoveries, Colonel Craig convoyed government and other supplies through Southern Colorado and into

New Mexico, stopping south of Trinidad to build a wagon-road over the Raton mountains. Some years later he became possessed of a part of the Las Animas grant, and in the State movement of 1865, was the democratic candidate for governor, as against William Gilpin, republican. A few Mexicans had settled near the New Mexican border, on the Las Animas river, prior to 1858.

In 1854 Lafayette Head, recently lieutenant-governor of Colorado, came northward from Taos, New Mexico, with some fifty Mexicans, or rather New Mexicans. They formed the settlement of Conejos, where a Jesuit Mission or school was soon after established. The Apache and Ute Indians attacked and besieged the place in 1855. Other New Mexicans afterwards moved into this same Rio Grande valley of Southern Colorado, and engaged in sheep raising and farming. Major Head built the first flour mill in the southern part of the territory, in 1864. All of the settlements of the Rio Grande and Las Animas were widely separated from one another, as well as from the gold regions of the northern districts. The Mexican populations have ever been devoted Catholics, and but few of them can speak or write the English language. From them comes the Spanish nomenclature of Southern Colorado.

Outside of traders, train men, explorers, Pacific coast emigrants and Mexicans, and the Mormons of Utah, no white men had ventured far west of the Missouri prior to the Green-Russell party of Georgia, in 1858. The advent of these men in Missouri and Kansas caused others to move on to the Pike's Peak country. Prospecting was carried on with moderate success on the tributaries of the Platte river, east of the base of the mountains. The reports carried back to the States by the Russell party spread like wildfire, and thousands prepared to visit the new Eldorado in the following spring. This was the year after the great financial crash of 1857, when so many time-honored houses went down in the storm, and men were ready for almost any venture that promised to better their fortunes. The opportunity was afforded by the gold discoveries of what was termed the Pike's Peak gold region.

The pioneers of the fall of 1858 founded the towns of Auraria, Denver, Boulder, Fountain City, and one or two minor settlements. The ambitious character of these early settlers, some two hundred in number, is shown in their choice of one of their comrades to proceed to Washington to procure a territorial form of government, and of another to represent them in the Kansas territorial legislature. While the mission of the first was unavailing, that of the second resulted in the establishment of a country called Arapahoe, embracing all of western Kansas. That territory then extended to the crest of the snowy range.

With the spring and summer of 1859 came a stampede westward to the land of promise such as has never been equaled except in the case of California. Over the broad expanse of six hundred miles of plain passed an almost continuous stream of humanity. The talismanic legend, " gold," had created a fever and enthusiasm that no distance nor hardship could repress, no danger or difficulty dispel. And so all routes over this ocean of dust and solitude were lined with caravans, and with pilgrims weary and footsore, but ever hopeful of the land and future before them That many were doomed to disappointment is told in the unwritten history of this as of all other mining excitements.

The roving, adventurous spirits that formed the vanguard in the settlement of Colorado came largely from the better and more enterprising classes of the East, West, and South. There was a smattering of good, bad, and indifferent characters, all equally desirous of bettering their fortunes, which, in many cases, could not have been worse. Probably over fifty thousand men aided in this eventful year to enlarge " that western trail of immigration which bursts into states and mpires as it moves." The wide-awake speculator, the broken-down merchant, the farmer, mechanic, gambler, or the wanderer from foreign lands, the cultured and the illiterate, all combined to swell the human tide that was setting in so strongly for the new land of gold out toward the setting sun. While many were admirably adapted to settle and reclaim a wilderness, large numbers soon became discouraged, and returned whence they came. But this could not arrest the progress of the oncoming multitude that followed. Probably nineteen-twentieths of these gold-seekers were as ignorant and inexperienced as regards mining as they well could be, and had but a faint idea of the work to be done or the experience to be undergone in this wild rush for wealth.

In the spring of 1859 the pioneers began to explore the rugged foot hills and mountains that extended on beyond the western border of the plains. Placer and creek mining was at the same

THE COURSE OF EMPIRE.

6

time prosecuted on all of the streams below the points where they left the hill country. Although gold had been found on South Boulder and on South Clear creek and tributaries a little earlier in the season, the grand discovery that gave the first undoubted assurance of value was that of John H. Gregory. This was made on the present site of Central and Black Hawk. When the news reached Denver and the valley that gold in plentiful quantities existed not forty miles away, there was a general stampede up the various creeks and cañons leading into the mountains. Gregory's discovery proved to be the outcropping of a great gold-bearing vein. The lode and district took their names from him. The Gregory has yielded more money than any other Colorado fissure. Thousands of men were soon encamped on Clear creek, Gregory gulch, and tributary streams, and rich surface deposits and vertical mineral veins were found in great numbers on every hand. Mining districts were organized, and subsequently subdivided, with local laws of their own framing and adoption. This was necessary, as these settlements were outside of the jurisdiction of any state or territory; and had the case been different, special laws for the pre-emption and government of an exclusively mining country would have been necessary. Between these mountain mining camps and the remainder of the inhabited world was a wilderness of plain on one hand and one of mountain and desert on the other—each as broad and boundless as an ocean.

Before the end of May the valleys of the streams that course through the mountains of the country that has since become Clear Creek, Gilpin, and Boulder counties were alive with men. Trees were felled, cabins erected, and sluice boxes constructed for washing the gold from the gravel and "pay dirt." Hand rockers were also used and arastras were subsequently operated. For this surface mining a plentiful supply of water was required.

Most of the more important early discoveries were made by men who had mined in Georgia or in California; many men who had never seen a mine before coming here were afterwards equally fortunate. In the districts of Gilpin county the miners' laws allowed the discoverer of a lode or vein two hundred feet thereon, while any other person could possess one hundred feet in length on the vein and no more. This course was adopted in most other sections. Such limited amounts of territory operated well as long as work was confined to no great depths below the surface. It divided wealth among a large number of people and kept money circulating freely. As greater depths were reached, the results were less and less satisfactory. When it finally became necessary to use steam machinery it was found that this subdivision of territory was a great drawback to the advancement of the country. Years were required in Gilpin county and vicinity to reach the time when the requisite consolidations of these small properties could be made that permitted profitable deep mining. For placer or gulch mining one hundred feet of ground up or down a stream were allowed, each claim being allowed a width of fifty feet. The results here were similar to those of lode mining as regards extensive operations.

As the summer of 1859 advanced the number of people in the above mentioned localities was too great for the opportunities offered, and prospecting parties began to move out in search of other fields. In July one of these passed southward over Mount Rosalia, and for the first time the South Park, radiant and beautiful in its summer garb, greeted the eyes of the gold hunters. Their discoveries on what they called Tarryall creek drew thousands in that direction, and the bustling and prosperous camps of Hamilton and Tarryall became great and famous. One hundred and fifty feet in length along the stream was the allowance to a claim there. This so disgusted the later arrivals, who were unable to secure their share, that they moved over to the Platte and established a camp, which they named Fairplay, where the ground was allotted so as to permit of a division among a larger number of claimants. Jefferson City, near Georgia Pass, was also a lively town, and one camp after another was established as the presence of golden sands or paygravel became manifest.

Early in 1859, W. A. H. Loveland and others founded the town of Golden. In Clear Creek county, Idaho was the leading town of the bar and creek mines. In Gilpin there was a cluster of towns adjoining or near one another. These included Black Hawk, Mountain City, Central, Missouri City, and Nevada. Further north there were lively times on the Boulder creeks and along the Saint Vrain and Left Hand creeks and tributaries. Gold Run yielded a hundred thousand dollars that summer. Late in the season gold was discovered on the headwaters of the Blue, over in Summit county. This is on the Pacific slope of the Continental Divide. A few small

CROSSING THE PLAINS IN THE OLDEN TIME.

CROSSING THE PLAINS TO-DAY.

and primitive stamp-mills were brought into the Gregory and Gold Hill diggings late in 1859.

As has been said before the gold hunters of " fifty-nine " were composed largely of the very best material the States could furnish. Men of enterprise and energy, these prospectors and explorers belonged to a class distinct in themselves, whose mission was to create what has been termed the mountain and plains empire. How well they and those that came after have accomplished the work the Centennial State attests. With these pioneers came those accompaniments of civilization, the printing press and free schools. The Rocky Mountain News issued its first number as early as April 23, 1859. Other newspapers in Denver and in the mountains had a varied career in these earlier years, but the only ones that still survive are the News of Denver and the Register of Central. Many of the journals of later date have also done good service and reflect credit on the State and her people.

In the spring of 1859 the Pike's Peak Express Company established a stage line between the Missouri River and the Rocky Mountains. The distance of seven hundred miles or more was soon after made in six days and nights, schedule time. This became the property of Ben Holiday in 1862, and afterwards of Wells, Fargo & Co. The main portion of the immigration was effected by means of wagon trains, and ox and mule teams.

This mode of transportation, occupying weeks or months, was in striking contrast to the rapid locomotion of the present plains travel, wherein the iron horse and palace-car play so important a part. The traveler of to-day can hardly appreciate the difficulties encountered at every step by those who " pioneer " the way for future generations and " rough it " in new and distant mining countries.

There were movements in 1859 looking toward the establishment of a territorial and state government. A state constitution was submitted to the people and rejected by a vote of 2,007 against to 649 for. In October, B. D. Williams was chosen to visit Washington to endeavor to secure the organization of a territory to be called Jefferson. County officers were chosen by those acknowledging the authority of the territory of Kansas, and a convention was elected and assembled for a state organization. State and county officers were finally chosen, but nothing eventually came of this provisional government.

CHAPTER II.

EARLY COLORADO HISTORY—THE PIONEERS OF 1860-63 AND THEIR
MOVEMENTS, DISCOVERIES, AND OPERATIONS—GULCH AND PLACER
MINING—PRODUCTIVE CHARACTER OF SURFACE DIGGINGS AND
GOLD VEINS—THE MINING CAMPS OF THE FRONTIER.

In the spring and summer of 1860 mining was continued with
redoubled vigor on streams and gold-bearing lodes from the Saint
Vrain to the Arkansas. New comers from the East were plentiful,
and many new sections were explored, with occasional rich discoveries. This season bands of prospectors crossed the Park range and
the main crest of the Rocky mountains and began mining in earnest
on the headwaters of the Blue and the Arkansas. California gulch
was washed for gold and began to yield its millions, and in Summit
county, Georgia, Humbug, Galena, and French gulches and Gold
Run astonished the country with their wealth. Other exploring
parties crossed the Sawatch range, and one venturesome band, led
by Colonel Baker, made an unprofitable trip through the San Juan
mountains and was ordered away by the Indians of that locality.

In Boulder several districts became very productive, noticeably
that of Gold Hill. Mining was exceedingly lively in the Gregory
and Russell gulch diggings of what is now Gilpin county, especially
after the introduction of a reliable water supply by means of the
consolidated ditch. Thousands of men were engaged in gulch and
lode mining. Sixty quartz mills, mostly of small dimensions, were
brought in and set at work. Thirty arastras were also employed, and
did good service as long as soft surface dirt was obtainable. Mining
affairs were lively on South Clear creek and tributaries, and over in
the South Park the gold yield was large and general prosperity prevailed.

In the spring of 1860 the owners of the Pike's Peak stage line
established what was known as the Pony Express. This served as a
daily fast-mail line between the cities of the Atlantic and Pacific
coasts, and was of great value to the business men of those sections

previous to the construction of the overland telegraph lines. The
scheme was a marvel of American enterprise. Previous to that time
over three weeks were required to convey mails by steamer from New
York to San Francisco. This Pony Express made the distance

THE PONY EXPRESS.

between the railway terminus on the Missouri river and the Pacific in
eight or nine days. Brave men and first-class stock were required,
for Indians and highwaymen were often encountered, and the relay
stations were sometimes burned and the stock run off. Almost the
entire distance of nearly two thousand miles to be traversed was one

vast solitude. No delays were permitted, and the mail-bags were kept on the move during the whole time of these long and lonely trips. Horses were changed at every station and riders at intervals of from fifty to seventy miles. The rapid time made caused the government to send the mails overland, and the overland stage and railway, established one after the other, were the results. The construction of the telegraph line to the Pacific in 1862 caused the discontinuance of the Pony Express.

In the summers of 1860–61, there were busy, bustling mining camps on the headwaters of the South Platte, and portions of the South Park were alive with prospectors and miners. These flourished while the placers and gulches were producing largely. As they gave out or failed to pay, the men who had located there abandoned them or moved on to newer diggings of this or other territories. In 1862, rich gold lodes were mined in Buckskin district, and the town of Laurette had a newspaper, theatre, nine quartz mills and, like other camps, numberless saloons, an occasional variety show, and all the gambling-houses that were necessary to make the fortune-hunter contented and happy. In four short summers the population and glory of Tarryall, Montgomery, Laurette, and other camps had departed, and few old timers remained to tell the story of the dead cities of the Park.

Beginning with the summer of 1860, and continuing for several seasons, California and Georgia gulches were enormously profitable. It is reported that many an oyster can of gold dust and nuggets was filled there in a single day. Diggings near Montgomery yielded an average of a pound of gold per day to the man, and Spring gulch, at Central City, produced largely.

Denver grew rapidly in 1860. It was the point of arrival and departure for nearly all who came or left the country, although Cañon City was of some importance in this way for the southern routes from the East to the mines. Brick buildings were erected and large business houses were established at the future metropolis. Among the latter were three banks, one of which is said to have charged from ten to twenty-five per cent. interest on loans per month. Clark, Gruber & Co. added a coining and assay department to their banking-house. The government purchased their establishment in 1862, since when it has been used as a United States assay and refining office. The rates of freight across the plains in those days were from ten to twenty cents per pound. This was less than in 1864–5, but from five to ten times present charges. Some hard characters found their way to Denver and the mines at this time, and several murders were committed by them, which induced the citizens to organize a temporary vigilance committee and do a little shooting and hanging on their own account. This had a beneficial effect. The surviving roughs left the country and order prevailed from that time forward. Auraria and Denver were finally united under one municipal government.

In the stirring mining camps and ambitious cities of the gold diggings frontier mining life could be studied in all its phases. There were many men of many lands in the rude habitations that lined the hillsides and gulches. Their histories would read like romances. One could never tire of listening to the annals of the "fifty-niners," and volumes could be filled with narrative and story of their deeds and adventures. These towns of log cabins, tents, and unpretentious frames had much the appearance of a military encampment. Saloons were numerous, theatrical troupes made regular trips from one point to another, religious services were often held in the open air beneath the mountain pines, and bands of music invited the miner to show or gambling-house at almost all hours of the day or night. Paper money was rarely seen, and gold dust was the universal medium of exchange. This was usually carried in buckskin pouches, and the price of an article purchased was weighed in dust on gold scales used in all business houses. Gold as it came from the gulches was usually valued at about eighteen dollars per ounce. The population of Colorado for many years was ever changing, fresh arrivals taking the place of those who returned to the East or moved on to other territories.

Placers and gulches are what are termed poor man's diggings, because little or no money is required to test their value or put them into producing condition. Every man knew what his claim was yielding when night came. As one writer puts it, "The expressions of satisfaction or disappointment in those early Colorado mining times, when the sluice-boxes were cleaned, would challenge the greed of the miser and the disgust of the spendthrift." Many streams were worked to great disadvantage. Some ground, which should have been operated by long bed rock flumes or hydraulics, was divided among too many owners to secure such improvements, and the miners were in too much of a hurry to get rich and leave the country to think of combining for the slow but eventually sure work necessary for such enterprises. Consequently abandonment followed sooner or later, and no further work was done until consolidations permitted of mining on a wholesale scale.

The amount of gold obtained, however, in the four summers of 1860–63, inclusive, was very large. Good authorities indicate the yield to have been from the creeks, placers, and gulches alone, about as follows, and some give much higher estimates : Boulder county, $400,000 ; Gilpin, $2,500,000 ; Clear Creek, $1,700,000 ; Park, $1,500,000 ; Summit, $5,000,000 ; Lake, $4,000,000. This is exclusive of lode mines, which were worked at all seasons of the year, and were immensely productive in Gilpin and in a less degree in most other leading districts.

Congress organized the Territory of Colorado February 26, 1861, embracing the same area as the present State. The first territorial governor, William Gilpin, arrived in Denver, in May, 1861. A census taken at this time showed a population of 25,329, of whom 4,484 were females. H. P. Bennett was elected delegate to Congress in September, being the first Coloradan admitted to a seat in that body. The nine counties previously referred to elected full sets of officers and a legislature was chosen.

Soon after the breaking out of the war of the rebellion numbers of men left Colorado to take part in the great contest. The population had been drawn largely from all sections, but the number who went South at this time was small. The first regiment of Colorado infantry, afterwards changed to cavalry, did good service in repelling the Texan invasion of New Mexico in 1862. That same year another regiment was organized, whose ranks were afterwards reinforced by the fraction of a third regiment. This force won no little credit for itself at the time of Price's invasion of Missouri in 1864. Colorado also had a battery, and late in 1864 a three months' regiment was raised for protection against the Indians of the plains. This did good service in annihilating a large portion of the Cheyenne tribe at Sand creek.

In May, 1862, John Evans succeeded William Gilpin as governor, and S. H. Elbert became territorial secretary in place of L. L. Weld. In the September following H. P. Bennett, conservative, was re-elected to Congress, receiving 3,655 votes to 2,312 for William Gilpin, republican, and 2,754 for J. M. Francisco, democrat.

In 1862-3 large numbers of miners left the failing gulch and placer diggings and what were then called the refractory lode veins.

OLD RANCHO AND TRADING POST ON THE BORDER.

Some went to the new camps of Idaho and Montana and others returned to the States. The gold product of these times was much larger, however, than in preceding years. The gold-bearing lodes of Gilpin were in many cases paying enormously and gulch mining was still very remunerative. The mines at Empire had just been developed and much gold was obtained by sluicing surface dirt as well as by quartz milling. The gulches of Summit county were generally very productive, and California gulch in Lake county was turning out a round million each summer. Some of the Park county placers had began to fail, but gold lodes were paying largely near Buckskin, Laurette, and Montgomery. The same was true of many localities in Boulder county.

The territory forming Gilpin county had been divided into many districts and a multitude of veins and claims had been recorded and worked more or less. Most of these veins were within a strip of country extending from Black Hawk to the upper end of Nevada and Russell gulches, embracing a length of but little over three miles. Located there were the lively wide-awake towns of Mountain City, Central, Missouri City, and Nevadaville, forming, with Black Hawk, almost one continuous camp. Here were such lodes as the Bobtail, Fisk, Gregory, Bates, Hunter, Kip and Buell, Winnebago, Casto, Gregory Second, Gunnell, Kansas, Burroughs, Gardner, Mercer

County, Kent County, Flack, Forks, American Flag, California, Illinois, Missouri, Alps, Pewabic, and the Patch diggings on Quartz Hill. The lodes were mostly divided off into claims one hundred feet long. Discoverers of veins were allowed twice that amount of territory. Further north in this same county were the active mining camps of Wide Awake and of the Perigo and Gold Dirt section, beside districts of less importance.

Very few of the men who came to Colorado knew anything of mining or milling. They had pretty smooth sailing, however, when engaged in such simple work as placer or creek mining, or while the soft surface dirt or decomposed vein matter held out. When a depth of from sixty to one hundred feet was attained on the lodes great difficulty was experienced by most mill men in saving gold enough to permit of any profits. The soft quartz had been succeeded by ore from which the gold could not be so easily extracted, especially by the amateur mill men usually engaged in the business. In many veins the rich top material had been succeeded by poor rock, and in some places the veins pinched up to nothing. Many believed the quartz had disappeared for good, and sold their claims at almost any figures they could get. So in some localities there was a suspension of work or of production for the want of ore, and in others on account of inability to extract the gold. There were other claims, however, that had not been worked deep enough to get below the decomposed mineral, and at all times there were large numbers of paying mines.

CHAPTER III.

MINING INVESTMENTS IN COLORADO IN 1863–4—HOW MINES WERE
BOUGHT AND STOCKED AT THE EAST IN THE GREENBACK ERA
—EASTERN MINING COMPANY OPERATIONS AND THE CAUSES
OF THEIR FAILURE.

The continued receipts of gold dust and bullion finally created an
interest at the East in Colorado mines. The result was that capitalists began to regard gold-producing properties with favor. The
sale of the Casey mine on the Burroughs lode, in Gilpin county, and
the organization of the Ophir Mining Company in New York, in
October, 1863, were followed by similar transactions one after another.
During the following winter, and in the spring of 1864, there was a
wonderful excitement over mining investments and mining stocks.
Mines—good, bad, and indifferent—were bought up in rapid succession. The more productive claims on the Gregory, Bobtail, and
Gunnell lodes brought one thousand dollars per foot.

The war had inaugurated a speculative era, in which men acquired
wealth with a rapidity they had never before dreamed of being able
to do. Success in one class of operations caused them to embark in
others. The rapid fortunes made in operating mines, and the steady
output of gold, led men into this class of investments. So, in the
days of gold speculation and fluctuating values, a mining stock
board was organized in New York, and mines were purchased and
companies organized. These were often stocked at enormous figures
and swung on values much higher than they would bear. As time
passed on the excitement increased, and so anxious were people to
possess a mine or some mining stock that the quantity of properties
fell short of the demand. Agents were sent out to Colorado to hunt
up and purchase mining claims. It is evident they were not very
particular as to the value thereof so long as they could show evidence
of a record or transaction of some kind. Yet when a company came
to be formed these Eastern manipulators stocked what they paid the
miner but a few thousand dollars for at a hundred times the original
prices. It mattered little, however, just then, for all stocks would

sell, and no one seemed to stop to consider the value of what was behind them.

Nearly two hundred companies were organized in various Eastern cities on mining properties of Gilpin, Clear Creek, and Boulder counties. The capital stocks of many of these mounted way up in the millions, and some of them were held for a time at par. It was the age of greenbacks, and as these promises of the government were steadily depreciating it was feared they would eventually become nearly worthless. This was one inducement for investing in anything that promised to give gold instead. While the results would have been more or less satisfactory with proper management, they could not but be disastrous when the properties possessed no value. Although Wall street had a brilliant and for the most part an unscrupulous set of operators in mines in those days, and the public was in a venturesome mood, this condition of affairs could not last always. The bottom finally dropped out of the market, and from that time forward people were as much too cautious regarding mines as they had previously been too anxious to obtain anything that went by that name.

Meantime very many mining companies had taken steps to work their properties, or at least get rid of their working capital as speedily or foolishly as possible. The entire history of these company investments and operations, with a few exceptions, could hardly have been worse. In the first place, claims of from sixty to two hundred feet only were usually bought on one vein, and as much more on another or many others, instead of making the entire purchase on one vein or lode. Many of these had paid handsomely as long as work was carried on near the surface, but it is an impossibility to successfully work such small claims separately to depths of many hundreds of feet. It took years of depression and abandonment before the time arrived when these false steps could be remedied by consolidation. Poor management, foolish expenditures, or a failure to work the mines, with high prices of labor and supplies, were the other main causes of the failures of the companies. Of course there were some claims that contained nothing of value; but this was not the case with very many of them. This has been proved time and again by Colorado miners, who have leased idle properties of these companies and made fortunes therefrom in one, two, or three years. Instances can be mentioned where some of these lessees have bought mines with the money they have previously made in leasing them. It needed men to operate them who understood mining, just as any line of business needs men at the head who understand it. The man with a process caught a great many of these companies. The stamp mills had been the reliance of the lode miners, and although they lost much of the gold, this was due more to poor equipments, lack of care, and unskillful work than from any fault of that system. With the hope of saving a higher percentage of the gold, many companies took up with the process of some professor or inventor. These process mills required a vast amount of machinery, and cost from five to twenty times what a quartz mill would to-day. When completed some would not save the gold, and all were too expensive to work. They broke up nearly all the companies who meddled with them. The working capital was usually expended in building a mill of some kind, instead of on the claim to see if it had anything that called for a mill. Staffs of heavy-salaried and incompetent officials, dishonesty, and inattention to business, generally wound up these companies, or their money and property, when they were not squandered in the ways abovementioned. To add to the misfortunes of the period, an Indian war broke out on the plains, and this caused freight charges to rise enormously. At this time the amount of machinery that was being transported to Colorado was enormous. It cost more to freight the inside works of a mill across the plains than a mill could be bought, and freighted, and put up for at the present time. As every company was erecting mills, works, and buildings at the same time, the cost of labor and supplies became very great, which the rebellion and Indian war aided to make still higher. The closing down of many companies and properties caused Colorado mining camps to wear a discouraging appearance in 1865–6.

Yet some of the lodes were so valuable that they continued to produce largely, and many companies operated them for years, with varying success. The condition of affairs was so different then from what it is now, that it was impossible to expect anything like the results of to-day. Since then successful smelting works for handling the richer ores, improved quartz milling, railways, bringing a reduction in cost of labor and supplies, and the knowledge which experience brings from many years of mining, have all come to aid the miner and render his labor profitable.

Careful investigation of the subject shows that not far from three and a half millions were paid Colorado men for mines in the first ten years of mining there. Probably as much more was expended for machinery, freights, and in working claims where no great returns were obtained. The remainder of the millions that were lost or invested in stock operations went to the eastern manipulators. It stopped in New York and at the East. As affairs were then managed, mining stocks proved what most railroad investments do to most stockholders—a losing venture all around. This need not be the case hereafter as regards Colorado mines. Purchasers or company managers should not be in too much of a hurry to build mills, but open the mine first and see if it can supply a mill with ore. They should entrust their mining and milling to experienced miners and mill men, instead of to worthless friends or relatives, and, in fact, conduct matters as they would in any legitimate business. The former are not likely to steal as much, if they were so disposed, as the latter would fool away. It requires as much ability and good judgment to operate a large mine as it does a manufactory or mercantile establishment. These facts are worth the attention of all men likely to be connected with mining operations.

In the spring of 1864 the plains Indians started out on the warpath, and for a time communication between Colorado and the States was almost stopped. Stages were often obliged to fight their way through or back to the nearest station, and were occasionally captured and their passengers massacred. Wagon trains encountered the same difficulties. Some of them containing supplies and mining machinery for the newly organized companies were abandoned on the plains. Scattering farm houses and numerous stage stations were burned, their inmates slaughtered, and the stock stolen. Troops were ordered west to protect the routes of travel, and a regiment of twelve hundred men was raised in Colorado. These, under command of Col. Chivington, attacked and nearly exterminated a band of hostile Cheyennes, which had a salutary effect on surviving Indians. The Cheyennes, Arapahoes, and other Indians continued their warfare on the whites in 1865, and renewed it at intervals down to 1870. Two railways had then been constructed across the plains, and the Indian fell back before the iron horse and other accompaniments of civilization. All of the plains tribes were removed to the Indian Territory in time. The Utes, of the mountains, have been friendly with the whites and hostile to most bands of their own race. By several treaties, dating from 1863 to 1878, they have ceded all of the mountain and park sections of Colorado to the

ATTACK ON OVERLAND STAGE.

whites, except a tract of country in the western part of the State. For these possessions they have received from the government various sums of money and annual allowances of cattle, supplies, and rations.

CHAPTER IV.

THE DISCOVERY OF SILVER AND ITS ADDITION TO THE KNOWN WEALTH OF THE COUNTRY—POLITICAL HISTORY—STATE MOVEMENTS OF 1864-7—MINING OPERATIONS AND GENERAL PROGRESS—FARMING, STOCK GROWING, AND COLONIZING—THE ADVENT OF THE RAILWAY AND RAILROAD BUILDING—ADVANCES MADE IN REDUCING ORES AND THE ADVANTAGES OF RAIL COMMUNICATION AND OF IMPROVED MINING, MILLING, AND SMELTING.

In the earlier years of Colorado mining, gold was the only metal sought for. No one thought of prospecting for silver. Consequently, the main portion of Colorado's mineral wealth was never dreamed of until more recent times. While many discoveries were made for several years previous, no great silver yield was obtained until 1870 and subsequently. The slow growth of this class of mining was due to a lack of proper ore-reducing facilities and to milling difficulties. Time has remedied these drawbacks, and all of the older districts are now supplied with effective mills, smelters, or amalgamating works. The first discovery of silver lodes in Colorado was made in Summit county. They carried much lead but not a large amount of silver, and, owing to their remote location, were never worked extensively. Late in 1864, float ore was found on McClellan mountain, near Georgetown, which proved to be rich in silver. This caused considerable excitement and some lively prospecting in 1865. Valuable discoveries have been made every year since, and flourishing towns and a large production has been the result.

For some time gulch and placer mining had been on the decline, and the miners had been leaving for the newly found diggings of Montana and Idaho. The ground that had been easiest to get at or handle had been largely worked out. This was not usually exhausted, for much of it has been worked over and over, with fair returns, ever since. But more extensive and systematic operations were required. Vast quantities of pay-dirt and gravel yet invite the attention of the miner and capitalist, and alluvial mining is once more on the increase.

In 1863, politicians began to agitate the State question. A convention assembled at Denver, July 11, 1864, and framed a constitution for the proposed State. Congress had previously passed an enabling act. The constitution was rejected by a vote of 5,006 to 4,219. In the following year another constitution, framed by a subsequent convention, presided over by W. A. H. Loveland, was adopted by a vote of 3,025 to 2,870. At the same time negro suffrage was defeated by a vote of 476 ayes to 4,192 nays.

On the 14th day of November, 1865, a legislature and state officers were elected. William Gilpin, a republican, was elected governor; G. A. Hinsdale, a democrat, lieutenant-governor, and George M. Chilcott, congressman. In 1864, John Evans and Henry M. Teller were named for senators, but the legislature of 1865-6 chose John Evans and Jerome B. Chaffee. Congress passed the necessary enabling act, but President Johnson vetoed it. A year after, the State movement received a quietus, when the necessary two-thirds vote to override the veto failed to be obtained in Congress.

A list of territorial and state officials from first to last will be found in the Appendix of this book. Also, the vote polled at most of the territorial and state elections.

In 1867, the process-mills having proved a miserable failure, the companies and miners generally returned to the quartz mills, as the only reliance for saving gold at that time. Many mills had been steadily in operation for years, but others resumed work in 1867-8. The result was that the output of gold from Gilpin county was very large up to 1870, and many mines would have paid handsomely, in spite of heavy expenses, had they been properly managed. As it was, the companies began to suspend work in 1869, and one after another of them shut down, until in 1873 but one or two were doing anything. As they left the field, however, the men who had been employed by them began to prospect or mine on their own hook. Some of them leased company properties and others left for the new silver camps of Georgetown and Caribou, and later, for Park county.

In the first decade of Colorado mining, the two leading cities were Denver, the territorial capital, and the mining camp composed of Central, Black Hawk, and Nevadaville. Each had two daily newspapers, and three banks, and churches, schools, and other evidences of civilization, such as any live town is expected to possess. Few places of much larger dimensions could boast of as enterprising populations or of as many citizens of superior abilities, accomplishments, or whole-souled qualities. There were miners, merchants, operators, and gold hunters, who had seen life in all its phases. Some of them were then on the high road to wealth; others had already lost or won several fortunes. The legal profession was also ably represented, as it has always been, and a class of politicians were coming into prominence, that, with business men, mining, milling, and railway operators, have since largely shaped the destinies of the State. It may almost be said, with one exception, that the little city of Central has furnished Colorado's entire representation in Congress for years. Mr. Chaffee was first sent to Congress as a citizen of that place, and Messrs. Teller and Belford reside there, as did Mr. Hill up to about the time of his election to the Senate. Gilpin county justly claims to be the mother of Colorado mining towns and camps. Her miners went forth to help develop new districts all over the mountains, and have exerted a very prominent influence in the direction of affairs wherever they have settled. Notwithstanding the thousands lost to the "old reliable bullion centre" by emigration, she contains more permanent residents now than ever before. As the old citizens move away new ones come to take their places in increased numbers. This is the history of all prominent lode mining districts in the Rocky mountains.

Denver organized a board of trade in 1867. That fall the Union Pacific reached Cheyenne, just beyond the northern border, bringing Denver within one hundred and ten miles of rail communication. This was a great advantage over being six times as far away, but the following year saw the beginning of work on the Denver Pacific. This was to connect the metropolis of the territory with the Pacific line at Cheyenne. The work was consummated in the summer of 1870. In August of that year the Kansas Pacific reached Denver, making two through lines to the East. The same season the Colorado Central railway was constructed from Denver to Golden, located at one of the main gateways of the mountains. The prosperity and greatness of Denver was then assured, and she grew rapidly from that time forward. Colorado was well represented at the World's Exposition at Paris in 1867.

Alexander Cummings succeeded John Evans as governor of Colorado in 1865, and was himself superseded in 1867 by A. C. Hunt. In 1869, Gen. Edward McCook became governor. He was followed by Samuel H. Elbert in 1873, but was again appointed in the following year. Then came the last territorial governor, John H. Routt, who was also state governor. In 1864, A. A. Bradford was elected delegate to Congress; then came George M. Chilcott, and then Bradford again. Jerome B. Chaffee was elected for the same position in 1870, and again in 1872. In 1874, Colorado chose a democratic delegate to Congress for the first time, when Thomas M. Patterson received 2,369 majority over H. P. H. Bromwell. This was mainly due to dissensions in the republican party.

The amount of creek and gulch mining grew steadily less as years passed on and the most easily accessible pockets and pay streaks were worked out. Yet most of the headwaters of the Blue and Arkansas and of Clear and Boulder creeks were still profitable to a limited number of miners, and have been so to this day. Recent operations of a more extensive character are at last bringing them into prominence again. From 1865 to 1870, more or less lode mining was carried on in nearly all of the gold-bearing districts then discovered. Many of them gave out temporarily, and have since been idle to this day. Others have had work resumed upon them within the past few years. Numerous lodes, especially in Clear Creek county, which had been worked for gold in former times and abandoned as unprofitable, were at length found to carry their main value in silver. As silver had not been looked for, the best part of their product had been lost. After silver mining became general, they were worked quite successfully.

So intent were the first settlers in the pursuit of gold that little attention was paid to farming or stock growing for many years. A few parties pursued those avocations successfully, however, for good prices could be obtained in the mining camps. Thousands of dollars were sometimes cleared in a season on a single mountain ranch. It was at first believed that the country was worthless for agricultural purposes. During the first winter at Denver no hay was obtainable, and the owners of cattle used in freighting turned them out on the prairie, as they supposed, to die. In the spring the animals were all found in good condition near the Platte river, and some thirty miles below Denver. This settled the stock question. After some reverses from dry weather, it was found that irrigation

by means of ditches was necessary to assure successful farming. In
1867–69 these industries had become so extensive that agricultural
and industrial societies and fairs were inaugurated at Denver and
Boulder. In 1870, several colonies were founded in localities

INDIAN ENCAMPMENT ON WHITE RIVER.

adapted to farming, and peopled by immigrants from the States.
The one at Greeley grew and prospered, and has since attained a
population of nearly or quite three thousand. The colonies of Longmont and Evans have also grown steadily. The German immigrants

of West Mountain Valley were less fortunate, and the organization finally broke up.

In 1871 the Denver and Rio Grande Railway was built from Denver southward seventy-five miles, and the town and colony of Colorado Springs was established at the terminus. Soon after the watering-place of Manitou was founded, and has ever since been the most fashionable pleasure resort of the State. The railway was afterwards extended to Pueblo, Cañon, El Moro, and over the Sangre de Christo range into San Luis Park. In recent years extensive irrigating ditches have been constructed from and near all the principal streams in Colorado, and farming and stock growing have been extensive and profitable industries. Crops are usually abundant and cattle and sheep thrive remarkably.

It came to pass as time went on that Gilpin county was one of the few mining camps where operations were carried on extensively. In fact, it was far ahead of any other district in number of mines and mills, as well as population and product. Most of Colorado's gold export came from there from 1867 to 1870. But all was not smooth sailing by any means. Great difficulty was encountered in saving the golden contents of the ore as the mines grew deeper and deeper. It is asserted that previous to that period the per cent. of the assay saved in most quartz mills ranged from 15 to 40 per cent. only. All outside of that was swept down the streams and lost. Somewhat better work was done in 1868 and 1869.

This condition of affairs could not result otherwise than in disaster, especially as high prices of labor, supplies, and material, enormous plains and mountain freights, bad management and poor mining all combined to exhaust the average product of the mines. Therefore, the establishment and successful operation of the Boston and Colorado Smelting Works, at Black Hawk in 1867-8, by Professor Hill, came very opportunely, and helped to prevent much loss and misfortune that would otherwise have occurred. So many works and processes had failed, that all innovations on the stamp mill method were regarded with a skeptical eye. Yet when Professor Hill continued operations steadily year after year, affording a cash market for the assorted or richer parts of the ore, the immense advantage of these smelters began to be appreciated.

The main bulk of the ores was too poor to admit of treatment anywhere except by raw amalgamation in the quartz mills, but it was found of great benefit to select the richer mineral and sell to the smelter, on account of the very high per cent. saved. Together the stamp mills and smelting works went on adapting themselves and their methods to the country, each working out their special mission. By handling both grades of ore as it came from the ground they made otherwise impossible mining operations profitable. This smelting company went on enlarging their works until, as railroads were constructed, they became almost as important to many silver districts as they had been to Gilpin county. Other concerns were also erected elsewhere. Still the leading gold district was in a very depressed condition up to 1875.

The construction of the Colorado Central Railway up through the mountains to Black Hawk caused several parties to start in to re-open some of the deserted and water-filled company mines. By 1876 the advantages resulting from the operation of the railway became manifest. It was apparently the salvation of the district, for expenses soon fell to such figures that mines, either active or idle, could be handled to advantage. But the grand success that has been brought about in Gilpin county cannot be attributed entirely to the railway and the smelting works, although their assistance has been invaluable. During all the years of failure and disaster, varied with an occasional rich bonanza, the miners and mill men had been becoming familiar with the mineral veins of the country, and were learning how to mine and mill to advantage. The companies who had continued work so long stopped a little too soon. These Gilpin and Clear Creek miners, after some delay, took up the job where they left off, and have made a success of it. So the change in the character of operations, and their present great extent and general success may be attributed to the railway, the smelting works, improved mining and milling, and a class of men with the nerve and energy to wrest victory from disaster.

Up to 1872, several silver mills at Georgetown had been run more or less extensively, of which the Stewart works had turned out the most silver. That year, Hall, Martine and Marshall began to purchase and ship high grade silver ores to Germany. This gave the miners much more of a competing market than they had previously enjoyed, and was the forerunner of the present advantageous ore-buying and shipping facilities. Discovery after discovery had been made on the lofty mountains around Georgetown, and notwithstanding the heavy cost of transportation and of treatment, the yield of ore and of silver increased wonderfully from 1870 forward. In 1872–3, some enormously rich mines were developed, and the product of the district for 1874 exceeded for the first time that of the sister county of Gilpin. Meantime several eastern reduction works had established agencies there for the purchase and shipment of ores.

In 1868 the Printer Boy and other rich gold discoveries in California Gulch turned attention to Lake county once more, although some inviting pockets of quartz near Granite had paid largely in previous years. About this time a company of Boston capitalists inaugurated heavy mining and smelting operations in Summit county, west of the snowy range. Other companies also worked silver mines there, but unsuccessfully.

The discovery of the Caribou silver lode in Boulder county, late in 1869, caused the founding of a town and flourishing mining camp there in 1870. Many veins were discovered, and the district became quite prominent and productive, and is still so. In 1871 came the excitement over the silver bearing deposits of the Mosquito range in Park county. These drew miners and prospectors from all quarters to the slopes and summits of Lincoln and Bross mountains. Owing to the lateness of the season when the more important developments began, and the severity of the winter, the full tide of prospectors did not set in until the spring and summer of 1872. Fairplay again revived and Alma and one or two other towns were soon after founded. So extensive were the deposits found to be that the smelting works at Black Hawk started a branch establishment at Alma. Park county has since been as famous for its silver product as it was for that of gold when the placers were all worked.

Owing to the bad manner in which gold mines had been operated, the cessation of work became a necessity in many quarters. The veins had usually been stripped of whatever of value remained in sight, and then work was abandoned. There was no thought of looking out for continuous development of ore reserves ahead, or of permanent operations of a lifetime character. In these later years this is not often the case, but it took time to bring about the change. The building of the Colorado Central from Golden up Clear Creek cañon to Black Hawk was the turning-point in mining affairs and general prosperity. That permitted of lower and

7

quicker transportation, of cheaper goods and supplies, and of a general reduction of expenses. It made it possible to work mines profitably that were losing concerns before. Several properties resumed work in that and the following year, but so much time was required to put them in order or develop them into pay that no notable advance was made up to 1876. That year the bullion product was a long way in excess of any former period and each season witnesses an improvement. In 1874 much of the business portion of Central was destroyed by fire, entailing a loss of over half a million. It has since been rebuilt.

In 1872–3 the mountainous country in southwestern Colorado, to which the term of the San Juan region has been applied, began to attract attention. This was of immense extent, and mostly composed of vast chains and spurs of mountains extending far above timber line. Exploring parties had ventured into this section a dozen years before, but no permanent settlements were made beyond the San Luis valley. The discoveries were such that the mountains were alive with prospectors in the summers of 1874–5, and quartz mills and smelters began to be erected. The Summit mountain gold mines attracted much attention, and so did the great silver belts, among which grew up the towns of Silverton, Lake City, and, later, Ouray.

Silver-bearing veins came to notice in what was then Fremont county in 1872–3. In the following years they were quite productive. Still more important discoveries have been made during the past two seasons, showing a remarkable amount of wealth where least expected.

For more than a decade subsequent to the early gold discoveries settlers had been moving into the southern part of Colorado from New Mexico. They were mostly of mixed Spanish and Indian blood, but a portion were descendants of Spaniards only. They engaged in pastoral pursuits, raising large herds of sheep. The amount of their farming was limited and of a primitive character. For years these Mexicans, as they are called, constituted almost the entire population of the southern counties. They have always secured a number of members in the territorial and state legislatures, and, as few of them speak or write the English language, interpreters have always been required. Owing to the rapid increase of American and foreign population, their political influence has been steadily waning.

CHAPTER V.

COLORADO'S POPULATION AND PROGRESS—ANOTHER AND SUCCESSFUL ATTEMPT AT STATEHOOD—COLORADO'S ADMISSION INTO THE UNION—THE FIRST STATE ELECTION—RAILROAD BUILDING AND GENERAL ADVANCEMENT—NEW AND RICH MINING DISCOVERIES AND MORE SMELTERS—WANTED A MINT OF COINAGE AT DENVER —CLOSE OF THE HISTORICAL NARRATIVE.

Probably one hundred thousand people had resided in Colorado for longer or shorter periods up to the year 1870. Yet so many left the territory from first to last that the population did not exceed from twenty-five to thirty-five thousand at any one time up to 1868. The census of 1870 showed the number of inhabitants, exclusive of the Indians, to be 39,864. From that time immigration set in steadily from the East, and the railways aided largely to bring this about. Rapid transit by rail was very different from making the long trip across the plains in coaches or in ox or mule trains. It was believed that the population had doubled in four years after the advent of the railway. The generous production of the mines, the harvests of the farmer, and the increase of the stockman had their effect, and eastern people began to move in this direction.

No attempt had been made to secure a state government for over six years up to that time, but in the winter of 1874-5 the subject was again agitated. The movement was successful this time in receiving the sanction of both Congress and the President. It was provided that in case a constitution was framed and adopted by the people that Colorado should not become a State before July 4, 1876. A convention was in session in the winter of 1875-6, of which Joseph C. Wilson was president, and the constitution framed was adopted July 1st by a vote of 15,430 to 4,053. On the third day of October state officers were chosen. There were 27,461 votes polled for governor, and the republican ticket was elected by majorities ranging from 491 to 1,728, Routt's majority over Hughes being 838.

James B. Belford, republican, became congressman for the short term ending March 4, 1877, and Thomas M. Patterson, democrat, for the two years succeeding. The first State legislature, consisting of 49 representatives and 26 senators, assembled at Denver in November, 1876, when the state government was inaugurated. Jerome B. Chaffee and Henry M. Teller, republicans, were elected United States senators. On drawing for terms, the former obtained that expiring March 4, 1879, and the latter that terminating in 1877. The legislature then elected Mr. Teller for the full term of six years from March 4, 1877. For full lists of officials and popular vote of elections see Appendix.

Great advances were made in wealth and prosperity in 1876. The older counties were progressing finely and the San Juan region was promising much for the future. An indication of the high opinion abroad of the State's capacity and resources was the construction of another through line of railway from the Missouri. The Atchison, Topeka & Santa Fe Company completed their road west to Pueblo this year, making Colorado's third outlet to the East. The last territorial legislature appropriated the sum of ten thousand dollars for the purpose of having Colorado properly represented at the World's Exposition at Philadelphia in 1876, and Governor Routt appointed Messrs. Decatur and Richmond commissioners.

The succeeding year was still more prosperous. The farmers, who had experienced two bad seasons, were then rewarded with bountiful harvests, which set them on their feet once more, or gave them heavy surpluses. The mines made a larger gain than had been known since the early discoveries and developments. Increased railway and ore reducing facilities were being supplied in various quarters. The Colorado Central Railway was extended into Clear Creek county as far as Georgetown, and north from Longmont, connecting with the Union Pacific at Cheyenne. In the south, the Denver & Rio Grande road was pushed on over the Sangre de Christo mountains to Garland, and afterwards to Alamosa, on the Rio Grande. But rapid as had been the progress, and handsome as had been the gain of previous years—the year 1878 eclipsed them all. This is true regarding financial improvement, as well as increase of population and production. The yield of gold and silver showed a gain of nearly fifty per cent. over the best previous year. The old districts that had been the main reliance in former times, all surpassed their previous records, with one exception, while Lake county came to the front and distanced every one of them. The production of that section had been small for several years; but the new carbonate mines of Leadville paid handsomely in 1877. Last year, however, their output surprised almost everyone. Yet, it was but a fraction of what will be recorded hereafter. As during the two preceding years, Colorado maintained her place as one of the few States extensively engaged in railway building. The Atchison, Topeka & Santa Fe railway was extended southward over the Raton mountains into New Mexico, and a heavy force of men were kept at work blasting a way through the Grand cañon of the Arkansas for the Leadville extension. This was the season of the railroad war for the possession of that route, in which the above-named company and the Denver & Rio Grande were engaged. The Denver & South Park road, which had been built as far as Morrison, in 1874, had its line completed from Denver up Platte cañon to the mouth of Hall Valley, at the close of 1878, or soon after. Central was also afforded rail communication this year.

The second biennial State election occurred October 1, 1878, with three tickets in the field. The republican nominees were elected by pluralities ranging from 1,923 to 2,890. The greenback nominee for governor received a total vote of 2,783. The republican candidate for governor was Frederick W. Pitkin, and the democratic W. A. H. Loveland. For Congress, Thomas M. Patterson was the democratic nominee and James B. Belford, the republican. The total vote polled in Colorado was from 28,876 to 28,900. See Appendix. The second legislature assembled January 1, 1879, and the State government was inaugurated January 14th. After an exciting contest, Prof. N. P. Hill received the republican caucus nomination, and was elected United States Senator to succeed Mr. Chaffee, for the term of six years, from March 4, 1879.

While the mines of Leadville were attracting attention far and wide, and causing a stampede for the land of carbonates all over the country, several valuable districts were developed in other quarters. Not far away great deposits of argentiferous galena were found in Summit county, and during the same fall of 1878 the unexpected discoveries of Silver Cliff drew large numbers of people and started a promising mining camp. The magic cities of these several localities are growing rapidly, and are evidently the forerunners of more to come among the mountains and valleys of western Colorado. There is seemingly no end to the mineral wealth of these mountains,

and each season witnesses the disclosure of some new district rich in
gold or silver.   The immense extent and value of Leadville's mines
and traffic is attested by the continual blockade of transportation
facilities, and by the fact that three different lines of railway are
all building in that direction.   It is further shown in the growing
ore production and the recent and projected addition of a score of
smelting furnaces.   The capacities of other districts are likewise
being duly appreciated.   Several extensive smelting establishments
have just been completed at Golden, which is so situated as to be a
natural receptacle for ores shipped for treatment from Gilpin and
Clear Creek counties.   The Boston and Colorado Company have
erected the finest works in America at Argo, two miles from Denver.
It is evident that Colorado will hereafter reduce her own ores and
turn out her own bullion to a far greater extent than heretofore.

What Colorado and the entire mineral region between the plains
of Colorado and Nevada require is a mint of coinage.   The government should establish this at Denver.   No other point can compare
with it in natural and general advantages for that purpose.   It is
located midway between British America and Mexico, and is the
most central point for Colorado, and for all the gold and silver
bearing territories not adjacent to the Pacific coast.   It is the
metropolis of a mining region whose production equals nearly all
others, excepting California and Nevada.   It is evident that Colorado will soon surpass even those favored localities.   A yield of
from sixteen to twenty millions this year, and as much more from
neighboring territories, whose bullion would be tributary to such an
institution, calls loudly for coinage facilities.   A product of ninety
millions since 1859 is one this State may well be proud of, especially
when it appears that work in earnest has but just begun.   Montana
has commenced shipping ores to Argo, recognizing that as a better
market than the East or her own local works.   The extensive
smelters of Argo, Golden, Pueblo, and Leadville, and the mills of
Gilpin and Clear Creek, are doing a combined business of immense
proportions.   Denver is the centre of a system of railways radiating
in all directions.   Supplies are as cheap there and expenses as low
as in any other place that could be selected.   Therefore, the government may as well do a portion of its coinage there as at any other
point, while the producing miner will be vastly benefited if relieved
from the heavy expense of bullion shipments to the East.

The United States geological and geographical surveys, conducted under the supervision of Prof. F. V. Hayden, by authority of the national government, have been an important factor in making known the nature and character of the immense region beyond the Missouri river. These have been carried on with the assistance of competent and experienced officials, army officers, civilians, and experts ever since 1869, and a very considerable amount of time and attention has been devoted to Colorado by members and divisions of the survey. The labors and reports of Messrs. Hayden and Wheeler have been of great value to the state and country.

In closing this brief narrative of Colorado's settlement, rapid growth and general progress, it is perhaps needless to speak of the prevailing prosperity or of the inviting opportunities for capital or labor there. The situation is beginning to be comprehended to a greater or less extent at the East as well as West. Something more definite regarding the State and her resources can be obtained by a careful perusal of this volume, whose remaining chapters will be devoted to descriptive and statistical matter and general information concerning the wonderful land of which so much has been told. A trip to Colorado would be far more effective, and the only way to obtain a true appreciation of her wealth, enterprise, and general attractions. The reader can then see for himself how new regions are explored, the wilderness settled up, and towns and cities built, how energetic and skillful miners go down into the depths for precious ores that the mill-man or the smelter subsequently turn into bullion. On the high plateaus and mountain sides, he will have an opportunity to breathe a purer air than he has been accustomed to, and can witness scenery grander and more beautiful than all the world besides can boast of. But of this, more hereafter.

MOUNT OF THE HOLY CROSS.

PART THIRD.

CHAPTER I.

COLORADO—PAST AND PRESENT PROGRESS AND FUTURE PROSPECTS—
GREAT MINERAL WEALTH OF THE ROCKY MOUNTAINS—MINING,
FARMING, AND STOCK GROWING—STATE AND COUNTY STATISTICS,
ASSESSED VALUATION, EDUCATIONAL FACILITIES, AND FACTS RE-
LATING THERETO—RAILWAYS AND RAILWAY BUILDING.

The remarkable advance recently made by Colorado in the development of mineral resources and the consequent accession of population and increase in production and wealth, have been among the most
noteworthy events in the history of the West. While every industry
of the State seemed to receive a fresh impulse some three years ago, it
was not until within the past twelve months that this progress was so
marked as to excite general notice. What have aided to fix the attention of the whole country and turn the tide of humanity Colorado-
ward more than all things beside are the wonderfully productive
bonanzas of Leadville, and while they seemingly form the principal
magnetic attraction, all parts of this matchless region will be correspondingly benefited. Nor should the intrinsic worth of other sections be overlooked in the prominence accorded the carbonate fields,
for all through these Colorado mountains an extent and variety of
mineral wealth is embedded and is now being explored such as has
seldom, if ever, been found elsewhere. The consequence is that
capital and labor are both moving in the direction of the legendary
star of empire, and gold and silver mining is attracting the world's
attention to a greater extent than for many years. Month after month
witnesses an increase in the volume of immigration as each successive disclosure is followed by others still more marvelous. So we

see people from all parts of the country, and even from Europe, coming to swell the population of this most thrifty of states, while yet other multitudes are contemplating a similar movement.

With the ever-occurring discoveries of new mineral veins and belts a steady and often rapid increase in the yield of bullion is recorded in the older districts. So, while the field of operations is continually enlarging by fresh accessions, mines that have been pouring out their hidden treasures for years are being opened for greater things in the hereafter. Rapid as has been the exploration of this wilderness of mountains of late, the present season is likely to eclipse all previous periods in that respect. There seems to be no limit to the wealth awaiting the advent of the miner, and as each new discovery is reported the fact becomes only the more evident that but little of the State has been half prospected, and the remainder almost entirely unexplored.

The extraordinary developments that have been and are being made are convincing men from abroad, in common with the most enthusiastic mountaineers, that Colorado's store of the precious metals exceeds that of any other State. At the same time it is generally conceded that a better field for investment is offered here than elsewhere, and that the State has a future before it of the most promising character. The supplies of gold, silver, and coal, although but little encroached on up to the present time, are seemingly inexhaustible, and lead and copper aid to a considerable degree to swell the value of veins carrying the first mentioned metals. Iron is also found in large quantities and may yet prove the source of an important industry, while the deposits of salt, lime, gypsum, fire-clay and other materials are all proving serviceable.

Colorado's agricultural and pastoral resources are quite extensive, and if the mining and city population becomes too great for home supplies, the bountiful fields of the neighboring State of Kansas are a never-failing resource. As it is, a ready cash market in the mines and business marts is afforded to both farmer and stock grower. While the extent of arable land is limited, compared with the State's total area, it embraces many thousand square miles, and additional tracts are being made available every year by artificial irrigation. The stock growing industry has been increasing in importance until the annual exportation of cattle, sheep, and wool makes a handsome showing. This industry has been remarkably and uniformly profitable, both on the plains and in the parks. For the past two years Colorado has raised as much wheat and five times as much beef as is needed for home consumption. Splendid farming and pastoral lands in western Colorado will in time be peopled by an industrious population.

The climate, mineral waters, and scenic attractions of Colorado, which may almost be considered as resources in themselves, have been sufficiently referred to in the first part of this volume. They alone will bring people and money to this section ; for many men of wealth are making this State their place of residence on account of its superior attractions and inducements in those respects.

The mines of Colorado have produced, from 1859 up to date, something like eighty-two millions, in round numbers, of which ten and a half millions were the result of last year's operations. The indications are now good for a yield of nearly twenty millions, and perhaps twenty-five millions, in 1879. The possibilities are so great that it is impossible to predict with accuracy. The farming products amount to several millions per annum, and the pastoral districts make an equally creditable return.

The State auditor gives the assessed valuation of real estate and personal property, according to the returns of 1878, at $43,072,648.26. The enormous growth of Leadville, Denver, and some other localities, and the State's gain in population and property since then indicate an assessed valuation at least one-half larger for the present year. As it was, the actual value of the property assessed last year, together with that which escaped assessment, must have approached $65,000,-000. The mines, which are the chief source of wealth, are not assessed nor taxed at all—nor can they be, according to the provisions of the State Constitution, for nearly eight years to come. Were these counted in the general valuation, the total would possibly run up to hundreds of millions. The assessed valuation of 1878 was divided among various classes of property, of which the principal are given below.

Land and improve-ments	$9,755,038 17	Horses	$1,914,339 50
Railways	5,013,685 83	Mules, etc	244,050 00
Merchandise	2,599,660 00	Cattle	4,928,147 50
Capital and manu-facturers	205,099 00	Sheep	1,026,482 25
Town and city lots	11,035,620 75	Money and credits	2,130,650 07
		Household property	902,062 00
		Bank & other shares	730,396 00

The counties, thirty-one in number, wsth their county seats, area,
estimated population in 1879, assessed valuation in 1878, and vote
at the last State election is given in the table below. The area of
the newer and a few of the older counties is estimated. Lake
county which contains Leadville, and from which Chaffee county
was set off last winter, probably has a valuation of over $4,000,000
at the present time, or nearly seven times that given for last year.
Denver and its county of Arapahoe have also greatly enhanced the
total valuation of property, and so have many other towns and
counties.

COUNTY.	COUNTY SEAT.	VALUATION, 1878.	AREA, Sq're Miles.	POPULATION, 1879.
Arapahoe	Denver	$11,076.761 00	4,800	31,000
Bent	Las Animas	2,279,376 00	9,126	3,000
Boulder	Boulder	3,097,320 00	792	12,000
Chaffee	Granite		1,240	500
Clear Creek	Georgetown	1,932,991 31	437	3,000
Conejos	Conejos	244,346 00	2,558	6,000
Costilla	San Luis	319,571 90	1,685	4,000
Custer	Rosita	500,654 00	1,100	5,000
Douglas	Castle Rock	951,713 00	833	3,000
Elbert	Kiowa	1,202,052 52	6,030	2,500
El Paso	Colorado Springs	3,076,335 00	2,628	9,000
Fremont	Cañon	946,363 00	1,268	4,500
Gilpin	Central	1,827,997 00	158	7,500
Grand	Hot Sulphur Springs.	63,866 75	4,278	500
Gunnison	Gunnison	62,014 00	11,000	1,500
Hinsdale	Lake City	564,396 50	1,528	4,000
Huerfano	Walsenburg	796,038 38	1,584	5,000
Jefferson	Golden	1,988,529 00	792	7,500
Lake	Leadville	603,858 92	400	15,000
La Plata	Parrott City	254,447 00	4,095	1,500
Larimer	Fort Collins	1,502,330 00	1,825	5,000
Las Animas	Trinidad	1,455,230 00	9,072	12,000
Ouray	Ouray	220,622 95	2,333	3,000
Park	Fairplay	796,239 00	2,222	3,000
Pueblo	Pueblo	3,069,639 00	2,412	9,000
Rio Grande	Del Norte	501,874 00	1,332	3,500
Routt	Hayden	74,661 00	5,000	300
Saguache	Saguache	637,607 00	3,312	3,000
San Juan	Silverton	255,358 00	726	3,000
Summit	Breckenridge	169,360 00	8,289	6,000
Weld	Greeley	2,583,827 00	10,494	7,500
	Total	$43,055,419 23		190,300

At the present rate of increase of population and wealth, the true
figures of many parts of the State would far exceed those given
above. New towns and mining camps are springing into existence
every month, and some of the farming districts and business centres
are growing rapidly. The immigration for April must have been

over ten thousand, and for May, fifteen thousand. The A., T. &
S. F. Railway alone brought in 936 people in the last week of
May, and there are two other through routes from the East. Before the end of summer the State may have a population of a
quarter of a million, and a valuation of one hundred millions,
exclusive of mines. With mines included, the valuation would be
at least three times that sum.

The following-named plains counties are largely engaged in
farming and stock growing : Arapahoe, Weld, Larimer, Jefferson,
Douglas, El Paso, Fremont, and Las Animas. Those devoted
mainly to stock growing are, Elbert, Bent, Pueblo, and Huerfano.
Boulder county is about equally divided between the plains and
mountains, the former embracing a fine farming district and the latter
rich in minerals. There are considerable farming and stock growing carried on in the mountain county of Custer, and in Saguache,
Rio Grande, and La Plata counties in the San Luis Park and San
Juan regions. Costilla and Conejos counties are mainly engaged in
pastoral pursuits. Of the mountain mining counties considerable
stock is raised in Park, Lake, and Grand, and more soon will be in
Gunnison, Routt, Summit, and Ouray counties. While farming is
pursued to some extent all through the mountains, it is proportionately small as compared with mining in Gilpin, Clear Creek,
Summit, Lake, Hinsdale, San Juan, and Ouray.

The growth of Colorado towns and cities is shown by the following, the census returns of 1870, for towns then in existence being
compared with careful estimates of number of inhabitants in 1875,
and on June 1, 1879 :

	1870.	1875.	1879.
Denver	4,759	17,000	28,000
Leadville	None	None	12,000
Central, Black Hawk, and Nevadaville	4,401	5,000	6,500
Pueblo and South Pueblo	666	5,000	6,000
Colorado Springs	None	2,500	5,000
Georgetown	802	4,000	5,000
Boulder	343	2,800	4,000
Trinidad	562	2,000	3,500
Golden	587	2,000	3,000
Greeley	480	2,000	2,700
Lake City	None	400	1,500

	1870.	1875.	1879.
Cañon	229	1,000	1,500
Del Norte	None	1,200	1,500
Silver Cliff	None	None	1,200
Rosita	None	1,200	1,200
Kokomo	None	None	1,500
Silverton	None	500	1,000
Brownville and Silver Plume	150	700	1,000

Leadville has grown from nothing to its present size in two years. Denver will expend over a million dollars in new buildings this year. Two mammoth hotels and ten or twelve hundred buildings and residences are in course of construction there.

No better evidence of Colorado's present and prospective capacities and importance can be asked for than in the continuous railway construction that is going on within its borders. Although railway building has almost ceased in nearly every quarter since the financial disasters of 1873, this is one of the few states where it is still vigorously prosecuted. During the past three years the mileage has been nearly doubled, and is still being increased. Various enterprises are projected, some of new roads and others of extensions of old ones that are likely to add considerably to the rail facilities before the year is out.

At the beginning of 1879 there were 1,218.6 miles of railway in operation within the limits of the State, or 174 miles more than a year previous. Of that amount 758.16 miles were of the standard broad gauge, and 460.44 miles of narrow gauge. Of this railroad mileage the Atchison, Topeka & Santa Fe has 259 miles, the Denver & Rio Grande 327, the Kansas Pacific 195, the Colorado Central 177, the Denver & South Park 75, the Boulder Valley 26, the G. B. & C. 5½, Denver Pacific 99, and the Union Pacific 9. Ten miles of track have been laid on the Denver & South Park road, additional to that given above.

The assessment of 1879 places the total taxable value of railway property in Colorado at $7,687,457. This heavy increase over the previous year is in accordance with the plan adopted for an advance of general assessments of all classes of property in the State. The consequence will be a much larger showing for the State's valuation than that noted in the first part of this chapter. It is evident that some 250 miles or more of railway will be constructed in Colorado during the ensuing year.

Colorado has ever been a liberal supporter of the press. No other section or community of anything like the same number of inhabitants contains as many newspapers. There are fourteen dailies with weekly editions, and forty-four weeklies—a pretty large list for a

DENVER HIGH SCHOOL.

population of less than two hundred thousand. The superior character of a very large portion of these speaks well for the State and its people. There are four well conducted dailies in Denver, and another recently established, three in Leadville, one in Central, one in Colorado Springs, two in Pueblo, and two in Trinidad. The News and Tribune of Denver are the largest, handsomest, and best dailies between Saint Louis and San Francisco. The first was founded in 1859, and the latter in 1867. There are many weekly as well as daily papers in the various towns and cities that are a credit to their owners and of substantial benefit to the localities where they are published. A full list of Colorado newspapers will be found in the Appendix.

Colorado has a public school system in no way behind that of any of the older States. It is modeled after the best established organizations elsewhere, with such improvements as have been deemed necessary. The plans and labors of its early originator and champion, Prof. H. M. Hale, have been effectually followed and continued by his successor, the present Superintendent of Public Instruction, Joseph C. Shattuck. The public school law of 1876—since slightly amended—provides for teachers of the very best classes, and for other regulations and requirements of the most systematic character.

GREELEY PUBLIC SCHOOL.

Owing to the transitory nature of the population, public schools did not receive the attention prior to 1870 which they have since been favored with. Still they were liberally endowed in the few large towns, and some excellent private academies had been established. In 1871 there were 160 public schools in the Territory, and 7,742 persons between the ages of six and twenty-one years, 4,357 of whom were enrolled. There were then 80 school buildings, worth $82,574, and $44,148.95 were paid for teachers. The progress which has since been made can be seen by a glance at the last report of the Superintendent of Public Instruction.

In 1878 Colorado had 26,473 persons between the ages of six and

twenty-one years, of whom 16,641 were enrolled in the public
schools, beside a larger number attending private schools and academies. There were 249 school edifices valued at $474,771, the
number of teachers employed was 567, and the total expenditures
for the year were $243,850.37. The figures for the present year
will be much larger. It must be remembered that much of the
population of Colorado is widely scattered, so that means cannot be
afforded everywhere for securing free school advantages. But in
every town, village, or settled farming or mining district schools
are in operation, and every city or town of importance has one or
more graded schools, with handsome and costly buildings for the
accommodation thereof—for nowhere is money expended with such
proportionate liberality on schools or churches as in Colorado.
Some of the leading counties made the following showing as
regards public schools in 1878 :

County.	No. Pupils Enrolled.	Av. Daily Attendance.	No. of Teachers.	Av. Cost per Month per Pupil.	Value of Buildings, etc.	Expenditures for Year.
Arapahoe.......	3,464	2,160	80	$2 28	$190,085	$77,100
Boulder.........	1,957	1,129	78	1 89	41,495	21,593
Clear Creek.....	945	493	17	2 07	29,450	6,968
El Paso.........	1,056	556	31	3 00	43,500	8,909
Gilpin	954	566	19	2 76	34,150	14,287
Jefferson	961	541	39	2 68	26,195	11,997
Las Animas.....	917	545	27	4 41	......	3,326
Pueblo..........	758	526	35	3 27	33,280	6,430
Weld	1,118	683	50	3 34	44,132	16,677

The average daily attendance would be larger but for the numerous private schools, academies, and seminaries, the scattered population in many sections, and the yet imperfect school facilities in some
of the Mexican districts. Several of the leading towns of the State
are now erecting school buildings that will cost from twenty to
thirty thousand dollars each, which will add greatly to the total
value of school property.

By territorial legislative enactments, provision was made for a
School of Mines at Golden, in 1870 ; for a Deaf Mute Institute at
Colorado Springs at a subsequent date ; and for a State University
at Boulder, and an Agricultural College at Fort Collins in 1874–6.
All of these were aided with appropriations for buildings and for
maintenance. The first two of these State institutions have been in

STATE UNIVERSITY, BOULDER.

successful operation for several years. In September, 1877, the State University began its educational work in the elegant buildings prepared for it at Boulder, and has since been most successfully conducted. The building for the State Agricultural College at Fort Collins is now ready for occupation. There are private and sectarian schools, colleges and seminaries in nearly all of the larger towns.

In subsequent chapters the farming and pastoral interests will be touched upon, and some facts and figures given relating thereto ; after which considerable space will be devoted to mining—the great industry of the State. Facts, figures and detailed statements will be given concerning mining and milling and the mineral resources of counties and districts.

CHAPTER II.

FARMING ON THE PLAINS AND IN THE MOUNTAINS — WHAT IS DONE BY ARTIFICIAL IRRIGATION—THE FINEST CROPS IN THE WORLD — FACTS AND FIGURES REGARDING THE YIELD OF CEREALS, VEGETABLES, ETC. — SUPERIORITY OF COLORADO WHEAT, BEEF, AND DAIRY PRODUCTS—LARGE PROFITS IN FARMING.

In the rush for gold in the earlier years of Colorado mining but little attention was paid to agriculture. That was considered too slow a method for accumulating wealth. Recent years have shown that it is not so slow as was supposed. A few of the pioneers, and less fortunate gold hunters, who were not disposed to leave the country, began to cultivate the soil. They were incited to do this from the occasionally high price of provisions, and in view of the fact, since everything consumed came from the States, that a scarcity might some time bring with it high prices to the farmer. It was not long until the lands bordering the streams on the plains and the valleys of the mountains were found to be extremely fertile.

The lack of a sufficient and regular rainfall acted as a drawback, until the true situation and resources of the region were understood. The disappointments attending early agricultural efforts led to experiments in artificial irrigation, so successfully conducted among the Mormon farmers of Utah. Then ditches began to be constructed from the rivers out onto the arid plains. The natural fall of the streams was from seven to one hundred feet per mile. These ditches, by the slight fall of two or four feet per mile, could, in the course of a few miles, be extended far out on to the sloping uplands bordering the stream. From these larger ditches water gates led into smaller or branch ditches, used as required. Thus regular and continuous supplies of water were obtained during all of the warmer months; for when most needed the streams were the fullest of water from the gradual melting of the snows on the mountains. The results of irrigation were so favorable, and the mines afforded such a high-priced ready cash market, that farming was more and more successfully prosecuted with each succeeding year.

While the amount of cultivated land was small during the first decade of the territory, farming had become an important industry in 1867-9 along the streams in Boulder, Larimer, Jefferson, and Arapahoe counties. The scattering farms or ranches of those days produced abundant crops, and each year saw the river bottoms slowly settling up with an industrious and thrifty population. In 1870 a more rapid movement began in the way of peopling the country, and in making what had been termed a desert bloom, blossom, and reward the husbandman. Several colony organizations were perfected in the States to the eastward, and hundreds of families were transported to the various localities selected for the purpose. Near the junction of the Cache la Poudre and the South Platte river the colony of Greeley was founded. That of Evans was established four miles further south, and that of Longmont on the Saint Vrain. These organizations were co-operative as far as the sale of lands, the construction of irrigating canals, and carrying on general improvements were concerned. Outside of that, the lands were owned and cultivated by colony members who had purchased them. Other colonies were also established, among them that of Colorado Springs in 1871.

In recent years, settlers have been locating on farming lands all along the valleys of the streams in great numbers, and the advance which this industry has made has been both rapid and gratifying. Farms large and small extend through all available localities, and the latest and most improved machinery and implements of husbandry are in use. Irrigating canals and ditches of great extent and value are constructed every year, and each season sees thousands of acres of land reclaimed and made valuable. The steady increase of population in the mining regions and trade centres more than keeps pace with that of the farming districts, thus insuring a ready demand for whatever may be offered. Severe losses were sustained in several seasons from grasshoppers, but not since 1876. The farmers have paid much attention to these pests and to their habits and movements, and are confident that the crops can hereafter be protected from serious damage.

The last two seasons were so favorable for farming that some very extensive land reclaiming enterprises have been carried through, and others of great magnitude are projected. New canals and irrigating ditches have been constructed from a score of streams, and the tillable belts of land are steadily growing wider. Some of these canals are six, ten, and even fifteen feet in width, several feet in depth, and carry a great volume of water for many leagues out on to the uplands. Reservoirs or lakes are prepared here and there, in order that the water supply may the better be economized, and in the general conduct of affairs the best interests of the farm, the dairy, and of stock are considered. Long experience, intelligent management, and adaptation to circumstances and locality are causes of the great success of the husbandman in this State. As new ditches are constructed, and additional areas supplied with water, these lands are purchased or pre-empted and settled on—and so the amount of tillable land is steadily growing larger. Still further gains and advances will be made this year with the completion of several irrigating canals.

The cost of constructing the main canals is usually borne by a neighborhood of farmers, and sometimes these enterprises are carried forward and operated by associated individuals, under a company organization. Although this system of irrigation necessitates a trifling expenditure for water rental, or the employment of a small amount of labor, it is believed that the flowing streams give back as much fertilizing material as is lost by cultivation, while the increased production of this method of farming more than makes up for all outlays incurred.

It is a well-established fact that heavier and more reliable crops can be obtained by the aid of artificial irrigation, taking one year after another, than where the uncertain natural rainfall is depended on. This is shown in Colorado as well as in other regions. The prosperous, well-to-do farmers along the South Platte, the Cache la Poudre, Saint Vrain, Boulder, Ralston, and Clear creeks, the Fountaine, Cucharas, and the Arkansas and Las Animas rivers are all illustrative of the truth of this statement. Rich, waving fields of grain now greet the eye where once were barren, uninhabitable wastes, and vegetables of such prodigious size and in such immense quantities are raised as would astonish those unaccustomed to the results of Colorado soil. Farming has often been enormously remunerative, and few that have followed it steadily have failed to accumulate money or property. Many men have well stocked farms of great extent and value, the results of a few years' industry and effort.

Colorado has from thirteen to fifteen thousand square miles of land that can be made available for agriculture, of which something like one-fifth is now under cultivation. The State Auditor's report of May, 1878, returned not far from 2,000,000 acres of land as taxable, with an assessed valuation, with improvements, of $9,755,038.17. This did not by any means include all lands under cultivation, as the assessors of many counties where considerable farming is carried on appear to have failed to make any return, while many localities are not represented by figures that come up to the true condition of affairs. Probably an accurate statement would make the number of acres of land under the above head over 2,500,000, and the valuation $15,000,000. Before the close of the present season these figures will be greatly enlarged. A single irrigating canal, that is to be still further extended, was so far completed in April, 1879, that the water was running therein for a distance of thirty-four miles. This already irrigates that length of territory for a width of from two to three miles—making over eighty-five square miles, or fifty-five thousand acres of hitherto untillable land available for cultivation. Many other enterprises of similar character are going forward.

The State Auditor's report of 1878 allotted the acreage of the farms of various counties, together with assessed valuation of land and improvements thereon, as appears beneath. These figures are far below the present facts in the case—and assessed valuations are of course lower than the actual value.

COUNTY.	Acres of Land.	Value with Improvements	COUNTY.	Acres of Land.	Value with Improvements
Arapahoe	119,538	$1,006,147	Huerfano	15,077	$72,520
Bent	63,159	117,516	Jefferson	128,252	801,298
Boulder	117,688	1,223,715	Larimer	55,532	419,540
Custer	16,818	143,269	Las Animas	229,210	403,011
Douglas	135,277	366,578	Park	47,046	237,165
Elbert	35,583	80,253	Pueblo	219,718	550,728
El Paso	223,757	773,290	Saguache	136,826	216,118
Fremont	64,924	281,288	Weld	140,307	709,920
Gilpin,	11,005	....			

While this statement does not make a very extensive showing, it must be remembered that it is under the actual condition of affairs, and that each season sees large additions thereto. It is given here in order that an idea may be obtained of the proportionate agricultural importance of different districts. Owing to the way in which stock and town property is sometimes apparently included, it is difficult to ascertain their relative standing in all cases. While a portion of the stock owned in the State might very appropriately come in under the head of farming, it will be considered under the head of stock growing, since no means are at the disposal of the author to obtain the figures on farm-houses, and on cattle and other animals, as distinguished from those raised especially for marketable purposes.

The annual farm products of Colorado are steadily increasing in quantity and value. Correct data of a detailed character have been difficult to gain, and reports from various sources are often conflicting. The farmers are not always willing to have the full extent of the wheat crop known, lest prices fall to a lower figure than might otherwise be obtained. Consequently, it is sometimes difficult to get correct estimates. Millers and speculators always figure out a much larger crop than the farmers are willing to acknowledge. The former are the buyers, and work for low prices, while the latter are the sellers, and of course want as much money for their products as it is possible to get.

The farming product of 1877 was far ahead of that of any preceding year. The season was a remarkably favorable one, and the acreage of land sown or planted was much greater than ever before. The result was that a large portion of the farmers, who had previously suffered losses from grasshoppers and from other causes, came out with a handsome cash balance in their favor, as did those who had newly embarked in the business. The good fortune attending the season of 1877 caused an increase of tilled land in 1878 of at least twenty-five per cent. In some sections the acreage in wheat was one-third greater, and in other fifty or sixty per cent. The harvest was not as bountiful, however, as in the preceding year. While the aggregate may have been somewhat greater for the entire State, the return of grain and some other crops per acre was considerably less. In the northern counties this was partly due to frequent rains just before harvest time, causing wheat to "rust." In southern Colorado no such misfortune was reported.

The average yield of wheat per acre has been from twenty to

twenty-five bushels. Possibly twenty-two bushels comes nearer the truth, taking one year with another. This includes the entire State and all localities, and is above that of 1878. There are many farms and belts of land that yield thirty, forty, and occasionally fifty bushels to the acre. This, of course, is far above average returns of the State. Colorado flour is the finest in the world. Quantities of it are shipped to Illinois and other States. Oats, rye, barley and other cereals do as well proportionately as wheat. Potatoes return all the way from one hundred to five hundred, and rarely seven

FARMING ON THE BOULDER.

hundred and eight hundred bushels to the acre. The average runs from one to two hundred. Vegetables of nearly all descriptions grow to prodigious size both on mountain and plain. The comparatively inexpensive system of irrigation constantly replenishes the soil. The water is let into the ditches and onto the land in June, when the streams are full of mineral and vegetable matter borne down from the mountains. The water goes down into the ground and leaves the mineral and vegetable substances on the

8

surface, adding to the soil.   The ground continues productive after years of cultivation, because the irrigation brings in new material. Corn does not thrive as well in the northern counties as small grains, owing to the chilly night atmosphere, yet the yield is considerable and steadily getting larger.   South of the "Divide" it does much better and large crops are raised—sometimes seventy-five or eighty bushels to the acre.   Large quantities of hay are cut and cured in the parks and in most of the larger plains and mountain valleys. The good prices prevailing in the mining camps make this an important article to the farmer and stock owner.

For a long time fruit culture in Colorado was deemed impracticable.   The experiments and experiences of the past few years show that fruit of various kinds can be raised successfully, and in some of the southern counties profitably and extensively.   There are thrifty orchards of apple and peach trees at and near Cañon City. North of the Divide much more difficulty has been experienced; but apple trees are made to grow and bear fruit when protected from the winds by other trees.   Several very fair crops of apples have been obtained in Jefferson, Boulder, Larimer and other counties.

The dairy has become an interest of no little importance within the past few years.   Owing to the nutritious character of Colorado grasses, the milk, butter, and cheese are of unrivaled excellence. Large quantities of these articles are sold in the numerous towns and camps.   Several cheese manufactories have recently been established in El Paso, Boulder, and Larimer counties.   There and in Arapahoe and Jefferson, more than elsewhere, are remarkably large numbers of superior cattle, many of them of the best blooded stock, and valued at very high figures.   Some of the finest cows and bulls of Eastern localities have been purchased and imported by these enterprising farmers of the far-away Colorado border.   There are finely-stocked dairy farms in other sections beside the counties enumerated, including Douglas, Fremont, Lake, and Saguache, but those named first take the lead.   At the state and county fairs the displays of Durham, Alderney, Hereford, Shorthorns, Jersey, and Swiss cattle, and of stock crossed therewith, are very fine.

There is a remarkably large amount of money invested in horse flesh in Colorado, and the average quality of stock is very high in some quarters. The liveries and private stables (especially the latter) of such cities as Denver, Leadville and Colorado Springs are of a very high order. On the farms are large numbers of horses, some of them splendid draft, work, or saddle animals. Good blood is as manifest there as among the fast trotters of the towns.

Colorado can make no such showing in amount of farming products as the Mississippi valley states, where farming is the main industry; but in the yield per acre, or in quality of wheat and beef cattle, and extent of stock farms, she far surpasses them. With little care or trouble these Colorado uplands and river bottoms turn out nearly or quite double what an equal area gives in Illinois or Iowa, and far more than is known in Minnesota or Kansas. While no accurate data of the annual farm production is at hand, the figures given below for the year 1878, while not official, are not far out of the way. They are estimates based upon statements received from farmers and millers:

COUNTY.	Acres in Wheat.	Yield per Acre.	Number of Bushels Wheat.	Value.
Larimer	8,350	18	150,000	$150,000
Boulder	16,460	18	300,000	300,000
Weld	9,333	15	180,000	180,000
Jefferson	6,818	22	150,000	150,000
Arapahoe	5,000	20	100,000	100,000
Elsewhere	2,000	15	30,000	30,000
Total North Divide	48,991	18 6	910,000	$910,000
Fremont	3,200	25	80,000	$80,000
Las Animas	10,000	23	230,000	230,000
Saguache and Conejos	2,000	25	50,000	50,000
Other Sections	2,500	16	40,000	40,000
Total South of Divide	17,700	22.6	400,000	$400,000
Total of State	66,691	19.6	1,310,000	$1,310,000

Boulder and Larimer, which generally give the largest yield per acre in the State, went far below their usual return last season, and for the first time, perhaps, the southern counties gave a higher average than the northern ones. Las Animas county yielded 50 per cent. more wheat than ever before. The value of the crop is rated at one dollar per bushel, which is the ruling price at this time, but more than the market rates of last fall and winter. A rough estimate of the more important streams figures up as follows: Poudre and Big and Little Thompson, 200,000 bushels; Saint Vrain, etc., 160,000; Boulder creeks, 100,000; South Platte, 200,000; Clear and Ralston creeks, 100,000; Bear, Plum, and Cherry creeks, 60,000; Arkansas river, 120,000; Purgatoire, Apishapa, etc., 230,000; Saguache, Rio Grande, etc., 50,000.

Over 300,000 bushels of corn were raised, of which 75,000 bushels grew in Las Animas county and nearly or quite as much more in Fremont. At seventy cents per bushel, the value was $200,000. There were about 250,000 bushels of oats raised, worth $125,000; nearly 150,000 bushels of barley, worth $80,000; and 50,000 bushels of rye, worth, say $30,000. The potato crop ranged from 400,000 to 500,000 bushels, worth $350,000. There were probably 50,000 tons of hay cut and cured in the valleys of the plains, parks and mountains. This varied greatly in price, being far more valuable in the mining camps than on the plains. The total value may be placed at $800,000. Garden produce probably counted up $250,000, and the dairy product of milk, butter, cheese, with eggs, etc., $350,000 more. The total agricultural productions of Colorado for 1878, exclusive of stock, may be summed up, as follows:

Wheat	1,310,000 bush.	$1,310,000
Corn	300,000 "	210,000
Oats	250,000 "	125,000
Barley	150,000 "	80,000
Rye	50,000 "	30,000
Potatoes	450,000 "	350,000
Hay	50,000 tons	800,000
Garden produce		250,000
Butter, cheese and eggs, milk—dairy product		350,000
Total		**$3,515,000**

Wages of farm hands usually range from $15 to $20 per month, with board, for the entire year or season, or about the same as female domestic servants receive. Laborers hired especially for harvesting receive from two to three dollars per day and board. There is quite a difference in the prices received for farming products, according to locality. No country has a better market, and one beauty of this is that it is right at home. Hay is usually from $20 to $30 per ton in the mountain mining camps, and about half that sum on the farms of the plains and parks. By the cental, or hundred pounds, potatoes ranged during the past year or two from $1.50 to $1.75; corn from $1.50 to $1.75; wheat, $1 to $1.70, or from seventy cents to one dollar per bushel; flour, $2.20 to $3 per hundred; oats, $1.75 to $2.50.

Before the railways reached Colorado there were occasional scarcities of articles of food. A single potato crop of a mountain farm near Central cleared for its owner $17;000 one year when potatoes did not do well on the plains. Many years ago receipts were often very large, from the sale of crops on such large ranches or estates as those of Col. Craig and others. A leading farmer, near Denver, who, from his penchant for potato culture, has been called the Potato King, usually raises from 40,000 to 60,000 bushels annually from 200 to 300 acres of land, and has received for his crops all the way from $40,000 to $70,000. He plants those varieties that are found to do best, and, as in most parts of the State, many grow to prodigious size. The highest reported yields of any extensive potato crops run from 500 to 800 bushels per acre. These are exceptional cases; but two and three hundred bushels to the acre are common returns.

Magnificent crops of the finest quality of wheat ever grown are usually harvested in the fertile and beautiful valleys of the Boulder creeks, and of Ralston, Saint Vrain, Poudre, Clear, Bear, and Saguache creeks, and in parts of the Las Animas, and Arkansas and Platte valleys. The profits of a farm in those localities are often many thousands of dollars annually. Some farmers have hundreds of acres in wheat, and harvest from 5,000 to 15,000 bushels per annum. From three to six times as much land is usually sown in wheat as in oats or corn. The most approved sowing, planting, and harvesting machinery are used, and steam threshing machines are moved from one place to another, as their services are required. These machines handle from 40,000 to 90,000 bushels each in the more populous districts. In July, 1877, over $75,000 worth of farming machinery was sold in Boulder county alone.

Greeley colony has over 35,000 acres of land under ditch, most of it in a high state of cultivation. Some fifty or sixty square miles of

territory were made available for agriculture by the recent completion of a section of twenty miles of the Larimer and Weld Canal.
The total length will be fifty-four miles, and a tract of country
thirty-six miles long, and from three to ten miles wide, will be
irrigated. The canal starts from the Cache-la-Poudre river, at the
Colorado Central Railway crossing, and continues eastward until the
Denver Pacific is crossed. A part of this land was pre-empted, and
some is being sold at from $3 to $10 per acre.

Western Colorado is beginning to be settled up by miners and
farmers. For many years the great Sierra Madre acted as a barrier
to immigration and advancement; but population is moving in that
direction at last. Beside the wonderful mining discoveries of that
region, the farming and pastoral resources are considerable. There
are fine parks and numberless valleys enclosing the streams. These
are extremely fertile, and will prove very serviceable and valuable
now that a demand has arisen for their products. The Gunnison
river alone has from 50,000 to 100,000 acres of farming land available for irrigation that is lower than San Luis Park, and which
yielded 20,000 tons of hay last season.

CHAPTER III.

STOCK GROWING—THE NATURAL ADVANTAGES AND LARGE PROFITS
RESULTING THEREFROM IN COLORADO—THE BEGINNING OF A
GREAT INDUSTRY—RAISING CATTLE, SHEEP AND HORSES ON
THE GREAT PLAINS AND IN THE PARKS AND MOUNTAINS—
STATISTICS RELATING THERETO.

Colorado is one of the best grazing regions of the world. Her
pastoral lands are of immense extent, and so profitable has been the
avocation of stock growing that this industry has begun to assume
immense proportions. The exports of beef cattle are exceeded only
by those of Texas, while her sheep and wool products, which interest is not yet as fully developed, are fast approaching the extent of
those of California and New Mexico.

The plains of Colorado will not feed as many cattle, sheep or
horses to the square mile as lands in many of the older States, but
the almost limitless area, combined with its winter as well as summer
supporting qualities, render it particularly advantageous. It is only
in case of severe storms that cattle on these plains require hay, grain,
or feed, and no stock men supply it even then unless it be one of the
few engaged in raising stall-fed animals. Yet the quality of Colorado beef is far above that of Texas or most other extensive stock-
growing countries. This is due to the superior character of the
grasses, of which the "gamma" and "buffalo" are the most common species. The former grows ten inches high, and has a single,
round stock with oblong heads. The other grows closer to the
ground, being but about three inches high, and is very curly.
There is still another kind called bunch grass, which keeps green at
the roots all winter. Colorado grass starts about the first of May,
and continues to grow until about the middle of July or August,
when the dry season commences. It then dries up and cures as it
stands on the ground, and having no frosts to cut it, it retains its
strength, and stock keep fat on it all winter.

Strangers passing through the country in the fall and winter
wonder what the stock find to eat, for it looks to them like a

barren waste. Yet the results of letting the cattle run at will are highly satisfactory and extremely remunerative. Unlike the eastern grass, which turns to ashes or decay after the frosts come, these upland species are as fine in January as hay in the mow. The dryness of the climate helps them to survive the winters. A heavy fall of snow usually evaporates in a day or two, and rains are so short and infrequent that the moisture is readily absorbed.

In case of storms, stock can find shelter under the bluffs and in the many small valleys and ravines, while the clusters of pines, piñons, and cottonwoods almost serve the purpose of barns and stables. There have been winters when a single storm of great severity has occurred, followed by the snow crusting over. At such times the loss of cattle was quite extensive, and of sheep much larger. The storm of December, 1878, was an instance, and led many men to take steps for the better protection of stock. Winter feeding will probably be followed in many localities in time of storms and heavy snow-falls. The increase of cattle, allowing for all losses, is placed at eighty and even as high as eighty-five per centum on the whole number of cows. Others have estimated it as low as seventy-five. The value of four-year old steers ranges from $23 to $30. Cows are not rated quite as high. With the aid of corn or grain crops, about double the above prices can be obtained.

The shipment of cattle to Chicago, Kansas City, and elsewhere began some years ago, and later that of dressed beef in refrigerator cars became quite an item. In 1877 some 80,000 cattle were forwarded by rail, and some 88,000 in 1878 and in the ensuing winter. The rapid influx of population created an increased home demand, which it is said called for 20,000 head last year. The cattle exported or consumed were steers, mainly four-year olds. The increase of cows is, of course, large, as these are retained for breeding purposes. The sales of 108,000 head, at an average of $25, gives $2,700,000. Add to this the increase of female calves and the total of receipts and addition to stock represents something like $3,500,000 for the year.

Of the Eastern cattle exports 24,500 went by way of the Union Pacific, 19,800 by the Atchison, Topeka & Santa Fe, and 18,700 by the Kansas Pacific. The main shipping points are Julesburg and Cheyenne on the first named road, Grenada, Las Animas, Pueblo, and Rocky Ford on the second, and Deer Trail, Hugo, Denver, and Wallace on the third.

The cattle men of Colorado usually started in the business by securing a quantity of Texas cows—"long horns," as they are called—and a suitable number of bulls, of American or foreign breeds. Some of the finest bulls in the world have been brought to Colorado. Most of them are of the Durham, Hereford, Jersey, Canadian, and other fine species. Their average value runs from $100 to $150, but some are worth several times those figures. Until recently Durham bulls were generally brought to Colorado in preference to others, but now the white-faced Herefords are the favorites, and are being introduced extensively. It is claimed that they are more hardy than Durhams or short-horns. By crossing these with Texas cows the increase is very much superior to the latter, and a second cross with the half-breeds still further improves the stock. So the pastoral ranges of Colorado have at last come to support large numbers of first-class cattle, as well as thousands of the less valuable Texans. Colorado beef is pronounced the best that finds its way to the Eastern market that is not stall-fed. Cattle lose flesh in the winter, and consequently poorer beef gets into the home market in February and March than at other seasons. Stock on the dairy farms and in the agricultural sections is sheltered, fed, and cared for to a greater extent than those on the regular stock ranges.

Notwithstanding the fact that cattle and sheep are able to obtain their own subsistence for the entire year, the avocation of stock-growing is attended with no little care and labor. During the winter the cattle roam at will over the plains, and different herds mingle together, and perhaps wander for long distances from their original ranges. With spring comes what is called the "round ups," when all the cattle of large tracts of country are driven together in one vast herd, and with their increase separated and driven to their former ranges by their owners.

These "round ups" are important occasions with cattle men, and usually occupy their time from late in April to July or August, when branding time begins, and continues until the beef shipments of autumn and early winter. The cattle often scatter over the plains into adjoining counties, fifty or one hundred miles away from their starting-place. To complete the "round up" the ground has to be gone over two or three times, although most of the stock is secured

THE ROUND UP.

the first trip. There is a law, as well as rules and regulations, for the guidance of stock-growers. These district off the country and designate the points of assemblage.

On or near the 25th day of April, when the time comes for the "round ups" to begin, the stock men in each of the sixteen districts assemble together with their herders at their respective places of rendezvous and begin to drive the cattle from the creeks and branches to the main stream or river. Gradually the scattered herds are gathered together. After many days and weeks from twenty to two hundred thousand head are massed together in a comparatively small space of territory. Then comes the separating and driving away of the stock of various owners, each of whom can distinguish his property by the brands placed thereon in the previous season.

After the country has been scoured over until the last of the wanderers are driven in and assigned to their owners, the latter return to their respective stock ranges, when the work of branding follows. Every cattle man has a peculiar brand, separate and distinct from that of his neighbor, in order that he may know his property wherever he finds it. By the time fall arrives cattle are fat and in prime order for market, and shipments begin and are continued until the surplus steers are disposed of. Large numbers of yearling steers are driven in from Texas, and kept on these prairie ranges until they are four years old, when from $40 to $45 are sometimes received for them.

A State board of cattle inspection commissioners was provided for by the last Legislature. Early in 1872, the Colorado Cattle Growers' Association had been fully organized. Since then it has held its annual sessions at Denver or in some other prominent town, and has been of no little service to the industry which it aims to advance, regulate, and represent. A cattle association for southern Colorado was organized in 1877. The first purely blooded live stock farm in Colorado was that established by Captain J. S. Maynard, in Weld county, in 1870, with a start of thirty-six thorough-bred short-horns. The same year, Childs and Ring brought a short-horn herd into El Paso county. Stock and animals of similar character had arrived in Saguache county in 1868, and in Huerfano, Park, and Lake in 1869. The growth of the cattle interest can be appreciated from the fact that but 145,916 were assessed for taxation in 1871, while 483,278 was the number in 1878. There are probably nearly 900,000 head in the State at the present time. It has been claimed that assessment returns of live stock for many sections have been far too low to give any just idea of the extent of this industry. Consequently the numbers and value of cattle and sheep of leading stock counties for 1879 are given as estimated by prominent dealers and owners :

NAME OF COUNTY.	Number of Cattle.	Value.	Number of Sheep.	Value.
Bent.............................	125,000	$2,000,000	20,000	$190,000
Weld..........................	95.000	1,500,000	65,000	145,000
Elbert.........................	90,000	1,500,000	100,000	225,000
Arapahoe.....................	60,000	1,000,000	87,000	190,000
El Paso	33,000	550,000	230,000	500,000
Las Animas...................	40,000	600,000	210,000	420,000
Pueblo........................	36,000	600,000	100,000	210,000
Larimer.......................	27.000	450,000	70,000	160,000
Douglas.......................	40,000	650,000	40.000	85,000
Huerfano.....................	24,000	380,000	180,000	360,000
Saguache.....................	25,000	400,000	25,000	55,000
Conejos.......................	10,000	150,000	120,000	230,000
La Plata......................	50,000	900,000	30,000	65,000
Other Sections..............	200,000	3,100,000	570,000	1,385,000
Total..................	855,000	$13,680,000	2,002,000	$4,220,000

Ten years ago Colorado had less than twenty thousand head of sheep. To-day there are something like two millions or more. The State has millions of acres of land that can never be irrigated, and consequently can only be used for grazing. The sheep industry is young yet, but is fast approaching cattle-growing in importance, and will soon be followed to a far greater extent. Colorado possesses many advantages for sheep-growing over Eastern or even Pacific coast States. Sheep live the year round on the open prairie. While numbers of them have died off from exposure to snow-storms of unusual severity, such disasters are of so rare occurrence that little attention has been paid thereto. Yet shelter of some kind is desirable from these storms, as well as a reserve of ten or fifteen tons of hay to every thousand sheep. The herders take the sheep out on the prairie at sunrise and remain with them until dark, when they are driven into corrals or fenced enclosures for the night. One man herds from two thousand to twenty-five hundred head in one band. If the range is fresh they will do well in bands of that size, but a somewhat smaller number will thrive better. Mexican sheep can be run in larger bands than the graded ones. Sheep are usually through lambing about the tenth or fifteenth of June, when shearing commences. Shearing is generally done by the head—five cents for Mexican sheep, and six cents for one-half and three-quarter bloods. The Mexican sheep shear from two and a half to three pounds per head, half-breeds from four to five pounds, and three-quarter bloods from five to eight pounds. The shearers go from place to place in bands of from six to fifteen men at the above prices. All they have to do is to catch their sheep, shear it, lay the fleece on the folding and tying table, when a man takes it, folds and ties it, throws it to the sacker, who sacks and marks the sack, and it is ready for shipment. Most of the wool is sent East to commission houses, that sort and grade it before selling. A good shearer will shear from seventy-five to one hundred Mexican sheep and from thirty to forty grades. It will be seen that the cost for help is wonderfully small.

Good authorities estimate the number of sheep in Colorado at nearly or quite 2,000,000. The increase is very rapid. Allowing a value of $2 per head in the Mexican counties, and of $2.25 elsewhere, and the total value would be from $4,000,000 to $4,500,000. It is claimed that last year's wool clip was 5,000,000 pounds, which at 17 cents per pound would be $850,000. Add to this the increase of lambs, valued at $700,000, and something like $300,000 for sheep consumed or marketed, and the total products or receipts from the sheep industry would be $1,850,000 for 1878. For 1879 this should be much greater; possibly 700,000 pounds of wool, worth $1,200,000, nearly 800,000 lambs worth $1,200,000, and $300,000 for sheep marketed or consumed. This gives a total of $2,700,000 as the receipts and increased value for one year. This is a remarkable showing for a business that employs but a very few thousand men, and a large portion of them merely herders at low wages. The distance from an Eastern market has so far acted as a drawback for the shipment of sheep or mutton, except into the mining camps and large towns.

Thus far, the business of sheep-raising in Colorado has been very profitable. A flock of 1,800 ewes, costing $4,500, were placed on a ranch in Southern Colorado. In eight years 1,600 sheep were killed for mutton, and consumed on the ranch, and 7,740 were sold for $29,680. There are 14,800 head on hand, worth, at $3 per head, $44,400. The wool clips paid for shepherds and all current expenses.

The result shows a net profit over the original investment of $69,520, equal to 193 per cent. per annum for eight years in succession. Per contra, out of a flock of 1,200 very fine selected ewes, worth $4 per head, 800 died during a storm of two days last March. The 400 that survived raised last summer more than that number of lambs. The dog is a valuable auxiliary in the care of sheep. The "Scotch collie" surpasses all others in his natural aptitude for this work, and oftentimes one well-trained sells for $150.

Many of the sheep men have two ranges for their herds—one for summer and the other for winter. The herder usually collects the sheep at night on a side hill, and sleeps by them. They lie quietly unless disturbed by wolves, who are the most troublesome in stormy weather. Shepherd dogs are very useful in the protection and herding of sheep, and are born and raised, and die with them. Lambs are weaned about the first of October. Sheep will travel about three miles out onto the range and back to water or the herding grounds each day. Those coming to Colorado to engage in the sheep business should go onto a sheep ranch, and stay there long enough to understand all about the methods of conducting the business. In selecting or taking up land for sheep-growing, plenty of range or room, with hay land and a water supply are requisites for successful operations. Good sheep should be purchased, to begin with, as they are the cheapest in the long run, and close attention must be given to the business in order to make money and build up a fortune.

While large numbers of the sheep of Colorado are of the American breeds, hosts of them are of the Mexican species. Still larger numbers are of mixed blood, obtained by crossing the long-legged, gaunt, coarse, light-wool Mexicans with Merino rams. The Cotswold has not been crossed so successfully with the full-blood Mexican, but makes fine stock when crossed with the three-quarter Merino. This brings size to the sheep, weight to the fleece, and length of staple. Since Colorado has been found to be the sheep-growing State of the West, large herds have been driven into her borders from other sections. California has been a heavy contributor, on account of the small expenses and large profits attending sheep raising here as compared with the Pacific slope. Thirty thousand sheep were driven in from that State but a few months ago.

CHAPTER IV

SOMETHING FURTHER ABOUT FARMING AND STOCK GROWING—AGRI-
CULTURAL AND PASTORAL LANDS OF COLORADO—SOME EXTEN-
SIVE STOCK FARMS—THE ANNUAL REVENUE FROM FARMING AND
STOCK GROWING.

The foregoing chapters on farming and stock-growing will enable
the reader to make a very fair estimate of the extent of these partially developed but rapidly growing interests. The values represented and the results obtained can be briefly summarized. The
value of farms, cultivated lands, improvements, and property, exclusive of live stock, may be set down at $12,000,000. The vast
tracts of land utilized as stock ranges are not included in that estimate. The value of horses and mules on farms and stock ranges
may be set down at $1,000,000, and of dairies and domestic cattle,
$1,000,000. In the regular stock-growing interests the value of
cattle may be placed at $12,680,000; of sheep, $4,300,000; and of
horses, $1,100,000; other property in stock interest, $500,000.
Here is a total capital representation of $14,000,000 in the agricul-
tural interests, and of $18,580,000 in stock, exclusive of that in-
cluded with the farm valuations. Nearly all of those sums were
the growth and accumulation of a few years from small investments
of money or muscle. The value of horses and mules outside of the
farming and stock sections, something like $3,000,000, is not in-
cluded in the above figures.

The receipts, gains and profits of the farming industry for 1878
was not far from $4,000,000, including increase of dairy and other
stock. Those of stock-growing were about $6,200,000. Of this
$2,700,000 came from sales of beef cattle, and $800,000 on growth
and increase of herds, and $300,000 for sheep consumed or marketed,
$1,200,000 for increase of herds, and $1,200,000 for wool sold.
This $6,200,000 represents the returns and gains of some 40,000
people, men, women and children, living on farms and stock
ranges. The figures for 1879 will be much larger.

The agricultural, pastoral, and mineral sections of Colorado can be outlined somewhat as follows: The eastern third of Colorado, made up of the great plains, may be classed as pastoral land, outside of that bordering the streams, which is available for both farming and stock growing; elevation from 3,500 to 6,000 feet, excepting the timbered divide south of Denver, which is somewhat higher. The pineries of the latter have furnished a vast amount of lumber, but the plains away from the streams are barren of timber. Central and western Colorado is made up of mountains more or less covered with timber.

To the northward are the fine farming and grazing counties of Weld and Larimer, and south of them Arapahoe and Boulder. The last, beside gold and silver mines, has vast measures of excellent lignite coal that are already producing largely and which extend into Weld and south into Jefferson county—the same belt leading southward to New Mexico. Coal also appears here and there in the parks and valleys of the mountains of central and western Colorado. All through the northern part of the mountain sections are fertile valleys and grazing lands. Many of the former are too elevated for crops, excepting oats, rye, potatoes, and other hardy vegetables. There are countless farms or ranches all through the mountains, some of them of considerable extent and of great fertility. In the little mining county of Gilpin, the annual farm and dairy products must exceed seventy-five or eighty thousand dollars. The Rollins farm at Rollinsville alone has a strip of meadow and valley land amounting to three or four square miles in extent, which produces heavy crops of hay, vegetables and of the hardier grains. There are similar farms all through the hill country of Boulder, Jefferson, and Park counties. On some of these the hay crop returns thousands of dollars per annum.

Western Colorado will be settled up within the next few years to come both for pastoral and agricultural purposes according to elevation and character of land. There is a large area that can be made available in the counties of Routt, Grand, Summit and Gunnison.

That part of Colorado extending from the Middle Park and the vicinity of James Peak and Central southward through Clear Creek, Summit, Park, and Lake to Chaffee county and the vicinity of Trout Creek, Granite, and the Twin Lakes, comprises some immense ranges of mountains, with valleys and parks intervening. The latter are, in some cases, well adapted to grazing, but are mostly too elevated for agricultural purposes. The principal valleys are South Park, with an altitude in the western part of from 9,500 to 10,000 feet above the sea; the Upper Arkansas valley, 9,000 to 10,600 feet: the lower section of the latter near Chalk Creek, Cottonwood, and the South Arkansas, which is from 1,500 to 2,500 feet lower, and produces fair crops; the Blue River basin, 8,700 to 10,600; Ten-Mile Creek, 9,500 to 11,000; the Blue River Valley, 7,800 to 8,700. The timber found on the inclosing mountains is spruce and pine, valuable for lumber, while cottonwood is found along the streams. Mining is the great business of this section, and but few supplies can be raised outside of Chaffee county, except in the way of beef. Large herds of splendid cattle are kept in the parks. The mountains include the great Snowy range proper, or Continental Divide, with its spurs, such as the Front and Park ranges. West of the Arkansas

ON THE A. T. & S. F. R. R.

the main Divide is called the Sawatch range. This is the highest average mountain range in North America. From the western slope of this flows the Gunnison and its tributaries, whose valleys improve, in an agricultural point of view, as the descent toward the western ocean continues. Luxuriant grasses are found there, and large crops of hay were cut last season. In the park, near Gunnison City, an irrigating ditch is being constructed that will water six thousand acres of land. Early in May grass was four or five inches high on this slope.

Further down the mountain valley of the Arkansas, and within the limits of the new county of Chaffee, is a fine stock section, and a very fair farming district. Wheat and other grains are raised there as well as vegetables. The elevation runs from 7,300 to 8,800 feet, with mountains on either side. Still further down is Pleasant Valley; elevation, 7,000 feet. In the valley of the Platte, in the lower part of the South Park, stock growing is quite successful; elevation, 8,500 to 8,800.

Wet Mountain Valley in Custer county has fine farming and grazing land, and is pretty well occupied with ranchmen and stock owners. This is just east of the Sangre de Cristo range and adjoins the Sierra Mojada or Wet Mountains. In and near it are the mining camps of Silver Cliff and Rosita. The elevation is from 6,700 to 8,300 feet.

The San Luis valley or park is over one hundred miles long, and from forty to fifty miles wide near the centre, but gradually closes up toward either end. From the east the grand old Sangre de Cristo range rises far above the spruce and pine forests that line its lower sides, and to the west are the foot hills and spurs of the San Juan Mountains. San Luis Valley slopes slightly towards the centre, where the streams that enter it from the mountains sink and disappear in the great swamp known as San Luis Lake. What is remarkable about this strange locality is, that the streams, after coursing through the park for some distance, gradually grow smaller and smaller, and divide or disappear, as if drank up by the earth, until the waters are entirely absorbed in the great sink. Little irrigation is required in the northern part of this park, and in some portions none at all. The northern half of this great valley, together with some of the mountain sections, comprises the county of Saguache. A stream of the same name comes down from the hills to the westward, and in the fine farming and stock district watered thereby, is the well-to-do village of Saguache. The amount of farming around it has been steadily growing, until the crops comprise some 50,000 bushels of oats, 20,000 of wheat, 50,000 bushels of potatoes, 15,000 tons of hay, beside vegetables in great numbers. The yield of wheat is reported at from 25 to 40 bushels per acre, of oats at twice as much, and of potatoes 200 to 400 bushels. From 60 to 100 square miles of land can be and in time will be cultivated on the Saguache side of the park. Elevation above the sea, 7,500 feet. Further south are other streams and farming districts, and then comes the Rio Grande itself. In time this can be made one of the leading farming sections of the State, for this river can furnish an immense amount of water for irrigating purposes. Portions of this park are thickly covered with grass, and support many cattle, and other parts are almost barren, and can sustain but little animal life. The southern half of San Luis Valley is mainly peopled by Mexicans and their descendants, with a sprinkling of Americans and Europeans. Alamosa, however, is an American town. Conejos and Costilla counties were gradually settled from New Mexico in two decades following 1854. Sheep growing is extensively prosecuted, and there is some farming done, and a fair quantity of wheat and other grains are raised. Most of San Luis Valley is from 7,000 to 8,000 feet above sea level. There are flour mills at Saguache and Conejos.

There are fine farms and stock ranges in the Animas valley south of Silverton and the San Juan silver mines, and near the New Mexican border. This stream flows southward into the San Juan river, and is nearly parallel with the La Plata and Mancos. This is in southwestern Colorado, and should not be confounded with the Rio Las Animas or Purgatoire of the Trinidad section, and which flows northeasterly to the Arkansas. The quantity of cattle, horses, etc., and of cultivated land in the Animas valley is already large, and settlers are coming in steadily. The elevation is from 6,000 to 7,000 feet.

The cost of irrigation varies with different localities. In some sections it is as low as three and five cents per acre and in others as high as ten. Ditch companies have charged from one to three dollars per inch for water. Ditch agents and superintendents are hired by the companies or owners to attend to water-leases, repairs, and collections.

Among the irrigating canals is what is known as the Big Greeley Ditch on the north side of the Cache la Poudre river. This is 36 miles long, with 3 to 3½ feet depth of water, and is 25 feet wide on the bottom at its head, diminishing to 15 feet at Greeley. Its fall is from 2½ to 3½ feet per mile. Total cost $66,000. The ditch south of the same stream is 11 miles long and 12 feet wide at the bottom, with 2½ feet depth of water. The Big Evans ditch on the south side of the South Platte river has a length, with its branches, of forty-five miles. The main trunk is ten feet wide on the bottom, with from 1½ to 2 feet depth of water. Grade five feet and four inches to the mile. There are many others, large and small, all over the farming sections, with grades all the way from two to ten feet per mile.

The men longest in the cattle business in Colorado are the best off financially, showing that the accumulation of wealth in this industry is only a matter of time. When John W. Iliff died, in 1878, he owned more cattle than any other man in the State—the accumulations of many years in the business. His herds numbered something like 30,000 or 40,000 cattle, valued at over half a million; thousands of calves were branded, and from 5,000 to 7,000 steers or oxen shipped East every season. His ranch or cattle range was 156 miles long, extending from Greeley eastward to Julesburg, and from the Platte river south to Lodge Pole creek. Of this immense range, Mr. Iliff had purchased some 20,000 acres. At the chief rendezvous, forty miles from Julesburg, were houses, sheds, corrals, chutes, and facilities for handling and branding stock. There are sections of inclosed land on this territory, some twenty houses, and mowing machines, wagons, and farming tools, beside nearly two hundred head of horses. From thirty to forty herders are employed. Eighty Durham and Hereford bulls are located on the Patterson ranch alone. N. R. Davis, of the same county of Weld, rebranded over 6,000 cows or heifers last season, and sold 1,500 head of fat steers.

It is impossible to mention all of the leading stock men of the State. There are large numbers who own from five to ten thousand head of cattle, others who own still larger numbers of sheep, and others still whose wealth is divided among both cattle and sheep, with here and there large herds of horses. In El Paso county alone there are thirteen men, each of whom have flocks of from five to ten thousand sheep, and one firm has nearly or quite fifteen thousand. Some of the heaviest sheep growers are in Las Animas, Conejos, and Huerfano counties. Single stock farms in northern and central Colorado have from two to three thousand head of fine horses.

The wool shipments from points in Colorado, in 1878, amounted to about 4,000,000 pounds, of which about one half came from New Mexico, via wagon trains to the southern railway termini. These shipments embraced 1,250,000 pounds at El Moro, 500,000 at Alamosa and Garland, 600,000 at Colorado Springs, 200,000 at Fort Collins, 200,000 at Greeley and Cheyenne, 500,000 at West Las Animas, 100,000 at Pueblo, 100,000 at Cañon, 100,000 at Walsenburg, and 450,000 at other places.

Estimates of the wheat crop of different years have varied greatly. The "Colorado Farmer" placed the wheat crop of northern Colorado at 450,000 bushels in 1876, at 750,000 bushels in 1877, and at 900,000 in 1878. Wilbur, after personal inspection, footed up the acreage of wheat in the Boulder and Saint Vrain valleys, in 1877, at 13,399. The "Greeley Tribune" estimated the acreage of wheat, in 1877, at 32,500 in northern Colorado, with a yield of 731,250 bushels, and 17,500 acres in southern Colorado, with a yield of 393,750, allowing for an average yield of 22½ bushels per acre.

Flour mills, some of which turn out fine brands of flour, are at work in Pueblo, Lake, Larimer, Boulder, Jefferson, Arapahoe, Fremont, Saguache, Conejos, and other counties. Las Animas, Jefferson, Arapahoe, Larimer, and Weld have three mills each. Boulder county has six mills, two of which are at Boulder, two at Longmont, one a little further down the Saint Vrain, and one at Saint Louis. These six mills convert over 300,000 bushels of wheat into about 120,000 one hundred pound sacks of flour. Boulder county crops were below the average last year, wheat giving an average of only 18 bushels per acre, oats 30, and corn 25. The wheat average of 1877 was 23½. In the spring of 1878 Boulder county had 3,583 horses, young and old, worth $235,000; 223 mules, worth $30,000; 9,106 cattle, worth $160,000, and 2,354 sheep, worth $8,000.

The first cattle-grazing enterprise of the Pike's Peak region came about in this way. Colonel John D. Henderson arrived from Kansas late in December, 1858, with a load of groceries and liquors. His first trade secured a large island in the Platte river, below Denver, in exchange for two barrels of whiskey. The bargain was considered a good one all around, as plain drinks were then twenty-five cents and mixed ones half a dollar, while land was somewhat plentiful. A commodious house, extensive cattle corrals, and a bridge were constructed, and Henderson Island Station became a great rendezvous and stopping place for mountain-bound emigrants. Preparations were made for the accommodation of stock, and in the winter of 1859-60 Henderson herded over two thousand head of cattle, used but one hundred tons of hay (cut in the previous summer), and lost but seven head. Somewhat later he sold the place to Major R. B. Bradford for ten thousand dollars, went to Missouri and raised a regiment for the Union army.

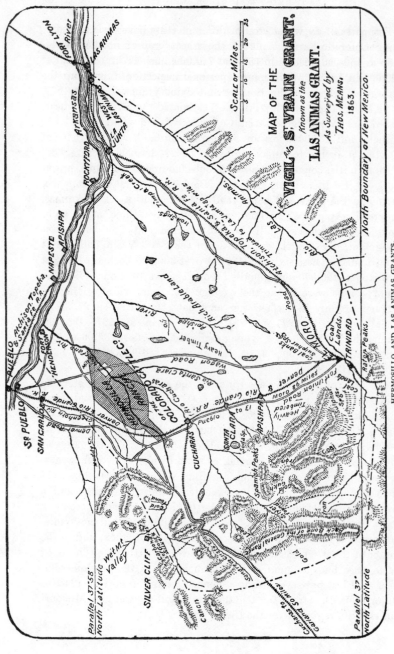

MAP OF THE
VIGIL No. St VRAIN GRANT,
Known as the
LAS ANIMAS GRANT.
As Surveyed by
THOS. MEANS,
1863.

Scale or Miles.

HERMOSILLO AND LAS ANIMAS GRANTS.

Among the large land grants or tracts of land bestowed on or confirmed to individuals by the national government were the Craig grant, south of Pueblo, the Gilpin grant, in San Luis Park, and the Nolan grant. Only a portion of the original claim of Craig has yet been conveyed to him, and the great Las Animas land grant of the Mexican government has never been ratified by the United States government, excepting so far as the Craig estate goes.

Attracted by the splendid fishing and hunting, wild scenery, fine climate, and great stock capacities of the Rocky Mountain region, many Englishmen of means have taken up their abode here; others sojourn at Denver and the mining districts portions of the time, or visit the watering-places and hunting grounds at favorable seasons. Among them the Earl of Dunraven settled in Estes Park, which he is converting into a magnificent estate and summer resort. The natural scenery and surroundings are of the most beautiful and attractive character.

Probably the finest large stock ranch of the State is that recently purchased of Colonel William Craig by the lately organized Colorado Cattle Company. This valuable tract of land is a part of the grant of over four million acres made by the Mexican Government to Colonel Ceran Saint Vrain. Saint Vrain was a French nobleman of a wandering, adventurous disposition, who had adopted Mexico as his place of residence, and received the above princely domain for patriotic services rendered that country. He came to America after the overthrow of Charles X, in 1830, and in time became the leading spirit and business man of New Mexico. Government contracts, freighting, trading, brewing and distilling sometimes brought him a revenue of a quarter of a million in a single year, and it all went as fast as it was made.

Some years after the American conquest, Colonel Garland, who was the military commander along the Rio Grande and Arkansas, experienced no little difficulty in suppressing the warlike Indian tribes, while the Mexican population was considered none too loyal. At Garland's request, Saint Vrain consented to raise a volunteer regiment to aid in restoring order, but stipulated that a regular army officer of his own selection should be detailed to assist him. William Craig, a West Pointer of the class of 1853, and then a young lieutenant of Garland's regiment, was chosen, and the volunteer force was organized. It attained a high degree of discipline and efficiency, and Craig was the actual leader and commander in the hundred encounters and skirmishes that took place before the Indians were subdued.

A strong friendship ever afterwards existed between the Frenchman and the young army officer, and resulted in Craig's purchasing that portion of the great Las Animas grant bordering the Huerfano and tributary rivers on very favorable terms. After the close of the war of the rebellion, Colonel Craig resigned his position in the regular army, and took up his abode on the estate just referred to. It proved a very profitable venture, and in succeeding years over one hundred thousand dollars were expended in buildings, stock, and improvements. The beauty of the place, when clothed in its summer garb of emerald and wild flowers, caused its owner to give it the Spanish name of Hermosillo. In the unsuccessful state movement of 1865-6, Colonel Craig was the democratic candidate for governor, when William Gilpin, another pioneer of the western wilderness, prior to the gold discoveries, was the republican nominee. Another regular army officer, Major George W. Schofield, bought ten thousand acres of the Hermosillo Ranch, and sold to P. T. Barnum, the great showman, and D. W. Sherwood, who made a great deal of money from stock-growing in the last ten years. Both properties are embraced in this three hundred and fifty thousand dollar purchase of the Colorado Cattle Company, and pass under the name of Hermosillo. With these vast tracts of unsurpassed grazing lands, and fertile meadows and grain-fields, go ten thousand thoroughly crossed steers, a multitude of cows, one hundred Kentucky and Canadian bulls, and horses and other stock. There are 91,000 acres in the government grant, beside half a million more in the upland country behind, which, from its lack of water, must ever be a dependency of the former.

Beside the above, twenty thousand steers will be purchased and placed upon the ranch this season, where they will be fattened for exportation. Additions will be made to the number of cows, bulls, and other stock, the design being to raise beef cattle for the home as well as for the eastern market, and to make this the most complete and extensive stock ranch in the Union.

There is no better land that the sun shines on than this. For more than fifteen years the late owner raised splendid crops of grain and vegetables from the four thousand acres, more or less,

RESIDENCE OF COLONEL WILLIAM CRAIG, HERMOSILLO.

which he had under cultivation. The average yield of wheat has been nearly or quite forty bushels to the acre, of corn seventy-five to eighty, of oats seventy-five, and vegetables were wonderfully productive. Acequias, or irrigating ditches, are now being constructed from the rivers that course through the plains and valleys, which will increase the area of available farming land to 10,000 acres. This will permit of feeding grain to the stock during the last three months before shipment, thus insuring beeves of unsurpassed excellence—for no finer beef graces the table than that fattened on Colorado grass and grain.

On this same estate are some 15,000 acres of timber, while much of the open country is dotted with piñon trees, affording stock protection in time of storms. Outside of the timbered and cultivated portions, the entire surface of the country is covered with rich and nutritious gamma and buffalo grasses. These afford sustenance at all seasons of the year, winter and summer, for the climate of this country south of the Arkansas Divide is warm and temperate.

The ranch is 140 miles south of Denver, 20 miles from Pueblo, and is nearly rectangular in shape. The Denver & Rio Grande Railroad passes through the southern portion of the property, and the Atchison, Topeka & Santa Fe runs within eight miles of the northern end. The railway shipping facilities are consequently excellent. The Colorado Cattle Company was organized in Bridgeport, Connecticut, and is composed of some prominent citizens of that place and New York. The officers are D. W. Sherwood, president; H. B. Hammond, treasurer, and J. M. Toucey, C. S. Bushnell, O. B. Jennings, A. S. Treat, C. B. Hotchkiss, and Samuel Grumman, directors.

The profits accruing from raising, fattening, and producing stock in Colorado can be seen from the following tables, based on the experience of actual workings. The increase of a herd of four thousand cows for seven years is shown, with an allowance for losses of twenty per cent. One of the greatest sources of profit is buying two-year-old steers, keeping them a year or a little longer at almost no additional expense, and selling them at an advance of ten dollars or more per head. This branch of the business is even more profitable than raising cattle. This schedule is made with reference entirely to grass fed cattle, but fattening with corn and other feed grown upon the ranch will be an additional source of large and never failing profit.

COWS.

YEAR.	Number of Cows.	Number of Calves.	Number of Heifer Calves.	Value when yearlings, at $10 per head.	Increased value when 2 years old, at $5 per head.	Increased value when 3 years old, at $3 per head.	Value when 3 years old, at $18 per head.
One	4,000	3,200	1,600	$16,000	$8,000	$4,800	$28,800
Two	4,000	3,200	1,600	16,000	8,000	4,800	28,000
Three	5,600	4,480	2,240	22,400	11,200	6,720	40,320
Four	7,200	5,760	2,883	28,800	14,400	8,640	51,840
Five	9,440	7,552	3,776	37,760	18,880	.....	56,640
Six	12,200	9,856	4,928	49,280	.....	.....	49,280
Seven	16,096	12,877	6,498 at $6 per head				38,628
Original Cows, at $18 per head							72,000
							$366,308

STEERS.

YEAR.	Number of Steer Calves.	Value when yearlings, at $10 per head.	Increased value when 2 years old, at $6 per head.	Increased value when 3 years old, at $10 per head.	Value when 3 years old, at $26 per head.
One	1,600	$16,000	$9,600	$16,000	$41,600
Two	1,600	16,000	9,600	16,000	41,600
Three	2,240	22,400	13,440	22,400	58,240
Four	2,880	28,800	17,280	28,800	74,880
Five	3,776	37,760	22,656	.....	60,416
Six	4,928	49,280	.....	.....	49,280
Seven	6,498 at $6 per head				38,628
					$364,644

Total product in 7 years of 4,000 cows, costing $72,000, including cost of Cows............... $730,952
The profits or increase, on the seventh year alone would be....................... 254,792
Or 50 per cent. on the entire capital of $500,000. Each subsequent year the increase of profits is enormously enhanced.

Each year, also, from 3,000 to 5,000 head of steers can be bought, and sold a year later, at a profit of $10 or more per head, which item alone would pay double the expenses of the entire ranch.

In the extreme southwestern part of Colorado, and near the Utah and New Mexico boundaries and the Arizona corner, are a succession of fertile valleys, as remarkable for their agricultural as for their stock-growing capacity. These valleys are watered by streams issuing from the great San Juan Mountains, and flowing southward into the San Juan River or into one another. Mountains and hills intervene, and several streams are walled up at intervals with huge cañons, but withal there are numerous tracts of valuable land which lay so low that wheat, and other grains and vegetables are raised successfully; across a portion of these valleys and divides is an immense coal belt of superior character. It is believed that this section will, in time, be the smelting depot for much of the San Juan silver region, and that a railway will be built in from Alamosa, Pagosa, and the east. As it is, a good market is afforded the farming and stock products of this county of La Plata. Animas City is the leading town.

Last season the lands already occupied by settlers in these valleys numbered 20,640 acres of farming land, outside of stock ranges in bordering hills. This was before the strip of land known as the Indian reservation, and since ceded to the United States, was open to settlement. As it was, there were forty-five farms, with 7,200 acres in the twelve-mile valley of the Animas, twenty-one farms, with 3,360 acres of tillable and hay-land along the Rio Florida, and forty-three farm locations and 6,880 acres of land on the Los Pinos. The more westerly streams have not been settled up so thickly. In the La Plata valley only five ranches or farms were occupied, with an acreage of 800 acres; in the valley of the Mancos were seventeen farms, with 2,720 acres. On the northwest slope the Rio Dolores has nineteen farm locations, with 3,040 acres. There are also large stock ranches. The late Indian reservation is being settled up rapidly. Some 40,000 head of cattle are owned in this section, and one farmer on the Animas has seven or eight thousand sheep.

A Mormon settlement, mainly composed of proselytes from Europe, was started in Conejos county early in 1879. The colony has 3,000 acres of land, on which the town of Manassa is being built. The location is seven miles north by east of the village of Conejos, and the number of inhabitants is 156, with more on the way. Polygamy is not practiced there, nor will it be.

PART FOURTH.

CHAPTER I.

MINING FOR THE PRECIOUS METALS—GROWING IMPORTANCE AND
INVITING CHARACTER OF THIS GREAT INDUSTRY — LODE AND
PLACER MINING AND THE VARIOUS MODES OF OPERATION—VAL-
UES, WEIGHTS, AND MINING TERMS.

Gold and silver mining is evidently as old as the first gathering
of the human race into nations and the earliest approaches towards
civilization. Neither profane history nor tradition refers to an
epoch that antedates the use or search of the precious metals. Their
discovery, obtainment, and use appear to have exerted a refining
influence, and peoples engaged in their production and circulation
were proportionately progressive in wealth and power.

The significant fact is taught by the history of mining in all countries that well-defined metalliferous veins are continuous in depth,
and that they are productive as long as machinery and appliances
of the requisite power can be obtained for moving ore and water.
Barren masses of ground may be encountered, but the vein matter is
never permanently lost. No true veins have been known to give out
for any great length of time, and when work has ceased on once
largely productive mines it has almost invariably been brought
about by other causes than the complete exhaustion of the lodes.
It may have been from inadequate drainage facilities or hoisting
machinery, or from caving of ground or unforeseen disasters, but
rarely from long-continued poverty of ground. Thus we see mines
still profitably operated in Europe that were worked centuries ago,
and thousands of feet of depth attained in prosecuting this remunerative industry. In the Comstock lode of our own country immense

bonanzas of rich ore have been penetrated and made to yield their millions at depths of from a quarter to a half mile below the surface, and still the work goes on. An instance of the confidence in which metalliferous veins are held in the old world is shown in the recent completion, after ninety-two years' continuous labor, of a tunnel over twenty miles in length that had been driven solely for the purpose of draining a mine that had been operated almost from time immemorial.

The progress made in recent years in overcoming the difficulties enumerated is as wonderful as the production it has so materially aided to increase. In a short period of time as great an advance has been made in mining operations as was previously known in centuries. This is best exemplified in the mammoth works and production of the great Comstock mines, whose yield has been unparalleled in the world's history. Since the temporary decline of that great treasure-vault the rapidly developing mineral belt of Colorado has been gradually securing the attention that once centered elsewhere. Vast and varied as are the developed resources of the Rocky Mountains, the discoveries that are constantly being made indicate that the beginning only has yet been heard of.

Colorado's metalliferous veins already greatly outnumber those of any other state or territory, and many of them are of surpassing richness. While a rival of what the Comstock was has not been developed to a certainty, it is evident that several Colorado mines will produce more money within the next few years than a like number in any part of the world, while there is a probability of a production almost equal to that of the Comstock bonanzas of 1874–8.

Until recently, mining outside of the placers has been mainly confined to what are termed true fissure veins of great uniformity and varying size. Immense ore bodies, like those of a few Nevada mines, were not encountered, but more continuous veins and less intervening barren ground were met with. Pacific coast miners say that production cannot be forced up to as large figures in these mines as in a few of the Nevada type, but that lodes of Colorado are more permanent and reliable for continuous work. The best of these fissures may not be able to produce as much for short intervals as some of the huge deposits of the western mines, but they often surpass them in a record of ten or twenty years. The great discoveries of eighteen hundred and seventy-eight have put a new face on the situation, and now Colorado, in addition to the old continuous veins, can boast of huge ore bodies and enormous deposits that will compare with those of any country in size and value. In fact, the world, to-day, cannot show anything superior to the Colorado developments that have followed the temporary decline of the Comstock.

The growing importance of the mining industry, its immense production, the rapid accumulation of fortunes, and the well-known prosperity of some mining regions, have created so widespread an interest in gold and silver mines that any information relating thereto is beginning to be eagerly sought after. There has ever been a fascination and romance attending the search of the precious metals, and time intensifies rather than diminishes the feeling. Under the magic influence of gold and silver discoveries a spirit of enterprise has been engendered that has brought about the accomplishment of results as unexpected as they are grand and wonderful. The wilderness is peopled, states are founded, and almost an empire established where the presence of civilized man was unknown but a few short years ago.

Gold mining comes under two heads—lode and placer, and silver mining is included in the first of these. Lode-mining is much the most important interest of the two in Colorado, since the quantity of the precious metals contained in quartz and ore is many times that of the gold of alluvial deposits. When a gold district is discovered, the first work is usually done in the placers and gulches, where the work is more simple, and the gold readily obtained. Less money is required than in lode-mining, where quartz mills or a market for ores are demanded. Silver lodes usually require still further time for development and for the procurement of the necessary reduction works.

There are an immense number of metalliferous lodes or veins already discovered in Colorado, and every month witnesses additional discoveries. A large majority of these are silver bearing, accompanied with copper or lead. The main value of some is in the gold they contain, and others carry all of these metals and iron, as well as other materials. What is sometimes termed a fissure vein, and is considered to be identical with a lode, is a body of gold or silver bearing quartz or ore filling a crack or crevice of the foundation rock with which a country or district is underlaid. These veins vary in

width from several inches to many feet.   Some have been proved to
have a length of thousands of feet, and others of several miles horizontally.   They extend downward into the earth for unknown distances.
The ore bodies contract or close up at intervals, but no well-defined

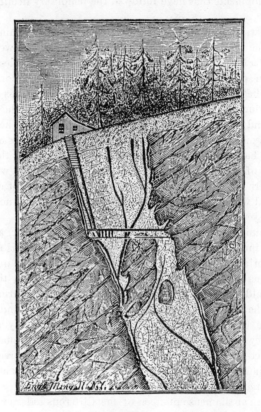

A LODE OR VEIN.

veins are believed to have given out entirely.   Some of them have a
perpendicular direction, and others are nearly flat or incline heavily.
Most of the argentiferous mineral bodies of the Park or Mosquito
Range appear in the form of egg-shaped or irregular deposits instead
of veins.   Some of the Leadville carbonates are claimed to be in the
shape of deposits and others are evidently in the form of veins.

Alluvial deposits consist of sand, gravel, and dirt, produced by the disintegration of the silicious, granitic, and other igneous and metamorphic rocks, and transported by the agency of water from the mountains above or around them. These are handled by one of the methods known as placer, gulch, creek, or bar mining, but to all of which the term placer is loosely applied. Gold is disseminated through the gravel or pay-dirt and lodges in considerable quantities on the rocky beds of streams. It is washed therefrom by water and secured in pans, flumes and sluice boxes, quicksilver being used to retain it where swift running water is used. No roasting, smelting, or milling is required, as where the gold is firmly embedded in the vein matter of lodes.

In operations of great magnitude large sums of money are often expended in bringing the requisite water supply to the desired placer diggings. When no water supply exists close at hand, one must be obtained from a distance, in order to work over these surface deposits. This often compels the building of miles of ditches and flumes. Powerful hydraulics are also used for the purpose of driving water with great force into the hill-sides, and tearing them down more rapidly than could otherwise be done. These placers and gulches call for appliances of varying extent and capacity, from those just referred to down to the ordinary sluice-box, the pick and shovel and the still more primitive hand-rocker and pan. Creek mining is carried on along the stream, and on their bed rocks far beneath the gravel and boulders immediately underlying the water.

In gulch mines, a flume composed of sluice-boxes is laid in the ravine or gulch, extending up to the bank or head of the excavations. Hose, hydraulics, or falling water from a flume above are used at this point to wash the bank or hill-sides down into the sluice-boxes. The latter are from one to four feet high and wide, and of uncertain length, and overlap one another. On their bottoms are fastened strips of board for riffles, or round blocks sawed from trunks of trees, and of a thickness of two or three inches. These, with quicksilver placed therein, aid in catching the gold dust and nuggets which the swift running waters sweep along with the dirt, gravel, and boulders. The gold being heavier than the other materials, sooner or later sinks to the bottom before it reaches the end of the sluices. It is always the intention to run the flume on the firm "bed-rock" as it is called, which underlies the gravel of the hills and

GULCH MINING—SLUICING FOR GOLD.

streams. Some of these flumes are run for hundreds and even thousands of feet before bed-rock can be reached, on account of the nearly level character of the ground worked. In other places the fall is so great that bed-rock, even if twenty-five or fifty feet deep, can be reached in a short distance and still retain the requisite incline to the sluice-boxes. Once a day, or as often or seldom as desired, the water is turned off and the gold taken from the sluice-boxes. This is called a "clean up."

In bar and creek diggings sluice-boxes are used, and the stream is turned from its natural channel, the boulders or heavier stones removed and shafts or pits are sunk until the permanent granite or bedrock of the country is reached. The gold in such localities is usually found extending up and down the course of the stream in a narrow streak or strip of ground. Drifts are excavated along this pay streak, and the gravel, dirt, and rock overlying the same are raised to the surface or packed in the drift as an adjoining and parallel one is opened. These drifts are run from six to seven feet high and wide, and are supported by heavy timbers, which keep the gravelly, rocky bed of the stream, often from fifteen to fifty feet thick, from caving in. If no "pay streak" is found on sinking the shaft, it is prospected for by running drifts as already noted. The water which continually leaks into the mine from above is removed by pumps, sometimes of great capacity.

In recent years, placer operations of great extent have been inaugurated in Summit, Park, Lake, Routt, and Ouray counties, and there are some extensive mines of this character in Clear Creek and Gilpin. These are supplied with hydraulics, great flumes, and other facilities for handling vast amounts of dirt and gravel. The rapidity with which the ground is worked permits of large profits where they would not be possible under the old systems so long in use.

Lode mining is very differently conducted from placer operations. After the decomposed surface material has been passed, gold is not so easily extracted as from pay-dirt and gravel, and silver ores are usually much more difficult to handle. Hard as are most ores, the enclosing rock is still harder, and the miner's difficulties do not end with blasting, breaking, and raising the ore to the surface; for then comes the reduction of the ore, and this calls for costly machinery, and for skill and experience in conducting the same,

and in operating the milling or smelting process in order to secure
the desired results.

The requisite entrances into the domains of mother earth, for the
purpose of breaking and securing the ore, are made by digging and

LODE MINING NEAR THE SURFACE—SHAFT AND LEVEL.

blasting out perpendicular shafts and horizontal levels or excavations
on the vein. To do this, hand or machine drilling and blasting powder and high explosives are brought into play. As work progresses
solid timbers are required to brace the sides of the mine. These
timbers, logs, or stulls extend from wall to wall, and keep them from

falling in. For fifty or one hundred feet below the surface man power and the windlass are sufficient for hoisting the ore, waste rock, and water. After that horse power is required, which is used with a " whip " or pulley, or more generally by a whim or large drum of timber, around which the rope winds and unwinds as the bucket ascends or descends. This usually answers all purposes down to a depth of two hundred feet or more, when the steam engine and accompanying hoisting is used. Sometimes the whim is dispensed with, steam following man power and the windlass. When greater depth is gained and the mine is enlarged there is more ore to handle and the water becomes more troublesome. More powerful hoisting works are then required, and huge pumps are a necessity.

As levels are extended and the vein material is broken down, iron tracks are laid, and the ore is conveyed in cars from various parts of the mine to the shaft, where it is placed in buckets and hoisted to the surface. From there it is assorted and taken to the mill or smelter. There are a number of requisites in lode mining, the development and working of mineral veins, and in the treatment of ore after it has left the mine, both in stamp mills and reduction works, that will be more fully explained hereafter. The entire business requires no little ability, care, and skill to insure success, even if the mine is a good one. The operations are much more difficult and intricate than in gulch mining, where the miner can clean up his gold every night instead of waiting for the results of the somewhat tedious processes of shipping, milling, and smelting.

In past ages the gold has found its way from lodes on the hillsides down into the streams or outlying ground, where it has been gradually working its way through the loose gravel onto the hard bed-rock, and that is where the richest streaks are found. The gold is usually as fine as powder, but is often found in coarser particles and in nuggets or lumps of various sizes. It is not free from impurities and consequently does not come up to the value of artificially refined gold, which is worth very near $20.67 per ounce. Placer or gulch gold in Colorado is worth from $17 to $18.50 per ounce. Large nuggets of gold have been found in Summit and Gilpin counties. One was found below Black Hawk, some years ago, that, with its attached rock, was much larger than a hen's egg and sold for $240.

Although nuggets or particles of gold are often seen in the quartz, the precious metal is usually disseminated through it so as to be

invisible to the naked eye. Beneath the surface the ore is so hard as to require the aid of ponderous stamps, driven by water or machine power, to crush it to the requisite fineness for washing or raw amalgamation or for roasting and smelting. Even then the stamps do not always pulverize it fine enough to admit of successful raw amalgamation.

IN THE MINE.

The most brilliant example of the superior profits attending mining for the precious metals as compared with those obtained in other avocations is afforded in the record of the two bonanza mines of the Comstock lode. Those mines cleared more money in four years than any two firms or companies in other lines of business have done in a generation of time since the world began. The most noticeable accumulations of wealth in mercantile and manufacturing pursuits cannot compare, in point of time and amount, with the larger fortunes acquired, at various times, in North and South American mining history.

As many names and terms are used in mining regions that are unknown or unfamiliar elsewhere, the following collection of definitions are given; likewise something concerning values, weights, and measurements. All of these should be carefully read and referred to when words used are unintelligible.

WEIGHTS AND VALUES.

A ton of gold or silver contains 29,166.66 ounces.

A ton of gold is worth $602,875.

A ton of silver, at the standard rate of $1.29,29, would be worth

$37,709.57, but at the present price of silver, $1.10 per ounce, it would be worth only $32,083.32.

The standard of gold and silver for United States money is 900 parts of pure metal and 100 parts of alloy in 1,000 parts of coin; that is, a dollar is nine-tenths pure metal.

Standard gold is worth $18.60,465 per ounce U. S. gold coin, 21 3-5 carats fine.

Standard silver, $1.1636+ per ounce. The term "fineness" expresses the quantity or proportion of pure metal in 1,000 parts.

The value of an ounce of gold, pure, is $20.67,183, or approximately $20.67; 23.22 grains of pure gold equals $1. The standard gold dollar 25.8 grains troy, and the silver dollar 412.5, and the trade dollar 420.9 grains.

Pure silver has 371.25 grains to the dollar; hence the value of one ounce should be $1.29,29+ instead of the present varying bullion price of $1.10 or $1.15. Had the former been the ruling price, as in bygone years, Colorado's silver product of 1878 would have had a valuation one million greater than it was.

The British standard of coinage is 11 parts of gold to one of alloy, and of silver 37 parts of silver to 30 alloy. Quotations of the price of silver on the British market is made on that basis, viz.: of 925-1000 fine, while American transactions are made in the pure metal. This accounts for the lower rates per ounce of the former.

One pound "troy" weight equals 822.857 of a pound avoirdupois; 7,000 troy grains equal one pound avoirdupois; 437.5 troy grains equal an ounce avoirdupois; 175 troy pounds equal 144 pounds avoirdupois; 175 troy ounces equal 192 ounces avoirdupois; one avoirdupois pound equals 1.215,278 pounds troy.

One troy pound equals 22.8156 cubic inches of water.

One cubic foot equals 7.4805 gallons.

One meter equals 39.370,797 inches, English measurement.

One decameter equals 32.80899 feet, English measurement.

One hectometer equals 328.0899 feet, English measurement.

One kilometer equals 3,280.899 feet, English measurement.

It is estimated that the gold coin, bars, and bullion, in circulation in the world are worth $3,500,000,000; equal to the debt of Great Britain. If this was in one mass it would make a twenty-five foot cube. One cubic foot of gold weighs 1,200 pounds, and is worth not far from $300,000. Silver is about one half as heavy as gold, a cubic foot of silver weighing about 600 pounds, worth about $10,000. There is about the same value of silver in the world as gold, viz.: $3,500,000,000.

DEFINITIONS OF MINING TERMS.

Adit. A tunnel on a vein or lode—a passage for water under ground.

Amalgam. Quicksilver and other metals, usually gold or silver, and sometimes both combined.

Arastra. A Spanish-Mexican ore-reducing machine, consisting of a hard circular platform, upon which the ore is deposited, the crushing being by means of a revolving sweep, to which huge flat stones are attached.

Bed Rock. The bed of a metalliferous deposit, commonly applied to the slate underlying auriferous gravel.

Blind Lode. One that shows no surface croppings.

Bonanza. A Spanish term, signifying in good luck, prosperity; a large and rich ore body.

Boulders. Huge rocks, weighing from a few hundred pounds to many tons, that by the force of water have been carried along the river beds until the sharp edges are worn away.

Blossom Rock. Float ore, found upon the surface or near where lodes or ledges outcrop, and from which they have become detached.

Breasting. Taking ore from the face of a mine, or head of a drift.

Bullion. Gold and silver uncoined and unmanufactured.

Cage. The elevator used for hoisting and lowering the ore cars, men and materials of a mine.

Country Rock. Rock on either side of a lode or ledge, usually barren—the permanent rock, enclosing a vein.

Cap Rock. The formation overlaying the pay-dirt or ore.

Carboniferous. Containing coal.

Chute. An incline or opening from one level to another through which to slide or pass ore.

Conglomerate. Pudding stone, composed of gravel and pebbles cemented together.

Contact lode. A lode lying between two different kinds of rock, as for example, porphyry and slate.

Croppings. Ledge matter lying upon the surface, or the outcroppings of a vein.

Crosscut. A drift run at right angles to the ledge, for the purpose of ascertaining its width, and to otherwise prospect it; also an opening or level driven across the ground from one vein to another.

Cupriferous. Containing copper.

Debris. Sediment from hydraulic or other mines; masses of rock and other materials detached from the sides of mountains and piled up below.

Denudation. Rocks laid bare by running water or other agencies.

Deposit. A body of ore distinct from a ledge; a pocket of gravel or pay dirt.

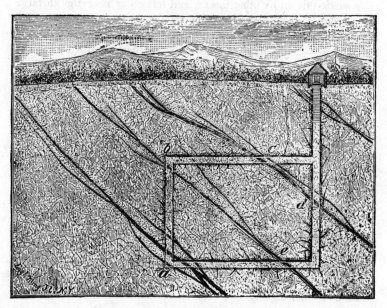

VEINS, WITH SHAFT AND CROSS CUTS AND WINZE.

Detritus. A mass of substances worn from solid bodies by attrition, and reduced to small particles.

Development. Work done in opening a mine; such as sinking shafts and running levels.

Dead Work. Work of putting a mine in order, and driving shafts and levels in search of "pay," or to open up a mine.

Disintegrated. Separated into integrant parts without chemical action.

Drifts. Tunnels leading off from the main shaft, or from other tunnels or levels through and along the vein.

Drift Matter. Earth, pebbles, and boulders, that have been drifted by water, and deposited over a country while submerged.

Dump. The place where ore is deposited after being taken from the mine ; a pile of either ore or waste rock.

Face. The extreme end of a tunnel, drift, or excavation, where work is prosecuted.

Float Rock. Fragments of a lode that have been floated by water or carried down by other means, and left on or near the surface ; ledges are sometimes found by tracing up the "float."

Flume. Boxing or piping for conveying water.

Free Gold. Gold easily separated from the quartz or dirt.

Forced Production. When a mine is worked so as to produce a larger product than can be maintained ; is done sometimes with large ore reserves.

Flux. Any substance employed to promote the fusion of minerals.

Fossils. Petrified organic remains.

Foot Wall. The lower wall or side of a lode or vein.

Gangue. The matrix ; quartz is commonly called the gangue rock of gold and silver ores, though it may be of other material.

Grizzly. Bars set in a flume in hydraulic mining, to screen out the large stones.

Gulch. A ravine.

Hanging Wall. The upper wall ; the rock or wall resting on the lode or vein.

Horse. A mass of wall rock or other barren matter, obtruding into an unbearing lode or fissure.

Incline. A slanting shaft.

Inch of Water. A miner's inch of water equals a discharge of 95 cubic feet per hour ; one cubic foot to $7\frac{1}{2}$ gallons ; a discharge of 712.5 gallons per hour, about $2\frac{1}{2}$ cubic feet per minute ; the water that will run out of an opening one inch square, or section under a head of six inches.

Jumping a Claim. Taking illegal possession of a mine by force or otherwise.

Lava. Melted rocks and minerals ejected from volcanoes.

Ledge. Synonymous with lode or vein.

Level. Drifts from the main shaft, or from one shaft to another; an excavation run on the lode or vein, or ore body at distances of from fifty to one hundred feet from each other, and high enough for men to work in.

Litile Giant. A movable nozzle attached to hydraulic pipes.

Locate. To establish the possessory right to a mining claim; the property secured being designated "claim" or "location."

Lode. A longitudinal fissure or chasm filled with ore-bearing matter and having well-defined side walls; lode, lead, vein, and ledge are synonymous; a mineral vein in the country rock.

Mine. A mine comprises a certain amount of territory on a lode or vein, together with the makings or developments, which generally consist of shafts, levels, tunnels, or adits, winzes, and stopes; there may be connected with this appliances or machinery on the surface for hoisting the ore and water; there may be several mines on one lode or vein.

Mica. A shining mineral of various colors that can be split into thin layers.

Ounce. An ounce of gold, as generally used in this book, means an ounce of stamp mill retort, worth from \$14 to \$18; pure gold is worth \$20.67; an ounce of silver varies in value; is now worth \$1.10 or \$1.15.

Petering. The pinching or giving out of an ore-body.

Piping. Washing gravel in a hydraulic claim by discharging water upon it through a nozzle.

Placer. Alluvial deposits; earth containing gold dust.

Plant. The interior works of a mill; the stamps or crushers, furnaces and pans, vats, tubs, machinery, etc., of an ore reducing establishment.

Plateau. A plain or flat surface.

Porphyry. A barren ore, stratified reddish, purple, or greenish rock, in which are imbedded crystals.

Primary or Primitive Rock. Consists of the various kinds of slate, quartz, serpentine, granite, and gneiss; they are the lowest group of rocks, are irregularly crystallized, and contain a few animal relics.

Prospecting. Hunting for mineral lodes or placers.

Pan or Panning. Usually to wash the dirt from the free gold with a pan; the pan resembling an ordinary milk-pan.

Pulp. Pulverized ore, generally very fine.

Prospector. Searcher for gold and silver deposits or lodes.

Reducing. Separating from foreign substances; the reduction of ores consists in extracting from them the metals they contain.

Reserves. Ore reserves are the vein material still standing in the mine between the shafts and levels that have been driven in or through the vein.

OVERHAND STOPING—IN THE ORE RESERVES.

Retort. This is the term applied to the bullion extracted from the amalgam, by placing the latter in a cast-iron retort, expelling the quicksilver by heat; the quicksilver also being saved by condensation.

Regulus. The impure metal; melted ore containing all its metallic ingredients.

Salting a Mine. The act of introducing rich ores into a mine, or gold dust into a claim, for deceptive purposes.

Schist. Clay slate.

Secondary Rocks. Those above the primary and below the tertiary; made up chiefly of sand, clay, and pebbles cemented together, and containing many organic remains; they consist principally of chalk, green sand, clay, limestone, marl, sandstone, etc.

Shaft. A vertical or incline excavation for prospecting or working mines.

Slag. Scum, dross, the excrement of a metal; vitrified cinders; waste from smelters.

Slimes. The finest of the crushed ore and gangue from mills.

Sluices. Boxes or troughs through which gold-bearing gravel is washed; also used at the foot of the tables in quartz mills for catching the fine particles of gold.

Strata. A flat bed or layer of rock, earth, mineral, etc.

Stoping. Breaking ore from a stope or section of ground in a mine; between or above levels.

Stopes. Ore stopes are the same as ore breasts, except that the former means the ore overhead or underneath, the latter in front, or on the sides; ore broken under the feet is "underhand stoping," broken from above "overhand stoping."

Stull. Platform of timbers between levels for strengthening the mine by supporting the walls, and for storing ore and depositing wall rock and waste material upon.

Stull timbers. The large timbers placed across the vein or lode from one wall to another, to support the lagging upon which the ore or waste is placed.

Strike. A find; a valuable mineral development made in a sudden or unexpected manner.

Sulphuret. Combination of sulphur with a metallic, earthy, or alkaline base.

Sump or Sumph. A pit sunk at the bottom of a mine, to collect the water. It may be the bottom of a shaft.

Superficial Deposits are composed of such metals and ores as lie on or near the surface, intermixed with soil, sand, gravel, etc.; they are also called washings or stream works, these metals and ores being gathered by washing with water; much gold, all platina, and some tin and cinnabar are collected in this manner.

Tailings. The auriferous earth that has once been washed and

deprived of the greater portion of the gold it contained; this
term is also applied to the sulphurets and slimes that escape
from the mills.

Tertiary Rocks. Those lying above the secondary, and below drift,
containing sandstone, clay beds, limestone, green sand, gypsum, rock salt, lignite, etc., with animal relics.

Tributors. Miners who pay a percentage on the ore or returns they
obtain from a mine by sinking, drifting, or stoping.

LODE MINING—UNDERHAND STOPING.

Trend. The course of a vein.

Upraise. Running a drift upwards, or rising above a shaft or
level instead of sinking.

Winze. A shaft connecting one drift or level with another, but not
reaching to the surface.

Wall. Boundary of vein, lode, or ledge, and inclosing the same. In
mining parlance, "Wall rock," "Trap rock" and "Casing"
mean one and the same thing.

CHAPTER II.

COLORADO'S MINERAL RESOURCES—THE GREAT ROCKY MOUNTAIN GOLD
AND SILVER BELT—ITS INNUMERABLE VEINS AND VAST PRODUC-
TION—AN INVITING FIELD FOR INVESTMENTS—FACTS AND INFOR-
MATION FOR CAPITALISTS—MINING NOW AND IN THE OLDEN
TIME—COMPARATIVE COST OF MINING AND MILLING—REDUC-
TION OF EXPENSES—ABOUT LODES, CLAIMS AND TITLES.

The mineral resources of Colorado are already known to be enormous in quantity, and yet further discoveries are constantly being
made. They constitute the main wealth of the State, and are continually growing more productive and remunerative. Gold, silver,
lead, copper, and coal are extensively mined. Iron, salt, zinc, mica,
and other materials abound, and some of them will yet cut an important figure. Metalliferous veins are encountered in clusters and
belts all through the mountains of this vast region. Coal occurs at
intervals along the plains, near the base of the foot-hills, and here
and there in the mountains and river valleys. A mineral belt,
carrying one or both of the precious and some of the baser
metals, extends almost across the entire State, following to some
extent the northerly and southerly course of the Rocky Mountains.
It also appears in the flanking ranges and outlying foot-hills east and
west of the Continental Divide. Each season proves this mineral region to be of greater extent and value than was previously known, and
the entire mountain system of Colorado may yet be dotted with
mining camps at no great distance one from another.

A belt, showing but slight interruptions, has been traced from the
North Park and the northern part of Boulder county, south through
Gilpin and Clear Creek, thence southwesterly through Summit, Park,
Lake, Chaffee, and into Gunnison counties. It approaches the point
where the great Sawatch or main range divides into the Sangre de
Christo on the southeast and the San Juan Mountains on the southwest. The belt appears at intervals in each of these mountain systems or their outlying spurs and valleys down to the New Mexico
boundary.

In the San Juan Mountains, which form the Continental Divide in the south, it is rich in silver veins, extending all through the counties of Hinsdale, San Juan, and Ouray. Gold is also found there, as well as in Rio Grande county. The gold and silver bearing deposits of the Sierra Mojada and of the hills and valleys skirting the Sangre de Christo range are fast bringing Custer county into notoriety.

IN A SILVER MINE.

The Sawatch range extends from the point of union of the more southerly mountain systems northward to the Mount of the Holy Cross and the headwaters of the Arkansas, and is but another name for a portion of the main Rocky Mountain divide. It forms the dividing line between Gunnison county and Chaffee and Lake counties, and also separates Summit from the latter. Rich mineral discoveries have been and are still being made on both its eastern and western slopes, silver being the predominating metal.

East of this and of the upper Arkansas valley is the Park range of mountains, separating the latter from South Park, and uniting with the main range at Mount Lincoln. This, with its foot-hills, is enormously productive. On the western slope are the world-renowned carbonate deposits and veins of Leadville, immeasurably rich in silver and lead, and the gold veins and alluvial deposits of California Gulch. On the range itself and its eastern slopes are vast numbers of deposits and veins. Silver predominates there, but gold, copper and lead are mined. Down in the park are gold placer mines.

Northward extends the main range, which, all along its course between Summit and Grand counties on the western slope, and Park, Clear Creek, Gilpin, and Boulder on the east, is more or less rich in silver veins. Its extending foot-hills possess veins and alluvial deposits rich in gold. The outlying mountain spurs, hills, and gulches are also ribbed with metalliferous veins, some productive of silver and copper, others of silver and lead, and others of gold and silver, with one or both of the baser metals. Close beside each other on this eastern slope are the famous mining districts of Clear Creek and Gilpin. The latter has produced most of Colorado's gold, and the former gave much the larger part of its silver for years, up to the time when Leadville came to the front. Both counties, however, have gold and silver mines, and so has Boulder, whose telluride veins, carrying the precious metals, are something rarely encountered elsewhere.

Westward, over among the mountains and valleys of Summit, Grand, and Routt counties, are numerous argentiferous and galenous veins and gold-producing gulches and placers. Some of these have been worked for years, and others are of recent discovery, such as those of the Ten Mile range.

The great central mineral belt of Colorado has a width of from twenty to forty miles, but often branches off to the right or left and again contracts, so that the breadth is by no means uniform. Continued discoveries indicate that its extent is by no means ascertained. It is impossible to make anything like a close estimate of the wealth that lies embedded in these mountains, where constant developments show that only the beginning of it has been found.

Mining in Colorado in former years and at the present time are two very different undertakings. Ten or fifteen years ago most of the men engaged in mining or milling were novices in the business,

10

and could not work understandingly and to the best advantage. Labor was usually scarce and high priced, and much of it of little value. The country was remote from railways and the base of supplies. Warlike Indian tribes often blocked the routes of travel and impeded the slow-going mule and ox transportation. It usually cost as much to freight machinery from a railway terminus to the mountain mines as it did to buy it of the manufacturer. Nearly everything consumed was imported from distant states and localities. In some years freight charges alone amounted to what will now pay both purchasing and shipping rates. The methods of extracting the gold from the ore were at one time so imperfect that the greater part of the treasure contained therein could not be saved. Lode veins were originally divided among too many distinct proprietors— the claims being too short to work profitably to great depths with steam machinery in each one of them—and consequently requiring consolidation of many under one management to insure success.

A great change has been wrought in recent times by railways and cheap and rapid transportation, by reduced expenditures of labor and supplies, by improved mining and milling, and by economical and systematic management, and a fair priced market for the miners' ore product. All of the beef, and nearly all the grain and vegetables now required at the mines are raised in the State, thereby greatly cheapening the means of living. Long experience has made practical miners, while a steady influx of skilled workmen has kept the labor market fairly supplied. Mill men and smelters, by long experience, have become thoroughly acquainted with the character of the ore and mineral, and can, therefore, handle them to much greater advantage than in former times. In the older districts the consolidation of properties has obviated serious difficulties that recent mining laws have prevented in the newer ones. The settling down to continuous work and a permanent life-time residence, in place of temporary operations and a mine stripping, abandonment, emigration policy, has also helped matters amazingly. All of these and deep mining and intelligent broad gauge operations are bringing about results such as were never achieved a decade ago. The cost of labor and supplies in 1864-5, as compared with those of to-day in Gilpin county, is shown in the following table. In other districts prices are now the same as in Gilpin where rail facilities are afforded, and a half dollar more per day where they are not. Other articles

are slightly dearer. The figures of 1864-5 represent coin values as
well as those of 1879. The greenback values paid at the former period
were vastly higher. The left hand column represents the charges
when the eastern company operations were most numerous and
extensive and when the failures and suspensions began.

	1864–5.	1879.
Miners	$4 00 to $5 00	$2 00 to $2 50
Foreman	5 00 to 7 00	3 00 to 3 50
Laborers	3 50 to 5 00	2 00
Head masons	9 00 to 12 00	4 50
Other masons and helpers	5 00 to 7 00	3 50 to 4 00
Carpenters	5 00 to 6 00	3 50 to 3 75
Flour, per sack of 100 pounds	12 00 to 19 00	2 25 to 2 50
Lumber, per M	40 00 to 46 00	23 00 to 25 00
Hay, per ton	50 00 to 70 00	23 00 to 25 00
Powder	6 00 to 9 00	3 65
Fuse, per M	15 00 to 23 00	6 50
Candles, per box	10 00 to 15 00	6 25
Rope, per pound	30 to 45	15
Quicksilver	1 10 to 1 60	48 to 50
Machine Oils	80 to 1 30	35 to 40
Sheet Copper, per pound	60 to 75	30 to 32
Iron, per pound	18 to 24	4½ to 5
Sheet Iron, per pound	17 to 24	4 to 5
Nails, per pound	16 to 22	5
Shovels, each	1 80 to 2 35	1 10 to 1 40
Wood, per cord	8 00 to 12 00	5 50
Milling Ore, per cord	35 00 to 50 00	20 00 or less.

There were times when the prices of labor and some supplies varied
greatly. Wood and timber is dearer in Central City than anywhere else in the mountains. In Gold Dirt, near Black Hawk,
at Caribou, Ward, Leadville, Ten Mile, and all of the southern and
western counties, wood usually sells at from $2.50 to $3.00 a cord.
Lumber sells in the same localities at from $30 to $35 per thousand
feet. Carpenters and mechanics at Leadville have been getting ten
or fifteen per cent. more than the figures given in the table, and
lumber has been higher there. This is due to the wonderfully rapid
growth of the place.

There has never been a time or locality more favorable for individual or company investments and organizations than this year of

1879, among the mines of Colorado. With a reasonable amount of ready capital to open and push mining development, a harvest is very sure to follow that cannot be blighted by floods, frost, nor insects, nor increased or diminished in value, but one that is sure, substantial and enduring—the pure metal itself. This product in reality represents the basis of all prosperity and wealth.

The mineral resources of Colorado of every description have hitherto been imperfectly appreciated, because but slightly developed. Recent discoveries and the results of well-directed labor, aided by superior mechanical and scientific processes, are attracting the attention of sagacious capitalists in this and foreign countries. The present rate of progress, development, and discovery will place Colorado ahead of all other sections in the production of the precious metals before the close of another year.

Mining, with the help of moderate capital, is one of the most certain and profitable industries in which men of enterprise can engage. The more thoroughly and systematically mines are worked, and the greater the milling facilities for the reduction of ores, the more satisfactory will be the amount of bullion produced. Colorado is now amply supplied with milling, reducing, and smelting facilities in all but the very newly discovered districts. Gilpin, Clear Creek, Boulder, and Park counties and the San Juan region and Leadville have all the works required for the extraction of the precious metals produced at present, and these are located within their borders or in localities not far away. Summit and Gunnison counties have been and are still receiving similar establishments. Good prices are paid for ores, and milling charges are as small as in any other state or territory. This is vastly beneficial to the miner, and quite the reverse of the condition of affairs a few years ago.

For the most part mining has been conducted by men of limited means or no means at all when they started in. These mountaineer prospectors and miners have worked out their own salvation, and have made their state rich and famous almost by their own unaided labors, strong hands, and characteristic energy and enterprise. But little outside capital came in to help them during the fifteen years of the State's greatest progress. What has been secured is due to the splendid showings and remarkable returns previously made, and which would have been much greater had these western pioneers had the means to begin with to conduct operations, instead of waiting in nearly all cases to make it out of the ground.

Capitalists in the older states, where rates of interest are low and speculative enterprises uncertain and more hazardous than mining for gold and silver, can strike the path to certain fortune if they will organize companies controlling ample ready means to develop mines, intrusting the management to honest and efficient business men and practical miners. This done, and the better classes of property secured, and there would be no such thing as failure, but success would be inevitable.

The day of unsuccessful experiments and losing investments has gone by. Colorado has the mines, and at last her miners and mill men know how to work them and how to reduce the ores. Skilled labor is on the ground, and metallurgists and mineralogists thoroughly acquainted with their professions and the character of veins and deposits encountered. With their assistance and that of judicious investments, intelligent direction, and proper economy, the capitalist need fear no loss.

Careful investigation of the subject shows there has been immeasurably less loss from capital wisely invested in mines, and generally far greater profits than have been realized in any commercial or manufacturing pursuits, or in railway stocks or operations. With the largest mineral belt in the world, unsurpassed rail connections within and without, ample reducing works, a first-class ore market, cheap supplies, and countless veins of a very high average value, the Rocky Mountains certainly afford the true field for future investment, and rare opportunities for success.

For years after gold mining began in Colorado the laws adopted by the miners and ratified by the Territory and Congress provided that a lode should be 1,400 feet in length, and that the discoverer thereof should be entitled to one claim of 100 feet on the vein, and another of 100 feet as a bonus for discovery. Each additional locator could pre-empt but one hundred feet on that vein. It was also provided that this location carried with it twenty-five feet of surface ground on either side of the centre of the vein, if this did not invade neighboring claims previously entered. Afterwards the laws were changed for subsequent locations, so that a discoverer could have 1,400 feet in length on the vein, instead of 200. Later, there was a short period when the discoverer could obtain 3,000 feet. No great number of locations were made under that law, and at length the present law was adopted, allowing a discoverer to pre-empt 1,500 feet on a vein, extensions taken up in the same manner by the same or other parties. In 1874 the Colorado legislature enacted that all locations made thereafter in the Territory should carry with them 150 feet of surface ground on either side of the centre of the vein (if such claims did not enter on ground already located), except in the four counties of Boulder, Gilpin, Clear Creek, and Park, when seventy-five feet either side of the centre of the vein should be the rule. None of these laws interfere with lodes discovered prior to their adoption.

After a government title or United States patent has been issued for a lode the owner can hold it against all comers and claimants, whether he works it steadily or allows it to remain idle forever. It cannot be relocated, nor is there danger of losing ground or terri-tory secured in this way through litigation or opposing claims. Some years ago these titles carried with them the land for twenty-five feet on each side of the centre of the lode and vertically downward.

The owner can follow his vein anywhere so that he does not go outside of his end lines. At the present time, seventy-five feet on each side of the centre of the vein is allowed in Boulder, Gilpin, Clear Creek, and Park counties, and outside of them 150 feet.

There are five United States land offices in Colorado, located at Denver, Central, Pueblo, Del Norte, and Fairplay. Up to April 1, 1879, the Central City office had issued 765 government patents or titles for lodes or mining claims. Of these patents Gilpin County ob-tained 274; Clear Creek, 334; Boulder, 135, and Summit, 22, besides a few issued direct from the General Land office. At the same time there were 372 mineral entries on the Central City office books, likely to be issued soon. Whole number of mineral applications, 1,480.

The average cost of procuring a government patent or title is $125 when the location embraces 1,500 feet by 150, and over $160 when 1,500 feet by 300 are included. The former class embrace 5.16 acres of land and the latter 10.33. The costs include $25 for the Sur-veyor General, $45 for the Surveyor's patent, $12.50 for certified copies and abstracts, $10 for filing, $18 for publishing, $15 for notary fees, and from $30 to $60 for land. The law contemplates that five hundred dollars' worth of work shall be done on a vein before application for a title can be made. This is in order that the owner may prove up and ascertain the course and dip of his vein. Some little time is required to apply for and secure title papers—generally several months.

In regard to relocating abandoned lodes, section 15 of the Mining Laws says: "The relocation of abandoned lode claims shall be by

HAND DRILLING IN THE MINE.

sinking a new discovery shaft, and fixing new boundaries in the same manner as if it were the location of a new claim; or the re-locator may sink the original discovery shaft ten feet deeper than it was at the time of the abandonment, and erect new, or adopt the old boundaries, renewing the posts if removed or destroyed. In either case a new location-stake shall be erected. In any case, whether the whole or part of an abandoned claim is taken, the location certificate may state that the whole or part of the new location is located as abandoned property." The discoverer or re-locator has sixty days after disclosing the lode before sinking a ten-foot shaft; hence, he should employ that time in ascertaining the exact direction of the strike of his vein, if necessary.

Probably not less than one hundred thousand locations have been made from first to last in the various recorders' offices of Colorado of what purport to be lodes, ledges, claims, or deposits. A large portion of these may not prove valuable enough to work. Others are abandoned or left idle because paying mineral has not been found and others are unworked at present, owing to remoteness from reduction works, ore markets, or for lack of roads and inaccessi-bility. But a few thousand lodes are steadily worked at this time, but the number of active properties is rapidly increasing. Nearly all sections but Gilpin possess the fifteen hundred feet locations. There are over 15,000 in Clear Creek county, embracing fourteen, fifteen, and thirty hundred feet locations. There are thousands of claims recorded in Park, Lake, and Summit counties, and a vast number in the San Juan region.

Where the number of lodes and mines is so great as in Colorado it is of course impossible to mention but a small portion even of those that are being worked. The design of this book is not to give a complete list of locations or of mines, but to show in a general way what Colorado possesses, what her people have accomplished and what has been and can be done in the Rocky Mountain region in the way of mining, farming, and making money. The figures and statistics of the state at large and of counties are very extensive and accurate. A few mines in every large district will be described at length, and in some cases their production will be published. There are other properties as valuable as some of these, that want of space, time, and opportunity to gather statistics of prevents the author from noticing at length. The character of the latter class may be judged from what is said of the others. Before the summer is over discoveries may be made as rich and extensive as any previ-ously reported. This mining region is in a state of transition and grows and develops faster than the world is aware of. A mine that is unknown to-day may become famous to-morrow or next year.

CHAPTER III.

Several methods or processes for the extraction of the valuable
metals from the ore or rock are in use in Colorado. Some ores are
found to be best adapted to one kind of treatment, and others require
a very different style of reduction. There is the stamp-mill raw amalgamation process, for low grade gold ores ; then comes a number of
smelting and reduction processes, for rich and for medium grade
ores ; copper matte smelting, adapted to all except ores very rich
in lead ; smelting with lead riches, and the blast smelter, which is devoted to silver-lead bearing ores handle a large part of the values
of the mining product. There are mills devoted to chlorodizing-
roasting and amalgamation ; others to chlorination and leaching,
and chlorination and lixiviation has been more or less in use.
Recently Silver Cliff silver ores are treated by raw amalgamation.

The system of wet crushing and raw amalgamation, by means of
stamp or quartz mills, is used on the great mass of what are termed
free gold ores. A considerable portion of the gold is lost, and most
of the silver and copper, but owing to the fact that no roasting or
smelting is required, this method, by its cheapness, is the only one
adapted to the low grade ores, of which most gold-bearing veins are
composed. Nearly nineteen-twentieths of the gold-bearing ores of
Gilpin county are handled by this process, and about twelve-twenti-
eths of the entire gold product is obtained therefrom. The richer
mineral is sold to the smelters. The same process is in use in Boulder, Clear Creek, and Park counties, and the San Juan region. The
cost of treatment, where steam power is used, is from two to three
dollars per ton, or from fourteen to twenty dollars per cord. The
smaller figures represent the expense where the operator handles his
own ore, under the most favorable circumstances. When water

power can be used, the outlay is still less. Custom mills charge from $2.25 to $3.00 per ton, or from $18 to $20 per cord, varying with the season, mill power used, and character of ore.

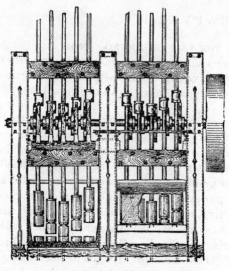

TEN STAMP QUARTZ MILL.

The stamp mill process is very imperfect, but has been vastly improved during the past fifteen years, as far as operations in Colorado are concerned. At one time only from fifteen to forty per cent. of the gold contained in the ore was saved, while from fifty to seventy per cent., and occasionally more, are saved at the present time. One mill claims a saving of over eighty-five per cent., including returns of buddled tailings. Blankets and pans help to increase the returns.

The mill proper consists of a solid frame work, heavy iron stamps and attachments, propelled by steam or water power by means of a horizontal shaft and connections. Mortars, inclined tables, and other accessories go to make up the contents of the establishment. The framework is upright, as are also the iron stamps, which are made to rise and fall by means of cams or arms extending from the revolving shaft above. The stamps rise from twelve to eighteen inches and drop on the ore in iron mortars or troughs beneath from twenty-seven to thirty-five times per minute. These mortars are several feet long, and from twelve to fourteen inches high, and nine or ten deep, and rest on solid wooden foundations. They are placed between the upright wooden posts of the frame; the stamps, usually five in number, that rise and fall thereon form what is termed a battery. The mortars are the receptacles for the ore, which is shoveled or fed into them as fast as it can be advantageously crushed by the stamps, at the same time that a constant stream of water flows in the same direction. Some mills have but a single battery of five stamps; others have ten or twenty, and there are some that have fifty and seventy-five.

On the side of the mortars where the ore feedng is done, the framework is boarded up some distance, and on the other side are sheet iron screens, through which the pulverized ore and water is forced on to the sloping copper plated inclines or tables below. Quicksilver is fed into the batteries and onto the tables when the mill man deems it necessary. This retains most of the gold on the tables while the pulp or slimes from the batteries are being carried onward by the water to the buddling tanks or stream beyond. The stamps are stopped, the water turned off, and the mortars and the plates of the tables are cleaned once a day, or once in several days, and the amalgam, or gold and quicksilver combination, is taken to the retort-room. Here it is skimmed and cleaned and pressed in a cloth so as to get rid of as much of the quicksilver as possible; the remainder is retorted and the crude bullion sold at the banks at from fourteen to eighteen dollars per ounce, or shipped in other ways. Gold from different mines varies in fineness and value, the quantity of silver accompanying it having much to do with this. The average fineness of Gilpin county bullion or retort gold is 787 parts pure gold, 198 parts pure silver, and 15 parts copper. The bullion obtained is from one-fourth to one-half of the amalgam, but rarely the latter. The quicksilver, after being condensed, is saved for future use.

After the pulverized ore leaves the batteries it is usually washed over two sets of inclined tables—the lower ones being covered with blankets. Some mills use pans, modeled after the principle of an arastra. The pulp or slimes, on leaving the mill proper, are generally worked over or concentrated by washing or buddling, when the concentrates are sold to the smelters. This often adds a dollar or two per ton to the total receipts from the ore. Formerly, no effort was made to save anything beyond the tables. About one ton of these tailings can be saved and sold to every ten tons of ore crushed.

The stamps used in these mills weigh from five hundred to seven hundred pounds, are generally ten or twelve feet high, and consist of a stem, head, shoe, and a collar, by means of which the cam raises them. The stem is made of wrought iron, and is from two to three inches in diameter, while the shoes attached to the lower part of the stem, and which come in contact with the ore, are thicker, and are made of steel or hardened iron. These stamps crush the ore to a pulp or powder, and much of the gold contained therein falls to the bottom of the mortars, and is taken up by the quicksilver placed there. Other portions of the gold are caught on the tables, blankets, and in the pans. The stamp-mill affords the only method of treating the low grade ores, of which the veins are mainly composed. Something like 140,000 tons are crushed in the Gilpin county mills every year. The smelting works are the destination of the high grade mineral, from which they save nearly all of the gold, silver, and copper.

The first quartz mills were brought into Colorado late in 1859. They were primitive affairs, with wooden, unplated tables, and had only from three to six stamps each. Up to this time the surface dirt and soft outcroppings of the veins had been shoveled into and washed in sluices, while other material was treated in arastras. Copper plates on tables and cyanide were not used at first, and few of the mill men knew anything about treating ores. It took a decade to bring quartz milling into even passable shape in Colorado, and nearly another to get it up to its present partly satisfactory condition.

This detailed account of the quartz mill is given because it is the basis of some other processes, and enters into their construction more or less. All ores must be pulverized before the silver and gold is extracted, and this is done either by stamps or by crushers and rolls. One or the other is found in all reducing, smelting, sampling and concentrating works.

Smelting with lead riches, is carried on at the works of the Golden and Valley companies at Golden, Hunt & Company's at Orodelfan, and at some points in the San Juan section. The lead comes out in bars, and the silver and gold in other bars. No copper is saved.

Chlorodizing-roasting and amalgamation is carried on at the Caribou mill at Nederland, and the Farwell reduction works at Georgetown, and has been used elsewhere. The ores are first broken in Dodge crushers and Cornish rolls, dried, sampled, and assayed, and then crushed dry by stamps, after which they are roasted in revolving iron cylinders, and then amalgamated in pans. Separation then takes place in the melting-room, and bars containing from $1,500 to $1,800 each, and of a fineness of from 800 to 900, are melted ready for shipment.

The pulverized ores are placed in the cylinders in charges of 3,500 pounds more or less, and the cylinders are then revolved at the rate of one revolution in two minutes. After four hours, from six to eight pounds of salt are introduced for every one hundred pounds of ore. Caribou ores require only from eight to eleven hours of roasting, and Georgetown ores from ten to twenty, according to lode. From 2,000 to 2,500 pounds of the roasted ore goes into each amalgamating-pan or leaching-tub at one time. In the pans, mullers do the grinding, and after one or two hours from 350 to 400 pounds of quicksilver are added, when the grinding continues from eight to twelve hours longer. The pulp is then thinned by water, and the specific gravity of the quicksilver and of the silver it has attracted causes it to seek the bottom of the pans, when it is drawn off, the pulp or dirt discharged, the amalgam still adhering removed, and the pans made ready for another charge. Retorting and melting into bars closes the proceedings

Chlorodizing-roasting and leaching is carried on at Georgetown and elsewhere. Works of this description have been operated at Rosita. The same kind of crushers, stamps, and roasting cylinders or furnaces are used as in the process just described, and the work is the same until the ore has been roasted. It is then placed in large agitating tubs, partially filled with a concentrated solution of hot water and salt kept in motion. This liquor dissolves the chloride of silver, and with the silver in solution is siphoned off and conducted into and through a series of tanks containing upright copper plates setting at intervals one behind and below another. The silver precipitates itself on these copper plates, when the brine or liquor is pumped back again into the agitating tubs for use.

The blast smelting furnace is used on ores carrying a high per cent of lead. When no roasting is required, as on carbonate ores, the process is rapid and somewhat simple. Skilled labor, attention, and experience are required, however, or disastrous results are likely to ensue. These furnaces are constructed of sheet iron and are usually circular in shape and of much greater height than diameter horizontally. Some are of square or oblong shape. They are built so that ore, coke, charcoal, and slag or iron are fed from an upper floor into the body of the furnace, while the lead and

REVERBERATORY FURNACES FOR ROASTING ORE.

silver bullion and the slag make their way from separate outlets at the base of the furnace and in the story below. The hot liquid, composed of lead and silver or other metal, is ladled out into the molds made for the purpose, and cools into bars called base bullion. The interiors of these iron furnaces are lined with brick made of fire-clay.

A reverberatory furnace is constructed of brick. The various compartments, hearths, or chambers, in which the fires are kept up and the pulverized ores roasted, are lined with fire-brick. These furnaces are often forty or sixty feet or more in length, and are divided into connecting hearths. The ore, while being roasted, is moved along from one hearth on to another, by means of long iron shovels, reaching into the furnace. These furnaces are used in the large smelting works, except at Leadville.

No Colorado silver ores have been found in large quantities that can be treated by the cheap raw amalgamation process outside of the recent discoveries at Silver Cliff in Custer county. The same is true of ores nearly equally rich in both gold and silver. By that process the free milling gold ores are handled in custom mills at a charge of $2.25 and $3.25 per ton. All other classes of ore have been treated, by some one of the processes mentioned above, outside of that just named, and are purchased on the basis of a charge of from $25 to $40 per ton, and an allowance for loss in treatment. Cheaper reduction is effected at Caribou and a few places where the mines have mills of their own, and the Leadville carbonates can be smelted at lower rates now or in the hereafter.

As silver ores rich enough for such outlays cannot be found as plentifully as ten dollar gold ores, it will be seen that the drifts, shafts and excavations of a silver mine, although equally expensive, give up less available ore in a given breadth or distance than those of a gold mine. Consequently it must cost more to mine a ton of silver ore of the requisite richness than one of gold, since better ore must be had for silver reduction than for gold. The surpassing richness of much of the former ore is what sets things even, and often proves wonderfully profitable for a time. In Gilpin it costs from $2 to $5 to get out a ton of gold ore. In Clear Creek it costs from $12 to $40 for a ton of silver ore.

Years ago it cost one hundred dollars a ton to simply mill silver ore in Georgetown. A little later that sum would pay for mining,

TUBS OR VATS FOR LEACHING ROASTED ORE.

milling, and hauling. At present, these items cost from $50 to $60 per ton, and less where the ore bodies are large. The same work costs more in some districts and less in others. In the San Juan region there are many miners that pay more for shipping their ore to a market—which, in the absence of roads, is mainly done on the backs of pack-animals—than they do for mining or smelting it. Twenty-five dollars a ton for transportation is not an unusual figure there. Mines in northern and central Colorado, along the line of, or in close proximity to railways, avoid heavy shipping charges.

The raw amalgamation process for silver ores is somewhat on the same basis as that for free milling gold ores, with pans in place of tables, and can be prosecuted only where the silver has already been chlorodized in the rock by the hand of nature. In the volcanic formation at Silver Cliff such has been the case, and consequently the above cheap and rapid method is going into use in that district. The process includes dry crushing by the ordinary stamps. The pulverized ore then goes into large pans, where water and quicksilver are applied. Here the pulp is kept agitated a requisite time, as in pan amalgamation described in Caribou and Georgetown mills. When thoroughly amalgamated, the charge is drawn and the amalgam retorted and the silver melted into bars of a fineness of about 900. This system is called by some western men the Washoe process, because used so extensively in that Nevada silver district. In order to save the charge of thirty or forty dollars per ton that must be paid for smelting or roasting, as with other ores and processes, the owners of the Racine Bay and Silver Cliff mines have been treating ores by this cheaper method at the Pennsylvania works at Rosita. Those works include crushers, dry stamps, revolving roasting cylinders, and pans and tubs. For treating Silver Cliff ores, the roasting part of the process is omitted, for nature has already chlorodized them. The result is it costs only from $3 to $5 per ton to handle these ores. A large stamp and pan mill is to be erected at Silver Cliff, and then this method of treatment will handle nearly or quite as much ore as any other, except that of the similar gold quartz mills.

Concentration is a method of separating the valuable portions of low grade ores from the gangue, in order that the miner will have the expense of smelting a smaller number of tons while securing nearly the same total value. There are two systems of concentration, known as dry and wet. Each embrace a great deal of machinery.   There are crushers, rolls, stamps, screens, jigs, hoppers, tables, elevators, etc., in one or both processes. The Krom, or dry process, is represented in the Clear Creek Company mill at Georgetown and elsewhere, and the Collom and other methods at Black Hawk, Silver Plume, Idaho Springs, and Spanish Bar. The machines known as frue vanners are used in Boulder county, in Salina, Ballarat, Nederland, and Gold Hill district. By the above named mills the crude or low grade ore is dressed and separated, so as to leave only marketable and paying mineral in place of rock too poor to sell to the smelter.

In seven years up to the summer of 1878 the adjoining counties of Clear creek and Gilpin gave a combined product of over $23,200,000 out of Colorado's total yield of $35,000,000 for that period. Gilpin gave about $12,200,000, nearly all in gold, and Clear Creek $11,000,-000, nearly all in silver. They will turn out together nearly or quite $5,000,000 in 1879. Clear Creek cañon is their natural outlet, and the mouth of this cañon and beyond has become the smelting depot for their richer ores. Golden and Argo are two of the great ore-reducing centres of the West.

The confidence of capitalists in these gold and silver mines is evinced by the great smelting enterprises carried on at the above mentioned points. Some of these smelting works have just been established; others have been enlarged. During the year three new ore-reducing concerns have been started in Golden. These, together with the works that have long been operating there, extend along the Colorado Central railway and the banks of Clear creek, and the name "Smelter's Row" has been applied to the locality.

The Valley Smelting Works were erected at Golden last winter by Gregory Board & Co., who have since been conducting them so successfully as to necessitate more furnaces. The proprietors of these works for a long time operated those controlled by the Golden Smelting Company, and for the first time made a financial success of them. The process embraces roasting, smelting with lead, and refining. The plant is quite extensive, and includes several roasting, smelting, and refining furnaces. The roasting furnaces are double, each equal to two ordinary ones.

Large quantities of ore are received from Leadville, Gilpin, Clear Creek and Boulder counties. From twenty to thirty tons can be handled daily, according to character of ore. Good prices are paid

Golden Sm. Co. Works.

Malachite Works.

French Smelting Works.

Valley Smelting Works.

SMELTERS' ROW—GOLDEN.

for the gold, silver, and lead contained in ores. For the first three months of 1879 $26,197.43 were paid for ores and tailings from Gilpin county alone. This indicates a bullion yield at these works during the year of over $150,000 from products of one county, and there are other districts that are said to be drawn upon just as heavily.

Not long ago America was visited by capitalists, miners, and metallurgists from France. After a general inspection of the western mining regions some of these gentlemen came to the conclusion that Colorado had the brightest and most permanent future before it, and concluded to embark in the smelting business there. Golden was selected as the most feasible point of operations, for that was at the gateway of the mountain districts having the largest amount of ores adapted to the copper matte process.

The French Smelting Works were completed in the summer of 1879. They were constructed after the most improved methods which skilled labor and experienced metallurgists could suggest and are a model of their kind in many particulars. The plant embraces a large calcining furnace, with three superincumbent soles forty feet long, two matte furnaces, three special furnaces for the separation of the precious metals, five main stacks, a Blake crusher, a pair of Cornish rolls, ball pulverizer, a forty horse-power steam engine and boiler, and all of the accessories and necessary arrangements for works of this kind.

The five separate buildings of these French smelting works are constructed to treat for the present five or six hundred tons of ore monthly. The matte and furnace products of many other works that are sold in this country under difficulties, and which are shipped to the east, or to England, Germany, or anywhere in Europe, with little profit on account of high freight, will be treated as a specialty in this establishment.

The French Smelting Works at Golden will realize an important progress in Colorado, because they will also treat the ores and furnace products, heretofore possessing a limited demand on account of their impurities and refractory composition (bearing zinc, antimony, arsenic, etc.), rendering them of less value to the miners. At the head of this establishment is J. Guillardon, assisted by efficient metallurgists and workmen from France.

The ores are first crushed, sampled, and assayed. The sulphur in gold-bearing ores is got rid of by kiln or heap roasting in the open air.

Piles of ore are underlaid with wood, which is set on fire. The sulphur in the former is thus ignited and continues to burn for a month or two, or until entirely consumed. Silver ores, not containing enough sulphur to maintain combustion without the aid of other substances, are roasted in reverberatory furnaces and then smelted in the same manner as gold ores. When smelting has been carried on long enough, the furnaces are tapped and the molten lava let out onto a sand floor. This contains pits, into which the heavier part of the output naturally gravitates. This is called matte, while the worthless part, called slag, flows over the floor and is broken up and carted away as refuse. The matte is then crushed and roasted in another furnace, in order to expel what sulphur remains and to form a sulphate of silver. It is then put in vats, where hot water dissolves this sulphate. After leaching, the solution runs into wooden vats lined with copper. The latter metal liberates the silver from the solution. The silver thus precipitated is gathered at intervals, washed and pressed into cakes and melted and run into bars. After the silver has been precipitated, the solution passes into other tanks containing scrap iron, which separates the copper from the solution, and the latter flows on to waste. The separation of gold takes place in this department. The reverberatory furnaces are constructed of brick and iron, are lined with fire-clay brick, and are heated by wood, coke, or coal—the latter being used generally in the furnaces of the plains' cities. The same kind of furnaces are used in reduction works of other descriptions.

The Golden Malachite Company recently began operations under the management of Professor W. T. Sapp. Gold, silver, and copper ores are bought and treated, mainly of the grades too poor to stand the expense of smelting. The ores are roasted, and muriatic acid is manufactured from the sulphur contained in them; also blue vitriol and copperas—the copper is leached out and the residue or matter containing the precious metals is sold to the smelters. The sulphuret ores of Gilpin county are the kind especially desired and sought after for the process used here. One hundred and twenty-five tons have been handled a month from that district, and now that the daily capacity of the works has been increased to fourteen tons, the business will be larger. Much ore has come from the O. K. and National mines, near Central; from fifteen to twenty tons of copper are produced monthly, and the acid chamber turns out from four to six thousand pounds of muriatic acid daily. The prices paid for sulphuret ores containing no lead are : for ores running less than one ounce in gold, six ounces in silver, and not under six per cent. copper, $10 per ton and upwards, adding $1 per ton for every additional per cent. of copper, the ore to be delivered on board cars at Black Hawk, viz.: ore running 66-100 of an ounce in gold, 5 ounces in silver and 7 per cent. copper, $10 per ton is paid; ore running same in gold and silver, and 10 per cent. copper, $18 per ton; ores running over one ounce in gold, six ounces in silver, and six per cent. copper, and not exceeding in value over $2 per ton, $20 an ounce in gold, silver at New York quotations, and $2 for every per cent. of copper, less ten per cent. and $20 for treatment, delivered on board cars.

The first smelting was done at Golden in 1872. After some suspension of work, the Golden Smelting Company became owners of and remodeled or enlarged the original concern. The value of gold, silver, and lead, produced in 1876, was reported at over $150,000, and at $275,000 in 1877. This was the product of ores purchased from Gilpin, Clear Creek, Boulder, and from what is now Custer county. A small amount came from Park, in the latter year. The process is smelting with lead.

Last year business was much better, and in the summer and fall the capacity was enlarged to eighteen tons daily. The product of the year 1878 was $384,122. From Gilpin county ores was obtained $60,865 worth of gold and $22,936.75 worth of silver. Clear Creek sent $204,403, nearly all silver; Boulder, $48,123 in gold and silver; Park, $14,498 in silver, with a small amount of lead, and the Leadville carbonates turned out $33,896. The latter have since been coming in large quantities. The total product of the works from first to last has exceeded one million.

The great buildings in the upper portion of Golden erected for, and for a time operated as, smelting works are now occupied by the Golden ore buying and sampling agency of Messrs. Netter, Matthews & Co. Ores are also bought and shipped from Denver. This firm has dealt largely in ores from all quarters, but especially in those of Clear Creek and Custer counties. The mill of Matthews, Morris & Co., in Georgetown, sampled, purchased and shipped more ore in 1878 than any other engaged in that line of business with possibly one exception. The mill at Golden is supplied with all machinery and appliances for the conduct of a large business.

The smelting works at Argo are the successors of the Boston and Colorado Company's long established operations in the mountains. Professor N. P. Hill was the founder and has ever been the managing director of that company's smelting establishments. He began work at Black Hawk, in January, 1868, with one calciner and one smelting furnace. All around him were wrecks of preceding attempts at ore reduction, but, while encountering many difficulties in the earlier years, there has never been an interruption of work, general progress or success.

As the ore-supplying mining districts became more numerous and extensive, the furnaces and working forces were increased, and in time a corps of assistants had been secured such as is seldom met with, and whom it would almost be an impossibility to replace. The rare business and executive qualifications of the general manager have been ably seconded by those whom he has called to responsible positions, while the State has shown its appreciation of services rendered its main industry by awarding him a seat in the United States Senate.

This copper matte method of smelting, old and tried in other lands, has required many adaptations to the numerous and varied ores it has had to deal with, and as now conducted at this establishment can be termed the Colorado more appropriately than the Swansea process. When Professor Richard Pearce took charge of the metallurgical department, away back in 1873, the production of the first absolutely pure silver bullion in the West began. Before that the valuable metals had been sent from Black Hawk across the ocean to Swansea, in the form of copper matte, where they were purchased, separated, and refined. Since 1875 the gold has also been parted and refined in Colorado, and by a method of Mr. Pearce's own invention.

In 1873 branch works were started at Alma, among the Park county silver mines, and in 1876 an ore buying agency was established at Boulder. In 1877-8 the capacity of the Black Hawk works was over fifty tons of ore daily, instead of ten or twelve, as at the beginning. The working force had increased to a hundred men, the annual production of bullion from a coin value of $193,490 in 1868 to one of over two millions, and the average stock of ores on hand represented a value of three quarters of a million. Ores were coming in steadily from almost all parts of the State, and began to arrive from Montana, even, a thousand miles away. But the question of fuel was becoming a serious one, a more central and generally accessible locality was desirable, and as it was necessary to again enlarge the works it was deemed best to build entirely anew, and near the coal measures and the railway centre of the plains.

A location was selected two miles from Denver, to which the very appropriate name of Argo was applied, after the good ship in which a hero of Grecian mythology is reputed to have set sail in search of the golden fleece. The new works were so far completed in December, 1878, that several furnaces were fired up, and soon after all business, except roasting ores on hand, and sampling, purchasing and shipping, was discontinued at the old place at Black Hawk.

The works at Argo were constructed after the most approved plans which long experience and the necessities and advantages of the situation could suggest. The result is the finest and most extensive gold and silver reducing establishment in the world. This will be enlarged hereafter, but already possesses a nominal capacity for treating 120 tons of ore, or a practical capacity of 100 tons daily from one year's end to another, with the following enormous plant: 30 great kilns for roasting and desulphurizing the ore, and requiring wood for fuel; 10 ore calciners or roasting furnaces; 8 ore smelting furnaces; 8 calcining furnaces in the refining department; and five melting furnaces; together with engines and other necessary machinery. Two hundred men are employed, more than a quarter of a million in bullion is turned out monthly, and one hundred tons of Cañon and El Moro coal are consumed daily, beside a small quantity of wood. The stock of ores carried on hand exceeds $1,000,000 in value. Ore and coal trains pass over side tracks from the adjacent Colorado Central railway into the yard and receptacles prepared for them.

In the great ore building, 450 feet long by 120 wide, are scales for weighing loaded and empty cars, steam engines for propelling the ore-crushing and sampling machinery, and ten calciners—each roasting 9,600 pounds of ore every twenty-four hours. Adjoining are thirty roasting kilns, and a smoke-stack 100 feet high, that carries off the sulphurous fumes of both calciners and kilns. The products of all the different furnace buildings are conveyed from one to another in cars over connecting railways.

THE BOSTON AND COLORADO SMELTING WORKS AT ARGO.

In another building nearly 300 feet long and directly opposite
are eight furnaces that smelt 100 tons of roasted ores into five of
matte every twenty-four hours, while the refuse remains in
what is called slag. After the slag has been skimmed off of the
matte, the latter is transferred to another massive building, pulverized by crushers and rollers and roasted in the calciners of the refin-

A TON OF PURE SILVER.

ing department—eight
in number. A line of
vats is the next recep-
tacle, into which contin-
uous streams of hot
water are conveyed by
pipes. This hot water
holds the silver in solu-
tion, and in a series of
tanks below, the silver is
precipitated or retained
on lines of standing cop-
per plates from which it
is removed every week.
The bright, pure flaky
metal is secured in im-
mense crucibles, and is
shoveled into buckets
and conveyed to the
melting furnaces, five in
number. There it is
melted into solid bars
of an average weight of
about 1,700 ounces,
valued at $1,900 more or less. The copper and gold are saved
separately from the silver, the copper being secured on scrap iron.
The gold bricks vary in value from $15,000 to $27,000 each. Centrally located is the handsome structure used as the headquarters and
offices of managers Hill and Wolcott.

All of the buildings are of cut stone, covered with roofs of corru-
gated iron, and outside of the works are buildings for the employees
and their families. This village has three hundred people, with a
school and church,

The production of the works for four years in the various metals, and by counties, was as follows:

1875.

COUNTIES.	Gold.	Silver.	Copper.	Total.
Gilpin	$357,000	$94,000	$51,000	$502,000
Clear Creek	4,000	438,000	.....	442,000
Park	41,000	618,000	19,000	678,000
Boulder	113,900	74,000	.....	187,000
Fremont.............	......	126,000	.....	126,000
Gold and Silver, San Juan and elsewhere	......	......	.....	12,000
Totals	$515,000	$1,350,000	$70,000	$1,947,000

1876.

COUNTIES.	Gold.	Silver.	Copper.	Total.
Gilpin................	$594,000	$132,000	$78,000	$804,500
Clear Creek	5,400	529,000	.....	534,400
Park	39,000	458,000	14,000	511,000
Boulder	86,000	49,000	......	135,000
Fremont	......	102,000	......	102,000
Other Sources.........	......	......	......	11,000
Totals...	$724,400	$1,270,000	$92,500	$2,097,000

1877.

COUNTIES.	Gold.	Silver.	Copper.	Total.
Gilpin................	$591,500	$137,500	$86,000	$815,000
Clear Creek	6,500	707,000	3,000	716,500
Park	38,000	221,500	8,000	268,000
Boulder	169,000	90,500	.....	259,500
Custer................	14,500	76,500	.. ..	91,000
Other Sources........	.....	......	... ..	4,000
Totals...	$819,500	$1,233,000	$97,500	$2,154,000

1878.

COUNTIES.	Gold.	Silver.	Copper.	Total.
Gilpin	$608,500	$181,000	$79,000	$868,500
Clear Creek	4,500	559,500	2,000	566,000
Boulder	178,000	73,000	......	251,000
Park	16,500	114,000	4,000	134,500
Custer.............. ..	83,000	52,500	......	135,500
Montana Territory	.....	254,000	36,000	290,000
Other Sources.........	3,500	10,000	......	13,500
Totals.............	$894,000	$1,244,000	$121,000	$2,259,000

The currency value of the company's bullion product previous to 1879 was as follows:

1868	$270,886	1875	$1,947,000
1869	489,875	1876	2,097,000
1870	652,329	1877	2,154,000
1871	848,571	1878	2,259,000
1872	999,954		
1873	1,210,670	Total	$14,568,162
1874	1,638,877		

This company now does its smelting entirely at Argo. It has ore-buying agencies with sampling mills at Boulder, Black Hawk, and Alma, and receives ore from nearly every mining district in Colorado. Now that the capacity is about double what it was at Black Hawk, it is likely that the bullion product will show a proportionate increase.

CHAPTER IV.

COLORADO'S MINING PRODUCT FROM THE EARLY DAYS TO THE PRESENT
TIME—A MASS OF STATISTICS—THE YIELD OF GOLD, SILVER, LEAD,
AND COPPER—EIGHTY MILLIONS, AND TWENTY MORE COMING IN
SEVENTY-NINE—TONS OF GOLD AND SILVER.

No definite record was kept of Colorado's mining product prior
to 1868, and the estimates of miners and bullion shippers alone
remain to base a statement of the yield of the earlier years on.
Neither the mints nor express companies handled anywhere near all
of the gold produced in those days. A published statement of
Colorado's output has appeared in print once or twice in recent
times, but it is wide of the mark. The amounts given for the early
placer mining times are too small, and those for the nine years up
to 1872 are too large.

The excess from 1863 to 1869 was evidently as much as six
millions, and for the three years succeeding the latter date at least
three millions. The figures given for the latter period were like
those furnished by Colorado men to Professor R. W. Raymond for
his annual reports. The yields for both periods were originally
computed on a currency basis, when gold ranged from $1.30 to
$2.50, and after the lapse of years were rated as coin values. The
express agents of Wells, Fargo & Co. always furnished their figures
on a currency basis, and so did all Colorado bankers, smelters, mill
men and miners, unless the words "coin value" were given. The
figures in this book represent coin values unless otherwise stated.

The placers and gulches of Lake, Summit, Park, and Gilpin
counties yielded largely for several summers, beginning with that
of 1860, and when they were on the decline, the lode mines, mainly
in Gilpin county, came to the front. These were doing well in
1862, and still better in 1863-4. Lodes and placers gave a varying
yield, however, from 1860 to 1865. Besides the above named
counties, both classes of mining were prosecuted in Clear Creek and
Boulder. The product of the territory dropped to low figures in
1866, and there was no heavy increase from that time until the

silver mines began to be extensively worked in 1870. What gain there was should be credited to the revival of lode mining in Gilpin county in 1868–9, and in a less degree to the then new discoveries in Lake.

The custom of counting the yield of mill gold in ounces may have been caused or strengthened by the continual variations between the values of the gold and greenback dollar. Such variations are shown in the price of silver, whose valuation per ounce should be $1.29, instead of $1.10, or $1.13. The reduction in the price of silver bullion has been a source of much loss to silver miners. The silver product of Colorado in 1878 would have had a valuation nearly one million larger, had silver been held at the same rates as prevailed prior to 1876. As has been stated elsewhere, all figures given in this book represent coin values unless otherwise stated. The reduction of numberless items and tables from currency to coin was a job of enormous proportions, but has been perfected.

The reader can rest assured that outside of the estimates for the earlier years, the figures of the Colorado gold and silver yield are in the aggregate correct and reliable. The tables of the production of the entire State, and of most of the counties for several years past, are the only accurate ones ever published, having been revised from the author's widely copied newspaper reports and statements. The best attainable information indicates the following yield of Colorado mines down to 1870—all gold, excepting about $330,000 in silver, and perhaps $40,000 in copper.

YEAR.	COIN VALUE.	YEAR.	COIN VALUE.
1859	$500,000	1865	$2,525,000
1860	3,250,000	1866	1,575,000
1861	3,250,000	1867	1,750,000
1862	3,400,000	1868	2,000,706
1863	3,400,000	1869	2,482,375
1864	3,350,000		

The following tabulated statement shows Colorado's production of the four valuable metals and the total yield prior to 1879:

COLORADO'S MINING PRODUCT PRIOR TO 1879.

(*Coin Value.*)

YEAR.	GOLD.	SILVER.	COPPER.	LEAD.	TOTAL.
Previous to 1870	$27,213,081 00	$330,000 00	$40,000 00	....	$27,583,081 00
1870	2,000,000 00	650,000 00	20,000 00	....	2,670,000 00
1871	2,000,000 00	1,029,046 34	30,000 00	....	3,059,046 34
1872	1,725,000 00	2,015,000 00	45,000 00	$5,000 00	3,790,000 00
1873	1,750,000 00	2,185,000 00	65,000 00	28,000 00	4,028,000 00
1874	2,002,487 00	3,096,023 00	90,197 00	73,676 00	5,262,383 00
1875	2,161,475 02	3,122,912 00	90,000 00	60,000 00	5,434,387 02
1876	2,726,315 82	3,315,592 00	70,000 00	80,000 00	6,191,907 82
1877	3,148,707 56	3,726,379 33	93,796 64	247,400 00	7,216,283 53
1878	3,490,384 36	6,341,807 81	89,000 00	636,924 73	10,558,116 90
Total	$48,217,450 76	$25,811,760 48	$632,993 64	$1,131,000 73	$75,793,205 61

Nearly 80 tons of pure gold, 770 tons of pure silver, 2,110 tons of copper, and 16,150 tons of lead.

Mining in the mountains of Colorado dates back nearly twenty years prior to January, 1879. The figures of her bullion yield previous to 1868 are based on estimates of miners, express shippers, and others, as no reliable data has been published. Coin or gold, instead of currency values, are considered. This is done in order that the proper comparisons may readily be made between figures of the present specie payment period and those of the greenback era. Statements of the bullion yield of nearly all western states and territories have heretofore been made on a currency basis. This gives a wrong impression among those who pay little attention to such subjects. The actual difference between coin and currency may have been ten per cent. one year and sixty another.

The first half of 1879 may not bring the grand total up to more than $83,000,000, but the last half is very likely to run it up to a round $100,000,000.

From the foregoing it will be seen that in a little over four years, up to 1864, the yield of gold was $13,800,000. This embraced the lively times of placer and gulch mining, and of lode mining by the pioneers and individual miners.

From 1864 to 1870, inclusive, a period of seven years, the yield was $16,121,435. This was when the companies organized at the East did most of the mining. During the year 1864 the Colorado miners were selling out and quitting work, and the companies were beginning. In 1868–70 there was a great deal of mining done by Colorado miners, and the silver districts were beginning to produce. Up to 1871 the silver yield was about $1,000,000 and that of copper $80,000. Most of this came out in 1869–70. From that time silver mining made rapid strides, and from the beginning of 1872 has given a larger product than gold mining.

The total yield of Colorado from the beginning of 1871 to 1879, a period of eight years, was $45,556,124.57. Nearly all of this was the result of individual work by Colorado miners. Eighteen hundred and seventy-eight gave $10,558,116.90 of this amount, and the last three years $23,915,306. The year 1879 may see as large an output as the preceding three years, and again may be considerably under twenty millions. Below are comparative statements of the yield of the leading mining counties by years, from 1870 to 1878, inclusive:

COLORADO MINING PRODUCT BY COUNTIES—
1870-'71-'72-'73.

NAMES.	1870.	1871.	1872.	1873.
Gilpin	$1,552,000 00	$1,400,000 00	$1,389,289 00	$1,340,502 00
Clear Creek........	481,354 08	869,046 34	1,503,291 00	1,204,761 00
Lake...............	125,000 00	100,000 00	133,000 00	230,000 00
Park...............	60,000 00	100,000 00	250,000 00	459,000 00
Boulder...........	130,000 00	250,000 00	346,540 00	390,000 00
Summit...........	150,000 00	66,000 00	125,000 00	106,000 00
Other Products	171,645 92	274,000 00	50,000 00	297,737 00
Total of Colorado..	$2,670,645 92	$3,059.046 34	$3,790,000 00	$4,028,000 00

COLORADO MINING PRODUCT BY COUNTIES, 1874-'75-'76.

COUNTIES.	1874.	1875.	1876.
Clear Creek.......................	$2,203,947,00	$1,780,054 31	$1,982,548 28
Gilpin	1,531,863 00	1,520,677 13	2,105,544 78
Park..............................	596,392 00	716,258 62	550,044 84
Boulder........	539,870 00	605,000 00	547,085 20
Lake	223,503 00	104,258 62	90,900 00
Summit...........................	126,108 00	122,413 78	350,000 00
Fremont......;....................	....	294,827 58	251,121 06
The San Juan Region.............	... .	90,517 24	244,663 66
Other sources and unaccounted for	40,620 00	200,380 55	70,000 00
Totals...............	$5,362,383 00	$5,434,387 02	$6,191,907 82

COLORADO MINING PRODUCT FOR 1877.

COUNTY.	Tons of ore treated or exported.	GOLD.	SILVER.	LEAD.	COPPER.	TOTALS.
Gilpin	147,000	$1,963,485 07	$161,255 38	$1,000 00	$82,256 64	$2,208,037 09
Clear Creek	19,503	96,500 00	1,984,077 91	123,000 00	3,000 00	2,306,577 91
Park	4,040	108,000 00	489,959 32	10,000 00	8,500 00	616,459 32
Boulder	10,000	356,722 49	234,602 86	2,000 00	......	598,325 35
Lake	3,700	55,000 00	423,930 00	76,400 00	......	555,330 30
Custer	2,000	196,000 00	155,081 34	....	......	354,081 34
Summit	500	150,000 00	40,000 00	....	......	190,000 00
The San Juan Region	9,500	105,000 00	237,472 52	35,000 00	......	377,472 52
Other sources	......	118,000 00	....	....	......	118,000 00
Totals	200,258	$3,148,707 56	$3,726,379 33	$247,400 00	$93,796 64	$7,216,283 53

The coal product was about 160,000 tons, worth $600,000.

COLORADO MINING PRODUCT FOR 1878.

COUNTIES.	Tons of ore treated or exported.	GOLD.	SILVER.	LEAD.	COPPER.	TOTALS.
Lake.............	21,746	$117,946 00	$2,591,054 71	$443,924 73	....	$3,152,925 44
Clear Creek...	22,000	134,000 00	2,275,105 85	98,000 00	$4,000 00	2,511,105 85
Gilpin........	157,000	1,574,864 36	225,936 75	1,000 00	79,000 00	2,280,901 11
Boulder.........	11,500	445,500 00	223,623 50	....	....	679,123 50
Park........	4,500	78,200 00	328,498 00	4,000 00	6,000 00	426,698 00
Custer.........	4,000	285,000 00	167,500 00	....	....	452,500 00
Summit........	1,500	165,774 00	125,000 00	30,000 00	....	320,774 00
The San Juan Region....	15,000	89,000 00	385,089 00	60,000 00	....	534,089 00
Elsewhere.........	....	200,000 00	....	.	....	200,000 00
Totals........	227,246	$3,490,384 36	$6,341,807 81	$636,924 73	$89,000 00	$10,578,116 90

The coal product of 1878 was 200,630 tons, worth about $800,000.

In 1878, the mines of Colorado turned out a little over 5¾ tons of pure gold, 193¾ tons of pure silver, 5,930 tons of copper, and 9,989 tons of lead.

No definite record of the placers, creeks, and gulches of Colorado was kept when their yield was heaviest. It is believed that their total yield up to 1879 exceeded $20,500,000 in gold dust. Taking that sum as a correct estimate and the yield of the placers would compare with that of gold lode veins up to 1879, as follows:

Yield of gold from lode mining.................. $27,717,450 76
Yield of gold from placers...................... 20,500,000 00

Total gold........................ $48,217,450 76

The yield of placer mining, as compared with that of both gold and silver mining, up to 1879, figured on the same basis, would be as follows :

Gold, silver, etc., from lode veins................. $55,293,205 61
Gold from placers, as given above............... 20,500,000 00

Total of silver and gold............. $75,793,000 00

The yield of the placers up to 1865 is estimated at $13,500,000, and from the beginning of that year to 1879, at $7,000,000. The present placer yield does not by any means form so large a proportion of the total as it once did. In 1860 and 1861 it comprised more than half of Colorado's product, and lately only about five per cent. of it. This kind of mining was at its lowest ebb in 1872, when the production was but little over $200,000. Since then it has increased so as to maintain about the same per cent. of the State's yield year after year. This gain is due to operations of great extent that have been inaugurated in many counties. It is not impossible that the placer yield of 1879 may reach three quarters of a million. Placer and gulch mining outside of some limited underground work cannot be carried on in Colorado in the winter. The available season for work commences some time in May and continues until late in October or early in November. The more elevated the locality the shorter is the season. This limited time for operations and the delay in starting in anew every spring is one of the causes of Colorado's small placer yield as compared with California. The alluvial or placer deposits are small however compared with those of the latter state. Yet many of them cannot well be exhausted in one or more generations.

CHAPTER V.

THE MINES OF BOULDER COUNTY—THE GOLD, SILVER, TELLURIDE,
AND COAL BELTS—REVIEW OF THE MOUNTAIN MINING DISTRICTS
—BRIEF NARRATIVE OF OPERATIONS—THE YIELD OF THE
PRECIOUS METALS FROM 1859 TO 1879—-DETAILED STATEMENTS
OF PRODUCTION—MINES, MILLS, AND SMELTERS.

Boulder county embraces a combination of mountain, valley, and
plain that reverts in the highest measure to the advantage of its
people. Its mineral deposits are of great extent and variety, and its
agricultural sections are extremely fertile, and in a high state of cultivation. Flourishing towns and beautiful farms dot its surface, and
mines and mills are profitably operated all over the mountain
sections, from the sunny plains at Boulder back to the snow-barren
summits of the snowy range. On the plains are extensive coal
measures, which will be referred to more in detail in another place.
The farming sections have already been described. The mines and
the mining industry will be the subject matter of the few succeeding
pages.

The mineral deposits of Boulder are very extensive, and embrace
a wonderful variety. First there are alluvial deposits in creeks and
gulches, but these are of limited extent and mainly worked out.
The gold and silver lode veins, and the coal measures are the main
source of wealth. The former are located on the mountains and the
latter on the plains.

The lode veins of Boulder county may be classed under three
heads—silver, gold, and telluride; the latter carrying both
metals. They are generally of the kind referred to as "true
fissures," very many of them having well-defined walls and seemingly unending depth. They commonly occur either in gneiss or
granite rock, or between the two. There are exceptions, however,
both regarding formation, regularity, and continuity. There is a

multitude of them, good, bad, and indifferent. Some thousands of locations have been recorded, and the number worked with a profit is large.

The alluvial gold deposits of the gulches were operated by the pioneers, and more or less every summer since. Some are abandoned, however. Some large gold-bearing lodes were discovered in 1859–60, and for several years quartz mills were turning out a great deal of bullion. After considerable depth was attained, more difficulty was experienced in reducing the ores and extracting the gold than is usual with free gold ores of other counties. This caused companies or individual owners to stop work. Process mills also brought disaster in certain localities. Long before the discovery of silver at Caribou, mining affairs were at a low ebb, although work was never entirely suspended in Ward district.

The productive character of the silver mines at Caribou turned attention once more to the entire section, and prospecters, and miners who had not found anything valuable near the Boulder creeks, began to move out over the hills to the northward. While looking for gold and silver bearing veins, they often encountered mineral of a strange and peculiar appearance, which was passed over as worthless. After a while Professor J. Alden Smith and others began to test this mineral, and found it to be of the telluride species, carrying gold in remarkably large quantities.

Tellurium is a metal that has been discovered in very few places, and Colorado miners were as little acquainted therewith as they had been with silver a few years before. Its existence in Colorado was first known in 1873, in the Red Cloud mine on Gold Hill. Ores from this vein could not be made to produce well in the stamp mills, although assays demonstrated the presence of gold in large quantities.

After their true character was ascertained, the owners commenced shipping ore to the smelters, large returns were obtained and men began to flock in to the district and to prospect for tellurides. Many discoveries were made in the succeeding two or three years, and the production and rich pay streaks of the Cold Spring, Red Cloud, American, Slide, Keystone, Magnolia, John Jay, Melvina and other veins created more excitement than did the Columbia, Horsfal and Hoosier gold lodes a dozen years before, or the Caribou silver finds of more recent times.

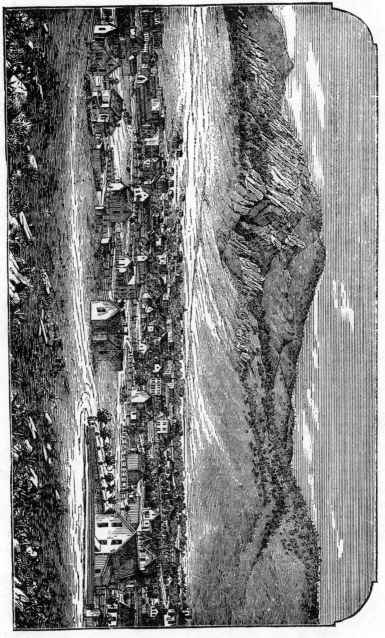

BOULDER.

These mines built up the towns of Sunshine, Salina, Providence, Ballarat and Magnolia, and caused a return of population to Gold Hill and James Creek. While many of these discoveries are no longer worked, some valuable gold veins have been found and operations have been resumed on some of the long idle mines that paid so well in the early days. Between the gold, silver, and telluride belts the mining portion of Boulder county is enabled to show a steady development and a gain in production.

Several mines of Boulder county yielded large amounts of gold from 1859 to 1865, inclusive. The Columbia lode, in Ward district, paid largely for a time, especially those parts since known as the Ni Wot and Baxter properties. The Horsfal mine on Gold Hill was also very productive, as was the Hoosier and some others. The yield of gold for the entire county, up to 1870, may be safely set down at $950,000. The gold yield had been decreasing for some time when the Caribou silver mines began to be developed. In four years, 1870–4 inclusive, before the telluride mines began to be generally worked, Caribou district had probably yielded nearly $700,000 in silver, and all other districts $270,000 in gold. From that time the gold product was much larger. The total yield of Boulder county up to January 1, 1879, was not far from what appears in the following table:

Prior to 1870........	$950,000	1874.....	$536,582 00
1870................	130,000	1875..............	605,000 00
1871................	250,000	1876..............	547,085 20
1872................	346,540	1877...............	593,325 35
1873................	390,000	1878..............	679,123 50

Total for twenty years, $5,027,656.05, of which $3,082,931 was gold and about $1,944,000 silver. The present yield indicates a product of $800,000 in 1879.

The product of 1875 embraced $266,000 in silver from Caribou district, probably about $70,000 from the few gold lodes and from the gulches, and $269,000 from the telluride veins, whose product was mainly gold. The total product may be set down as $305,000 in gold, and $300,000 in silver.

In 1876 the silver product of Caribou was only about $80,000, and of the county possibly $120,000, leaving $427,085.20 as the gold product, mainly from telluride camps.

The mining product of the county for the years 1877 and 1878 was as follows :

1877.		1878.	
Gold.............	$356,722 49	Gold..............	$454,123 50
Silver............	234,602 86	Silver.............	223,000 00
Lead.............	2,000 00	Lead..............	2,000 00
Total........	$593,325 35	Total........	$679,123 50

Last year Boyd and other smelters purchased about $25,000 worth of Lake and Clear Creek county ores and Gilpin stamp mill tailings for fluxing purposes. That amount is deducted from the export and output of Boulder, which was actually $704,123.50.

The yield of 1877 passed through the following mills, smelters, and avenues :

	Tons of Ore.	Value.
Silver bullion—New Jersey, at Caribou.........	600	$100,000
Gold bullion—Gulch and stamp mill gold.......	3,000	60,000
Gold and silver bullion at Boyd's smelting works, Boulder...............................	1,800	150,000
Ores smelted at B. and C. works at Black Hawk.	1,800	248,325
Ores smelted at Golden smelting works.........	200	20,000
Ores shipped to West Denver works............	75	5,000
Other shippers and consumers, and crude ore concentrated.................................	50	10,000
Total tons and value.................	8,125	$593,325

The concentrating mills reduced the bulk of some 3,500 tons of low grade ore down to one-third of that amount, and then sold to the smelters, as appears in the above figures.

The gold and silver mining product of 1878 passed through various channels, in amounts as follows:

Gold and silver bullion from Boyd, Hunt. etc.........$120,000 00
Silver bullion from Caribou......................... 130,000 00
Silver bullion from Washington Avenue mill......... 15,000 00
Gold dust and mill retort........................... 65,000 00
Gold taken out of county outside of banks and express, 25,000 00
Ore sent to Boston and Colorado Works at Black Hawk, 251,000 00
Ore sent to Golden Smelting Co..................... 48,123 50
Ore sent to Omaha, St. Louis, and elsewhere.......... 50,000 00

Deduct from above $25,000 due ore of other counties.

The ore product of 1878 was not far from 11,500 tons, of which all but 1,500 were handled in the county. About 1,000 of the first amount were concentrated into less than two or three hundred tons, and then mainly shipped, so that they eventually appear in the second or export figures. The quartz mills treated about 4,000 tons of ore, yielding an average of about $15 per ton. The silver ores exceeded 2,500 tons, and were mostly treated at the Caribou mill, with an average of $66 per ton. Others went to Boulder, Black Hawk, and Golden, and smelted from $80 to $200 per ton, and occasionally $200 to $600 and more. The telluride mines are supposed to have yielded nearly 3,500 tons. Most assorted ores gave from $100 to $400. Crude ores, before concentrating, contained only from $15 to $50. The tellurides went to Boulder, Golden, Black Hawk, and Argo. The last two places represent the Boston & Colorado Smelting Company, whose purchases yielded $74,782 in gold and $42,608 in silver in 1876, about $160,952 in gold and $86,190 in silver in 1877, and $178,000 in gold and $73,000 in silver in 1878.

The mines that appear to take the lead at present are the Caribou, Native Silver, Seven-Thirty and some others at Caribou, the Melvina Slide, and Smuggler in the telluride belt, and the Golden Age gold mine. The Cold Spring, Keystone, Mountain Lion, Last Chance, and some other telluride mines are reported to be producing largely again. Some of the gold lodes of Ward district, such as the Columbia, Celestial, Utica, Stoughton, and others, are beginning to pay once more. There is more than usual activity in Caribou, Ward, Gold Hill, and Central districts. The last embraces the Left Hand, James Creek, and Ballarat sections. Magnolia is also reviving. There has been a steady improvement nearly all over the county for the past twelve months.

Many quartz mills, smelting and reduction works, have been in operation in Boulder county since mining began. The varied and novel character of some of the ores, and the refractory nature of others, offered a fruitful field for experiments, and for the trial of various processes, resulting in failure and loss. The old stamp mill methods, melting with lead riches and cupeling, and chlorodizing and amalgamating are the processes by which the ores are handled at present. The frue vanner concentrating tables had a big run two years ago, and some twenty or more were in use, but most of them are now idle or discarded. Other concentrating mills are at work. The smelting and reduction works of Boulder county that are at work are stated below.

Name.	Location.	Character or Process.	Reducing Capacity in Tons.	Plant.
Caribou Cons. Company...	Nederland.	Stamping, chlorodizing roasting and amalgamating......	15	15 stamps, 4 cylinders, and 10 pans, etc.
J. H. Boyd.....	Boulder....	Smelting with lead and cupeling............	8 to 12	Crushers, 10 stamps, reverberatory and smelting furnaces, and cupel furnace.
Hunt, Barber & Co.........	Orodelfan..	Smelting with lead and cupeling............	4 to 8	Crushers, reverberatory, waterjacket and blast furnaces, and cupel furnace.
Pomeroy.......	Ward......	Stamping, roasting and amalgamation, and concentration..	5 to 8	Stamps, 2 cylinders, 3 pans and concentrating tables.
Atchison Co....	Salina.....	Concentration, smelting, and amalgamation.	4 to 6	Stamps, furnaces, etc.
Washington Avenue	Sugar Loaf District..	Conc., chlor., roasting, and leaching with copper; dry concentration..	8 to 10	10 stamps, cylinders, leaching tubs and vats, and concentrating machinery.

The raw amalgamation stamp mills, for treating the low grade gold ores and quartz, have a total crushing capacity of 130 tons daily, but only about half of them are usually at work. They are as follows:

Name.	Location.	Character.	Calibre.
Baxter..............	Ward District.......	Raw amal..........	20 Stamps.
Ni Wot.............	" "	" "	50 "
Humboldt...........	" "	" "	10 "
Pomeroy............	" "	" "	15 "
Brainard............	Central "	" "	10 "
Golden Age.........	" "	" "	25 "
Corning Tunnel.....	" "	" "	15 "
Hetzer..............	Nederland District..	" "	15 "
First National......	" " ..	" "	25 "

Total, 9 mills and 185 stamps.   There is also a small quartz mill in Sugar Loaf district.

The concentrating mills (mainly for telluride ores) now at work are the Melvina or Everitt mill at Salina, and the Black Cloud mill, near that point and Gold Hill.   The Van Fleet mill at the Smuggler mine is also run occasionally.   Pomeroy has concentrating tables in his mill at Ward, and the Washington Avenue mill operates the dry concentration process.

Boyd, and Hunt Barber & Co. treat gold, silver, and telluride ores. Their bullion is mixed gold and silver, in which the former largely predominates.   The Boston & Colorado Smelting Company have a sampling mill and ore-buying agency at Boulder.   This handles large quantities of ore, shipping to Argo.

There are two idle silver mills in the Caribou district.   One of these belongs to the owners of the No Name and Sherman mines. It was operated only in portions of 1875-6.   The other was built at Caribou in 1876 and is called the New Jersey mill.   This turned out considerably more than one hundred thousand dollars in 1877-8; but has not been at work for ten months.   It contains ten stamps, roasting cylinders, vats and tubs for copper leaching.

CHAPTER VI.

BOULDER COUNTY MINES—THE SILVER BELT ON THE HEADWATERS
OF THE BOULDERS—STORY OF A GREAT SILVER MINE—THE
CARIBOU, ITS RECORD, YIELD, AND PRESENT CONDITION—HARD
MONEY, AND PLENTY OF IT—THE NATIVE SILVER, SEVEN-
THIRTY, NO NAME, IDAHO AND OTHER LODES OF THE CARIBOU
DISTRICT.

Up to 1870 the forest-clad hills up towards timber-line and the
headwaters of the Boulder creeks had seldom been visited. While
hunting for deer, Samuel Conger had located a gold lode there away
back in 1864, but never did much work on it. Years after he saw
some Nevada silver ore, and was struck with its similarity to rock he
had stumbled over in his lonely hunting excursions among the pines
near Arapahoe Peak. He induced some Gilpin county men to ac-
company him on a prospecting trip, and the result was the discovery
of silver. Conger struck the outcroppings of a vein which he called
the Poor Man, and William Martin and George Lytle found a lode
just above, which they named the Caribou. This was on the last
day of summer, 1869.

An assay of the " blossom rock," made at Central, caused them to
return with pick and shovel, and blaze a trail to their new camp.
Supplies were furnished by three ranchmen named Mishler, McCam-
mon, and Pickel, who were partners in the discoveries. The others
carried these winter supplies in on their backs, and over the deep
snows. Conger traded his interest in the Caribou in such a way as
to become the sole owner of the Poor Man. Before winter came on,
one load of ore was sold for good figures to the smelters.

Martin and Lytle built a cabin on the spot where the town of
Caribou now stands, and kept at work on the mine whenever the
weather would permit. The locality was close to the snowy range,
and ten thousand feet above sea-level, and storms and snows were of
frequent occurrence. When summer came the owners constructed a
wagon-road, and began to break ore and team it to Prof. Hill, at
Black Hawk, twenty miles distant.

Reports of the value and quantity of the ore soon became noised abroad, and a stampede ensued for the new district. Many lodes were found that season, some of which paid handsomely, and a town sprang up in the adjacent valley, which, after the big vein, was called Caribou. Among other mines that sold ore in 1870, were the Idaho, Boulder County, Trojan, No Name, Sherman, Spencer, Sovereign People, Poor Man, and Seven-Thirty. The entire tract of country was called Grand Island Mining District.

In the fall of 1870, A. D. Breed, of Cincinnati, purchased the western half of the Caribou lode for $50,000, and constructed a road to and began the erection of a mill at what is now called Nederland. Up to January, 1871, the main shaft had reached a depth of 200 feet, and $70,000 was said to have been obtained from sales of ore. Breed completed his great silver mill late in 1871, and by October 1, 1872, had mined 3,650¾ tons of ore. The discoverers also made money on the eastern half of the lode.

In the spring of 1873 the Mining Company Nederland was formed in Holland, and purchased the Caribou mine and mill property at the nominal figure of $3,000,000, although the actual cash payment was but a little more than half that sum. The Holland organization encountered trouble from the start. It is said that Breed stripped the mine of much of its rich ore after the examination and before the property was turned over. Some of the Company agents were of no benefit, and contentions, mismanagement, and debts caused a cessation of work at the close of 1875, and the disposal of the mine at sheriff's sale, to Jerome B. Chaffee, in October of the succeeding year. During 1873-'4-'5, the mine had yielded largely, and if properly conducted would have paid handsomely. From the date of discovery to the time when the company closed down, the yield was not far from $750,000, of which sum $130,000 came from 1,800 tons of ore in 1874, and $210,703 from 3,819 tons of ore in 1875. Tribute workers are said to have taken out about $25,000 during the spring and summer of 1876. The mine was then 470 feet deep, and over 3,250 square fathoms of ground had been broken or excavated.

Since Mr. Chaffee and associates acquired the property, they have recovered the mine from the bad condition in which it had been left, and have steadily pursued the policy of development until the ore reserves are of immense extent. Although the work is almost entirely confined to sinking and drifting, the product and profits are now rarely equaled. Eben Smith, who has operated important mines nearly all over the State, has been the superintendent since the purchase in 1876. The results are a mine and mill in splendid condition and working order, and the beginning of the payment of regular dividends, with no probability of stoppage.

Where work has been confined to development without drawing on the ore reserves, the output of a mine does not by any means show what it is capable of doing when production is "forced." Since entering the great ore bodies of the present lower workings, however, the returns have been very creditable. In sinking and drifting $26,449.80 were received for ore sold up to October 1st, 1877, and $83,507,31 for the year succeeding. The actual yield of this ore, for which $109,957.11 was paid, may have exceeded $150,000. The mill was started up in February, 1878. For a year ten stamps and three cylinders were kept at work, on less than half the force formerly employed. Since March, the increased production of the mine has caused the mill to be run to its full capacity. The product was 13,034 ounces of silver in November, 17,190 in December, and over 92,000 for the four succeeding months. This silver, not being refined at the mill, is worth about one dollar per ounce. Here is a yield of $122,000 in five months. The mine yielded $27,000 in May, and about $25,000 in June, and the entire monthly expenses are reported at less than $9,000. Total yield of mine to July, 1879, about $1,100,000.

The superintendent is confident of being able to continue for years to mine fifteen tons of ore per day, or over four hundred per month —the full capacity of the mill—without exhausting or even reducing the reserves, and to pay from ten to fifteen thousand dollars in dividends every month. The average yield of Caribou ore at the mill, just as it came from the mine, has been $66 per ton. Assorted lots of from one to seven tons each, sold at the Boston & Colorado smelting works, gave from 235 to 666 ounces per ton. Thirty-nine tons sold at near the same dates averaged over 300 ounces. Pieces of ore are found every day that will assay among the thousands.

The Caribou pay vein varies in width from two to eight feet. It is remarkable for its great size and comparative uniformity of value one month with another. It pitches toward the north, and is the

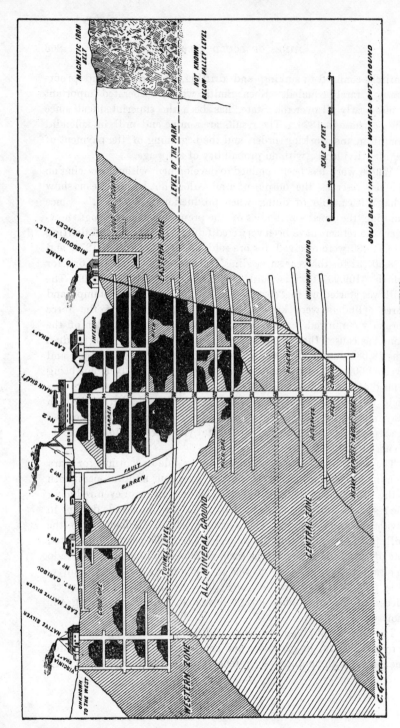

CARIBOU MINE—LONGITUDINAL SECTION.

great mother vein of the hill. The course and direction of this and neighboring veins are such that the Caribou will be found to absorb several of them before much greater depth is attained. In fact several have already merged into this great ore channel, as branches of a tree connect with the parent trunk. Other feeders and blind lodes have been discovered, by means of cross cuts driven north and south, all pitching in the same direction. The result of the union of two or more veins is to increase the quantity and quality of the ore. Late developments go to show that the Caribou vein is richer at great depths than near the surface. The best ore ever mined there was raised within the past few months in solid blocks, ten or twelve inches long and wide.

About sixty men are employed in the mine. Most of them are engaged on contract or on tribute work; others receive $2.50 per day for their labor. The cost of drifting or running levels by hand-drilling varies from $12 to $18 per foot, according to hardness of ground and size of vein, and eight dollars is the lowest price ever paid for drifting. Where machine drills are used, the cost is thirty three per cent. less. The main shaft is sunk with the aid of the latter at $40 per foot; with hand-drills the cost was $60. This shaft is five feet wide by fourteen long inside of timbers; has a double hoisting copartment or bucket-ways, and will be 810 feet deep as soon as the present "lift" is sunk. A duplex Wood patent air-compressor, capable of running four machine drills, that strike from 500 to 700 blows per minute, is used. In rock of the unusual hardness of that of Caribou Hill the amount of time and money saved by this system of rock-drilling is strikingly apparent. It is claimed that twice as much ground can be broken in a given time by using these machine drills as by hand-drilling.

As sinking and drifting are five times as costly in this mine as stoping is, expenses will be vastly reduced when breaking down the ore reserves. Mining costs but $9.15 per ton, according to past experience. Ore is hauled to the mill at a contract price of $2 per ton. Milling expenses, including all outlays for labor, fuel, salt, chemicals, etc., as per monthly statements, are only $8 per ton. This makes a total cost of $19.15, or say $20 per ton. It takes a big vein and favorable ore to admit of such small figures. The average yield of the fifteen tons of ore mined and milled daily has been $66. Allowing a return of $60, and the per cent. of profits on

12

the gross yield is over sixty-six per cent., or at the rate of $16,000 per month. As the ore has recently been getting richer, the yield will be even better than this.

The developments of the Caribou mine comprise seven shafts one hundred feet apart, with a total of 2,200 feet, and thirteen levels, connecting the main shafts, of a combined length of over 5,000 feet. tunnel 700 feet long intersects the mine from the north at a depth of 300 feet. The main shaft is reported to have reached a depth of 810 feet with a newly started level within ten feet of the bottom. This shows that the mine has been deepened 340 feet in a little over two years.

The Caribou main shaft is covered by a structure of great size, containing steam hoisting machinery of the most powerful character. The total length, including both hoisting and engine departments, is 180 feet. The former encloses two shafts, and contains blacksmith and tool shops, air compressors, assorting floor, tramways, cars, office, etc. In the latter, are an eighty-horse power steam-engine, two tubular boilers of one hundred-horse power, operating a hoisting gear of four drums of five feet diameter, each of independent action and capable of storing 3,000 feet of two-inch rope. Steam is also furnished for a new twelve-inch cylinder, four-inch water plunger Knowles pump of double action, located in the mine and draining the same. There are also large buildings and machinery over shafts two and five.

The Caribou silver mill is located at Nederland, four miles from the mine, on account of abundant water and fuel facilities. The main building is 165 feet long by 100 wide, and is terraced in five floors for automatic handling of the ore. In the upper end of the mill is the ore room, where are located a Blake crusher of forty tons daily capacity, and three automatic feeders of twenty tons daily capacity. Adjoining and on the next lower floor is the stamp room, with fifteen stamps, weighing seven hundred and fifty pounds each, for pulverizing the ore by dry crushing. Then comes the cylinder room, where four Bruckner cylinders are kept slowly revolving while the ore within them is being roasted and chlorodized. On the next lower terrace is the pan room, where the roasted ore is placed in pans with water and quicksilver, and kept in motion until amalgamated. There are ten of these amalgamating pans and four settlers for the same. In the melting room, to which the amalgamated silver

CARIBOU MILL AT NEDERLAND.

is taken for retorting and melting into bars, are two retorts and a double melting furnace, ten amalgamating pans, and four settlers for the same. In apartments near the furnaces are a hundred horse power engine, and two boilers of one hundred and fifty horse power. In the building there are also elevators, ore hoppers, dry kiln, cooling floor, water and steam pipes and connections. Close by is a finely equipped assay office, a weighing house, office and residence building, stable and other buildings. This mill can handle fifteen tons of Caribou ore every twenty-four hours. The process used is referred to elsewhere. Outside of the mine itself, the mine buildings, machinery, mill and lands are worth $150,000, and originally cost over $200,000.

The Caribou Consolidated Mining Company was organized in 1879, with a capital of $1,000,000, in 100,000 shares of $10 each. Its property consists of 1,400 feet on the Caribou lode, patented ground, situated on the northern slope of Caribou Hill. The officers of the company are ex-Governor A. G. Curtin, of Pennsylvania, president; John T. Graham, secretary, and treasurer; Eben Smith, superintendent; and A. G. Curtin, James B. Metcalf, H. H. Hollister, P. W. Holmes, and Eben Smith, trustees.

The Native Silver lode is considered the western extension of the Caribou. The ore shipments are of unusually high grade and large in quantity. In developing this lode Adin Alexander is said to have taken out nearly $25,000. He sold it to ex-Governor Curtin, J. T. Graham, Senator Cattell, Secretary Robeson, and others of Pennsylvania and New Jersey, who organized the Mining Company of New Jersey thereon. A silver mill was then erected at Caribou, and in 1877, not far from $140,000 was obtained for the silver product of the ore mined and milled. The process was chlorodizing-roasting and leaching with copper. After John T. Graham's retirement from the management in March of that year, eastern men unacquainted with the business, conducted affairs unsuccessfully and work ceased. This was not from lack of ore or from any fault of the mine. In the summer of 1878, Graham started up the mine and mill again, and recently had the shaft of the former carried down to a depth of 360 feet. The mill did not run long, but Joseph Irwin has continued to work the mine on tribute with great success, having taken out some $40,000 altogether. The yield of the mine since discovery has been about $200,000. There is said to be more ore in sight than ever before.

In June, 1879, John T. Graham bought the entire property of the Mining Company of New Jersey, including the Native Silver mine and the New Jersey silver mill. Some idea of the rich character of much of the vein can be had from the fact that the average price received for ore shipped in five consecutive months of 1877–8, was $188. Later than that, on the 12th day of May, twelve tons and 991 pounds brought $2,541,38; six tons and 1,667 pounds yielded 289 ounces of silver per ton, and brought $236,98 per ton; two tons and 387 pounds carried 255 ounces, and brought $206.55 per ton. and three tons and 937 pounds brought $142.88 per ton.

The Seven-Thirty is west of the Caribou and was for a long time considered its western extension. The patented location is 3,000 feet in length. When Gilbert Lehmer purchased and took hold of it in January, 1878, the shaft was 136 feet deep. He ordered steam hoisting machinery and soon began a systematic development of the property. The first year's operations gave a yield of $35,000, over $5,000 coming out of a very small space of ground, and a very large proportion of the receipts of the mine were profits. Within the past three months the sales of ore have also been quite large and more ore is in sight than at any previous time. The working force embraced for a long time twenty-five men and upwards, but has lately been increased to forty. The ore vein has varied in thickness from a knife-blade up to eight feet in width and has yielded from 53 ounces to over 800 ounces of silver per ton, beside poorer material. From 30 to 35 tons of high grade ore are sold monthly. The ore body appears to take the form of a nearly perpendicular chimney at and east of the main shaft. The latter was 300 feet deep not long ago, with five levels extending east and one or two west, making altogether nearly 700 feet of drifts. The longest of these was then 302 feet east and west of the shaft, but all of the workings are being extended. There are also several winzes. In former years the previous owners, Moore, Brewer, Hupper, and Burger, took out a considerable amount of money, reported to have been between fifteen and twenty thousand dollars. A Knowles' pump was lately put in the mine.

The Poor Man lode is just below the Caribou, approaching it to the westward at an acute angle. The workings are intersected by the Caribou tunnel, and the mine approaches a depth of 300 feet, with numerous levels. The vein has been from one to two feet wide in much of its course, with ore yielding from one to three hundred dollars per ton. In 1874–5 one hundred and fifty-two tons of ore sold for $21,504, with a profit of $12,000.

The Sherman has a very rich vein, often from six to twelve inches wide. This lode was purchased by the same men who bought the No Name in 1874. There were 300 tons of ore sold in 1876, that averaged $270 per ton.

The No Name has a northeasterly and southwesterly direction, and the ore obtained from the mine has come from a point at and below the point of intersection or union with the Caribou. The shaft is 528 feet deep. The original owners, Donald, Shaw, and associates, sold over $50,000 worth of ore in a little over three years, and then disposed of the property to L. M. Bates of New York, for $55,000. Afterwards William Fullerton, A. G. Dun, and M. A. Smith, of the same locality, became owners and still retain possession. The yield in 1874–6, inclusive, is said to have exceeded $60,000. Since then the property has been worked on lease, and the yield is supposed to have been somewhere between forty and fifty thousand dollars. These parties built a chlorination and lixiviation mill on North Boulder creek, in 1875, and operated portions of two years on ores from the No Name and Sherman mines. The No Name has yielded some enormously rich ore, some of it showing native silver in large quantities. The two mines may have produced, from first to last, nearly $250,000. Joseph Irwin, who has for years been conducting some of the leading mining operations of the district, and who has been operating the Native Silver mine, has worked the No Name on lease. The ore was often extremely rich at and below the intersection of the veins.

The Idaho yielded $9,000 within a few weeks after its discovery in 1870, and showed a remarkably rich pocket of ore. It had too many proprietors, and interests in it have changed hands until three of the discoverers of the Caribou have come to be the main owners. Mishler, McCammon, and Martin put up a large shaft house with steam hoisting machinery a few years ago, but have not worked the property much of the time. The pay seems to run in pockets, and the mine is troubled with a great deal of water.

On Caribou Hill, above the Caribou, are the Mount Vernon, Grand View, Arizona, Ontario, Spencer, Columbia, and Missouri Valley. Most of these have produced considerable money. The Grand View has a shaft 130 feet deep. The ore comprises high and low grades, The Spencer has been turning out rich ore, and the Missouri Valley has a good record. Near Caribou are the Silver Point, Brick Pomeroy, Northwestern, Great Western, Centennial, Amanda, Watson, Thatcher, and Potosi, the last located in the centre of town.

On the same hill as the Idaho is the Monitor. This has been worked to a depth of over 200 feet. A very large body of rather low grade ore was not long since developed, said to be capable of returning a good profit. Mill returns of from sixty to one hundred dollars have been obtained, and some far richer ore is met with.

The Fourth of July lode is of great size, but its pay material does not seem to be concentrated enough to insure rapid development. The various owners are confident of success, however, and those of one location have been driving a tunnel to cut the lode at great depth. The lode appears to extend clear over the snowy range. One shaft has just reached a depth of 210 feet.

The Boulder County is a large, strong vein, situated nearly midway between Caribou and Nederland. It has been worked more or less ever since 1870. Assorted ore has been sold at the rate of many tons per week at good figures, usually yielding from $90 to $120 in silver and nearly $20 in gold. There is a great deal of low grade ore that has been concentrated at Nederland. The Trojan and Sovereign People lodes have both yielded rich ore.

CHAPTER VII.

BOULDER COUNTY MINES—GOLD HILL, CENTRAL, MAGNOLIA, SUGAR
LOAF, AND WARD MINING DISTRICTS—THE TELLURIDE BELT—
GOLD, SILVER, AND TELLURIUM VEINS—SOME ACCOUNT OF PROM-
INENT MINES— THE MELVINA, SMUGGLER, SLIDE, COLD SPRING,
COLUMBIA, GOLDEN AGE, KEYSTONE, AND OTHERS.

The telluride belt is about twenty miles long and several miles in
width, extending from the Smuggler on the north almost to South
Boulder creek on the south.   Within this belt are numberless telluride veins, and some regular gold and silver lodes.   Telluride ores
have been found in very small seams or pockets in one lode, and in
bodies or veins in another, but when large the ore is generally of
low grade with occasional rich mineral.   Some have continuous veins
of high grade ore, and have yielded a great deal of money and
profit.   Most of them are mainly made up of ore too poor to smelt
and too refractory to treat in the cheap stamp mills.   Concentration
answers as a remedy or great benefit on some lodes and will not
answer on others.   Smelting is the only mode of extracting the gold
and silver.   The telluride mines of the entire belt have yielded something like a million dollars since work first began on them in 1873,
'4, '5, '6.   The ore sold has generally been very rich.

Tellurium is a metal of no intrinsic value in itself, but owing to
its combination with the precious metals, veins carrying it are often
extremely profitable.   It gives the mineral in which it shows itself so
different an appearance from other gold and silver ore as to be
readily distinguishable.   American miners had never encountered it
before discovering it in Colorado, as it is found in but few places in
the world, and Boulder county prospectors had been passing over
these veins and their blossom rock for years without dreaming of
their value.

The crevices of telluride veins are often of good size, but the
amount of mineral that pays for mining and smelting is generally
small compared with gold or silver veins.   As much of very rich

mineral can be found in these classes of lodes as in the tellurides, while the available ore of lower grades is vastly greater. Some of the leading telluride mines show continuous veins several inches wide of extremely rich ore, sometimes widening out to pockets, and bordered by poorer material that is often concentrated into marketable ore, but nearly all of them require as large a force to assort, separate, and "hand dress" the product as they do underground miners. The rich part of the veins are more likely to be from half an inch to four inches wide than of larger size. The Melvina and Smuggler are two of the lodes that are larger and better than the average. The Cold Spring, Slide, American, Last Chance, John Jay, Red Cloud, Keystone, Victoria, and others have also shown fair sized veins and pockets. There are a large number of lodes that have yielded by close assorting a few hundred pounds of ore that were worth from less than a dollar up to several dollars per pound, but the trouble is to get a ton of such material at one time from any one mine. Still, it has been done occasionally from some of those named. The combinations of tellurium are many, of which the more important are sylvanite, carrying nearly twice as much gold as silver; petzite, over twice as much silver as gold; calavarite, or telluride of gold; altaite, or telluride of lead; and tetradymite, or telluride of bismuth. The native or pure metal is rarely found. The value of the gold in the above greatly exceeds the value of the silver. Lodes of this character often carry several feet of low grade ore that cannot be made available.

Gold Hill mining district contains a multitude of lodes and some gulch diggings, and has turned out a great deal of money since 1859. Gold Hill rises far above the surrounding country, and is bordered by Left Hand Creek and Gold Run. On this hill are the Horsfal, Columbus, Red Cloud, Cold Spring, Victoria, Cash, Saint Joe, and Slide veins. The district has probably produced half a million altogether.

The Cold Spring is a telluride lode of great value, close by the Red Cloud, and is bordered by a large porphyry dike, in a gneissic formation. Its yield in 1874–6, inclusive, was $50,000. It has not been worked steadily but is developed by a shaft over 400 feet deep, and by several levels. The ore reserves contain several times the value of the mine's past product. The mine is paying and has a fine set of steam hoisting machinery. The vein varies from a few inches to two feet. The assorted ore runs up in the hundreds, and one ton brought several thousands of dollars. It is one of the most valuable of the telluride veins. The owner is Truman Whitcomb.

In 1873–4 the Red Cloud yielded in much the same manner as the Cold Spring has done, but gave out at a depth of several hundred feet. The Columbus has been worked at times by a large force of men, and so has the Cash and Saint Joe. The Victoria has been opened extensively, has extensive buildings, and has been paying profits.

The Horsfal is a free gold vein, which is said to have yielded nearly a quarter of a million in the first few years of mining in Colorado. When a depth of over two hundred feet was attained difficulty arose among the owners, and the ore became more difficult to reduce, and the mine shut down. It was idle for many years up to late in 1878, when work was resumed and development commenced again. The results are said to be so satisfactory that the mine is likely to be worked steadily from this time forward.

The Black Cloud mine has been extensively developed, and is owned by a company of the same name. It carries gold and silver, gray copper, zinc-blende, sulphurets and copper and iron pyrites. A mill was erected last year for handling the ore at Summerville, one mile from Salina. Its concentrating capacity is given at twenty-five tons in twenty-four hours. The lode is worked through a tunnel intersecting the vein one hundred feet deep, below which a shaft is sunk on the vein one hundred feet further. The location of the mine is on a high hill on the opposite side of Gold Run from the Hoosier mine.

The Slide lode is located on the north side of Gold Hill, and was discovered by J. G. Pell, in July, 1875. It was afterwards sold to W. A. Campbell and Colonel Seymour. The vein lies between metamorphic gneiss and a dike of porphyry, and has a width of several feet, with several pay streaks and seams of rich ore. It has all the indications of a heavily mineralized fissure. Tellurides of gold and silver, iron and copper pyrites carrying the precious metals, and fine gold are found with a quartz gangue. The lode is extensively opened and is intersected by the Corning Tunnel, 950 feet from the mouth of the latter. In the first two years of work, 80 tons of selected ore sold for $28,927, or at the rate of $350 per ton. A large amount of ore containing less than $40 per ton had also been mined, but is still being found with the richer ores. The yield of 1878 is said to have exceeded that of either preceding year, and the yield of April, 1879, is reported at over $14,000. The mine has not been operated steadily, owing to connection with another company, but will be hereafter.

The discovery of the Sunshine lode in 1874 was followed by the opening of the Charcoal, Osceola, Grand View, American, White Crow, Sheridan, Nil Desperandum, and others, and the building of the town of Sunshine, six miles from Boulder. The American took the lead and became quite famous. It was purchased by Hiram Hitchcock, of New York, and superintended and developed by Professor J. Alden Smith. A remarkable vein was uncovered, with wonderfully rich streaks of telluride combinations, such as sylvanite, petzite, calavarite, and also ruby silver and free gold. From twenty-five to thirty men were usually employed—one half of them being required to separate the rich mineral from the poorer ore or gangue. Many tons of ore were sold monthly, at prices varying from $400 to $600 per ton, and small lots milled at the rate of from four to seven thousand. There were portions of the mine where the vein varied from three to twenty inches in thickness. This included ore carrying from $30 to $60 per ton, as well as the more valuable and marketable varieties. The yield ran into the thousands some months, and few telluride veins have turned out as much money altogether. The best years were from 1874 to 1877. The shaft is over 400 feet deep and from twelve to eighteen hundred feet of levels have been driven. Sinking is progressing.

The Melvina mine is located on Melvina Hill, between Gold Run and Four Mile Creek and Salina. It was discovered by Henry Meyring, who dug a prospect hole and located the lode. In July, 1875, Henry Neikirk received an interest for developing it. It was then not known to be valuable. His first month's operations resulted in uncovering a telluride vein of surpassing value, when over $8,000 were received for ore sold to the smelters. The pay vein was soft material, and sometimes gave several dollars in gold per pound. The mine kept on producing steadily, and the world has seldom seen such proportionately large profits. In February, 1876, ore was sold that brought $15,800, and the expenses were only $800. Only eight men were at work, most of them being owners in the mine. In the monthly shipments the ore has usually been assorted in three lots, and there would usually be a few hundred pounds that yielded at the rate of from two to nine dollars per pound, or from $4,000 to $18,000 per ton. In the first fifteen months of work the mine had yielded $84,600 from the labor of eight men, including the proprietors. In that time 151 tons had been sold and the average value was over $560 per ton. While a pretty continuous vein of ore was maintained, the best material came in or was found at depths of 50 feet, 200 feet and the present lower workings, where the width was from six to eight inches. In four months, ending May 1, 1877, there were 60½ tons of ore sold for $31,830, of which $24,200 was profit. Up to March the actual yield had been about $100,000 and the profits $65,000. These extremely rich lots of ore were largely obtained by assorting from the entire crevice matter, although there had been parts of the mine where a solid streak six or eight inches wide had been composed entirely of the high grades. Gradually large amounts of ore had accumulated at the mine that would not pay for smelting. As a mill had been established at Salina for concentrating tellurides—that is separating the mineral from the gangue or waste rock—some of the Melvina dump pile was tested. The result was one ton of dressed concentrates containing $270, and another ton containing $430, instead of ten or twelve times as much crude ore, with only fifteen or thirty dollars' worth of gold in each ton. This led to the leasing of the Everitt concentrating mill, which has lately been purchased by the Melvina owners. Both concentrates and high grade mineral is sold to the Boston & Colorado Smelting Company. Up to May 1st, 1878, the receipts for ore sold exceeded $130,000, and the supposed ultimate yield $155,000. The receipts for the year 1878 were $90,000, indicating a yield of $100,000, and the profits must have been 75 per cent. of the receipts. Last winter twelve men were at work, breaking and raising about 235 or 250 tons of ore monthly. Most of this was low grade, and ten or twelve tons of it were dressed down into one at the mill. In different portions of the mine the high grade pay vein has varied in width from five to ten inches, and the accompanying low grade from fifteen to twenty-five, and from thirty to forty. The total ore receipts of the Melvina for the four years of work ending July, 1879, would probably foot up $230,000, and the actual smelters yield $280,000. The lean ground encounted at times in sinking has given away to good ore, and the mine is especially rich at depths of 420 and 470 feet.

The richness of much of the ore is as remarkable as the large total yield and small working force and outlays required. Henry Neikirk, Henry Meyring, Melvin Bailey, and Marion Kessler have all made fortunes out of this richest of the telluride veins.

The Wren lode is considered the extension of the Melvina, and is situated further down the hill towards Salina, where what is probably the same vein is called the Baron. Last month the Wren main shaft was down 240 feet, with levels at depths of 166 and 225 feet, and sinking is continued and drifting pushed on towards the Melvina. It is thought the same body of ore that is paying in the latter will soon be fairly entered by the deep shaft of the Wren. Meantime there had been from fifteen to twenty inches of ore suitable for concentrating and a small amount of high grade. The latest reports are to the effect that the shaft has fourteen inches of mineral, averaging $100 per ton, and that Hunt & Barber paid $96 per ton for one lot of this ore.

The Baron lode was discovered in 1875, but it is only lately that its true value has been developed. The crevice between walls is five feet wide, containing four veins of mineral or tellurium, each from one to three inches wide. Four men were at work in May, and received $1,500 for ore sold in drifting eleven feet. Twelve tons of the low grade ore, averaging $30 per ton, concentrates down into one ton of marketable mineral, with a loss of only thirty per cent. Most of the high grade ore sold brings $400 more or less, but small lots contain from $5 to $8 per pound. The owners are C. C. Eddy, Sr., C. C. Eddy, Jr., F. R. Eddy, and A. R. West.

The Great Eastern lode is about two hundred feet southwest of the Melvina, and is opened by a shaft 175 feet deep. It has paid well.

Central mining district extends along Left Hand and James Creeks, and adjoins and separates Gold Hill and Ward. It contains both free gold and telluride lodes. Near Jamestown the John Jay, Last Chance, and Longfellow are prominent telluride veins. The Summit lode shows a very large crevice. The Mountain Chief is on the divide between the two creeks. At and near Springdale are some productive telluride lodes, such as the Big Blossom, Grand Central, J. Alden Smith, Louis, B. F. Smith, Rip Van Dam, Hecla, Ellen, King William, and Gladiator. These have sometimes been enormously rich. The Bondholder is a profitable free gold lode The Golden Age and Standard free gold mines are in this district, and further north is the famous Smuggler. At Springdale are seltzer springs, similar to those of Germany, and a fine hotel. The country is well timbered.

The Last Chance has produced a great deal of rich telluride ore. One lot of three tons was sold not long ago that brought $980 per ton. Last year two tons sold for $1,267, two and three-fourths tons for $2,337, two tons for $951.15, and four and a quarter tons for $1,749.61. One lot carried $530 in gold and $22 in silver. The John Jay was discovered late in 1875, and has yielded many thousands of dollars. An Illinois company that bought property at Jamestown, last fall, has sold ore that yielded $200 per ton.

The Golden Age is one of the best mines in the county, and the most successfully operated of those having free gold milling ores. It has been steadily developed for thirty months or more, and has paid good profits from the surface down to the present depth of between 230 and 300 feet. A fifteen stamp mill was erected early in 1877, and this was since enlarged. Since January, 1878, twenty-five stamps have been crushing some fifteen tons of quartz daily. The product for last year was 2,200 tons of quartz, yielding over $40,000. Since then the mine has been opened in better shape, and the yield has been proportionately larger. During the month of April twelve men were at work at the mine, and about sixty cords, or over 400 tons of quartz were mined and milled, with a yield of $6,900. There were 390 ounces of gold, worth not far from $17.75 per ounce. Much the larger half of the yield must have been profit. The mill contains, besides stamps and tables, two iron Bartola pans. There are said to be several thousand cords of ore in sight. The vein matter is a pure white quartz, containing a very light trace of anything beside gold, and streaks and nuggets of the yellow metal are constantly met with. The mine has produced more handsome free gold specimens than any other in this part of the State. The yield is usually from an ounce to an ounce and a half of gold per ton. It is reported that both mine and mill were sold in May to Messrs. Pike, Parmly & Shedd, of Chicago, for $194,000. Hiram P. Walker, the late owner, purchased the mine of the discoverer, "Indian Jack," some thirty months ago.

The Smuggler is one of the few very productive telluride lodes. It not only yields quantities of very rich ore but also carries a large, strong vein, with occasional pockets of great size and varying richness. If worked systematically, so as to keep ground and ore reserves opened in advance of immediate necessities, it would make a much better record than it has done, and be a source of greater profit to the owners. For a long time it has been worked on temporary leases and tribute work, which, in the end, cannot fail to result in injury to the mine and its owners.

In April, 1876, Charles Mullen, a veteran prospector, wandered up into the hills near Long's Peak, and on a gulch near the south fork of the St. Vrain, discovered what he called the Smuggler lode. The quantity of mineral and the enormous assays convinced him that he had "struck it rich" enough to insure a fortune. General Lessig and W. A. Christian were also partners in the discovery. A great deal of ore was mined and sold that summer, which yielded all the way from one hundred up to one thousand dollars per ton. Mullen sold out his interest to Kennedy, Eaton, Freeman, and Flowers, of Greeley, and went to the Centennial.

Afterwards Freeman and Flowers sold, and Christian disposed of one-half of his interest to a son of the late Dean Richmond, of New York. The entire property comprises the Smuggler, Wamego, Careless Boy, Sweetheart, and two other veins, and their government patents cover the entire hill. The first is the main source of production.

There seems to have always been a great deal of trouble about the mine's management. Perhaps it had too many owners. One of them estimates the yield of gold and silver up to December, 1877, at $186,000. The receipts in 1878 were $81,400, indicating the actual yield of the ore at the smelters to have been $95,000. The receipts for January last were $4,600. The total yield in less than thirty-three months after discovery is given at $286,000.

In January, 1877, a small lot of ore was sold that assayed 285 ounces in gold and 214 in silver. At the same time second-class ore yielded 13 ounces of gold and 15 of silver, and third class 3½ ounces of gold and 6 ounces of silver. Forty men were at work. In April of the same year nineteen tons of ore were sold to Boyd, at Boulder, for $7,600, and low grade ore made the total yield $2,000 more. The expenses were $4,600. Fifty-two men were at work, and numerous shafts and levels were being driven.

In time a large amount of ore of poor quality had accumulated, and four frue vanner machines were put up at the mine for concentrating purposes. In January, 1878, Boyd paid $7,000 for ore, much of which contained over $400 per ton. In March the main shaft was 130 feet deep, and the vein had been opened for a length of 440 feet, and was intersected by the Careless Boy tunnel, 270 feet long.

In the summer of 1878 six parties were leasing on different portions of the property, some of them paying from 25 to 50 per cent. royalty on gross receipts. They and their employees numbered forty men altogether. Their receipts for ore taken out in thirty-five actual working days of July and August footed up $20,492.34, indicating an actual yield of $24,000. Here was an average return of $14 and over to the man for every working day. J. P. Maxwell received $8,654.34 for one lot of ore, and $5,127.35 for another lot of 3,026 pounds. Some lean ores that were concentrated by the frue vanner machines sold for $578.16. The ore sales for August were $8,900, and for six weeks ending October 15 about $17,500. These were the exceptionally good months. The yield was much less at other times. It is said that the royalty for the year exceeded $40,000. For some time the main shaft has been sunk on fifty per cent. royalty, the ore-body being unusually good at that point.

The crevice sometimes opens out into a pocket several feet wide, and a width of two feet is not unusual. This includes rich and lean ore and gangue rock. The telluride ore itself has been from three to eighteen inches wide for long distances, but is not all high grade. Last winter about twenty-five tons of ore were sold per month, that yielded from three to four hundred dollars per ton. The poor grades of ore are very plentiful, but it is claimed that two or three hundred tons can be dressed down into marketable mineral monthly. There is a rich, but very crooked streak of tellurides outside of and nearly parallel with the main vein.

Three tunnels intersect and drain the upper part of the vein. Below that the main shaft extends 240 feet, with several levels. Fifty feet below the tunnel the vein has been opened several hundred feet each way, and much further nearer the surface. There is more silver in the southern part of the vein than elsewhere. Some lots of ore sold from the mine yielded $2,400 in gold to $100 in silver, while others gave the same amount of silver and but two or three hundred dollars in gold. The Smuggler is the largest of the telluride veins, and the Melvina is the only one that has given a higher average quality of ore in quantity.

Sugar Loaf district lies northward from Caribou and Nederland, and contains a variety of silver, free gold and telluride veins. There is also some creek mining on Four Mile.

The Washington Avenue silver lode, six miles north of Nederland has been opened with hundreds of feet of shafting and levels. The ore is of rather low grade, but there is plenty of it. Within the past two years a dry concentrating mill has been erected with reduction works. The latter contain stamps, Bruckner roasting cylinders, and leaching vats and tubs. This reducing mill has been operated at intervals during the past year or more, and was at work at last accounts. Some $10,000 worth of bullion was shipped in 1878. There are two shafts, 300 feet deep and 500 feet apart, with levels. One mile further north is Pennsylvania Gulch, where are a number of gold and silver veins that have been more or less worked; among them the Dolly Varden, Geneva, Sacramento, San Francisco, and Webster City. In Sunbeam gulch are the Logan and Clipper lodes. The Comstock and Pickerel are large veins.

Extending through Sugar Loaf Mountain is a great vein located by the Blake brothers as the Lindley and Crown Point. The same parties own the Ogallalah. Among the active mines of Sugar Loaf district are the Grey Copper, Vucleus, Logan and Isabel, rich in silver, and the Yellow Pine and the Doss telluride vein.

Magnolia district is situated among the mountains near Boulder creek, and from six to ten miles above Boulder City. It was opened in 1875–6, and afterwards experienced dull times, but now shows considerable activity. Within a year such valuable telluride veins as the Keystone and Mountain Lion and the Sac and Fox have resumed work and production, and are said to be paying handsomely. These are operated by steam-hoisting works, one engine for the first two and one for the last two mines.

The Keystone and Mountain Lion are on the same vein, and the hoisting is done for both by machinery over the 230 foot shaft of the former. The Mountain Lion lower workings are still deeper below the surface of the sloping hillside. The pay vein is from half an inch to six inches wide. About five tons of ore are sold monthly, at $350 and upwards per ton. Twelve men clear over $10 daily on this Mountain Lion mine, after paying the owners twenty-five per cent. of the receipts. The total yield has been $40,000. That of the Keystone has been much larger. Twelve men are also at work there. Rich sylvanite is found, and the marketable ore runs from $100 to $1,500. Both mines have long levels and ore in fair quantities.

Ward district is situated high up towards the snowy range, and not far from Long's Peak, and has been very productive in gold. No telluride lodes are reported in this section. The total yield is believed to have been over half a million dollars, mainly from the Columbia lode. The Stoughton, Celestial, Utica, Ute, Humboldt, and others have also been quite productive. Mining has been carried on there ever since 1860, and most of the gold was obtained in the first six or eight years. Affairs went on very successfully until the surface quartz was exhausted. The ores at great depths appear to be much more refractory than in Gilpin county. Being of low grade, the average vein matter will not pay for smelting, and as the stamp mills do not seem to succeed, operations have failed of success on some of the leading properties. Considerable quantities of ore are mined that are so valuable that it pays to mine and smelt them. Concentration is said to help matters, and a process of that kind is in operation in connection with a quartz mill. There appears to be a revival of work with several mines and stamp mills.

The Columbia is the great vein of this district, and is often found to be of tremendous size. It has been located and opened for a long distance, and is divided among many owners. The best developed and heretofore the most productive portions are known as the Ni Wot and the Ward Mining Company or Baxter properties. The entire lode has probably yielded $350,000, coin value.

The Ni Wot mine, on the Columbia lode, was purchased by an Eastern company some fifteen years ago. A large fifty-stamp mill and other buildings and hoisting works were erected, at a cost of $150,000, in the days of high freights and prices. This mill was burned and replaced in 1866 by one of equal capacity, costing $55,000. Most of the product of this mine came out within a few years of that date, but for some cause the company was not financially successful. In after years W. A. Davidson, the company superintendent, became the owner of the property. This embraces 1,500 feet on the vein, covered by government title and shaft houses, steam hoisting machinery, barns, office buildings, boarding houses, and a fine fifty-stamp mill. There is also a set of chlorination works. The first 200 feet of depth worked below the surface gave most of the product of the mine. The crevice often had a width varying from twelve to twenty feet, and for a time milled freely. Work has been stopped and resumed since then several times, and the workings had attained a depth of 445 feet in 1877. Up to that time the yield is given at $300,000 currency—probably $250,000 coin value. No sinking was done after the year last named, but the mine and twenty-five stamps in the mill have been operated for some time. The reports in April and May, of 1879, were to the effect that the mine was "in good pay", and yielding considerable ore. Large quantities of ore were mined in the last eighteen years that yielded all the way from $8 to $250 per ton.

The Ward Mining Company own a part of the Columbia lode, and have a twenty-stamp mill. The yield was much smaller than that of the Ni Wot, but the mine is extensively opened with shafts and levels. At times there has been from six inches to twelve feet of crevice-matter and ore, largely made up of pure copper pyrites, assaying from $20 to $40 per ton, but difficulty was experienced in saving the gold in the mill. A few years ago, Supt. E. K. Baxter put up steam hoisting machinery and sunk the shaft to a depth of 500 feet. Ore was found, but the mine has not been steadily worked. Claim Number 8 is another property, and has yielded $15,000 within a few years. It was lately cleared of water and is again worked.

The Humboldt is a large, well-defined, gold-bearing quartz lode, with a pay vein of from one to two feet in width. It has been proved up and located for a length of 7,500 feet, and embraces four different properties. The main shaft has attained a depth of considerably over 200 feet, and a large force of miners is employed there, and in connecting levels. There is a large shaft-house with steam hoisting works, also a mill with three Pomeroy concussion tables, ten stamps and steam-engine. The Celestial mine is producing ore that yields in the stamp mills from $100 to $150 per cord. Six and a half tons of smelting ore lately sold for $594, and a ton of concentrated tailings for $43.

The Pomeroy mill at Ward has lately received some additions, and now contains ten stamps, two Bruckner roasting cylinders, three amalgamating pans, and two concentrating tables, all supplied with steam power by two engines.

CHAPTER VIII.

GILPIN COUNTY MINES—THEIR LOCATION, HISTORY, AND PRODUC-
TION—THE SPLENDID RECORD OF TWENTY YEARS—$30,000,000
IN GOLD—RESUMPTION OF WORK AND DEEP MINING—FACTS
AND FIGURES REGARDING GOLD MINING—THE GOLD PRODUCT
BY YEARS—THE QUARTZ MILLS AND WHAT THEY ARE DOING—
SOMETHING ABOUT STAMPS.

Gilpin county extends from the junction of North and South
Clear creeks westward to the Snowy range. Boulder county borders
it on the north, Jefferson on the east, Clear Creek on the south, and
Grand on the west. Its territory is made up of rugged hills, divided by deep valleys and ravines. It was once heavily timbered,
but those portions in and near the towns, mines, and mills are so no
longer. The population is mainly embraced in the three contiguous
towns of Black Hawk, Central, and Nevadaville, which extend in
the order named up North Clear Creek, Gregory Gulch, and tributary
streams. Outside of these are scattered mining camps and farms,
and around them a great deal of land that has never been of any
value except for the timber that grew upon it.

Rising abruptly from the dividing ravines and city streets are a
number of lofty hills, among which the mines are located. From
Black Hawk westward to Nevadaville are Bates, Bobtail, Gregory,
Mammoth, Central City, Casto, Gunnell and Quartz hills, which, with
their intervening gulches, are intersected by numberless metalliferous
veins or lodes, the sources of the golden millions of the past and
present. From these lodes, that are traced along the surface for
distances of from a few hundred feet to one or two miles, gold was
washed by the rains and floods of former ages into the recently
profitably mined creeks and gulches. The lodes are divided among
many owners, each of whom has more or less extensive underground
workings that go to make up a mine.

The main rock or formation of Gilpin county is a gneissic one,
but granite occupies most of the territory where the mineral veins

are found. Some veins lie between granite and gneiss. Hornblende occurs in dikes, and there are occasional patches of porphyry. There are two main systems of lodes in the gold belt, those having an east and west direction, which are much the most numerous, and those extending almost northeast and southwest. Of the former class are the Bobtail, Kansas, Gardner, California, and of the latter the Gregory, Bates, Leavitt or Buell, and Fisk. Some veins are nearly or quite perpendicular, and others incline ten, twenty, and even forty degrees therefrom. Some dip to the northward for several hundred feet, and then change their course to the opposite direction. The veins termed gold-bearing are composed of copper-iron pyrites, or sulphurets of iron and copper, carrying gold, and a less value in silver. The gangue includes quartz, feldspar, crystals, and other matter. Many veins contain galena, and some of them in large quantities. The vein matter is usually decomposed near the surface, and down to a depth of seventy or eighty feet. This is called surface quartz. The gold contained therein is more freely extracted and more frequently visible than in the vein material of greater depths. Many silver veins north of Black Hawk have a south of east strike. This is also the case with many of the gold lodes. Copper is present to a greater or less extent in nearly all Gilpin county lodes. Two or three per cent. of some ores are copper, and more rarely five, ten, and fifteen per cent. Gray copper and ruby silver are found in the richer ores of the new silver district, and a great deal of lead in those between Black Hawk and Clear Creek county.

The main portion of the gold-bearing veins are located in an area less than four miles long, by one wide, and in the midst of this is the almost continuous city known under the names of Black Hawk, Central, and Nevadaville; but many valuable gold lodes and all of the silver district is situated outside of this. This gold belt continues northerly into, and nearly through, Boulder county, and southwesterly into Clear Creek as far as and beyond the Freeland mine, on Trail Creek. Of the precious metals contained in the ore, the proportion of gold is larger, as compared with silver, in the veins near Gold Dirt and Black Hawk, and smaller in those on Quartz Hill and toward and beyond South Clear Creek. Thus, on the western end of Quartz Hill lodes contain more silver than they do one mile further east. There are exceptions to this, however. This is shown in assays, in smelting

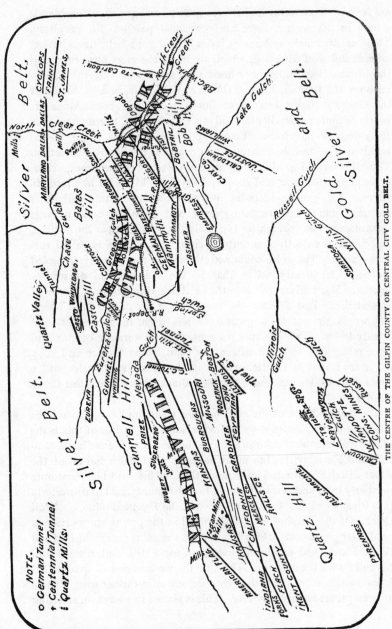

THE CENTRE OF THE GILPIN COUNTY OR CENTRAL CITY GOLD BELT.

returns, and in the difference in value per ounce of stamp mill retort. Near Idaho Springs and Trail Run, lodes on the same belt carry nearly as much silver as gold, and some have increased their silver yield as depth was gained.

It has been ascertained that the retort gold as it comes from the mills runs pretty much as follows in fineness: Bates, .746 in gold, .241 silver; Bobtail, .849 to .866½ gold, .128 to .140 silver; Briggs, .803½ to .816 gold, .172 to .180 silver; Buell, .800 to .860 gold, and .120 to ·140 silver; Burroughs, .820 to .833½ gold, .158 to .166 silver; Illinois, .781½ gold, and .211 silver; and Kansas and Kent county about the same. The value of Bates gold retort is $14.30; of Bobtail, $17 to $18; Briggs, $16.30 to $17.00; Buell, $16.70 to $18; Burroughs, $16.50 to $16.90; Illinois, $15.90; Kansas, $15 to $16; Kent County, $14.50 to $15; Gold Dirt, Ophir, and Perigo, $17.50 to $18; Dallas, $14 to $14.50. Continued tests show that the average of all the Gilpin county gold mill retort, or bullion handled, contains about 787 parts gold, 198 silver, and 15 copper.

What is termed the new silver belt of Gilpin county extends to the north and northwest of Black Hawk, across North Clear Creek and other hills, from York Gulch, Chase Gulch and Wide Awake to the Dory Hill. The first silver discoveries of that locality were made late in May, and in June and July, 1878. Prospecting has continued since, and hundreds of lodes have been located—some of them of proved value. One or two already appear to rank with first-class silver veins of the Georgetown and San Juan districts. Silver lodes were worked with profit in Silver Gulch, near the smelting works of Black Hawk, from nine to eleven years ago, and more recently in Willis Gulch and Virginia Mountain.

Mining in Gilpin county fairly began in the summer of 1860, with the completion of the Consolidated Ditch and the introduction of many stamp mills. Before that, work had been done by sluicing, rocking, and panning, and by means of arastras. In a year or two the more productive gulches had been worked over, the decomposed vein matter in the leading lodes had been exhausted, and the mill men were at a loss to know how to get gold in paying quantities from the solid ore, or "iron" as it was termed. At one time nearly all of these mills were idle, but afterwards the ore was handled with less difficulty. In 1862-3 many rich "strikes" were made on claims that had shown nothing but barren rock after the surface pockets were exhausted. The Gregory, Bobtail, Bates, Kansas, Burroughs, Gunnell, Gold Dirt, and Perigo were paying enormously for much of the time up to 1863, when the eastern companies began operations. The gold product continued to be large until 1866, when many companies had discarded the old stamps, and were spending their money in putting up and testing process mills. On returning to stamp mill crushing in 1867-8, business revived.

At this time the district possessed a population such as has rarely been gathered together in so small a compass, and remarkable for enterprise, intelligence, and sterling qualities. Operations were carried on by numerous companies, whether they paid expenses or not, and leasers and owners of mines were making money at intervals all over the hills. There was eastern money as well as western gold to help matters. A large number of mills and stamps were in operation in 1868, and, in the summer of 1869, nearly 700 stamps were operated, but not continuously. In November, 1869, when several water mills had closed down, there were still 29 mills and 624 stamps at work. Outside of the companies, the California and U. P. R. lodes, worked by Gilpin miners, were paying largely.

The companies on the Gregory, Bobtail, Bates, Hunter, Burroughs, and other lodes were suspending operations in 1869-70-71, and their employees began to lease some of the same company properties, and to start up other mines new and old that had been idle. Quartz Hill and Nevadaville were the more active localities in 1870-71, when nearly all the mines or claims on the Kansas, Burroughs, California, Gardner, Flack, Prize, Suderberg, Jones, Roderick Dhu, Illinois, and some other lodes were in full blast. From 1871 to 1875 the Buell mine was the leading producer of the lower part of the county.

In these years large numbers of miners left for the new silver districts of Georgetown, Caribou, and of Park county, which some of their own number had been discovering. Gilpin county has furnished explorers, settlers, and colonists for every new mining camp that has been started, thereby earning the title of "the mother of Colorado mining camps." Those who remained at Central and Nevadaville finally exhausted the pockets and ore bodies of many leased mines, and left them to fill with water, and in bad condition for succeeding operations, as they were poorly timbered, and many of them "in cap."

The entire district had a dull appearance in 1873–4, but the previous record and known value of the lodes caused several Central men to resume work on their own or leased properties. The success which rewarded their nerve and enterprise caused others to do likewise. Time and money were required to remove water and sink or drift into new ore bodies, but a few years brought about a great increase in production and prosperity. When many of these reopened mines got fairly to producing, in 1876, the county's gold yield was larger than at any former period. Since then every month sees great improvement and progress. These results are largely due to the enterprise of such Colorado men as Briggs, Fagan, Sullivan, Buell, Fullerton, Kimber, Mackay, Young, Standley, Thatcher, Holman, and others, whose faith in the mines has been proved to have been well founded.

Many old properties are now worked under one management. Some lessees have made enough money to buy the mines of the owners, the companies, or their successors, and others have retired in one, two, or three years, with a fortune. These were the mines that the companies could not make pay. If these company stocks had been made assessable, as in California and Nevada, the mines would probably have been worked steadily, and eventually have paid a profit—where the agents were good for anything. Non-assessable stocks permit of the dog-in-the-manger policy—for some stockholders will not advance money when it is needed for exploration, development, or machinery—while sure to come in for their share of the dividends if any money is made. All that is left for those stockholders who are anxious to have work progress, is to pay for it, and take all the chances on loss and only a part of those on gain, or else let the mine lie idle. The latter has been the course generally adopted.

In Nevada, men who will not pay their assessments are sold out, to give room for those who will. Had this not been the case the great bonanzas of the Comstock (whose yield and profits for five years were the grandest in the history of mining) would never have been found. The best way for these old companies to do (that are not working their properties) is to sell out for any price, for their claims are usually too small to work successfully by themselves. The only other sensible move would be to buy up adjoining claims, and so procure territory enough to pay for deep mining. It should be re-

13

membered that it takes just as much machinery and steam-power to work 100 or 200 feet of the vein to a depth of 1,000 feet as it would to work 1,000 feet of territory to the same depth. The only old companies that have operated since their formation, in 1864, with hardly an interruption, are the Consolidated Bobtail and New York & Colorado; and the reason is largely due to the fact that they had more than the usual quota of contiguous property on one vein, and have subsequently increased it by purchase. As to the stocks in the old defunct companies, they may be considered utterly worthless. Any mining company organized in 1864–5 in Gilpin county which is not now at work is never likely to make any money. Stockholders should consider their stock worthless.

The permanent and healthy character of the revival in mining in this district is shown by the large number of mines supplied with steam-hoisting works. Steam machinery indicates deep mining, extensive operations, probably extensive production, and, at all events, a high estimation of the value of the property. No heavy mining work can be carried on without steam-power. There are now forty-four different mines in the district operated in this way. Some of them have engines of from forty to one hundred horse-power each. One engine answers for a long stretch of territory, and for what was once several separate properties. Out of these forty-four mines, the Consolidated Bobtail, the Briggs-Gregory, and the N. Y. & C. Gregory, the Gunnell, and Monmouth-Kansas are each supplied with one, or several hoisting engines of great capacity, beside additional ones for the great pumps with which they are supplied. In place of three or four active steam-hoisting works on Quartz Hill, as in most previous years, there are now twenty — most of them put up during the past twenty months on mines that had been idle for years.

For twenty years Gilpin county has been the leading gold district of Colorado. In that time it has probably turned out more bullion than any other one gold mining locality in America. So uninterrupted has been this outflow of the precious metals that the county has justly earned the title so often applied to it, of the "Old Reliable." This production has been going on ever since the arrival of the pioneers in Gregory Gulch, in 1859, and is much larger now than at any former period. There are more valuable lodes in the immediate vicinity of Central, Black Hawk, and Nevadaville, than in any section of equal size in the known world, and there are more mill stamps in operation than anywhere else. Various causes have prevented all of the profitable or valuable mines from being operated at any one time, but the closing of one was usually followed by the reopening or discovery of another. No suspensions are reported of late, but more than a score of mines have lately resumed specie payments, and more are to follow. Parts of or all of every valuable lode (with a few exceptions) are now in active operation, and the time is not distant when every mine on these lodes will be worked separately or with consolidated properties. The unfailing character of so many hundred veins, and their combined and continuous production, long ago caused this, the smallest of Colorado's counties, to be considered the richest district of the State.

Below is a statement of Gilpin county's mining product prior to 1879. The figures for the years previous to 1868, are estimates. From that time they are reliable and are very accurate for the past four years. Any productions or shipments made in or through Gilpin from mines of other counties does not appear in these figures. For several years prior to 1879, the actual bullion and ore shipments exceeded $3,500,000 per annum, but large portions came from outside ores treated at Black Hawk.

YEAR.	COIN VALUE.	YEAR.	COIN VALUE.
1859	$250,000	1869	$1,680,000
1860	900,000	1870	1,552,000
1861	750,000	1871	1,400,000
1862	1,200,000	1872	1,389,289
1863	1,600,000	1873	1,340,502
1864	1,800,000	1874	1,531,863
1865	1,500,000	1875	1,533,909
1866	750,000	1876	2,105,544
1867	1,000,000	1877	2,208,037
1868	1,305,000	1878	2,280,871

Total to 1879........................$28,077,015.
Currency value of yield to 1879........ 35,000,000.

Of this amount very near $27,000,000 was in gold, not far from
$690,000 in silver, over 470,000 copper, and a very little lead. It is
estimated that more gold has been wasted in milling, and has been
washed down the creeks and gulches than has been saved. By
October, 1879, the total product of Gilpin will have exceeded
$30,000,000.

The production of the county in 1868-9 was as follows, coin
value :

SOURCES.	1868.	1869.
Mill and Gulch Gold......................	$1,175,000	$1,380,000
Boston and Colorado Smelting Works......	193,000	367,400
Other bullion.............	50,000	50,000
	$1,410,000	$1,797,400
Deduct for Clear Creek....................	105,000	117,000
Total for Gilpin....................	$1,305,000	$1,680,400

The production and sources of reduction and export for 1872-3-4,
was as follows :

SOURCES.	1872.	1873.	1874.
Stamp Mills...................	$959,439 00	$710,996 00	$1,044,575 89
Boston and Colorado Smelting Works	419,850 00	510,635 00	483,928 57
Other sources, exports and works....	10,000 00	118,871 00	3,358 54
Total value......	$1,389,289 00	$1,340,502 00	$1,531,863 00
Tons of ore handled.................	100,000	90,000	115,000

The average number of stamps at work in 1872 was not far from
430; of 1873, probably 400; of 1874, over 470. There were several
mills that did not keep steadily at work.

The county's product in 1877-8 came through the following sources:

SOURCES.	1877. TONS ORE.	1877. VALUE.	1878. TONS ORE.	1878. VALUE.
Stamp Mills..............	140,000	$1,289,142 33	140,000	$1,283,569 36
Placers..................	......	45,000 00	......	35,000 00
Boston and Colorado Smelting Works......	5,000	779,894 76	5,500	868,500 00
Golden Smelter..........	1,200	80,000 00	1,500	83,801 75
Mill tailings to Boulder, etc.	......	14,000 00	......	10,000 00
Totals..............	146,200	$2,208,037 09	147,000	$2,280,871 11

The tonnage of mill tailings is not counted above, but the value is. It amounted to from 7,500 to 9,000 tons each year.

The yield in the various metals for four years was as follows:

	1875.	1876.	1877.	1878.
Gold...........	$1,390,253 90	$1,878,818 34	$1,963,485 07	$1,974,934 36
Silver..........	97,409 00	151,569 50	161,255 38	223,936 75
Copper.........	44,155 80	70,672 64	82,296 64	79,000 00
Lead..	2,100 30	4,484 30	1,000 00	1,000 00
Total.......	$1,533,909 00	$2,105,544 78	$2,208,037 09	$2,280,871 11

The express shipments of mill and placer gold, which are substantially the same thing as the shipments of the three Central banks, have always been considered as an indicator, from month to month, of what the mines of Gilpin county are doing. The amount is almost entirely the product of ores crushed in the stamp mills. From $25,000 to $40,000 only come from the gulches and creeks of Gilpin, and smaller amounts from the same sources and from lode mines in Clear Creek county. The express shipments of 1876 were larger than those of 1878, but the heavy increase of productions by the smelting works and in gold taken away by private parties brought the county's total product for the latter year ahead of any previous time. The bank and express shipments of 1875, '6,'8 were as follows:

	1875.	1876.	1878.
January	$86,149 56	$104,984 15	$102,154 00
February	62,817 50	111,411 00	91,494 00
March	75,526 76	124,305 37	102,544 00
April	78,219 80	102,902 49	98,800 00
May	73,359 92	107,194 89	103,194 00
June	95,403 25	105,734 50	100,484 80
July	92,272 80	100,184 03	98,476 56
August	102,615 21	118,081 52	120,900 00
September	96,340 81	145,870 91	99,502 00
October	94,450 86	93,894 47	124,592 00
November	96,818 01	99,592 54	107,536 00
December	114,223 67	107,084 65	125,892 00
Total	$1,068,198 15	$1,321,240 52	$1,275,569 36

Gilpin county ores are treated either by the stamp mill or by the smelting process. Most of them contain too little value to stand any other treatment than that of stamp milling.

One smelting process saves very nearly all of the gold, silver, and copper, and another nearly all of the gold, silver, and lead. Since the last reduction in smelting charges, gold ores are bought at a price, allowing for a charge of twenty-five dollars per ton, and ten per cent. deduction from the assay for waste, etc. On ores containing one hundred and twenty dollars in gold, thirty dollars in silver, and ten in copper or lead, the miner would receive $110 for his ton of ore. The same ore treated by amalgamation in stamp mills, would return but $70 or $80, allowing for a saving of sixty or seventy per cent. of the gold and very little of the silver or copper. But most of the ore mined contains but fifteen or twenty dollars of all the metals per ton, and the stamp mills that handle it for two or three dollars per ton comprise the only means of profitably extracting the gold. The ore of a mine is now divided into separate lots, a few tons of very rich mineral being sent to the smelter, to ten, twenty, or thirty times as much crushed in the stamp mill. By this means as much money is made in gold mining as on smaller but richer silver lodes.

The stamp mills crushed about 21,000 cords, or 108,000 tons of ore in 1875, of an average yield of $9.70. The average yield of 1876 was a little over $10, and that of 1878 was $9.12. This decrease was not due to growing poverty of ore but to closer assorting, and sending a larger proportion of the rich ores to the smelters. From seventeen to nineteen quartz mills were at work in 1878 with from 550 to 630 stamps. The average number of stamps at work in 1876 was 560, and in 1878 it was about 590; yield nearly $1,300,000.

Over a hundred small quartz mills of five, ten, and fifteen stamps each, arrived in Gilpin county in the earlier years of mining. Only a portion of them were ever at work at one time, and on one occasion nearly all were idle. Some were worn out long ago, others were sold to the foundries for old iron, a few were moved to other districts, and many went to make additions to the more pretentious mills of later days.

Gilpin county quartz or stamp mills, as now conducted, may save sixty or seventy per cent. of the gold contents of ordinary ores, and very little of the silver or copper, or say half of the ore's total value in the three metals. Better work is done on some quartz and poorer on others. Thorough tests in several mills, where only one kind of ore is treated and that low grade, show a saving of from seventy-five to eighty-seven per cent of the gold. A mill stamp, as run in Colorado, will crush three-fourths of a ton of ore every twenty-four hours, and ten stamps will crush one cord or seven or eight tons in the same time.

Several mills have recently resumed work, and others have been enlarged. One new mill has been completed and another is being constructed, beside a concentrating establishment. Early in May,

1879, nineteen mills and 624 stamps were at work, and in June 662 stamps, and later 672. In July twenty-two mills and 735 stamps were at work; names, capacity, and location given below:

No.	NAMES.	No. of Stamps.	LOCATION.	TOWN.
1	Randolph..................	50	North Clear Creek	Black Hawk.
2	New York..................	50	" "	"
3	Kelty......................	38	" "	"
4	Richman (California)........	50	" "	"
5	Cons. Bobtail..............	75	" "	"
6	Cons. Bobtail............. ..	20	" "	"
7	Briggs	50	Gregory Gulch....	"
8	New York and Colorado....	40	" "	"
9	Wain and Reynolds.........	25	North Clear Creek	"
10	Kimber (Cal.)..............	35	" "	"
11	Bostwick and Wheeler.....	25	" "	"
12	Fullerton (Lower)...........	20	" "	"
13	Fullerton (Upper)....... ...	33	" "	"
14	Arrighi	10	" "	"
15	Wheeler	25	" "	"
16	Lewis and Aulsebrook	25	Nevada Gulch ...	Nevadaville.
17	Monmouth-Kansas.........	60	" "	"
18 19	} Mackay Mills..............	37	" "	"
20	Waterman..................	20	Eureka Gulch.....	
21	Tucker....................	32	Russell Gulch.....	Russell.
22	Hendrie and McFarlane.....	15	Gamble Gulch.....	{ Independence District.
	Total..................	735		

The Cashier mill will have 50 stamps, including 15 of the old Lake mill, and will begin work in September. This will make 810 active stamps in the county. The New York mill was built in 1879, the Hendrie mill in 1878, and the Tucker mill was rebuilt and nearly trebled in size last winter. The Kansas and other mills were greatly enlarged within the past few years, and a new Mackay mill is in course of construction. The old Winnebago mill may soon resume work. Among the few idle but serviceable mills are the Buell, of 60 stamps, and the Illinois, of 22. The Fullerton mills resumed work with the reopening of the Gunnell mine.

Outside of stamp mills the present ore treating facilities in Gilpin county are no longer extensive. The Boston & Colorado smelting works, that grew at Black Hawk from a single furnace and smelter to mammoth proportions and the leading ore establishment of the State, are used only for sampling and roasting purposes since the building of the great works at Argo. The Humphrey mill concentrates ores, but has not been at work steadily. The Winnebago concentrator is nearly or quite completed.

An example of the work a custom quartz mill can do is shown in the record of the Randolph. In 1878 it crushed 1,704 cords, or 11,920 tons of ore, which yielded 7,349 ounces of retort gold, worth $16 an ounce, or $117,584 altogether. In the first quarter of 1879 there were 449½ cords crushed, yielding 1,996½ ounces, or $31,944, a return of 4.43 ounces to the cord. This was the work of fifty stamps. The Wain twenty-five-stamp mill crushed over 860 cords, with a yield of $58,000.

The following Gilpin county mines employ the number of mill stamps following their respective names—each stamp crushing about three-fourths of a ton every twenty-four hours: Bobtail Cons., 95 stamps; East and West Bobtail, about 30 stamps—total, 125; California (Standley), over 60 stamps; Hidden Treasure California, 60; Gardner lode, 20 stamps—total on one vein, over 140; Fagan-Kansas, 60 stamps; other parts of Kansas, 30—total, 90; Gregory (Briggs), 50; other parts, 45 to 50—total, nearly 100. The Gunnell will soon be supplying 60 or 70 stamps. The Fisk supplies 30 stamps; Kent County, 37. The Flack, Forks, Alps-Mackie, and Cashier are expected to employ many stamps at an early day.

The reader can judge of the amount of ground excavated among these mines from the fact that all of the prominent lodes have several shafts on them many hundred feet deep, that there are long levels extending therefrom, and that all extensive mines have vast excavations, caused by the removal of ore and rock, and where the walls are kept braced apart by huge timbers. There are places

where this worked-out ground extends (for the few feet in width
between the walls of the veins) hundreds of feet vertically and
horizontally. There are seven or eight shafts on the Kansas lode
over 300 feet deep, two of them about 600, and one 1,000 feet deep.
The Burroughs and California-Gardner are opened in a similar
manner, and so are the Gunnell, Gregory, and Bobtail.

About fifteen hundred men have usually been employed in and
about the mines, mills, and works of Gilpin county, and the result
of their labors is a product of over two and a quarter million dollars
in bullion per annum. This, if equally divided, would give $1,520
to each person directly engaged in obtaining it; or allowing an
expenditure of half a million for machinery, mining and milling
supplies, and other outlays, and there would still be $1,166 to each
employee, or nearly $300 for each man, woman, and child in the dis-
trict. As the operations in many mines for a year or two have been
mainly of a preparatory character prior to the heavy production now
setting in, the results hereafter are likely to be twenty per cent.
better than those given above. The three banks of Central have
very nearly three quarters of a million of deposits from the miners of
the district, which is a very large sum when the fact is considered
that so much is continually expended in opening mines, in expensive
buildings, and machinery, and in permanent town improvements,
beside moneys sent out of the State to friends and relatives. Every
year there are nearly or quite one hundred and thirty or forty thousand dollars sent away in the shape of money orders through the
post office of Central, and nearly or quite as much at Black Hawk
and Nevadaville. All of these facts indicate how profitable and
enduring the mines of these mountains are. No eastern town or
county can show average returns to the whole population any where
nearly as large as are known in all leading Colorado mining camps.

CHAPTER IX.

THE GREGORY AND BOBTAIL LODES AND THEIR PRODUCTIVE MINES—
MILLIONS OF GOLD AND TONS OF BULLION—THE MILLS, HOISTING
WORKS, AND PUMPS OF THE BIG MINES—FIGURES OF COST AND
CURRENT EXPENSES AND ANNUAL AND TOTAL YIELD—HOW FOR-
TUNES WERE MADE.

The Gregory lode stands pre-eminent as the first found and the
most productive of Colorado mineral veins.   While not yielding as
much at present as some of the later discoveries, its total output
from first to last still surpasses that of any American lodes excepting the Comstock and two or three others on the Pacific slope.   Its
surface outcroppings were first panned and tested for gold by the
pioneer prospector John H. Gregory on the 6th day of May, 1859.
This discovery proved the existence of gold in these mountains in
paying quantities, and at once brought in an army of gold hunters.
The surface dirt was exceedingly rich, and large amounts of gold
were sluiced therefrom.   The vein has always produced larger or
smaller quantities of gold whenever worked in the more central portions.   It has been located and claimed for nearly a mile, including
extensions, but the productive and developed portion is embraced
in 2,440 contiguous feet of ground.   This extends from the summit
of Gregory Hill northeasterly across Gregory Gulch into Bates Hill,
and embraces what are now known as the Narragansett, Consolidated Gregory, Briggs, and New York & Colorado properties.
The Gregory vein material has maintained a width and continuity far above the average, and has, consequently, yielded
immensely.   The width between walls has usually been several feet,
and sometimes ten or twelve and even twenty.   The distribution of
the ore is variable, occurring in seams of from a few inches to two
or more feet, with intervening bands of poor rock, and sometimes
for short distances it has pinched out or given place to vein matter
of barren quartz and feldspar.   There have been huge bodies of ore,
extending for hundreds of feet in length and depth, and very broad

in places. The walls are not regular, being sometimes smooth and well defined and again rugged and uneven. The inclosing rock is granitic gneiss, showing much mica in some places and little in others. The retort gold from the Gregory is of higher value than the average of the county, indicating that the proportion of silver is small. Seams and pockets of ore of surpassing richness have occasionally been found in both upper and lower workings, and a large amount of nugget and wire gold. On the northeastern slope of Gregory Hill is a parallel and branch vein of the Gregory, called the Foot and Simmons, which is evidently the same as that known further east by the name of Briggs. This is separated from the Gregory by a granite wall from a few feet to seventy in width.

The lode, like others in the early times, was staked off in claims one hundred feet long. Gregory, the discoverer, secured two of these, which he soon sold to E. W. Henderson and A. Gridley for $21,000. The purchasers cleared $18,000 from the first summer's work, and other men were making money above and below. After a time the surface dirt was exhausted and the owners were disconcerted at the appearance of the solid iron pyrites or barren cap rock. All difficulties were to some extent sooner or later overcome, and some portions of the lode would return to "pay" as others grew poor and unproductive. Claims or parts of claims changed hands several times between 1859 and 1863. James E. Lyon, Pullman, of palace car fame, Wilkes Defrees, Joseph E. Bates, E. W. Henderson, John Bruce, Benjamin Smith, D. S. Parmelee, J. S. and C. H. Briggs, and Lee, Judd & Lee were among those who owned and operated properties there prior to the sales to Eastern men and companies. The last named firm tried to sell their claims for $6,000 in 1862, when they were not paying expenses. They could not find a purchaser and so kept at work. They soon after struck a rich ore body that widened to twenty feet. It yielded over three hundred thousand dollars, two hundred thousand of which was profit, up to April, 1864. Then they put the property into the Black Hawk Mining Company, organized in New York. The five hundred feet adjoining and extending up the hill were bought in June, 1864, for the Consolidated Gregory Company at the rate of one thousand dollars a foot. Other claims sold at lower rates. The Narragansett Company was organized on the adjoining four hundred feet southwesterly. The Briggs Company was organized on the claims immediately west of Gregory Gulch and the Smith & Parmelee and the New York & Colorado on those northeast of it.

The following will show how productive and profitable were the Briggs and Black Hawk claims at one time, notwithstanding it was in the era of high prices and heavy expenses. In 1867 the Black Hawk company obtained 12,193¾ ounces of gold, worth in currency $279,647.76, from about 12,000 tons of ore, showing an average yield of $23.30 per ton, with an outlay of $194,425.63, or at a total average expense of $11.43 per ton, or over double the cost at the present time. Gold was at $1.37. The pump then broke down and the water prevented further mining operations until a new and powerful pump was placed in the shaft. During the year ending July 1, 1869, when the company closed business, the yield was $154,135.76, the outlay $92,381.78, and the profit $61,753.98. In four years and six months previous to 1869 the Black Hawk three hundred feet produced $1,358,149. In four years and eleven months the Briggs two hundred and forty feet yielded 534,615. During these years gold ranged from $1.33 to $1.50 in currency. The expenses in the Black Hawk property in 1867, in coin value, were $8.17 for mining, $2.48 for milling, and $1.05 for teaming; this makes a total of $11.50, or $10.45 without teaming. In 1869 the cost was $11; it is now $4.50.

The Briggs Mine comprises the two hundred and forty feet known as the Briggs claims, and the three hundred feet formerly owned by the Black Hawk Company, and includes the diverging but nearly parallel Gregory and Briggs veins. Over the Briggs claims and shafts is a fine brick mill building, containing powerful hoisting works, pumps, and fifty stamps, with double issue batteries throughout, one-half furnished with automatic ore feeders. Here is the main shaft, 925 feet deep, driven a portion of the way forty feet long and ten wide. From this shaft levels are being driven at intervals through the entire 1,040 feet, including the 500 feet of leased ground, called the Consolidated Gregory. The amount of ore in reserve between these levels ready to be broken down is immense. Very little stoping has been done in the lower 450 feet of the Briggs property, and in the lower 600 feet or more of the Consolidated Gregory.

There is ore enough to keep fifty or seventy-five stamps at work for five years without sinking the shaft deeper. The machinery and appli-

Gregory Lode.

BLACK HAWK.

Bobtail Mill.

COLORADO—MINES OF GILPIN COUNTY.

ances are first-class, and embrace many improvements not yet introduced in many mines. Among the pumps is one which was put in by the old Black Hawk Company that is fifteen inches in diameter. The mine usually makes 140 gallons of water per minute. There are several shafts between five and six hundred feet deep. Both the Briggs and Gregory veins are worked, and are connected here and there by cross-cuts.

The Briggs brothers conduct operations at a less cost per ton of ore mined than any other firm or miner in the State. The yield of the mine for the last year or two has ranged from $11,000 to $16,000 monthly, and the profits are said to average over $6,000 per month for the entire year. When the expenses reach $9,000 per month about $5,500 go for labor, $2,300 for supplies, $1,000 for coal, $300 for powder, and $175 for candles. The working force, including both mine and mill, approaches one hundred men. A few men work on tribute—that is, pay a certain royalty or percentage on ore taken out from a piece of ground worked by them. Expenses are very low, the average cost, per ton, of mining being $1.90, of hoisting forty cents, and of milling $1.70, or $4.00 altogether. The hoisting and pumping machinery of the Briggs mine is of the most efficient character, and embraces great engines and boilers of one hundred horse power or less, one of which furnishes power for the fifty-stamp mill.

The mines on the Gregory lode yielded $225,934 in 1875, and $222,405 in 1876. The monthly bullion shipments of the Briggs portion of the lode have since increased. Its yield was about $134,000 in each of the years 1875-6, and $150,000 in 1877.

It is reported that the Briggs mine yielded $31,500 in the months of May and June, 1878 combined, with $18,000 profit, and that the yield of August and September together was $34,500. The sales of smelting ore ran from $6,000 to $8,000 per month nearly all of the year, and as the mill ore generally paid expenses, those figures may be supposed to represent the clear profit of the mine. Last year rich pockets and fine gold specimens were found. Three lots sold at one time returned as follows: 100 pounds yielded $32 per pound, or at the rate of $64,000; a few hundred pounds sold at the rate of $4,000 and $1,200 respectively. Other small lots gave at the rate of $7,669 per ton, $1,541 and $408; 156 pounds yielded $1,496 and $2,350 worth of gold was panned out of only 92 pounds of ore.

Such returns help along the profits, but the thousands of tons of mill ore yielding less than $8 a ton with a profit of $3.50 per ton and the hundreds of tons of ore that the smelter buys for $100 or so per ton are the reliances of the mine. As the mill is directly over the mine, and no hauling is required, nearly or quite all of the crevice matter is fed into the stamps. This and close sorting for the smelter are causes of the low grade of the mill ore. Of the two veins the Gregory averages the larger.

The New York & Colorado company own some 1,200 feet on the two veins northeast of the Briggs mine. This company absorbed the Smith & Parmelee company and took in its property. Eight hundred feet of the veins are developed by long levels extending from a shaft that is nearly 800 feet deep and gradually getting deeper. Over this shaft is a building containing a forty-stamp mill and fine hoisting works, propelled by an eighty-horse power engine, which also furnishes power for the Cornish pump. The yield of this mine was $76,310.75 in 1875, with a small margin of profit, and matters have continued in about the same way ever since. The ore is generally of low grade, but there is a great deal of it. The company's workings extend from Gregory Gulch under Bates Hill. These lower levels can be carried forward as far to the northeast as the veins extend.

The following is something like a correct statement of the yield of the entire Gregory lode from its discovery up to July 1, 1879, coin value. The currency value would approach $10,000,000. Some estimates go still higher.

Estimated yield by old owners up to June, 1864, coin	$3,500,000
Black Hawk, 1864–69	936,654
Briggs mine, 1864–69	368,700
Briggs mine, including Black Hawk, 1869–79	600,000
Consolidated Gregory, from 1864–79	500,000
Smith & Parmelee, 1864–69	375,000
New York & Colorado, which now includes Smith & Parmelee, from 1869–79	450,000
Narragansett, 1864–79	100,000
Total	$6,830,354

The Briggs mine, which includes the old Black Hawk mine, and the adjoining Consolidated Gregory, now worked by the Briggs firm, embrace the 1,040 feet in the central part of the lode. From the best data at hand it would seem that the yield of this 1,040 feet from discovery to July, 1879, was not far from $4,205,000, coin value, or $5,500,000, reckoning the currency values in which the gold was sold. This property is now said to have as much ore above the line of the deepest workings as has already been mined and milled by the upper excavations.

The Narragansett Company of New York own 400 feet of the Gregory lode, adjoining the Consolidated Gregory property on the southwest, and their buildings, on claims 11 and 12, are on or near the crest of Gregory Hill. This mine has been operated only at intervals and has never yielded as well as those described above. Last fall some practical miners obtained a two years' lease and have since been sinking and drifting with fair results. The deep shaft is down over 530 feet.

The Bobtail is one of the great lodes of Colorado, ranking next to the Gregory in past production. Its ore has been of a higher grade than that of its great neighbor, but until recently a smaller amount of ground had been worked, owing to unproductiveness near the surface. This is why the aggregate yield has been less than that of the Gregory. Yet the total foots up over $4,500,000. Much production was prevented by the closing down of the company claims with which the lode was too much subdivided.

The intersection of the vein by tunnel, the consolidation of different properties, and the reopening of them by deeper shafts and levels, has enabled the Consolidated Bobtail Company to work to great advantage and profit. From 1875 to the time when the Little Pittsburg mine began to produce so heavily, the Bobtail was the most productive of Colorado mines. It still continues to increase its product, and now that it has paid off the purchase price of numerous claims, and of a seventy-five stamp mill, beside rebuilding the latter and furnishing the mine with new shafts and splendid machinery, it will undoubtedly pay dividends much more frequently than heretofore.

The ground along the line of the Bobtail was very rich in surface material or "float," and was pre-empted in many separate claims under the name of Field or Bobtail soon after the Gregory discovery. The surface dirt was taken to the creek and sluiced for the gold it contained. Much of it was hauled there by a solitary ox, whose caudal appendage had been abbreviated. From this historic animal the lode took its name.

Some of the claims changed hands for trifling considerations prior to the spring of 1860. The vein or lode itself was not found until then, many believing the pay dirt previously obtained to be merely a wash deposit. One claim was given away that, long after, sold for $60,000. The vein proved enormously rich, and when it gave out in one place it opened out in another. In 1861–2–3 there seemed to be no cessation to the golden shower that some of the lucky owners encountered. This carried the workings down to depths of from 60 to 250 feet. Hundreds of dollars per cord were common returns at the stamp mills, where the amalgam gathered so fast on the tables that two " clean-ups " were made daily. Among the men who figured prominently in the Bobtail in those days were Joseph W. Holman, D. G. Wilson, B. O. Russell, L. D. Crandall, J. F. Fields, W. H. Hurlbut, the Cotton brothers, and John Sensenderfer. Hill and Armstrong and Hale and Patterson purchased interests in 1862, and made fortunes. Jerome B. Chaffee made his first great strike there. He and Eben Smith leased Sensenderfer's claim, which was "in cap." Early in 1864 they had cleared from that and from the working, purchase, and sale of another claim, over $100,000. Sensenderfer and other claim owners are said to have netted from one to two hundred thousand each in a few years' time.

In 1864 eastern companies purchased most of the best developed parts of the lode, in very small claims, excepting the Bobtail Gold Company. It survived and prospered when the others failed at depths of four or five hundred feet, because it had as many feet of territory on the lode as all of them combined. In the two years ending September 1, 1868, the Sensenderfer one hundred and twenty-eight feet, produced $197,155, which was mined and milled at a cost of $77,935, leaving a net profit of $119,220, or of over 60 per cent. Ten dividends of $10,000 each were paid previous to November, 1867. At that time mining, milling, and other expenses footed up an average expense of $13.50 per ton, coin value, as against $6 at the present time. The Bobtail, Field, and other claims also paid largely.

In 1872, when most of these mines were idle, the shaft-houses were burned, and the shaft timber work rendered useless and unsafe. The Bobtail tunnel was afterwards driven to intersect the lode and afford drainage and an outlet for the product of the mine. The Fisk lode was penetrated 574 feet, and the Bobtail 1,110 feet from the mouth of the tunnel. This was in 1873. Superintendent A. N. Rogers, who had had charge of affairs from 1864, then induced the company to reopen the mine on a large scale, and to purchase the adjoining company properties and the great Black Hawk Mill. This required time and expense, but the present yield, the thousands of cords of broken ore on hand, and the immense ore reserves in sight show the wisdom of these movements in place of suspending work or operating on a small scale. The Bobtail Company owned 433⅓ feet on the vein originally, and after many years bought the Sensenderfer, 128 feet, separated therefrom by the Black Hawk Company's 72 feet, the Brastow, 66⅔ feet, the Teller, 100 feet, and the Sterling, 66⅔ feet. In the course of several years these were all purchased, making 900 feet of territory, less 33⅓ feet owned by J. F. Field, beside the Branch lode and other claims.

A large excavation in the solid rock at the head of the tunnel, and 471 feet below the surface of the hill, contains huge engines and boilers for propelling the hoisting machinery and great pumps. A brick and iron smoke-stack extends up an old shaft to daylight. A splendid perpendicular shaft has been sunk some 400 feet below the tunnel level, 8 feet by 16 in the clear, divided in four compartments, one for sinking, one for pump and ladder way, and two for cage-ways, up and down which ascend the great iron cars loaded with quartz, men, or supplies. The cars, each loaded with two tons of ore, are run from the iron tracks of the various levels of the mine directly into these cages. They are then hoisted to the tunnel level and run out on another track to the ore building and daylight. Here the ore is dumped onto a floor below the track by the two halves of the car parting at the bottom. The hoisting machinery for the cage is as substantial as wood and iron can make it. The two drums are seven feet in diameter. Upon these are wound the flat steel wire ropes, of English manufacture, three inches in width and half an inch in thickness, with breaking strain of fifty tons, which are attached to the cages. These drums are driven by spur-gear, twelve feet in diameter and twelve-inch face. The engine driving this makes direct connection, and has reversible link motion.

The quantity of water that finds its way into the workings of this mine is immense, and much greater than in any other in Colorado. This is due to the fact that this hill and portions of another are drained by it, now that the shaft and levels have been carried forward to great depths and lengths. In order to handle this troublesome element the more effectively, two great Worthington pumps have been purchased and set at work, at an outlay of something like $10,000. These send nearly or quite 500 gallons of water to the surface every minute, or 72,000 every twenty-four hours, and are models of their kind.

The main shaft of the Bobtail mine, unlike most others, has not been driven down on the course of the vein, but perpendicularly, so that, at several hundred feet below the tunnel-level, cross cuts, from sixty to eighty feet long, are driven, in order to connect with the vein and its workings. This style of shaft is driven in order that hoisting by cages can be carried on to better advantage; another reason may be that, since the vein has once changed its course, it may do so again, and in that case come back to the line of the shaft once more.

The company keeps its seventy-five stamp and twenty-stamp mills steadily at work, with a yield the year through of about ten cords, or seventy-five tons daily. The larger mill has been rebuilt internally, and is a model of its kind. The quartz mills, the shops, offices, and ore buildings, with the great shaft, compressors, and machine drills, hoisting and pumping machinery, embrace what are known as permanent improvements, and must have cost a quarter of a million altogether. The mine has paid for these, as well as dividends, and there is money in the treasury. The mill may be enlarged by fifty stamps next year. A branch tunnel has been driven a long distance on the vein, and workings in one place extend west of the shaft a quarter of a mile. The depth of the mine below the surface is now over 815 feet.

The company employs over 200 miners, mill men, teamsters, and shop men. This includes those working on contract who generally make about $2.25 per day, or about the same as those receive who work for wages. The pay-roll foots up nearly or quite $13,000 every month for labor, exclusive of superintendent and assistants. Five steam engines, combining 200-horse power, are employed at the mills, including one used for the air compressor of the machine drills. There are five engines, combining about 225-horse power, in the mine. Two machine drills have generally been operated in the underground workings.

The receipts and expenditures of this company are given for 1876, not that they make as good a showing as those of later years, but because they are the only ones in the writer's possession. The receipts for that year were $232,206.70 for bullion from ore milled and $44,147.47 from ore sold smelters. Tributors paid a royalty of $1,253.25, and rents and interest on loans gave $629.37; total receipts, $278,236.79. Net profits of the year $46,976.80. The figures on expenses and profits for 1877–8 are not at hand, but are believed to make a better showing for the company than the above. To enable the reader to see what outlays are required in a great mine, the following statement is given :

The expenses for the year 1876 included $156,555.87 for mining, $51,154,21 for milling, $14,358.46 for drainage and superintendence; taxes and other expenses, $9,181.45. Of the mining expenses, mining contracts took $51,386.95; day labor, $49,052.98; candles, powder and fuse, $13,165.71; fuel, $4,853.77; timber and lumber, $3,165.94; and hardware, foundry work, and machinery, $12,591. In the mills fuel cost $9,878.09; hauling ore, $8,734.51; and chemicals and oil, $1,052.29. Something like seven-tenths of a ton of coal is burned for every cord, or seven and a half tons of ore milled, and the coal consumption at the mine and mill together probably exceeds three thousand tons per annum.

The Consolidated Bobtail Gold Mining Company has a capital stock of $1,136,630, in 227,326 five dollar shares. The trustees and officers are George A. Hoyt, president; John Stanton, Jr., secretary and treasurer; and E. C. Litchfield, Jerome B. Chaffee, L. H. Brigham, E. H. Litchfield, John Ewen, R. J. Hubbard, and Walton Ferguson.

Below is a four years' statement furnished by the company. It shows the amount of ore milled and smelted, of mill tailings dressed and sold, the average yield per ton and cord in ounces of gold and in dollars; also the cost of milling per ton and of mining per foot, fathom, and ton. Its completeness should insure for it attention. Few companies or miners keep so close or accurate a knowledge of just what they, their mine, ore and mills are doing, and in this the management deserves commendation.

CONS. BOBTAIL MINE—QUANTITIES, YIELD, AND VALUE.

	1875.	1876.	1877.	1878.
Cords of Ore milled	1,913½	3,225	3,511	3,276½
" " by Tributors	93½	70½	53	83
Tons of Smelting Ore sold by Company	574	395¼	350	402
" " " Tributors	111½	30¼	25	102
Tons of Dressed Tailings sold	545	981¼	1.149½	1,500
" " per cord Ore.	0.3	0.3	0.32	0.45
Ounces Gold yield per cord Ore	3.62	3.71	3.738	3.98
Currency value per cord Ore	$71 60	$71 85	$68 97	$70 26
Currency value of same, including} Tailings	74 22	74 68	72 31	73 75
Value of Tailings per cord Ore	2 62	2 83	3 33	3 49
" " sold, per ton	8 73	9 33	10 18	7 63
" Smelting Ore sold, per ton	83 60	88 53	109 64	118 10

The quantity of ore milled in the different years has been governed almost entirely by the number of stamps operated.

COMPARATIVE COST OF WORK.

	1875.	1876.	1877.	1878.
Drifting, per foot	$12 15	$10 18	$9 89	$9 45
Stoping, per fathom	26 50	24 33	23 07	22 48
Sinking, per foot (excepting No. 4} Winze—see below)	.....	10 76	12 88	12 85
* Passing dirt and filling buckets, per} cord	3 67	3 10	2 00	2 17
† Hoisting, per cord	.....	1 60	1 53	1 93
‡ Loading and Transportation (con-} tract with Tunnel Co.), per cord.	6 00	6 00	6 00	6 00
Assorting Ore, per cord	1 80	1 60	1 80	1 70
Hauling to mill, per cord	3 20	2 10	2 12	2 26
Milling expense, per cord	13 76	12 86	11 88	11 87
Dressing Tailings, per cord	.....	90	96	1 43

* Refers to new ground being opened.   † Does not include hoisting from winzes.
‡ Actual cost of loading, $1.00 per cord.

The increased saving of tailings adds correspondingly to cost per cord for dressing.

Mine openings during the year, 318 feet sinking winzes, 1,595.7 feet drifting and cross-cuts, 1,865.52 fathoms stoping, No. 4 winze was carried down double size to accommodate pumps. Average cost, $17.00 per foot.

Careful and oft repeated tests and assays in 1878, show that the quartz mills of the Consolidated Bobtail Company made the remarkable savings of 75.8 per cent. of the gold contained in the ore with the stamps and tables, and 87.96 per cent. of the gold and 6 per cent. of the silver, including both the product of the batteries and tables and of the buddled tailings. A higher per cent. of the gold contents of ores can be saved when they are of low or average grade like the Bobtail than when they are very rich. As will be seen by the tabulated statement the cost of milling, $11.87 per cord, would make the expense only $1.70 per ton allowing for seven tons in a cord and only $1.58 allowing for seven and a half tons.

The Bobtail Tunnel is owned by a company of the same name. This is a separate organization from the Consolidated Bobtail Mining Company, but comprises several members of the latter. Its revenues, mainly derived from tolls charged for taking the product of the mine out to daylight, have ranged from $15,000 to $19,000 per annum. This tunnel also helps to drain and ventilate the mine.

Below is a statement of the yield of the Bobtail vein for four years.

That the lode may have credit for all it produced, figures for company and individual receipts are given, and to these are added estimates of the yield of ore and tailings over and above what the smelter paid for them, allowing for coin value. This should give the actual yield. In those years ore must certainly have contained $35 or more per ton above the price paid, and tailings twice as much as was paid. There were nearly 4,200 tons of the latter. In the statement below the yield of tributors' ore, instead of the royalty, is counted. The yield of the Bobtail lode for four years would then have been $1,386,275.06, mostly on the company property.

NAME OF MINE.	1875.	1876.	1877.	1878.
Cons. Bobtail, Receipts of—				
Ore Milled, including Tribute full ore yield..... ...	$143,899 61	$232,206 70	$245,627 00	$236,191 58
Tailings sold...	4,777 85	9,155 06	11,701 91	11,445 00
Ore sold smelter	57,307 80	37,625 15	41,115 00	59,522 40
Total of Cons. Bobtail Company...........	$205.985 26	$278,986 91	$298,443 91	$307,158 98
Estimated yield of ore and tailings over prices paid for them....	35,000 00	85,000 00	40,000 00	45,000 00
East Bobtail................	1,900 00	2,000 00	14,000 00	72,000 00
Lake Claim, etc.............	12,800 00	20,000 00	10,000 00	
Total actual yield of entire Bobtail lode.....	$255,685 26	$335,986 91	$362,443 91	$424,158 98

Now that work has been fairly inaugurated on claims known generally as East and West Bobtail, the total product will be much greater. At present rate of production the East Bobtail alone is likely to yield $150,000, this year, and the entire lode may give $600,000.

It is evident that the entire ten or eleven hundred feet of this lode opened in former times had yielded over $3,250,000 coin value up to 1875, notwithstanding the cessation of work between 1870–74. The yield of the past four years added to that sum gives a grand total of $4,631,275.06.

The East Bobtail is the name applied to the mine on this vein adjoining the consolidated company property on the east. Little work was done there until recently, because barren ground prevailed near the surface. A shaft was sunk during the past few years to a depth of 740 feet. Ore was not found in large quantities until the shaft had been driven over 400 feet. A strong vein was then exposed, which continues downward and eastward beyond present workings. The milling ore is much richer than on other parts of the lode now worked, and the amount of smelting ore of high grade is remarkable. The latter has been over a foot wide for long distances, and the entire vein runs from two to five feet. The mill ore has been yielding nearly or quite $130 per cord, or $17 a ton. Recently two cords have been mined and milled daily, beside a ton of smelting ore. The latter sells at from $70 to $180 per ton. The amount of this kind of ore is very large, the lower levels showing a vein over a foot wide, flanked by from one to three feet of milling ore. This mine has probably given the largest profit while running levels without stoping of any mine in the county. The reports of only a few months are at hand. The ore-body was first entered late in 1877, when the receipts of three months were $12,237.75. In the succeeding January 44 cords of milling ore yielded $4,458.28, and 14½ tons of smelting ore sold for $2,140, and the month's profits were $4,598.28. Thirteen men were at work. The receipts of 1878 were $72,000, of which about one-half was profit. Since the 700 level entered the richer portion of the vein the yield and profits have largely increased. The month of March alone returned $14,371.73, and the total expense was but little over half that sum. The ore is richer in the lower workings than above, and there is plenty of it. The mine is evidently in condition to increase its yield, but already ranks among the large producers of the county. Some months have given an average profit of over three hundred dollars for every man employed.

East of this property is the Denmark, 1,425 feet, whose surface ore yielded as high as 23 ounces of gold. J. W. Holman has a government title for this. There is every reason to believe that it will become productive with the proper development, and cut an important figure hereafter. Its course crosses the Colorado Central Railway. A shaft has been sunk 140 feet deep.

West of the Consolidated mine are the Lake and the Whipple claims, which with others may be called the West Bobtail. The Whipple Company property lies at the point where the Fisk crosses the Bobtail, and the present lessees are getting very good ore at a depth of less than 200 feet. This mine was idle many years before 1878, but now keeps 15 stamps employed, and the intersecting Fisk claim as many more.

CHAPTER X.

The Gunnell ranks third among Gilpin county lodes in the production of gold. Its total yield is estimated at nearly two millions and a half. It was discovered by Harry Gunnell, in 1859, and paid enormously on the surface. The dirt on some claims of the eastern portion has been known to yield one hundred dollars in gold dust to the pan. Among the original pre-emptors were Harry Gunnell, J. F. Bailey, D. McLeod, C. Cooper, D. J. Sanders, A. P. Wright, Chase, Sewry, Morey, Getz, and Bashore, and later W. H. Doe, John Ralfe, John Scudder, John Hense, James White, Alexander and Coleman were owners of portions.

Early in 1864 the profitable claims on the lode were sold in New York, and companies were organized. The production was then very large. The Central Gold Mining Company paid John Armor, W. H. Russell, and John Scudder $80,000 for two hundred feet, and the Gunnell Gold Company bought four hundred and eighty feet of Warren Hussey, A. P. Wright, and W. H. Dodge for $300,000. The owners of the last, including W. H. Doe, made $30,000 from the gold product obtained by a postponement of the sale for one month. It is said that the entire lode had yielded half a million (coin and currency values) up to that time. The Coleman, University and other claims yielded a great deal of money when worked during the succeeding fourteen years. John Scudder now owns or controls much of that part of the lode

General Fitz John Porter was the first agent of the Gunnell Gold Company, and after him came John J. Fitzpatrick. In three years they took out gold of the currency value of $591,000, or about $400,000 coin. The heavy expenses of that period and mismanagement caused the company to shut down when the shaft was five hundred feet deep. Afterwards, New York men who had lent money to the company on its bonds, came into possession of the property. In 1872-3 the mine was leased, cleared of water, and made to produce $53,718 before work suspended.

In January, 1874, J. V. Kimber, William Fullerton, Richard Mackay, E. Clinton, and associates leased the mine, and at heavy expense placed it in working condition. Little ore having been found in sinking to a depth of 700 feet, a level was driven westward, which came into one of the finest bodies of ore ever opened in the county. The receipts for ore sold and milled in 1874-5 were $170,854.42, and $162,722 for 1876. In twenty-five months, up to February, 1876, the yield had been about $313,000. The profits of 1876 were reported at $66,151.69. In September of that year the shaft house and hoisting works were burned, and soon after the lessees bought the property of the bondholders for $50,000, being money they had cleared from the mine. A solid stone building was erected, and first class hoisting machinery and pumps were set at work. They afterwards purchased eight hundred feet of the western part of the lode of James C. Fagan. This was known as the Grand Army property. In 1877 the receipts were about $180,000, and the actual yield of the entire lode over $210,000. The mill gold was shipped every month in a single retort, worth from $14,000 to $16,000. The value per ounce is about $16. Work ceased in June, 1878, owing to litigation over the two hundred feet of ground, between the Gunnell Gold and Grand Army. This property was purchased early in 1879. A part of the Marine lode at the western end of the Grand Army was also bought.

The owners soon after began to free the mine from water, and to put up hoisting works on the Grand Army shaft. There are levels a quarter of a mile long in the mine, and the vein of several feet in width holds good in the lower westerly and central workings. The shafts are to be deepened, probably to 1,000 feet, and the usual number of 68 mill stamps will soon be at work again. An iron column one thousand feet long was received in May, and as much as is needed has been put in the seven hundred feet pump shaft. The property has been one of the best paying in the district.

The time may soon come when the eastern half of the Gunnell will be worked in the same systematic manner that prevails on the 1,180 feet of Fullerton and associates. The entire lode yielded over $650,000 in four years preceding the summer of 1878.

DUMP PILES OF A GREAT MINE.

The Cashier mine is situated on Mammoth Hill, one fourth of a mile distant from the railway depot at Central City, its easterly boundary terminating in Packard's Gulch. It was originally located and owned by Joseph W. Holman, by whom the preliminary developments were made, and became the property of the present company in March, 1878. Since then the opening of the mine has rapidly progressed under the direction of Mr. Holman as Superintendent.

The system of development adopted is the result of the best practical workings of the district. This contemplates a production of ore consistent with the location of the mine among the noted properties on the same vein, and in the near vicinity, which will undoubtedly place it foremost among the bullion producers of Gilpin county.

The contour of the ground is exceedingly favorable to economic workings, admitting of tunneling on the vein. A tunnel has been begun in Packard Gulch, and driven forward about 200 feet. This will reach the main shaft, near the centre of the property, 310 feet below the surface, and through it, when completed, the mine will be worked.

The principal part of the development has been made within the past year, and embraces a main shaft, down to a depth of 245 feet, west of present shaft workings, and two others further west, the first of which is down 50 feet and the other 119 feet. The last two are designed for winzes for future level explorations west. East of the main shaft, a surface winze connects the east adit at a depth of 60 feet and a depth of 120 feet below the rim of the main shaft. The adit has been driven west to a point where it connects and intersects the east 100-foot level from the main shaft. This adit, 446 feet in length, will be used for a tramway for all backstoping above a depth of 100 feet from the surface. To facilitate this and carry out the plans inaugurated, cars have been procured, an iron railway track has been put in, and the ore is backstoped and trammed through the adit to the surface. The present amount of levels that have been driven east and west from the deep shaft is as follows: 50-foot east level, 26 feet; 50-foot west level, 60 feet; 100-foot west level, 134 feet; east level (forming a portion of adit driven from the east), 446. The crevice in the bottom of the main shaft measures $5\frac{1}{4}$ feet between walls, and is saved for milling and smelting purposes. The ore thus far treated under stamps has yielded from $3\frac{1}{4}$ to 6 ounces gold per cord. There is a large amount on the several dumps that will be treated profitably with a mill near at hand. The various intersecting (blind) veins, spurs, and feeders of silver veins met with give promise, by their high assays in several instances, of an addition in lower workings of equal or greater value than the Cashier vein itself.

The company has delayed the construction of its mill until the mine should be opened to a capacity to supply it continuously, without interfering with the progress of the work. Miners can now be set at work in the back stops of the 100-foot level, and the body of ore already in sight in that level will be available before the completion of the mill. A mill site was purchased in Black Hawk, that controls the full water power of North Clear Creek. It is expected that the mill, now being constructed, will be in operation early in September. It is designed to be run both by water and steam, and to embrace the most approved features of the mills in practical operation in the district; 50 stamps will be first employed, but the buildings and machinery will admit of the addition of stamps as required to the number of 100.

Besides the Cashier mine, 1,500 feet on the vein by 150 feet in width, covered by U. S. Government patent, the company's property embraces the North Cashier and the South Cashier, parallel veins on either side, the whole covering an area 1,500 feet in length, by 400 feet in width.

The Empress mine is situated on Mammoth Hill, Gregory mining district, and is about one fourth of a mile distant from the Colorado Central railway depot at Central, and near the Cashier mine. This is evidently on the Fisk vein, which further east has been so productive in gold. Surveys and developments lead directly from one to the other, with the Treasury location intervening. The Empress property embraces 1,500 feet in length by 150 in breadth, and under former workings had been developed by shafts sunk to depths of one hundred and ten, sixty, and twenty-five feet, and 150 feet of levels, and the ore yielded from $4\frac{1}{2}$ to 9 ounces under stamps. It was acquired in March, 1879, by the Empress Mining Company, and since then the work of development on an extensive and systematic plan has been pushed forward as rapidly as possible, with a view to a large and continuous production as soon as requisite shafts and levels are opened. The Empress Mining Company of Colorado was organized on a capital of five hundred thousand dollars, in shares of a par value of two dollars, full paid and unassessable. The company headquarters are at 52 Broadway, New York. James Howell, mayor of Brooklyn, is president, and James Schenck secretary and treasurer. The ore has been milling five ounces of gold per cord, and two shafts are being sunk as fast as possible. The last mineral found assays $400.

The Emperor mine is situated on Mammoth Hill, between the Bobtail and Fisk veins, and opposite the Cashier, supposed extension the former, and the Treasury and Empress of the latter. It was located by Joseph W. Holman, of Central City, and consists of 1,500 feet on the vein by 150 feet in width. The vein is supposed to be the same as the "Minnie" and "Cotton." None other than the preliminary development have as yet been made on this property. The surface dirt has yielded under stamps the average of the surrounding properties.

The Washington mine, at Central City, Colorado, is situated on Gregory Hill. The property consists of 1,100 feet on the vein by 150 feet in width. The topographical features of the ground admit of tunneling on the vein from Packard's Gulch, striking some 300 feet below the surface a short distance in. The developments consist of several shafts, varying in depth from 10 to 60 feet, and an adit from the gulch driven 60 feet in, and are preliminary to the adoption of a large and systematic plan of operations in the near future. The dirt recently taken out yielded 11½ ounces gold to the cord under stamps, and the vein in all the different workings shows the characteristic features of the prominent adjoining and surrounding mines for the depth attained.

The Buell mining property embraces five thousand linear feet of veins, about half of which are covered by government patents. The Leavitt and its eastern extension, the Vasa, from which the U. P. R. pocket was mined, and the Kip are the main veins. There are many shafts, and an immense amount of underground work, mainly in the Leavitt, which has been the leading producer. The whole property is said to have yielded $800,000 currency, or $650,000 coin.

The Leavitt was reopened in 1871, at a point beneath Gregory street and gulch, Central City. At a depth of 50 feet an ore body of soft gangue rock was entered, ten feet wide, of an average value of $10 a ton. Subsequent work continued in ore, the vein widening and closing, but never giving out for long distances. At a depth of 130 feet a rich body of black, decomposed sulphurets was entered, having a width of four feet. Thousands of dollars were obtained at the Black Hawk smelting works for single lots of this ore—there being many tons in each shipment. Several tons were sent across the ocean to Swansea, and brought $300 per ton. The gangue rock, lying beside this in the vein, was worth $80 a cord. In one place there were over four feet of ore, carrying 15 per cent. of copper. The ore body was generally four to ten feet wide, but at a depth of 400 feet widened to 16 feet, averaging $10 under the stamps. Great pockets and seams of smelting ore were found. Unbroken masses of ore, weighing over one thousand pounds each and assaying $200, were occasionally raised. The showing was a remarkable one. From 40 to 100 stamps were employed in crushing the ore, varying in number as the product of one season or year increased or diminished. A great stone mill, with sixty stamps, and costing $100,000, was erected, and ore and shaft house adjoining. A splendid shaft was sunk 500 feet and over, with double compartments for cages and first-class hoisting machinery. The ore was cheaply mined, but expenses were greater in 1871–3–5 than now, and so a profit of only $150,000 was made, where a much larger figure could now be secured. In the last eight months of 1872 there were 7,917 tons of ore mined, that returned $105,185, currency value. The cost was $83,443, or $10.43 per ton, and the profits $21,742. Eleven months of 1873 returned 14,850 tons of ore, and $143,706.86 currency, with a profit of $46,878.86. The total expenses were then reduced to $6.52 per ton. This mine and mill should now be operated at a cost of less than $5 per ton, but has not been extensively worked of late, owing to the low grade of the ore-body in the bottom of the shaft, now 580 feet deep.

The O. K. is the southwesterly extension of the Leavitt or main Buell vein. Work was begun in 1875 by J. W. Hanna, the present superintendent of the O. K. Mining Company. Not long ago the main shaft had attained a depth of 325 feet, through an ore-body averaging 42 inches wide for its entire length. At the same time five levels were driven as follows: At a depth of 50 feet, 50 feet in length west; depth, 115 feet, 185 feet in length west; depth, 225 feet, 175 feet in length west; depth, 285 feet, 95 feet in length west; depth, 225 feet, 110 feet in length east. The levels are all connected by winzes from the top, affording the best of ventilation in the lower workings of the mine. The average of the mill ore has been three ounces gold per cord. By concentration, from returns, some of the ore averages six and one-quarter ounces. Levels are being driven to open up the ground to the east, and the shaft will soon be sunk 200 feet further. But little stoping has been done.

This company is organized on a capital stock of $500,000, in ten dollar shares. It owns 1,500 feet on the O. K. lode; also, the Winnebago mine and mill, and the Liberty lode. Concentrating works of the Collom wet process are being put up in the Winnebago mill to handle the low grade ores. There is a very large quantity of these in the O. K. mine, which, it is believed, can be advantageously handled in that way. Steam hoisting machinery is employed. The Malachite Company, at Golden, have been buying the common milling ores at seven dollars per ton. These ores carry five or six per cent. of copper, and the smelting mineral carries sixteen to eighteen per cent. When two or three car loads of ore were sent to Golden weekly the common grades brought from $90 to $100. But little stoping has been done, and there is a great deal of ore in sight.

The Gregory Second is considered the extension of the Buell on the northeast, and the Smith, in Chase Gulch, as the extension of the Gregory Second. The latter has been opened to depths of four and five hundred feet, and has yielded largely, and the Smith to a less amount.

The Bates is one of the main veins, and, although worked only at intervals, has yielded considerably over half a million. It was discovered by John H. Gregory, May 19, 1859, and was the second lode found in the mountains. Its surface dirt was extremely rich, and so was much of the vein. In 1863-4 ten Eastern companies were formed on different parts of the Bates. In those years the Baxter and Union company claims were among the most productive in the mountains, but other properties were very profitable. But little work has been done, however, since 1869-70, except by parties leasing on the Loker company mine on the Chase Gulch slope. The Union was idle mainly on account of a lawsuit concerning a money loan. It yielded $205,000 currency value in sixteen consecutive months of 1866-7, and the ore has never given out.

The same vein east of the gulch and on Mammoth Hill is called the Bates-Hunter. Southwest of Gregory street this is owned by several Central miners and has paid largely in places. A movement is on foot to consolidate this and the Bates lode in one great combination and mine them extensively. Six hundred feet of the Bates have already been secured, with $100,000 to sink a shaft 1,000 feet deep, run levels, and build a stamp-mill.

Still further southwest the German lode gave a yield of 3,900 tons of ore and $146,250 in two years. The Susquehanna company claim is worked to a depth of 310 feet by lessees, and the Kline claim to about the same extent.

The Fisk lode has yielded a large amount of money—some say as much as a half million. Two different firms are working several claims each, to depths of over 600 feet, and another property is nearly as deep. All are said to be making money. The vein is small, but rich, and the ground hard. In 1873-4 one of these properties gave nearly $60,000. The average yield of mill ore was nearly $20, and the expenses nearly $12. The smelting ore was of high grade. Further east the same vein is called the Sleepy Hollow, owned by M. Rasin, and developed to a depth of 265 feet within the past two years. This property embraces a length of 1,500 feet. Considerable smelting ore is sold, carrying more or less gray copper.

The Prize and Suderberg lodes are located on the upper portion of Gunnell Hill and close to Nevadaville. They approach each other from the west, and the claims where they unite were the scene of a great deal of trouble when the ore bodies of 1870–71 were paying so largely. The courts finally enjoined the Prize company, and after a time the Suderberg men exhausted much of the ground. In two or three years the yield exceeded a quarter of a million coin value. This was one of the richest large bodies of ore ever found in Gilpin county. The amount of high grade smelting ore sold was very great. There was over five feet of milling ore that yielded from six to twelve ounces of gold per cord. The Prize also yielded a large amount before work ceased. Afterwards Richard Mackay took out $75,000 from the Suderberg. These mines are now idle, but may not be much longer. The eastern part of the Prize, called the Commonwealth property, yielded some $371,000 during the same period.

The Jones is situated on a line and nearly west of the Suderberg. The vein is not as large as some, but is of very high grade. The McGonnigal and Phillips properties have maintained a pretty regular vein from the surface down 400 feet, and there is ore below the bottom of the shaft and lower level.   At one time fifty feet only of the Phillips claim netted over $4,000 in a few months' time and it is said that both properties are doing as well now.   The ore has milled all the way from nine to thirty-one ounces.   From nine to eighteen ounces per cord have been the returns of the past year.   Many tons of smelting ore are sold monthly at from $60 to $90 per ton.   The crevice matter is three feet wide, with one foot of rich solid mineral.

The Hubert is located near the Jones, and is thought to be on the same vein as the Suderberg.   It has been worked to a depth of 400 feet, and was paying a profit at last accounts.   Quite a large amount of ore has been taken from this mine.   The vein has usually been of good size and carries some high grade ore and considerable galena.

The Eureka is a large vein, is located on the hill of the same name.   It has been worked to a depth of over 400 feet and is supplied with good buildings and machinery.   Its owner, Alexander Taylor, mined large amounts of ore from it in previous years.   The crevice has sometimes been ten or twelve feet wide.   Among mines on Gunnell Hill are the Saint Louis, Pleasant View, Ashtabula, Whiting, and Butler, and on Casto Hill the Winnebago, Casto, Cincinnati, Comstock, Ellery, and Furnald.   The Maryland yielded $30,000 in one summer.

CHAPTER XI.

GILPIN COUNTY MINES—QUARTZ HILL AND ITS VEINS OF GOLD—THE
KANSAS, CALIFORNIA, GARDNER, AND BURROUGHS—THE STORY OF
THEIR WONDERFUL ORE BODIES AND LARGE PRODUCTION—THE
BIG STRIKES OF THE HIDDEN TREASURE, FLACK, AND FORKS—
THE KENT COUNTY, ALPS, AND ILLINOIS—GOLDEN DEPOSITS AND
FREAKS OF FORTUNE.

Quartz Hill is one of the grandest depositories of wealth that the
world possesses. Here is a network of mineral veins, spurs, and
feeders, and a number of great lodes, such as are rarely seen in any
country. Millions in gold have been taken from this hill and there
are millions in it yet. The two longest and most reliable of the
great fissures are the Kansas and that known in different portions
under the names of Indiana, Hidden Treasure, California, Gardner,
etc. These two veins are nearly parallel, but approach one another
on the west. The Burroughs is another nearly east and west vein,
which approaches and unites with the Kansas from the east. Above
the California is the lode known under the names of Mercer County
and Flack, another called the Kent County, and still further south
the Alps-Mackie and Pyrennes. South of the Burroughs is the
Missouri, and beyond that are the Kinney and the Roderick Dhu
and Borton veins (considered as the extensions of the Gardner), and
the Illinois and other lodes. Taking a more northerly course is the
great Forks lode. This is on the western part of the hill, along
with the Mount Desert, American Flag, and others. Further east
are the Camp Grove, Sullivan, Ute, Columbia, Lewis, Corydon,
Fortune, Fourth of July, and others too numerous to mention. The
total yield of the hill from first to last has probably exceeded ten
millions coin value, and the future annual production is likely to
reach a million and a quarter or a million and a half. The Kansas
and the California-Gardner, if worked extensively for a mile in
length, as they are likely to be, should yield that amount them-

selves, and the half dozen other leading veins of the hill ought to produce an equal sum.

Ever since the days of the pioneer miners the Kansas has been known as one of the main veins of the county. Few have been as continuous, reliable, or productive, and but three in the State have exceeded it in the yield of the yellow metal. It has been developed for a greater distance than any other in the county. Its eastern and western tracings are nearly a mile and three-quarters apart and near either end of Quartz Hill. In one of its shafts mining is carried on to a greater depth than anywhere else in Colorado, and possibly anywhere east of Nevada and Idaho.

Many individuals and companies own portions of this lode. Too much division has been the cause of the irregular manner in which it has been operated. Notwithstanding intervals when first one claim and then another were unworked, some two millions in gold have been obtained altogether and the indications are good for an increased annual yield hereafter. This is rendered certain by the increased amount of territory mined, many claims having been reopened during the past six months. After the stoppage of work by eastern companies the more centrally located claims were worked under lease, and the lessees retired with money on hand.

Since then the railway has entered the district, and opportunities for profit have grown better as expenses grew less. The success attending the resumption of work on the Fagan or western part of the lode, where several properties have been united in one, has at last caused the twelve hundred feet embraced in several mines further east to be worked again—and all with evident profit. The former has been one of the few great producers of the country ever since the close of 1873.

One mine after another had been closing down, as their lessees had stripped them of ore, and at the time James C. Fagan took hold of what had been the Kansas Colorado Company property, many had begun to despair of the district's future. Not so with the lessee and subsequent purchaser of this mine. He believed the gold was there and that a moderate outlay of money and muscle would bring it to the surface. The removal of the water from the mine and the deepening of the shaft one hundred feet proved his opinion to be correct. An outlay of twenty thousand dollars accomplished this and brought the property into paying condition, and subsequent developments have kept it there.   This and the entire western portion of the lode that has since been purchased have been worked in the most advantageous manner possible, under the personal supervision of one of the best mine managers in the state.   A splendid record has been made and large dividends disbursed, notwithstanding the fact that much of the profit has been required for additional property and for permanent improvements necessary on greatly enlarged operations.

Beginning with three hundred feet in length on the vein, the owners have extended operations vertically and horizontally until a depth of one thousand feet has been attained, and a large portion of a length of two thousand feet has been developed or partially explored.   Ore reserves of great extent have always been kept ahead of present requirements ever since the mine was fairly opened five years ago.   Since then about $550,000 worth of gold bullion has been obtained from the thousands of cords of ore milled or smelted, and the mine never looked better than it now does in the lower workings.   Had all needed milling, hoisting and pumping apparatus been at hand to begin with, and had production been forced to the utmost, the yield could have been much larger.   Such was not the condition of affairs, however, and consequently matters necessarily progressed slowly to begin with, and at intervals subsequently.   Yet the profits have been sufficient to procure all of the above requirements, to repay the heavy outlay of putting an idle and water-filled mine in order, to construct a great shaft, discover vast ore chambers, and to erect buildings and increase the mill's capacity fivefold, as well as to purchase the original property and many times as many feet of adjoining claims.   All of this called for an expenditure of over $120,000, and yet the profits to the operators, in excess thereof, have approached $100,000, making over $200,000 of net receipts above ordinary or current expenses.   With the present development and showing, all of the above figures may be more than doubled, with no further outlay for permanent improvements, except, perhaps, an addition to the mill's stamping capacity.

Levels from the Monmouth shaft extend along the vein far to the westward, and thus afford an outlet for that portion of the property.   Iron tracks are laid in these levels, over which cars convey the ore to the hoisting place.   As ground is worked out the rails are removed to newly opened drifts below.   On the surface are sub-

First High Grade Ore Body
Poor Ground
MONMOUTH KANSAS OR FAGAN SHAFT 1000 FT. DEEP
Granite or County Rock
worked out
worked out
Second High Grade Ore Body
400 ft. Level
240 ft east
363 ft west
Low Grade Ore
2nd Class Vein Matter or Lean Ground
500 ft. Level
out
Worked out
240 ft. east
600 ft. Level
1063 ft. west.
Low Grade
650 ft. Level
1300 ft. west
worked
720 ft. Level
900 ft. west
2 feet of ore
Solid crevice in face of drift 3 ft. wide.
185 ft. east
800 ft. Level
500 ft west.
Solid Ore
180 ft. E
860 ft. Level
340 ft. west.
915 ft. Level
225 ft. west
Crevice in face of drift 4½-5 ft. wide
Third High Grade Ore Body
Solid ore 4 ft & over
1000
Fine body of good ore

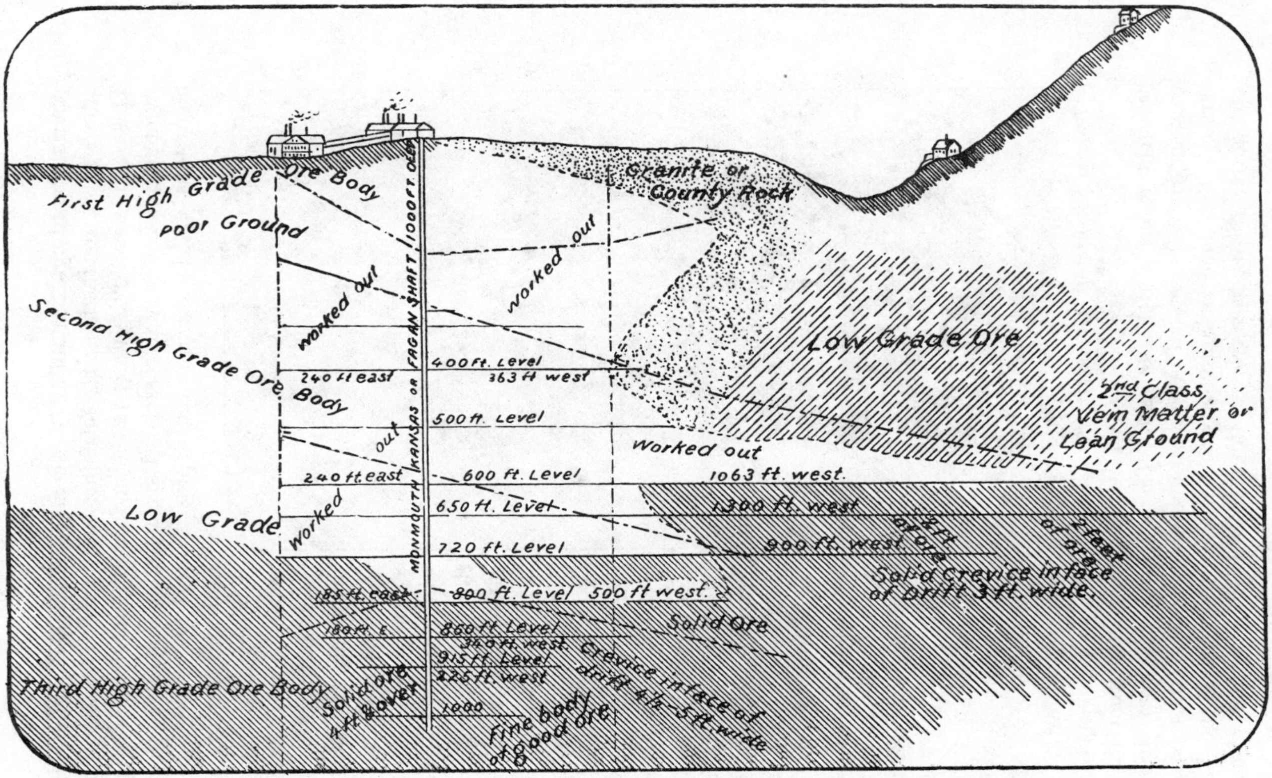

THE FAGAN AND MONMOUTH-KANSAS MINE—LONGITUDINAL SECTION.

stantial buildings containing powerful engines and boilers that
afford power for the hoisting machinery and great Cornish pump.
This pump elevates the water to the surface in four alternate lifts of
two hundred and fifty feet each. Its connecting rod alone weighs
many tons, and far down in the depths is the huge walking-beam
attached thereto. The
hoisting and drainage
machinery will answer
every purpose for five
hundred feet below
present workings.

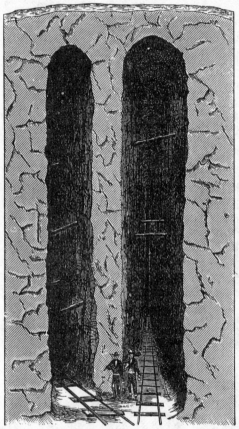

The mine itself is
substantially timbered
throughout, and is in
first-class condition.
Levels have been dri-
ven from the great
shaft at intervals as
far east as the property
extends, and westward
for varying distances.
Most of the vein has
been worked out to a
depth of five hundred
and fifty feet below
the surface, and for
several hundred feet
east and west of the
shaft, excepting some
low grade material.
The level 650 feet be-
low the surface has
been driven west of

DOWN IN THE DEPTHS. JUNCTION OF THE KANSAS
AND BURROUGHS.

the shaft over 1,300
feet, and from this a

cross cut enters a rich side vein. The 720 level has been driven
west nearly 950 feet. The western portion of both of these passes
through the same rich ore body that paid so well around the shaft
and nearer the surface two or three years ago, and which pitches

downward as it extends westward. Near the shaft the ground was poor at this depth. The 800 level has reached a length east and west of 700 feet, the 860 of 600 feet, and the 915 is 225 feet long west of the shaft. All of these are being driven through a fine body of ore. At the bottom of the shaft, 1,000 feet below the surface, and the deepest point where mining is carried on in Colorado, the showing is especially good. There appears to be paying ore enough in the stopes and between, beneath and ahead of the five lower drifts to keep the mill employed for several years without extending the shaft further. Yet it is proposed to continue sinking, in order that an equal amount of ore may continue to be kept ahead of milling requirements. The vein gradually widens from two feet at the 650 level to four and five feet in the lower workings, and is richer than the average of paying mines in this district. About seventy-five men are usually employed under ground and over twenty on the surface, at the hoisting works and mill.

Close by is an excellent quartz mill, into which forty-five tons of ore are dumped from cars every twenty-four hours. A twelve-stamp section has recently been superseded by one of twenty, bringing the mill's capacity up to sixty stamps and forty-five tons daily. This enlargement was rendered necessary by the increasing production of the mine. There is room for forty more stamps, without additional propelling machinery.

The Fagan, or Monmouth and West Kansas properties, as now opened, hold the key to much territory. The heavy dip of the vein, and its situation as compared with other nearly parallel but gradually approaching and more vertical lodes is such, that at great depths it cannot fail to gather them into one or more grand ore bodies. Since this became more and more apparent, the design has been to sink another shaft 1,800 feet west of that now used, and at a point where several of the main veins of the hill unite with or closely approach the Kansas. This will undoubtedly result in the finding of a still larger ore body than that now mined near the Monmouth shaft, where the Burroughs and Kansas unite. The lodes referred to on the more westerly location are the once productive Forks and others, and the Indiana. The latter is identical with the Hidden Treasure and California, which have lately been paying so handsomely. The Forks is a very large vein that has yielded a great deal of money. It pitches toward the north, while the Kansas, which is north of it, pitches equally as strongly toward the south. At the junction of these veins and below, an enormous ore body is very sure to be encountered by the shaft now being sunk.

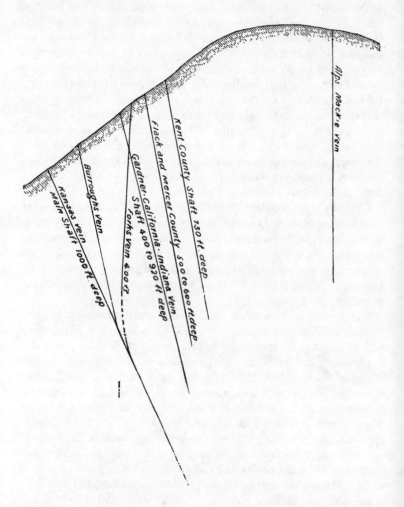

CROSS SECTION, SHOWING PITCH OF QUARTZ HILL VEINS NEAR WEST END.

The Kansas lode, for several hundred feet, or portions of that distance east of the Monmouth, is owned by the First National Com-

pany. Sullivan and Wheeler made money in leasing this ground in 1869–71. It was afterwards worked in the Fagan combination, and is still producing. The shaft is about 600 feet deep. East of this the University Company property has a shaft 590 feet deep. This and adjoining claims, making 659 feet, has lately been re-opened and worked by Newell & Co. It has turned out $200,000, currency value, altogether, mostly when worked by George Easterbrook, in 1871–72. A number of claims further east are combined and worked together, and beyond them is the Pease claim. Both of these resumed work not long ago, and both are paying. The mines are over 300 feet deep, and sinking and drifting continues. A thousand feet further east is what has been known as the English Kansas, because operated by an English company that bought it in 1871. It had just previously enriched three lessees in eight months' time. Further down the hill the Olga Kansas is worked, near where the Central City tunnel intersects it.

The California-Gardner-Indiana vein is one of the most productive in Gilpin county. It has been traced for a distance of over one mile, and has yielded altogether something near $1,750,000. These figures include the production of the Roderick Dhu and Borton, which seem to be an eastern extension of the Gardner. The California embraces that part of the vein between the Gardner and the Indiana, and is about midway between the nearly parallel Kansas lode and the summit of Quartz Hill. The Hidden Treasure mine is made up of claims on the California and Indiana. The latter is the westernmost part of the vein as far as opened.

The Hidden Treasure mine is remarkable for its large yield and profit and the size and value of its ore-body. The seven claims included in this property were formerly divided among many owners, and were worked years ago with varying success. The last attempt previous to 1878 to work the central claims was made in 1872, when ore in paying quantities was not found, and work ceased. The leading owner had no money to expend in further explorations, and the property remained idle until January, 1878, when he induced some miners to take a lease with him on adjoining claims, and thus work six hundred feet of ground together. The result was that the shaft was sunk but a few feet before a vein of rich ore was entered, and this grew large with depth until it proved to be one of the best ore-bodies ever opened in the district. The men who abandoned the mine six years before had stopped sinking just a few days too soon.

The mine began to pay in May, and two or three months later was attracting universal attention. The ore body has been from thirty inches to seven feet wide in the central portion of the underground workings, and there has generally been two feet of very rich ore. The returns in the stamp mills are from five to seven ounces per cord after smelting ore had been selected. There were months when from 100 to 130 tons of mineral sold at an average price of nearly $80 a ton. Last summer and fall the ore came from the vicinity of the 500 and 550 levels. Since then the mine has reached a depth of over 800 feet, with over 3,000 feet of levels, and the 700 level west is looking as well as any portion of the mine has done. The average number of men employed at the mine has been from forty to forty-five, and of stamps, sixty, showing a yield of a ton daily to every man employed.

The receipts from the Hidden Treasure up to February 1, 1879, almost entirely taken out in nine months, were $167,000, of which $67,000 came from sales of smelting ore. This indicates an actual output at the smelters and mills of over $205,000, or of $185,000 up to the end of 1878. The profits were $90,000, including the lessees' royalty. The mine comprises 500 feet, owned by A. M. Jones, S. V. Newell, and Johnson, and 200 feet on the Indiana, leased of T. Whitcomb. The yield continues good.

The California, as at present owned and located, embraces 1,033 feet, beside claims forming a part of the Hidden Treasure. For years after its discovery it was worked at intervals by various owners of claims. Among them were Joseph Standley and W. J. Stalker. As they had found a rich pocket at the surface, they felt sure, even after the vein disappeared, that they would find it again below. Consequently, they continued to sink the shaft. For a year or two the result was most discouraging, for the granite walls hung together most obstinately for two hundred and twenty feet. A ray of hope came at last, with the appearance of ore, and before many months money was as plentiful with the persevering owners as it had previously been scarce.

The California was the "big paying mine" in 1869, '70, '71. In three and a half years the currency receipts for ore sold and milled were $521,000, and April, 1870, gave $30,000. Within a year after the ore body was entered, Stalker paid Standley $75,000 for his half interest in this 350 feet of ground and purchased other contesting claims beside. From depths of from 300 to over 500 feet below the surface the ore was unusually rich. In 1872 the richer pay ore was pretty well exhausted, and the yield was small from that time forward. Stalker died and the mine was idle for several years after 1874.

Late in 1877, Standley, who had been engaged in the banking business, and in other pursuits away from Central, resolved to start up the mine. He acquired 1,033 feet on the vein at low figures, all of the claims then being idle, and prepared to mine on an extensive and systematic scale. He had plenty of money to operate with, the result of the former harvest, and so labored under no disadvantage in that direction. Quite an important item was the fact that he had more feet on the vein to get returns from than before, in case it turned out well.

But there was no ore in sight and the future yield was somewhat problematical. Standley went ahead, nevertheless, as if he knew it was there. He picked a first-class foreman and went up the hill to a shaft 370 feet deep, and several hundred feet east of the old bonanza. A solid stone building of ample dimensions was put up and steam hoisting machinery of the most effective and improved pattern was procured and set at work. The search was almost as long a one in depth as it had been ten years before, but Standley was better prepared for it than then. After sinking for a time in barren rock, levels were run and a good vein developed.

Over thirty thousand dollars were expended before the gold began to come out of the ground, and then sinking and drifting were continued without using up the ore reserves, in order to have deposits in this underground mineral bank as plentiful and substantial as in the owner's establishment elsewhere. The work of drifting and sinking gave ore enough in the summer of 1878 to keep first twenty, and finally thirty stamps at work. Early in 1879 the quantity of mineral increased so that the fifty-stamp Richman mill was leased. All this time the vein was exceedingly rich and the shaft going down, down at a rate seldom seen in Colorado mining.

With the spring of 1879 more stamps were required and the Kimber thirty-five stamp-mill was leased. The California now supplies over 60 stamps, or more than any other mine, except the Bobtail, and is

THE MONMOUTH-KANSAS GOLD MILL.

said to be making more money even than any of its prosperous rivals. The present production and condition of the property, and the immense amount of ore that has been developed and uncovered, show that the owner knew how to mine and went at it in the right way. The shaft is now 940 feet deep, and the deepest worked in Colorado, except that of its neighbor just below, the Kansas. The ore body varies from fourteen inches to nine feet in width, and mills from $60 to $90 a cord, and sometimes $125 or $150. This is after smelting ore has been selected. This sells at from $70 to $75, and occasionally at $100 to $160 a ton. There are hundreds of tons of this mineral stored in the shaft house. The vein has been opened by levels at depths of five, six, seven, eight, and nine hundred feet, for hundreds of feet from the shaft. The three hundred level also shows ore. The shaft has been carried down seven feet wide by sixteen long, and is twelve feet inside of end timbers. It has cost $30 a foot to sink and timber it. The mill retort gold from this ore is worth from $14.30 to $15.40. Thirty men were engaged in breaking ore some time ago and a larger force now. The ground has been worked out but little below the 500 level. The daily yield of mill ore is about fifty tons. The mine yields from $14,000 to $15,000 monthly, and cleared $50,000 in six months to July 1, 1879.

The Gardner is that part of the lode extending from the California eastward to the Roderick Dhu and Kinney, and embraces 1,154 feet in length, Of this S. B. Hawley owns the western 354 feet. The Hawley-Gardner 200 feet comes next, and then the 300 feet of the Clark-Gardner Mining Company, including the Utley claim. East of this is the Philadelphia and Colorado Company's 300 feet. These claims are said to have given an aggregate yield of half a million dollars. The two company properties have been the richest, but all have paid at one time or another, and none have been worked steadily.

The Clark-Gardner mine is owned by a company in Rome, New York, and has shown some of the best ore bodies in the district, but was not worked to the greatest advantage until recently. An effort was made to strip the mine of ore a year or two ago, and over $17,000 was taken out in two months, when the company stopped the operation. Ten years ago, when this company suspended work, twelve ounce ore had been found in the bottom of the shaft 405 feet deep. When the present superintendent. J. W. Brown, started up the mine, it was not in condition to lead to dividends without expenditures for sinking and drifting. It had been pretty well worked out down to depth of 320 feet for some distance each side of the shaft, and the best ore below had been removed. It is reported to have paid expenses, however, for twenty-five or thirty employees. The usual yield has been a cord and a half, or eleven tons a day, with mill returns varying from an ounce and a half a cord up to ten, or from $22 to $160. The crevice is from thirty to forty inches wide, but sometimes much larger. The last reports say the ore mills seven ounces. The mine is being systematically opened, and is economically managed. It costs only $15 a foot for sinking the shaft four feet by nine, $3 a foot for drifting, and $8 a fathom for stoping, contractors furnishing their own powder, candles, and fuse. Not long ago the shaft was 440 feet deep, and there were prospects of finding an ore body like that worked out above, or like that of the California. What is needed for success is the consolidation of the entire lode into one mine, worked by one shaft and set of machinery.

The Roderick Dhu has yielded a great deal of money when worked by companies and by lessees. Five hundred feet owned by John Scudder has at times shown an immense crevice, is 550 feet deep with long levels and excavations. The Borton is east of the Roderick Dhu and both are considered parts of the Gardner vein. Several hundred thousand dollars are said to have been taken out altogether from these two mines. The Kinney, leading out of the Gardner northeasterly, is said to have been paying a few men $1,000 per month.

The Burroughs extends from the western part of the Kansas lode eastward, making an acute angle with the latter, and is nearly parallel and about four hundred feet north of the California-Gardner. Ben Burroughs discovered it in May. 1859. Its history has been a chequered one, varying from "rich strikes" to suspension of work with change of owners and lessees. There are many separate properties, embracing altogether 2,509 feet, most of which are now worked. The richest portion is included in the 462 feet owned by the Ophir Company. Here Pat Casey made his "big raise" in 1862-3, and here a party of Cornish miners made fortunes in 1874-5. Casey was an uneducated Irishman—energetic, lively, and generous. After the claims he had bought on time of the Burroughs brothers "capped on him" and he had exhausted his funds and credit he discovered one of the richest bonanzas of the mountains by the accidental caving of a part of the mine. Wealth then rolled in on him in a steady stream, a large force of miners was employed, and Pat Casey's wild rollicking "night hands" are remembered to this day by old timers. This was the first property sold in New York in 1863. It brought $90,000. Casey afterwards got rid of his fortune and is now in the Black Hills. The Ophir Company took out an immense amount of money, but it did not make much difference to eastern organizations in those days how much a mine yielded—they were no better off for it. In 1868-9 when there was a large sum of money due the men employed, they worked the mine awhile and soon took out their back pay. The mine was full of water for years until six of these miners leased it in 1873. In twenty months they took out $160,000 and returned to Cornwall with $100,000 of that amount. The mine was then 714 feet deep. It was soon leased by other parties, but owing to the vein dividing they lost money and abandoned it at a depth of 1,000 feet. The Gilpin and La Crosse company claims have been worked steadily for some time by lessees. The vein splits in the latter about 350 feet below the surface, but is producing something at a depth of over 400 feet. The Burroughs vein has produced altogether nearly $1,250,000 coin.

The Flack is another famous lode, parallel with the California and Indiana, and probably terminating in the Mercer County. There have been times when rich ore was mined in plentiful quantities. Like the Forks, it has been idle most of the time for years. Long ago one of the shafts reached a depth of 580 feet. Several hundred thousand dollars are said to have come out of the vein. The Mercer County also paid well once. Work was resumed on it eighteen months ago, and the shaft deepened to 550 feet. The two main properties or sets of claims on the Flack have been worked for a year or two. Last winter steam hoisting works were erected over each of them, and sinking and drifting is now successfully prosecuted. The shafts are 640 and 350 feet deep.

The Forks lode, on the western portion of Quartz Hill, was at one time one of the most productive mines in the county, and could be made so again if reopened and worked as other prominent veins have been. It has a course north of east, and intersects the Flack and California. It pitches southward quite strongly, which would bring it into the Kansas at depths of from 700 to 1,000 feet. There is

15

evidently a bonanza along the line of junction. The Forks produced heavily in the first decade of its history, and was famous for the mammoth size of its vein, as well as for its profitable character. The deepest shaft is down 517 feet. Last fall work was resumed on the Wheeler claims. A new building with steam hoisting works was put up, and the shaft carried down to a depth of 350 feet, with rich mill and smelting ore all the way. It is said that over four hundred thousand dollars' worth of gold have been taken from the Forks lode. The vein carries considerable silver and lead.

The Alps-Mackie mine is situated on two contiguous locations on the lode of that name. There is also another vein that pitches in an opposite direction from that first mentioned and crosses it over three hundred feet below the surface. These and other lodes, with buildings and strong hoisting works for two shafts, belong to the Cleveland Gold Company, organized on the property in 1875-6, on the basis of a capital stock of $250,000. Previous to that time George R. Mitchell held the property for debts due from the Alps and Grenada Companies. The latter expended their working capital in a large mill and other improvements. The mine had paid handsomely at intervals, and the ore was often very rich. Within two months after the discovery in 1863, the receipts for ore milled was $17,591 from the Mackie claims alone. The profits were $9,399.87. There were 20¾ cords that gave an average yield of $552.68 per cord, and 17¾ an average of $345. The Alps claims yielded $54,537.14 in four months, with the wonderful average of $818 a cord, or over $100 a ton. The profits of both properties in these lots of ore in four months were $52,253, of which $42,853 came from the Alps.

The ore bodies yielded large amounts in subsequent years, but it seems the mistake of following the crossing vein led the company into unprofitable ground. The property had been unworked most of the time from 1870 to 1876.

In eighteen months of 1866-7-8, the yield was $78,415, and $10,654 soon after came from assorted waste materials of the stulls. After 1869 lots of smelting ore were sold at good prices. The following shows the product of the Alps-Mackie mine up to 1875, currency :

Mackie product from July, 1863, to October, 1863.... $31,449 15
    "   from October, 1863, to February, 1864.   41 792 18

Alps product from July, 1863, to December, 1863.... $54,537 14
      "   from December, 1863, to February, 1864.   37,911 16
Alps and Mackie product from July, 1866, to January,
      1867.................................... .....   78,415 41
Alps and Mackie product from March, 1868, to July,
      1868..   10,654 74
Alps and Mackie product from September, 1868, to
      September, 1869.............................   20,040 64
Alps and Mackie product from September, 1869, to
      March, 1870.................................   11.035 90
Estimated product of the mine not included in the
      above 75,000 00
                                                      _____
      Making the total product................... $360,836 32
                                                      ═══════════

The Cleveland Company has been developing the mine for some
time, and has deepened the shafts and extended the levels east and
west until at last another rich ore-body has been opened up. One
of the shafts is now down over 567 feet. The last reports were
extremely favorable, the ore milling twenty dollars a ton after
smelting ore had been selected. The latter sells at high figures,
and is similar to some of the rich quartz that brought up the milling average to such high figures before the days of smelting works.
Some extraordinary lumps of ore are found. Very high assays
were lately obtained. Ore is being mined in the 450 ft., 500 and
560 levels. The latter has recently opened out a vein three feet wide,
that yields about $23 per ton after the richer ore averaging $200 has
been selected therefrom. Two steam pumps are used in the mine.

The Jessie mine is worked to a depth of two hundred feet with
steam-power, and the R. D. Kenney, Gauntlet, Dutchman, Barnes,
and National are said to be paying. The Missouri is profitably
worked on two claims, and has yielded over $100,000.

The Illinois and Confidence lodes extend along the northeastern
slope of Quartz Hill, and is developed at that part bordering on
what was called the Patch Diggings, near the Roderick Dhu and
Borton properties. About three hundred feet in length of the Illinois, partly worked to a depth of two hundred and sixty feet, has
yielded not far from $300,000, currency value. A company made a
great deal of money there in 1867–8, and large mill and mine build-

ings, with fine machinery, were put up at a cost of $100,000. In 1869 B. S. Buell, one of the original owners, and others, came into possession of the property and worked it at intervals afterwards. The mine has paid profits in many different years. The cost of mining, milling, and hoisting, $5.00 to $7.00 per ton. In 1868, 1,500 tons milled $15.88 per ton, and forty tons sold for $112 per ton. Occasionally the vein widens, showing ore-bodies ten feet thick. The immense buildings over the mine and the two shafts contain a twenty-two stamp mill, shops, store-rooms, and offices necessary for an establishment of the largest kind, and a splendid set of hoisting works.

The Kent County is one of the leading veins of Quartz Hill, and is said to have produced several hundred thousand dollars. Richard Mackay, who has been one of the district's most skillful and prominent miners among such lodes as the Gunnell and Suderberg, owns the western 3,256 feet of the Kent County. This embraces most of the valuable portion of it. Since 1876 he has opened this mine in a very extensive manner to a depth of over 700 feet, with long levels at intervals of one hundred feet down to that depth. The vein is generally large and profitable, the ore-body varying from four to seven feet wide. Thirty-seven stamps have been almost entirely supplied from this mine for three years, and the yield of salable smelting ore has been as high as sixty tons monthly. The mill ore has generally yielded from four to seven ounces to the cord, and the smelting ore sells at from $50 to $100 a ton. The main shaft is covered by a large mill building, supplied with one of the best set of steam-hoisting works in the county. The production of the mine is not generally known, but many months of past years have given from four to five thousand dollars' worth of mill gold, and in one month the mine produced $11,000. Mr. Mackay is building a fine fifty-stamp mill for this mine.

The American Flag lode extends in a northeasterly direction through a part of the western section of Quartz Hill down into Nevada Gulch. It is a large vein and is said to have yielded over three hundred thousand dollars. It was worked only at intervals in the first decade of mining in the district, and has been idle for its entire length since 1872. The last work done was on the Clayton property in that and the preceding year, when the profits are believed to have been large. Previous to 1869 the American Flag

Company had worked two or three shafts on some five hundred feet of the property, to depths of from three to five hundred feet. The caving in of some of the underground workings had placed the mine in bad condition, requiring a considerable outlay of capital to resume work effectively.

Men were found, however, in the immediate neighborhood, who were willing to take hold of the property. The recent record of one mine after another that had been developed into producing condition were inducement sufficient for the resumption of work on the American Flag. In June, 1879, and association of Central and Nevada miners, bankers, and business and mill men, leased 550 feet of the company property, and since putting up the requisite machinery, have been clearing the mine of water preparatory to continuous work. This furnishes another instance of the confidence which Colorado men have in these mines. They show their faith in the country by putting their own money into its mines and fissures, even if large expenditures are required for preliminay work and exploration. If eastern company owners lack the nerve to work their own properties, these men that live around the mines are willing to invest their accumulations, their money and muscle on temporary leases only (where the permanent improvements they make must revert to the owners), confident that they will encounter no exception to the rule that a vein that paid well on the surface can be depended on for continuous production below. At the present rate, at which old mines are being reopened, there will soon be no idle ground in the county—and there are hundreds of veins studded with claims and shafts in this same gold belt, whose courses can be traced from any hill side.

The American Flag Company property embraces 550 feet on the American Flag and Bennett lodes, which are said to have yielded gold to the currency value of $300,000. The lease referred to in the last paragraph is of five years' duration—the company to receive twenty per cent. of the gross earnings of the mine, less $3\frac{1}{2}$ ounces of gold per cord of the milling ore. The capital stock of this company is 60,000 ten-dollar shares.

CHAPTER XII.

GILPIN COUNTY MINES—NEW MINING ENTERPRISES ON OLD AND
WELL-TRIED MINES---WYANDOTTE AND GOLD DIRT—HOW FOR-
TUNES WERE MADE IN THE LONG AGO—RICH POCKETS AND
LARGE VEINS—THE NEW SILVER DISTRICT—RICH ORE AND
GOOD LODES—THE VALUABLE DISCOVERIES OF 1878.

Among the productive localities of this gold region is Leavenworth Hill. It contains a perfect net-work of mineral veins, most
of which converge toward the centre of its eastern slope, as if some
mammoth deposit had been forced toward the surface in fragments.
Old miners say there were no better diggings than those of the surface
outcroppings of this locality. Much of the surface of the hill has
been dug over, and the vein material gophered out without system
for short distances downward. Thousands of cords of ore have
been milled, with a reputed yield of something like a round million.
The companies took out much gold, but the original owners more.

There has been no time since the first discoveries when all the
claims were idle, for men have been making money there every season. The properties were too much subdivided, however, to permit
of profitable deep mining, and until recently many owners held
their property at too high figures to permit of buying and consolidat-
ing to advantage. Within the past two years some of these men
have united and combined their claims with others purchased and
relocated, and the result is the Wyandotte Consolidated Gold and
Silver Mining Company, organized with a capital stock of six hundred thousand dollars, in shares of a par value of three dollars, for
the purpose of developing the dozen valuable lodes of the hill.
Among these are the Wyandotte, Elmer, Leavenworth, and East
Leavenworth, Gold Ring, Calhoun, and others, and the total number
of feet of veins covered by government titles is 12,270 feet.

A shaft is being sunk at a point where several of these lodes converge or unite, with the design of driving cross cuts in the underground workings so as to intersect and develop them. This shaft is

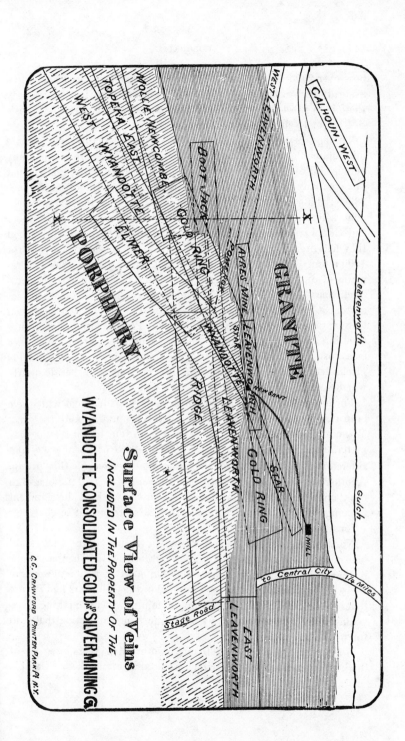

Surface View of Veins
INCLUDED IN THE PROPERTY OF THE
WYANDOTTE CONSOLIDATED GOLD ᴬⁿᴰ SILVER MINING Cᴼ.

C. G. CRAWFORD, PRINTER PARK PL N.Y.

now over 200 feet deep, and the crevice matter penetrated has shown a steady improvement as depth was gained. The last reports say there is five feet of crevice, and much ore worth $90 a ton. It costs $14 a foot to sink the shaft 5 feet by 9.

The figures of the past yield of the property of this company are not obtainable, owing to repeated changes of ownership of the many claims and of the mills where the ore was treated. It is known that one company took out three hundred thousand dollars from a space 230 feet long and an average depth of 90 feet on the Leavenworth vein, after the discoverers had previously made snug fortunes there. Individual troubles caused another company to suspend work when they had ore in the bottom of the Wyandotte shaft that sold for $300 a ton. The numerous crevice and shaft excavations and remains of dump piles are silent yet telling monuments of past productiveness. For years mill men, when short of ore, were accustomed to team away the refuse from the shafts that had been thrown away as worthless. Professor Pearce, when operating smelting works fourteen miles distant, obtained ore from this place at a cost of ten dollars per ton for freight alone. Very valuable pitch blende ore has been mined in the Leavenworth, beside quartz worth several dollars a pound.

For long distances bodies of ore from two to four feet wide have been developed in the two Leavenworth properties, and the great Wyandotte or Harsh vein has carried from four to ten feet of pay material within well defined walls. The presence of porphyry is considered a good indication of the mineral character of this group. Another year will undoubtedly see Leavenworth Hill take a high rank among gold-producing localities, for the work of development is going steadily forward with a uniform improvement in character of ore encountered.

Northward from Central and Black Hawk the Gilpin county gold belt makes itself especially prominent at Gold Dirt. There are veins in that locality that rival in size and value of contents those mentioned in preceding chapters. The yield of the Gold Dirt and Perigo lodes in the earlier years of Colorado mining was something marvelous. There were also many other mines in that section that paid for working.

Mining began there in 1860, and two or three years later one of the liveliest camps in the territory was fairly established. Gamble

Gulch was lined with arastras, quartz mills, sluice boxes, cabins, stores and saloons, and almost everybody had money who operated claims in that vicinity. The best days of the settlement were from 1862 to 1864, when some five hundred votes were polled in that precinct at the annual elections.

Some of the quartz gave up the precious metal so plentifully that little care was taken in milling or saving it, and the dumps and mill tailings were long after found to be quite valuable. Sluices and stamp mill coppers were lined and coated with gold, and dust enough could be panned from the surface dirt to satisfy the most avaricious prospector. Some idea of how loosely it was scattered about may be formed from the fact that when the camp began to break up, a miner obtained over a thousand dollars' worth of gold by cleaning up the fireplace and dirt floor of a deserted cabin where retorting had been done occasionally.

In 1864 a committee of Gold Dirt citizens, appointed for the purpose, approximated the yield of the Gold Dirt lode for the two preceding years at $930,000, in the varying currency values at which it had been sold. J. Q. A. Rollins had obtained $250,000 from a claim only 33⅓ feet long on the vein, and Hollister & Company $200,000 from an adjoining claim of equal size. Such a production from so little territory in so short a time has seldom if ever been equaled in Colorado. Fairbanks & Keene, on another claim, obtained $70,000; then came Grill, Hulbert & Co., with $150,000; Elliott & Fowler, $65,000; the Mulligan Brothers, $15,000; the Gold Dirt Company, $120,000; and Hall, Evans & DePeyster, $60,000. The banking house of Clark, Gruber & Co., of Denver, paid $150,000 for gold from the Hollister claim alone.

These claims were mostly sold to Eastern companies in 1864. The Hope Mining Company, owning on the present Ophir location, including the two small but rich claims noted above, made money until it embarked in a process mill operation. It took $125,000 to build this great mill, and then cost more to operate the imperfect concern than there was gold in the ore handled. Because no profit could be obtained in operating this mill the company concluded that the vein was worthless, and stopped work after having sunk through a large vein all the way in the lower sixty feet of the main shaft. A depth of 500 feet had then been attained, and men who worked there say the ore was of more than ordinary value.

The Perigo was worked by a score of different owners through as many shafts, and is said to have yielded altogether not far from $400,000. This yield, like that of the Gold Dirt, from mines worked without system or concerted action, indicates what could be done under happier auspices. Poor milling caused more gold to be lost than was saved. The superintendents of companies on these lodes came from entirely different pursuits at the East, and knew nothing of mining and cared less. Finally one mine after another shut down and the miners departed for more inviting fields. The yield of ore ranged from $150 to $600 a cord, and $300 were common returns at the Rollins mill.

It was the old story of abandoned and lost mines—lost by debts and taxes, or more frequently by relocation under the late congressional abandonment act. The camp fell to decay, and ruined mine and mill buildings were all that was left of the once flourishing but since deserted village of Gold Dirt. As the place was off of the traveled road it was seldom visited, and gradually became almost forgotten. The mines were there, however, and a few of the " old " timers believed they could be made profitable.

J. Q. A. Rollins owned some isolated claims on these lodes. He preferred to let them remain idle until he could secure adjoining properties, and thus be surer of successful mining. Owners of the latter paid no attention to the annual assessment work required by the congressional act of 1875. Rollins was aware of this, and relocated many of the idle mines and purchased others. In time he came to be the owner by government title of the lodes and timber and placer lands of the entire locality, and is now preparing to carry into effect his long-cherished plans of mining on a scale commensurate with the size and magnitude of the property.

The Gold Dirt vein west of Gamble Gulch is called the Savage, on which a tunnel has been started that will eventually attain a depth of 1,000 feet on the vein. East of the gulch is the Crown Point location, on the same lode, on which a tunnel is being driven that will be 400 feet deep after it enters the more easterly Ophir location. The most of the vein's past production has come from the Ophir and Virginia. The latter has but 300 feet of the lode, but has yielded not far from $400,000. A tunnel driven in the Perigo would eventually attain a depth on the vein below surface outcroppings of nearly 2,000 feet.

The Rollins property embraces 20,000 feet of lodes, whose surface locations include nearly all that part of the district that has been very productive. On the Gold Dirt lode are four locations— the Ophir, 1,500 feet; Virginia, 300; Crown Point, 1,500; and Savage, 1,500; or 4,800 altogether. On the Perigo lode, 3,200 feet are included, and 1,500 on each of the once productive Colorado (Maurer), the Comstock, New York, Surprise, and some other veins. Beside the lode veins covered by government patents are over 400 acres of patented placer lands along South Boulder Creek, Gamble Gulch and tributary streams—and the largest amount of mountain farming land in any one locality in this part of the State.

The Rollins steam quartz mill is located at Rollinsville, on a down grade from the mines. It is terrace built, 100 feet long by 65 feet wide, and has one of the finest water-powers in the State, the water being conducted along the upper side of the building in a flume or raceway. Here are twelve stamps and room for fifty more, and an eighty horse-power-engine.

There is no property in the State that offers greater inducements for the resumption of work than the Gold Dirt, and although it will take money to drain, open and outfit it, but a short time need be required to get it back again. With persistent development under economical management the same favorable results may be expected that are met with in the reconstructed mines around Central and Nevadaville.

The valley of the South Boulder is one of the most beautiful in the mountains, and affords a most charming summer resort, with its spacious hotel, green sloping meadows, streams and lakes, and adjacent hunting and fishing resorts. A wagon road leads over the snowy range to Middle Park, thirty miles distant. This farm, or series of farms, yields seven or eight thousand bushels of potatoes every season, hundreds of tons of hay, while rye and oats grow seven feet high.

At the head of Gamble Gulch, and between the new silver district and Gold Dirt, is the Golden Flint Mine. This was very productive at one time, but had been idle for a long time previous to last fall. Hendrie, Bolthoff and Macfarlane have since been operating it with quite a force of miners and the aid of steam-hoisting works. The shaft has been deepened and levels driven. The ore from this mine has yielded from four to twelve ounces of gold to the cord. The new fifteen-stamp mill, owned by the same men that operate the mine, has been engaged in crushing the ore.

The sections in and around Lake and Russell districts are more active than they have been in many years. The gulches are worked every summer for gold by the aid of water from the Consolidated Ditch. These and North Clear Creek give employment to about one hundred men, including many Chinese, who have been purchasing partially worked out claims. Gulch mining yields from $30,000 to $45,000 annually. The Paul and Harker claim, and one or two others, are worked by means of hydraulics. There are a large number of lodes operated—most of them lately idle—and much rich ore is being obtained. Among these are the Topeka, Fairfield, Spinney. Emerson, one or two mines on the Pewabie, the Saratoga, Nottaway, Williams, Justice, Powers, Aduddel, Caledonia, Gold Cloud, and Hazeltine. Just over the Clear Creek line, at the head of Virginia Cañon, are the productive Champion, Specie Payment, German, Trio, Clarissa, Virginia, Nabob, Racket, Monte Cristo, and others, Some of them will be noticed in a Clear Creek county chapter.

The Richardson lode, containing nine hundred feet, covered by a U. S. patent, is located on the south side of, and leading into the heart of the famous gold basin, Russell Gulch. The vein varies from one to four feet in thickness, and averages about three feet. Owing to internal and legal difficulties among the original owners it has been but little developed, and this only by the use of the primitive hand-power windlass. Five shafts, at short intervals one from the other, have been sunk along the vein, the deepest being about forty feet. The ores from the latter, many cords of which were produced in progress of sinking, gave the remarkable mill returns of $1,000 a cord and upward. In addition to this several tons of still richer ore were selected and sold to the smelters. From shaft No. 3 to shaft No. 5, a distance of two hundred feet, the vein averages one foot in thickness, worth from $30 to $80 per ton. Although the development is slight the vein shows so much valuable mineral that, if not one of the largest, it is considered one of the richest in the county.

The Williams lode was discovered long ago, and the owner to the more famous portion having died some years since, no work was done until Lester Drake and his sons took hold of it two years ago. Starting in without capital, they continued to make money by simply sinking and drifting. The ores carried both gold and silver in paying quantities, with a generous amount of copper. The richer mineral was sold to the smelter at from $60 to $150 per ton, more or less, and larger quantities of ore were treated in stamp mills, where little more than the gold was saved. The yield there was from $60 to $85 per ton for a long period. Up to the time when a depth of 315 feet had been attained, but little stoping had been done. In two years $42,000 had been received for ore treated, and experts say there was a still larger value in reserve in the mine above the lower workings. This refers to 550 continuous feet, sold in April, 1879, to R. F. Weitbrec and K. G. Cooper, of Denver, for $42,000, and which is now worked by the Gilpin County Mining Company, of their organization. Since then a shaft house, 30 by 50 feet, has been contructed, with engine, boiler, and hoisting rig, and the mine will be deepened and developed rapidly. Beside this property disposed of by L. & E. Drake, the more westerly part of the Williams vein is worked to a depth of 250 feet. Up to April last there had been removed from the Gilpin Company claims 522 fathoms of ground, with an average per fathom of $80.46, viz.: smelting ore per fathom, $53.64; mill ore per fathom, $26.82. This vein carries liberal quantities of gold, silver, and copper. A rich vein has been found in the Updegraph and Packard claims.

The Dallas lode crosses North Clear Creek a short distance above Black Hawk, and has been worked by shafts and excavations in the mountains on either side. The part in Silver Mountain and east of the creek carries more silver and lead than the western half of the lode. It has been traced up to the locality where the rich Cyclops and Fannie group of silver mines has been opened. The main production of the lode has come from the part in Dallas Mountain which is west of the creek. For two years the mine opened there has been very profitable. Various causes prevented vigorous development, but several shafts have been sunk and levels driven down to a depth of 120 feet. The vein has usually been from four to seven feet wide, with very little waste rock and considerable smelting ore, rich in gold, silver, and lead. One or two cords of ore have been milled daily for a long time, which gave returns of from four to eight ounces of gold, or of from $60 to $120 a cord. The record of four days' work taken from the receipts of the owners made the following: Besides $100 for smelting ore, three cords of ore yielded at the rate of $96.18 per cord; two cords at $106.50, and one cord and a quarter, $107.30; total, six cords and a quarter, $635.66; an average of about $100, or seven ounces per cord. It costs from $15 to 16 per fathom in these levels to mine or break down the ore and raise it to the surface—the latter being done by horse power, and a contrivance called a "whip." On a vein of this unusual width a fathom of ground, when broken down, will make about two cords, or sixteen tons of ore, showing a cost for mining and hoisting of $8 per cord, or $1 per ton. The expense of hauling a cord of ore to a mill, and of crushing it and extracting the gold, is $24. This shows a total outlay for mining, milling, etc., of $32 for a return of from $70 to $115. It cost only $200 to obtain the $635.66 from the six and one-quarter cords of ore noted above.

The mine has so far paid all expenses of development, besides leaving a considerable amount of surplus or working capital in the company's treasury. The shaft is being deepened and the levels extended as rapidly as possible, and when double their present length, they will, with the aid of the stoping ground, be able to pay big dividends to the owners. In the mean time, two cords of ore yielding $200 daily from the labor of seven miners, is a very good thing for any firm to have—and those were the returns at last accounts.

There are a number of tunnels in Gilpin county that are being driven to intersect lodes and to work the same. Some of these have been pushed forward steadily by the labor and money of business men and miners for many years. The Bobtail tunnel at the Bobtail lode has already been noticed. There are several that have not been extended for some time, and others, such as the Centennial, Black Hawk, German, Quartz Hill, and Central City are pushed forward more or less energetically. The La Crosse tunnel, owned by the company of the same name, passes into Quartz Hill something like 1,000 feet, 150 of which was driven last year. It is only from 180 to 200 feet below the surface above, and consequently can be of no great benefit in working mines.

The Central City tunnel was started by D. G. Wilson, who organized a company on the enterprise. It enters Quartz Hill just above the Quartz Hill tunnel and the limits of Central, and is headed in the direction of such main lodes as the Burroughs, Missouri, Illinois, and Roderick Dhu, which it will intersect some five hundred feet beneath the surface of the ground. Steam drills and an air-compressor are used, and are thought to do cheaper and better execution than hand drills. The eastern portion of the Kansas lode has been intersected, and the Fortune and Corydon, Lewis and Columbia are some distance ahead. The tunnel had penetrated the hill about five hundred and fifty feet at last accounts. The enterprise is a promising one, as old lodes can be explored and several blind lodes may be discovered. For drainage purposes this tunnel should be of great service.

The German tunnel is a home enterprise of Central business men, which has been driven nearly seven hundred feet into Mammoth Hill. There are many valuable lodes crossing the territory ahead of it, which will be intersected hundreds of feet in depth. Several veins have already been reached. The outlook is good for dividends when the Mammoth and other lodes have been opened.

The Centennial tunnel is in Mammoth Hill, is about four hundred feet long, and has crossed several blind lodes that have yielded large amounts of ore. The enterprise has paid well at times. The breast of the tunnel must be near the Tierney lode.

The Saratoga is a large vein, worked at the depth of one hundred and twenty feet by an intersecting tunnel, with levels extending therefrom. The soft iron-stained dirt and quartz is easily mined, and the mill gold is of unusually high value. The Silver Dollar mine is extensively opened by shafts and levels, and is reported as quite profitable. Its main value is in silver. The Powers is very rich in copper, carrying from ten to forty-five per cent. The vein carries enargite or sulphide of copper and arsenic.

In the silver belt of the southern part of the county is one very large vein, which extends from Willis Gulch clear over Clifton or Virginia Mountain, a distance of over a mile. It carries considerable galena, sometimes forty to sixty per cent, and a fair amount of silver. The developments of some portions are extensive, and the yield pretty large. This vein is known under the names of Aduddel, Serle, Clifton, and Rara Avis. Nearly all parts of it have been worked extensively. The Aduddel has been yielding paying ore for several years, and almost from the time of discovery. It carries considerable galena, and is a large, strong vein. Not far distant are the War Dance, and Rose and Plume. Last winter, while sinking a shaft on the former thirty-five feet, and driving a level fifty feet, two men obtained ore that sold for $2,674, and yielded $4,300. The vein carries from $50 to $90 in silver to the ton, and from $5 to $12 in gold. Later, from three to ten tons of ore were mined and sold per week. Henry Paul has valuable silver mines in this same section, where he has been lode and placer mining for years, and at the same time raising crops of grain and vegetables nearly 9,500 feet above sea-level.

THE BLACK HAWK SILVER DISTRICT.

This includes Silver Hill and the sections at and near Hughesville, Wide-Awake district, Bald Mountain, and the Harper Ranch. The first discoveries were made on Silver Hill, near the close of May, and in June, 1878, by Professor S. W. Tyler, assayer and engineer, and E. A. Lynn, an old time prospector. During the summer and fall, while lodes were being opened all around them, they worked their mines and continued to make an occasional discovery. They located the Cyclops and Fanny at the beginning. The Saint James was also one of the earliest veins recorded.

In August, the Hard Money at Hughes' ranch, a mile and a half from the Cyclops, was discovered; likewise the Boss lode on the Harper Ranch. All of the above have since produced regularly, and have paid well, at the same time that they have attracted many prospectors and miners to their districts, resulting in new discoveries. There are now over one hundred men at work and some five hundred locations have been made. Among these veins the galena ores seem to be the most valuable, but some ruby silver and gray copper are found. The best ore yields from 400 to over 1,000 ounces of silver per ton. Most of the silver discoveries are among the hills and mountains to the east and north of North Clear Creek. South and west of that stream is the great gold belt.

The Cyclops was discovered May 29, 1878, and is owned under the affix of numbers one and two, by Tyler and Lynn. The first ore was sold July first. Ten shafts have been opened to depths of from 20 to 100 feet. Six of these, at intervals of 100 feet, have yielded ore, and three of them are now paying handsomely. The ore vein varies in width from a few inches up to three feet, and generally carries from 100 to 900 ounces of silver per ton. Some of it shows streaks of ruby silver mineral of unusual size and value. Up to May 31, 1879, the Cyclops had yielded over 20,000 ounces of silver. Good profits have been divided, beside developing the property into its present productive condition.

The Cyclops has, beside rich vein matter, gangue of quartz and feldspar, or quartz, hornstone and calcspar, the latter with true silver minerals. The minerals or ores proper, are galena, zinc blende, and iron pyrites, and considerable proportions of ruby and brittle silver, occurring in solid streaks from one to eight inches thick, or scattered throughout a foot or more of quartz, in the latter class making up the second-rate ores.

The Fanny is just below the Cyclops, and is owned by Tyler, Lynn, Gray, and Pease. Its workings are confined to a shaft 100 feet deep and a 50 foot adit entering the same at a depth of 30 feet. The width of the vein is shown by the development to be from two to six feet, with a pay streak of from two inches to three feet in thickness, generally clinging to the north wall. The sixty foot level east shows for twenty feet in the floor an average of eighteen inches of pay, of which from two inches to one foot is solid mineral —galena—milling over 300 ounces of silver per ton, and the balance mixed ore—quartz, with mineral, sulphurets of silver and native silver—milling from 40 to 200 ounces. Total ground removed in shaft, levels, and stopes, 52 fathoms; portion bearing ore, 45 fathoms. The gross value of silver produced has been, in round numbers, $17,000; net return for same, in round numbers, $13,000. The net profit on same over all expenses has been 50 per cent., or $8,500. For every fathom of ground removed in the whole mine the average has been: Gross product, $230; net return, $173; net profit, $36.50. Per fathom of ore ground proper: Gross product, $266; net return, $200; net profit, $100.

The character of the ores of some of the best and richest of these silver veins is exemplified in returns of the Fanny lode. In the latter part of May, 1879, S. W. Tyler sold 9 tons and 358 pounds of ore for $1,832.93, and in the first week of June 4¾ tons for $1,212.65. Average receipts per ton, $218; average yield per ton, over $260. The four richest lots gave 608 ounces, 605 ounces, 490 ounces, and 470 ounces of silver per ton. The three poorest lots gave 71 ounces, 87 ounces, and 88 ounces per ton. Total receipts for sales of less than four weeks, $3,045.58. Expenses less than $1,000.

The Silent Friend, Humboldt, Mary Graham, and Joe Reynolds, on this same Silver Hill, are promising veins, but have not been opened extensively. The Mary Graham has a good vein of paying ore which is producing well.

Between Silver Hill and the Hard Money lode are many locations, of which the Toronto, Wellington, New York, and Emerald are the principal ones. The two first named have turned out much ore, yielding from 80 to 300 ounces per ton. The Wellington main shaft is 50 feet deep. This lode is of the unusual size of nine feet, and what are considered average samples of the crevice assay from 20 to 50 ounces of silver. Tons of assorted mineral have been sold, carrying from 200 to 1,000 ounces per ton.

The Hard Money is owned by Hunderman and Locke. Its size, great value, and profits, are making it famous. Its product, mainly obtained after October, and from then to July, is said to have been over $40,000. One report makes it 50,000 ounces of silver; another 55,000; the deepest shaft is 128 feet. The Philadelphia is nearly parallel with the Hard Money. The Rough and Ready appears to be nearly on a line with the Hard Money and Boss lodes; time may prove all three to be parts of one continuous vein. The Bonanza, a more recent discovery, bids fair to be a first-class vein. Many locations were made and some good lodes found all through this section too late in the year to permit of prospecting or continuous work. This summer will enable their value to be tested. The Boss lode, owned by Sayer & Owens, pays handsomely; steam hoisting works have lately been put up. Smith E. Stevens is driving the Silver Flag tunnel from North Clear Creek towards the silver belt and veins of the mountains above and beyond. Many veins will be crossed at great depth. The Queen Emma is a valuable lode.

The Rough and Ready lode has probably shown the richest ore in the district; specimens have assayed from 14,000 to 21,000 ounces, and small mill runs which yielded at the rate of several thousand dollars a ton. The Forrester and Fremont lodes on Bald Mountain have shown rich ore. There are more than fifty of these silver-bearing lodes discovered within a year that are yielding more or less money. The district will add considerably to Gilpin county's bullion product, and bids fair to rival most other Colorado silver camps in importance. The number and value of veins discovered in so short a time is remarkable.

CHAPTER XIII.

CLEAR CREEK COUNTY—MINES OF SILVER AND GOLD—DETAILS AND
STATISTICS OF THE GREAT SILVER DISTRICT—THE COUNTY'S
YIELD OF THE PRECIOUS METALS NEARLY $20,000,000—ANNUAL
STATEMENTS OF THE PRODUCT—GEORGETOWN, SILVER PLUME,
IDAHO SPRINGS, AND THEIR COUNTLESS MINERAL VEINS.

Clear Creek county includes the region drained by South Clear
Creek, and embraces the best known and best developed silver district of Colorado. It is bounded by Gilpin county on the north,
Jefferson on the east, Park on the south, and Summit and Grand on
the west. South Clear Creek and its branches sweep down the
cañons in and below the Snowy Range, forming long narrow valleys,
wherein the population mainly finds its abiding place. The steep
and rugged mountains that flank these valleys and ravines are ribbed
with veins of silver, often of immense value. Here and there are
newly built villages, thriving mining camps, or solitary cabins to
indicate the presence of the miner or prospector. The entire section,
up to elevations of 11,000 or 11,200 feet, is more or less thickly
covered with pine and other forest species.

South Clear Creek is formed by the union, four miles below
Georgetown, of the Empire and Georgetown forks. All around are
lofty mountains, and between rises a steep and rugged spur of the
range, which, beginning at the junction of the forks and running
south and west, is known under the names of Douglas, Colfax,
Democrat, Republican, Sherman, and Brown mountains. Opposite
Republican are Griffith and Saxon mountains. Two beautiful
streams, fresh from the springs and snows of Gray's Peaks and
Argentine and Geneva passes, unite at Georgetown to form the fork
referred to above. Between these extends a spur of the snowy
range. One portion is called McClellan mountain, and that overlooking Georgetown is known as Leavenworth. Close by Gray's
Peak is Kelso mountain. These elevations embrace the silver-bearing localities around Georgetown. North of the Empire fork of the
creek are Silver and other mountains, noted for their gold veins and
alluvial deposits. Further down South Clear Creek is the famous
silver locality of Red Elephant mountain, and opposite that of

GEORGETOWN.

Columbian mountain. Other lodes and veins, generally carrying gold, silver, and copper, are found at intervals from Mill City to Gilpin county, and from upper Trail Creek to Idaho Springs, while the streams are productive of gold. A large portion of the silver lodes near Georgetown, and for miles above and below, carry black sulphurets and gray copper. Ruby and native silver and silver glance are met with. The same belt contains many veins of the heavy galena, zinc blende order. From eight to ten per cent. of lead is a common occurrence, but from thirty to sixty per cent. is not unusual.

Georgetown is built at the head of a level valley, with mountains rising above it, covered with pine and ribbed with silver. Above Georgetown, and at the feet of Republican, Sherman, and Leavenworth mountains, are the adjoining towns of Silver Plume and Brownville. These and the still newer village of Lawson are the main settlements of this part of this great silver belt.

Gold was discovered on Chicago Creek, Spanish Bar, and above and below the present site of Idaho Springs in 1859. The Empire gold lodes and placers produced largely in 1862-4. The first silver discovery was made late in 1864, on McClellan mountain, and prospecting became lively all around Georgetown in 1865-6. The territory then possessed no means of treating silver ores, as the only successful mills at that day were the gold stampers. A few attempts were made to reduce the ores, and in 1866-8 chlorodizing-roasting, and amalgamation mills were erected, and a few smelters of small capacity. Then came the Brownville smelter, that turned out great silver buttons worth from ten to fifteen thousand dollars each. Joseph Watson, C. A. Martine, and Garrett, Hucpeden, J. O. Stewart, Schirmer & Bruckner, and Frank Dibbin, were engaged in ore reduction, and later Palmer & Nichols and the Stewart Reducing Company. After 1865 gold-mining declined around Empire and Idaho, but the silver mines began to produce largely in 1869, '70, '71. Among those especially prominent in the earlier years of silver-mining were the Equator, Terrible, Brown, Coin, Compass and Square, Anglo Saxon, Astor, Belmont, and International. For years many lodes near Georgetown, Idaho, and Spanish Bar were worked for gold whose value lay mainly in silver. Garrett, Martine & Co. made Colorado's first silver brick and firist practically tested the Bruckner roasting cylinder.

The great increase in the yield of the county in 1872 was caused by the developments or discoveries of rich ore in the Pelican, Dives, Maine, Phœnix, Colorado Central, Saco, O. K., and Hukill, and the growing product of the Terrible and other mines. The gain in 1874 was due to the enormous product of the Dives and Pelican at that time, and, to a less extent, to the development of many ore-bodies, veins, and pockets on Leavenworth, Republican, Sherman, and Democrat mountains. A multitude of lodes were discovered or reopened in those years, and the number worked at present is very large. Nearly 18,000 mineral locations, lodes, or claims had been recorded in this county up to a year or two ago.

Clear Creek county yielded the following values in the various metals prior to January, 1879 :

Total amount of silver	$14,316,907 99
Total amount of gold	2,840,661 05
Total amount of lead	351,000 00
Total amount of copper	20,000 00
Totals of all metals	$17,528,569 04

The yield of Clear Creek county from the time of the first discoveries to the present time will be found below :

CLEAR CREEK COUNTY MINING PRODUCT, 1859–1879.

1859 to 1868, gold product	$2,000,000 00
1866, silver	500 00
1867, silver	40,000 00
1868, silver and gold	141,820 35
1869, silver and gold	400,354 00
1870, silver and gold	481,354 08
1871, silver and gold	869,046 34
1872, silver and gold	1,503,391 43
1873, silver and gold	1,259,761 06
1874, silver and gold	2,203,947 97
1875, silver and gold	1,928,161 74
1876, silver and gold	1,982,548 31
1877, silver and gold	2,206,577 91
1878, silver and gold	2,511,105 85
Total yield to January, 1879	$17,528,569 04
Estimated total yield to January, 1880	20,000,000 00

	1871.	1872.	1873.	1874.
Silver Bullion.........	$396,011 24	$235,187 43	$345,263 46	$555,268 49
Gold Bullion.........	20,000 00	30,000 00	34,000 00	42,500 00
Ore shipments to Colo-rado Works.......	....	406,648 00	438,746 16	520,968 60
Ore shipped out of Colorado*	453,035 10	831,556 00	441,751 44	1,085,210 88
Totals.........	$869,046 34	$1,503,391 43	$1,259,761 06	$2,203,947 97

	1875.	1876.	1877.	1878.
Silver Bullion.........	$534,372 28	$473,414 00	$383,189 74	$389,871 70
Gold Bullion..........	70,000 00	85,161 00	70,000 00	115,000 00
Ore Shipped to Colo-rado Works.......	408,621 46	650,000 00	822,645 92	810,403 00
Ore shipped out of Colorado........	915,168 00	663,973 31	925,742 24	1,195,831 15
Total..........	$1,928,161 74	$1,982,548 31	$2,206,577 91	$2,511,105 85

PRODUCT OF THE DIFFERENT METALS, 1876, '7, '8.

	1876.	1877.	1878.
Silver.................	$1,837,387 31	$1,984,077 91	$2,275,105 85
Gold....	95,161 00	96,500 00	†134,000 00
Lead....................	50,000 00	123,000 00	98,000 00
Copper.................	....	3,000 00	4,000 00
Totals..	$1,982,548 31	$2,206,577 91	$2,511,105 85

* A large portion was shipped to Germany for treatment.
† Includes gold in lodes carrying both gold and silver.

The following statistics for 1876 appeared in the report of the author, published in the New York Engineering and Mining Journal:

Sources and Shippers.	Ore.	Ore.	Silver.	Coin Value.
	Tons.	lbs.	oz.	
Silver Bullion—				
From Judd & Crosby, Pelican, Clear Creek and Stewart Mills....................	3,500	....	401,198.9	$473,414 00
Silver Ore Shipped—				
Church Brothers & Co..........	2,073	775	381,573.8	450,257 03
G. W. Hall & Co...............	1,218	....	294,813	347,879 34
Matthews & Co.....	671	167	113,333.8	133,733 88
L. F. Olmsted..................	634	310	88,781.7	121,948 63
W. Bement.....................	451	463	60,276	....
Silver ores from Idaho, etc......	250	....	21,190	25,000 00
Other silver and lead ores, etc...	1,278	....	87,875	145,629 09
Concentrated Ores—				
Clear Creek Company—crude ore dressed...... ......:...	4,000	....	108,150.9	127,618 04
Gold—				
Gold from lode veins............	2,000	....	....	40,000 00
Gold, placer and bar...........	....	....	....	45,161 00
Total..................	16,075	1,715	1,557,193.1	$1,982,548 31

About 11,000 tons of ore were concentrated altogether. Deducting 2,500 tons of concentrated ore, credited above to mills and ore buyers, the amount of ore mined in the county will appear as 9,575 tons of high grade, and 11,000 tons of low grade ore (afterwards concentrated), or 20,575 tons altogether.

The smelting works at Black Hawk received ores to the value of $534,400, and those at Golden and Denver smaller amounts. Some 1,676 tons went to St. Louis, Pittsburg, and Wyandotte, Mich.

Rich discoveries were made just at the close of the year on Red Elephant and Leavenworth Mountains. The Free America and S. J. Tilden were prominent among these. The Dives and Pelican mines were the largest producers, and then came the Stevens, Baxter, Pay Rock, Colorado Central, Marshall Tunnel lodes, Chelsea Beach, Polar Star, Magnet, and Burleigh and Lebanon Tunnel mines. The Hamill and Chaffee mines, on Brown and Sherman Mountains, were this year consolidated with the Terrible of the English Company, with a capital stock of $1,500,000.

The product of 1877 came from or passed through the following channels :

	TONS OF ORE.	VALUE.
SILVER BULLION—		
Pelican, Clear Creek, Judd & Crosby, and Stewart Mills......	3,200	$388,189 74
GOLD—		
Dust from Creek Mines......	....	30,000 00
Retort, etc., Idaho and Empire Mills........ ...	3,200	60,000 00
ORE SHIPMENTS—		
Church.........	$1,503\frac{262}{2000}$	325,467 56
Hall & Co.....................................	$783\frac{1}{2}$	258,339 48
Mathews & Morris........................ ...	$1,035\frac{1039}{2000}$	204,755 07
Olmsted & Ballou............................	1,881	222,938 86
McCann & Co...............................	200	43,062 20
C. C. Co., Silver Plume, to the East, and Boulder	1,200	157,000 00
Other ores to Black Hawk, Golden, etc., silver and gold, less Summit County...... ...)	3,300	416,825 00
Totals............................. ...	$16,303\frac{301}{2000}$	$2,206,577 91

An allowance for low grade ores before concentrating would bring up the total tonnage mined to 19,503.

The Stewart and Judd & Crosby mills did but little work,

16

The Clear Creek Company's mills sampled, concentrated, and reduced ores. The Pelican Mill, after being repaired, ran ten months, mainly as a custom mill, by Napheys & Ballou. The Silver Plume Mill turned out 694 tons of dressed ore for the market, and 400 tons were shipped away. The Boston and Colorado Works, at Black Hawk, bought $645,500 worth of ore from Clear Creek county in 1877, all silver-producing, except $6,500 in gold and $3,000 in copper. The Golden Smelting Company bought ore to the value of 150,000, of which $20,000 was gold, $7,000 lead, and the balance silver, all coming from about one thousand tons of ore. General F. J. Marshall shipped to Pittsburg, St. Louis, and Wyandotte, Michigan, via the Kansas Pacific Railway, 362 car loads, or 3,982 tons of ore, valued at $800,000. About $15,000 worth of bullion was obtained at the West Denver Dry Ore Reduction Works from the Polar Star Mine.

The average value of the 11,903 tons of high grade silver ores was $160.44 per ton; of high and low grades, $127.80, and of all ores, including gold stamp mill quartz, $111.70. Some lodes carry a great deal of lead, from 30 to 65 per cent., and others carry a few per cent. of copper. Nearly or quite 5,000 tons of ore, too poor for smelting, were dressed and separated so that the mineral was retained in one-third or one-fourth of that bulk, and thus rendered profitable for reduction. Nearly all of this work was done by the Silver Plume wet concentrator and the Clear Creek Company's dry dressing works. Near the close of the year the Silver Queen Works, at Georgetown, and Miles' Works, at Idaho, began to dress ores.

The year 1877 was noticeable for the development of several very rich and valuable lodes. The more important of these were the Free America and Boulder Nest, on Red Elephant mountain, where a lively mining camp was started, the S. J. Tilden and Kirtley, on Leavenworth, and the Dunderberg on Sherman mountain. The Tilden gave the richest average ore of any mine in the district, and the Boulder Nest showed the largest very valuable ore body during the latter eight months of the year. Just at the close of the year the Dunderberg was opened. Among older mines that were large producers were the Pelican and Dives, the Pay Rock, Baxter, Terrible, Brown, Stevens, the Colorado Central group, the Hukill, and Specie Payment.

YIELD OF 1878, SHOWING PRODUCERS AND SHIPPERS.

PRODUCERS AND SHIPPERS.	Tons of Ore Handled.	VALUE.	TOTALS.
SILVER BULLION—			
Pelican Mill......	1,241	$155,241 00	
Clear Creek Company Mill*........	2,741	124,966 56	
Farwell Reduction Works.........	500	109,664 14	$389,871 70
GOLD BULLION—			
Dust of placers and retorts of lodes of Empire, Idaho, etc.....	4,000	115,000 00	115,000 00
ORE SHIPMENTS—			
Mathews, Morris & Co............	1,646	430,555 07	
G. W. Hall & Co............. ..	1,000	276,594 47	
Olmsted & Ballou.................	1,493	191,111 86	
Silver Plume Conc. Mill of Franklin Ballou*.....	1,788	116,481 22	
P. McCann..... ,.................	900	238,995 00	
Clear Creek Company.............	3,934	493,604 25	
J. B. Church.....................	715	145,000 00	
Ores sent to Golden, Black Hawk, and elsewhere, not included in the above†.................. .	2,042	113,892 28	2,006,234 15
Totals.................	22,000	$2,511,105 85	$2,511,105 85

* Mainly low grade ores before concentrating.
† This includes 1,400 tons or more of low grade ores concentrated at the Miles and Hukill Mills.

Of the ore shipments of 1878, $810,403.05 were the result of ores sent to and treated at works in Colorado outside of Georgetown, and $1,195,831.05 worth of ore went to various points East, mainly to Omaha, Saint Louis, and Pittsburg. Large amounts of ore are said to have been treated at the Omaha Smelting Works. Of ores treated in Colorado the Boston & Colorado Works obtained $566,000, the Golden Smelting Works $204,403, Boyd's Works about $10,000, and the Cañon Reduction Works $30,000. Of the gold bullion some $25,000 came out of the 25-stamp quartz mill at Idaho Springs, and about as much at the three stamp mills at Empire, only one of which was running steadily.

The 12,071 tons of silver ore, outside of the low grades concentrated, averaged $174.35 per ton. The average of all silver ores handled, high and low grades, including mixed gold and silver ores near Idaho, was $133.11. There were about 17,000 tons. The average of all ores, including the low grade stamp mill quartz, was about $112. The free gold milling ores yielded from $10 to $20 per ton. Over 5,000 tons were crushed.

The Dunderberg, on which mining began just at the close of 1877, yielded $255,000. The Boulder Nest, which began to yield about eight months earlier, produced over $200,000 in 1878. The Terrible, and other connecting mines are said to have turned out about $150,000, and the Pelican, Dives, Pay Rock and Baxter, each about $60,000. The Kirtley, discovered in October, 1877, gave a very large product, probably as much or more than any of the last four estimated. The Equator must have yielded between $75,000 and $100,000. The Free America was among the productive mines of the county. The Freeland shipped ore but a few weeks, and the Hukill product was not sent forward very extensively. Still their export was considerable. No figures have been given concerning the Stevens, but the return probably reached $80,000. The Colorado Central, S. J. Tilden, Frostburg, Brown, the Lebanon Tunnel mines and Specie Payment were quite productive.

The ruling Georgetown prices for ores last winter were about the same as those of Mathews, Morris & Co., which, rating silver at 1.18 per ounce, were as follows, per ounce of silver to each ton of ore:

30 oz.	6 cts.	80 oz.	60 cts.	180 oz.	79 cts.	350 oz.	89 cts.
35 "	19 "	90 "	64 "	190 "	80 "	400 "	90 "
40 "	27 "	100 "	67 "	200 "	81 "	450 "	91 "
45 "	36 "	110 "	69 "	210 "	82 "	500 "	92 "
50 "	42 "	120 "	71 "	220 "	83 "	550 "	93 "
55 "	46 "	130 "	73 "	230 "	84 "	600 "	94 "
60 "	50 "	140 "	75 "	240 "	85 "	700 "	95 "
65 "	53 "	150 "	76 "	260 "	86 "	800 "	96 "
70 "	56 "	160 "	77 "	280 "	87 "	900 "	97 "
75 "	58 "	170 "	78 "	300 "	88 "	1,000 and over	98 "

Mathews, Morris & Co. crushed, sampled, bought, and shipped at the Rocky Mountain Mill, in Georgetown, 1,646 tons and 409 pounds of ore, containing 372,024.9 ounces of silver, 58.4 ounces of gold, and 123 tons 1,112.3 pounds of lead. The total value was $430,555.07. The average contents of ore handled was 8 per cent. of lead, and 234 ounces of silver, or $270.82 per ton.

F. M. Taylor's statement of the Clear Creek Company's business at Georgetown shows that 2,741 tons and 510 pounds of ore were concentrated and sampled and sent to the reduction works of the company and to other ore buyers of Georgetown, beside 3,934 tons and 901 pounds concentrated or shipped; total tonnage, 6,675 tons 1,411 pounds, for which $300,976.67 was paid, making an average of $45 per ton. The average assay was 82 ounces of silver, making a total of 547,407.8 ounces of silver, of a value of $618,570.81. This represents value of both shipments and mill bullion product. The latter alone amounted to $124,966.56. The company paid out for labor $42,013.88, and for fuel $9,647.86.

Olmsted & Ballou deal heavily in lead-bearing ores as well as others. They operate the Washington Mill in Georgetown, which is supplied with the usual sampling and crushing machinery. The Silver Plume Concentrating Mill handles the lower grade ores. The combined business of both mills for the year was $302,519.32.

G. W. Hall & Co. is the oldest ore-buying, sampling, and shipping firm in the county. In 1872 General F. J. Marshall and C. A. Martine began to purchase the richer ores of the miners and ship them across the ocean to Germany for treatment. This was the actual beginning of a high-priced competition ore market for the Georgetown mines. Since 1875–6, the firm has shipped to American works only. It has probably handled from first to last over two million dollars' worth of ore.

P. McCann, with mills at Georgetown and Lawson, the latter in operation only seven months, handled 900 tons of ore, yielding $238.995. The ore averaged 235 ounces, or $265.55 per ton. Two hundred tons of ore contained 35 per cent. of lead.

The Miles concentrating mill at Idaho Springs is conducted by Harry Montgomery who has ore sampling and shipping works in connection therewith. The products are sent to Golden.

The ore reducing works in Clear Creek county that were at work all or parts of 1878 are as follows:

Name.	Character.	Daily Capacity in Tons.	Plant.	Time Employed.	Established.
Clear Creek Company, Georgetown..	Silver Red'g.....	12 to 15	10 stamps, 6 cylinders, leaching tubs.	Full year.........	1876
Farwell Red. Works,　　"　　:	"	6 to 8	10 stamps, 3 cylinders, amal. pans......	Last six months...	{1872 1878
Pelican Mill,　　"　　"　　:	"	10 to 12	10 stamps, 5 cylinders, amal. barrels......	First five months...	{1867 1874
Clear Creek Company,　　"　　:	Dry Concentration..	45	Crushers, screens, jigs, etc.	Full year...	1875
Colorado United M. Co............	Wet　　"	:	"　　　"	....	1877
Silver Plume (F. Ballou)..　......	"	45	Crushers, screens, jigs, tables, etc...	Full year.........	1875
Hukill Company (Spanish Bar)..　......	"	24	Crushers, screens, jigs, tables, etc	Last 4 or 5 months..	1878
Miles (Idaho)....　.....	"	15	Crushers, screens, jigs, tables, etc...	Most of year.......	1877
Sunshine, at Idaho........	Gold, raw amal.....	16	25 stamps with tables....	Full year.........	1877
Pioneer (Empire)............	"	12	16 stamps.............	Most of year......	1878
Knickerbocker, Empire.........	"	15	20 stamps...........	Latter part of year.	1865
Bay State, Empire............	"	11	15 stamps...........	Few months.......	1865

The ore sampling, buying, and shipping firms and mills of Clear Creek county are as follows :
Rocky Mountain Mill, Mathews, Morris & Co., Georgetown. Established in 1876 ; rebuilt from fire in 1877. Capacity, 30 tons.
Washington Mill, Olmsted & Ballou, Georgetown. Mill rebuilt 1872. Capacity, 30 tons in ten hours.
G. W. Hall & Co., Georgetown. Buildings used for present purposes since 1871-2.
Clear Creek Company Mill, Georgetown. Established 1876. Capacity, 40 tons.
J. B. Church, Georgetown. Established 1874. Capacity, 30 tons.
P. McCann, Georgetown and Lawson. The first established in 1877, and the latter in 1878.
Silver Plume Mill, Ballou & Co., Silver Plume. Established in 1875.
Harry Montgomery, Idaho Springs. 1876, for Golden smelters.

Probably two thousand men are directly engaged in mining, milling, and hauling ore in Clear Creek county, or in prospecting. Allowing for an outlay of $300,000 for mining and milling supplies, and the yield of 1878 would have returned over $1,100 to each man at work had it been equally divided. At the same time, this same labor proved up and vastly increased the value of many properties. Outlays for buildings and machinery are not counted above, as they are permanent improvements. The mines of Clear Creek county have averaged a return of over three dollars per day per man employed for many years, and in those years the value of mining property, with new discoveries, has been increased $20,000,000. It can hardly be an exaggeration to say, that while the average bullion return for nine or ten years has averaged three or four dollars per day to the men engaged directly or indirectly in producing it, that in that period each man so engaged has each day advanced the value of mining property an equal amount. The same industry has furnished the means or inducements for the growth of well-built and prosperous towns, for permanent improvements of various descriptions, and for the support of a large population.

The following very appropriate review of past and prospective work appeared in a late number of the Georgetown Miner: "For a period of about sixteen years, that enterprising individual, the 'honest miner,' has prospected and dug for the precious metals in our county with that energy and tenacity which is a distinguishing characteristic of 'miner men,' and, to some extent, is born of the circumstances in which he is placed. He has lived hard and worked harder, and with an undaunted brow has often faced the bitterest and sternest realities of life. He has gazed down the misty avenues of probabilities until what to others appeared to be the vague outlines of chance were to him all but an absolute certainty of his hopes. He has acquired fortunes with a few weeks' or months' labor, and often, with a generosity bordering on recklessness, he has squandered it again in but little less time than it took to accumulate it. On the other hand, he has toiled incessantly for years without taking out a single 'red,' but his faith still continues unshaken and his perseverance unimpaired. He has accomplished labors compared with which the cleaning out of the Augean stables would be but an ante-breakfast chore. He has penetrated to the very foundations of the eternal hills, and the innermost recesses of

'earth's gigantic sentinels' have echoed with the sharp ring of his
steel-impelling strokes and bellowed back the infernal roar of his
fiery persuasions. He has carved his way through sullen solitude
in search of metalliferous wealth, and a liberal and enlightened civilization has followed close upon his heels. If he has not discovered the secret of the transmutation of metals, he has unfolded their
rock-bound hiding-places; while mechanical and chemical science
have sprung to his aid and rendered him indispensable assistance in
their extraction. The brave and persistent miner has done all this
and much more; not with the magic wand of an eastern fairy, but
with a striking hammer, weighing from six to eight pounds, and
other implements necessary to his vocation.

"Notwithstanding the fact that he has accomplished so much, however, reason, experience and observation assure him that he is upon
the first round of his ladder. In this case it is the topmost round,
and however paradoxical it may appear, he must rise to wealth and
position by sinking. In his very natural and potent desire for gain
he instinctively grasped at that which came first within his reach,
and many were the rich surface 'pockets' that he legitimately and
profitably rifled. With this object in view he has burrowed in and
through the mountains, until the latter are dotted with the results of
his subterranean labors, but thus far he has rarely penetrated below
the streams which flank the bases of the secondary ranges of mountains. He recognized the fact that there was no necessity for descending lower while so much remained above. Surface chimneys
and pockets are not inexhaustible, however, and with their deflection
deep mining is the next step in the exploration of true fissure veins.
We would not insinuate that the surface deposits, or a tithe of them,
are worked out, but there certainly is not as many of them as there
were a dozen years ago, while the expense of downward development is much less now than it was at that time. In the matter of
deep mining—which is abundantly suggested by circumstances and
by the records of the development of mining properties in all parts
of the world—it must be admitted that the probability of realizing
a snug fortune with a small outlay of money and muscle, is less likely
to occur than in surface explorations, while it is equally true that the
former presents a more certain and satisfactory field for investment."

CHAPTER XIV.

CLEAR CREEK COUNTY MINES—THE GOLD AND SILVER COPPER-IRON BELT—THE HUKILL MINE—ITS HISTORY AND PRESENT CONDITION AND PROSPECTS—THE FREELAND—HOW A GREAT MINE WAS DEVELOPED—THE FIRST COLORADO PURCHASE OF THE CALIFORNIANS—MINING ON THE NEVADA PLAN—GOLD AND SILVER VEINS OF VIRGINIA CAÑON, SEATON HILL, AND IDAHO—THE TROPIC MINE —CREEK AND BAR MINING.

Clear Creek county is in reality one large and continuous mining district, extending from Gilpin county and Floyd Hill southward and westward to the "snowy range." The mineral wealth of the northeastern portion is mainly embraced in the extension of the great copper-iron gold belt of Gilpin, which carries much more silver here than there. This belt enters the county from the head of Virginia Cañon, and in Bellevue and other mountains, and crosses South Clear Creek and Chicago and Trail Creeks in the vicinity of Idaho, Spanish Bar, and Fall River. Near Black Hawk, Willis Gulch, and on Clifton and Seaton Mountains are silver-bearing galena veins. The streams of this section are worked for gold.

The two great mines so far developed in this copper-iron belt, and in this part of the county, are the Freeland and Hukill, but there are scores of lodes in the same districts, and great activity is displayed in their development. An idea of the capacity and character of the two lodes mentioned can be had from the fact that after a critical examination of many Colorado mines the Freeland was the first one purchased by Californians, and the Hukill was the second in which they became interested. Moderate figures may have had something to do with this, but the size, continuity, and reliability of the veins and their large ore reserves were the original attractions.

The Hukill mine is situated in Spanish Bar mining district, two miles above Idaho Springs, and is crossed by South Clear Creek and the Colorado Central railway. Its outcroppings, surface workings, tunnels, and mine and mill buildings are plainly visible from the railway and stage-road, and are the most extensive for miles around. The location on the steep mountain slopes permitted of tunneling in on the vein at various elevations above the creek-bed, and this is the way the Hukill was opened until it was deemed best to further develop it by attaining greater depth. Recent explorations near and under the creek prove the Hukill and Whale mines, that were so long worked on opposite mountains, to be on one and the same vein. This is indicative of greater worth than if the veins were separate and distinct. The largest and richest body of solid ore ever found on either location is that recently discovered in and now being explored from the new Whale shaft.

John M. Dumont began to develop the Hukill lode in 1871. It paid handsomely from the start, and work was steadily continued until few mines could show as much value in sight, and none better internal development. Little ore was sold outside of that removed in drifting and shafting. This paid all expenses, and a satisfactory profit beside. At the end of five years the mine was sold for $200,-000. The excavation of 1,600 feet of adits, drifts, and shafts had returned, beside a large amount of low-grade ore, 1,700 tons, that sold for $195,200. The cost was $167,140, and the profit $20,060. The average yield was $114.82 per ton. There were thousands of tons left standing in the mine between the levels. Some of this was removed by a subsequent operator—probably $70,000. Then the Hukill Mining Company came into possession of the property.

Through the action of the two leading stockholders, very important additional property was secured in June, 1878, at no cost to the company itself. This property was the Whale mine, mill, and placer claim, purchased of John M. Dumont and E. S. Platt. The transaction increased the company ownership to 3,188 feet—1,900 on the Whale, and 1,288 feet on the Hukill previously obtained. The brick mill building is an immense affair, built by an eastern company formerly owning the mine. A pan process was at first used, and later, smelting was carried on. The Hukill Company put in concentrating works that daily dress twenty-four tons of low grade ore down to eight or ten tons of salable mineral. Their capacity is being trebled or quadrupled, so as to handle past accumulations and future products. This mill is directly opposite the main entrance to the Hukill mine, and connected therewith by a bridge and railway crossing the stream; the Colorado Central railway, and a side-track therefrom, extends along the Hukill side of the creek, and on the opposite side is the new Whale shaft, also connected with the mill by rail. From this shaft underground workings will be carried at great depths under the creek and either mountain.

Not long ago, the same Californians who had bought the Freeland purchased a controlling interest in the Hukill company property. The manager of the former, F. F. Osbiston, formerly of the Comstock, and one of the most experienced of Pacific coast miners, was then appointed superintendent. Work has since been prosecuted on an enlarged plan, and with a degree of system and energy that will insure a large product.

There are now between four and five thousand feet of adits, levels, shafts and winzes on the property. An average force of sixty men is employed in the mine and mill. The Hukill shaft has reached a depth of 220 feet lower than the creek level. The last one hundred feet of depth has shown an unusually good body of ore, which a level is further proving up in the direction of the Whale. Last winter a drift from the shaft of the gold placer claim was extended under and beyond the mill, with the expectation of intersecting the Whale vein, which had previously been opened on the mountain side only. The vein was found, and proved to be the best ore-body yet developed. Its direction and location also showed that the Hukill and Whale were parts of the same lodes. Since then a new and vertical shaft twelve feet square has been started, resulting in the development of a wonderful body of ore. The vein has gradually expanded until at a depth of 100 feet, it is reported that the shaft and drift show a width of twelve feet of ore. Much of this is solid mineral that brings good prices at the smelters. Quantities of it sold at an average of $200 per ton, carrying over forty dollars worth of copper and the remaining value in silver and gold. There is also heavy lead ore in places running low in silver—also a large proportion of concentrating material. Small streaks and pockets have been found in both mines that have milled as much per ton as the high grade Georgetown mines, but the hundred dollar ore and about twice as much that concentrates from forty dollars up to one hundred has been the main dependence. From three to ten, and, rarely, twenty per cent. of the ore is copper. The inclosing walls are of mica schist and gneiss formation. The vein dips strongly to the northwest.

Since the company owes no debts and has large amounts of ore and ore reserves, and of supplies, machinery, and equipments, its future should be a prosperous one. Official statements show the product for the past two years to have been about $250,000. Most of the surplus of this has gone into permanent improvements. The total yield of the Hukill mine since 1871 amounts to about $515,000. The Whale turned out considerable money a long time ago, and the two mines combined are now in condition to greatly surpass their best former periods.

The Freeland is one of the great veins of the famous gold and silver belt and has few equals in the State or country in substantial worth and aggregate wealth. Its value, as previously demonstrated, has been vastly enhanced by the developments of the past few months. While the average yield of its ore is less per ton than in many silver lodes, the great width, uniform tendency, and seemingly limitless extent of the mineral body entitle it to a place in the front rank of the best of mines. But a trifle of all the ore so far penetrated has been removed or sold.

The vein is mainly composed of copper and iron pyrites, with occasional bodies of nearly pure galena, carrying 65 per cent. of lead and about 50 ounces of silver. Nearly 60 per cent. of the product is in gold, the remainder being credited to the silver and copper. From three to ten per cent. of the ore is composed of the latter metal. The ore is usually in the shape of a vein of copper-iron, rich enough to ship to market, flanked by poorer material and mixed mineral and gangue. The poorer grade requires concentration—from two and a half to three tons of crude ore being dressed down to one of salable mineral. About one-third of the ore brings good prices at the smelters without separation. Not taking into consideration the small per cent. of lead, the average value of shipping ores and concentrations is from $50 to $60 per ton. In the ground entered last year the ore-body was generally from one to two and a half feet wide. The two lower tunnels or adits have lately been passing through from three to five feet of ore, showing the vein to be of greater size at the furthest points from the surface. These widths are not in pockets, but continue for long distances, and at the tunnel breasts. There are also streaks of very rich ore that assay far above the average. The cheapness with which this great vein can be worked is remarkable, and combined with its great size renders it extremely

THE FREELAND MINE.

profitable. Mineral of this character is especially desirable to smelters of the copper matte process, on account of its fluxing qualities in the treatment of baser ores.

The Freeland lode is on a branch of South Clear Creek, a little over two miles from the Colorado Central railway, and four miles from Idaho Springs. It was recently purchased by California parties, and is superintended by F. F. Osbiston, a well-known mining manager and expert of the great bonanza firm. The property is over a mile long.

This California company are developing the mine with all possible dispatch, and has begun the construction of important permanent improvements on a scale that compares with the general magnitude of their operations. An immense mill will soon be completed, for the purpose of concentrating the poorer ores at the mine. This will separate the gangue or waste rock from the salable mineral. The wet process of concentration will be used, and one hundred tons of crude ore handled daily. There will also be a stamp mill, through which the low grade material will be run, for securing what gold can be saved before concentrating. A tram railway will be constructed from the mine and mill down Trail Creek, to connect with the Colorado Central Railway. There are thousands of tons of ore already outside of the mine, beside the vast unbroken ore reserves extending for hundreds of feet horizontally and vertically inside. To facilitate the output of the latter a great ore chute is being excavated between the various levels, so that all of the ore can be run out in cars on the lower level.

There is no more favorably located lode in the country than this. It can undoubtedly be worked on a larger scale and at less cost than any other in Clear Creek county. It intersects the mountains that rise on either side of Trail Creek and thus permits of tunneling in on the vein instead of the more costly shaft work. By this means the mine is drained and afforded a down grade outlet. The owners estimate the total cost of mining and concentrating the ore at the remarkably low figure of less than three dollars per ton. The present mining expenses and the large amount of stoping ground, with the known cost of concentration, seem to warrant this estimate. The ore will be shipped to Golden and Argo smelters for three dollars a ton. Then come the smelting expenses.

From the head of the Freeland tunnel the "back" is over 700 feet

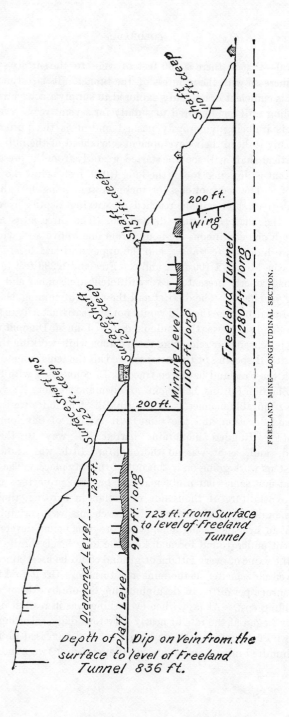

FREELAND MINE—LONGITUDINAL SECTION.

vertical—that is, there is 700 feet of vein to the surface—and this will increase with the progress of the tunnel. It is estimated that there is sufficient ore already explored to supply a concentrating and sampling mill one hundred tons daily for several years. All of the tunnels are being vigorously pushed and it is the purpose of the company to keep their developments far ahead of the mill capacity. A vertical shaft will soon be started westerly from the present workings that is designed to cut the lode 1,000 feet below the Freeland tunnel. The vein pitches or inclines, something less than forty-five degrees, and will be reached at varying depths by cross-cuts from the shaft and then drifted on. The three adits are going through one continuous ore-body, from one to five feet wide. They are two hundred feet apart, and the upper or Platt level is 970 feet long, the Minnie 1,100 feet, and the Freeland 1,280 feet long.

This property presented a very different appearance and valuation a few years ago. The district and the score of mining claims were abandoned because the gold would not save satisfactorily in the stamp mills—and silver was then unlooked for. John M. Dumont was gradually purchasing or relocating these claims while working the Hukill, and after disposing of the latter secured all the remaining territory on which the Freeland had been traced. In connection with E. S. Platt and Sheldon Collins, he began to open and explore the vein in the same admirable manner as on the Hukill. The lodes were similar in size and location, and the same adit system of development was adopted. Rugged mountains barred the way to the outside world, and, as it was no thoroughfare, little was known of the persistent work going on in this out of the way place. The enterprise was at first somewhat problematical, but the projector's confidence and expenditure of thousands of dollars in drifting, timbering, in roads, buildings, and permanent improvements, were certainly justified when an ever-increasing amount of ore was being developed. An efficient underground foreman kept the long levels solidly timbered, and the value of every fathom of ground could be ascertained from an assayer and smelter at the mine and furnace. Great forests of pine and spruce permitted of desulphurizing the ore by "heap roasting," at trifling cost. At last, when everything was in readiness, ore ship-ments began at the rate of nearly fifty tons daily. During this year or two of operations the working force had increased to more than one hundred miners and a pretty village of over two hundred inhabitants grew about the mine, with church and school, but no disturbing element in the form of a saloon. Dumont had practically a little kingdom by himself in this isolated and picturesque valley, for there were no competing mining interests and no work except that of his own direction. At length the adits were in on the vein from seven to ten hundred feet, thousands of tons of ore had been broken, and in the mountain were the largest explored ore reserves in the county. But concentration works were needed, so that all classes of ore could be made available as they came from the mine. At this juncture the Californians came along, examined the property, and paid a quarter of a million for it. The nature of the vein had already been proved; and the new owners began to crowd work with all possible dispatch. The result is that the ore-body is found to be so much larger and better near the heart of the mountain that they now consider the property worth three or four times what they paid for it. It has certainly improved wonderfully within the past three months.

What the future capacity of the mine may be is difficult to predict, but the present owners confidently expect to bring it up to two hundred tons per day within the coming year. This may seem an enormous product, but it is difficult for one who has not been there to appreciate the tremendous energy displayed in the mining operations now going forward—an energy and push characteristic of the live mining operators and great mining enterprises of Nevada. The California theory is that the more rapidly a mine is worked the more money is made—and it certainly leaves more time to make money. Accordingly these men do not propose to be any longer removing a given quantity of ore than is absolutely necessary. The Freeland and Hukill are operated by men of means, who have been engaged in similar work among the famous mines of the Pacific slope. If they are successful in this new field they will induce others to come. With the present showing in these mines, it would appear that there could be no such word as fail. Consequently an influx of California capital may be looked for with a considerable degree of certainty.

In the same belt is the Mayflower, which is being rapidly developed by a New York company, which employs nearly forty miners on this and the Lafayette. On the opposite side of the creek, and probably on the same vein as the Mayflower, is the Beauzy, also worked by purchasers from the East.

Around the head of Virginia Cañon, and midway between Central and Idaho Springs, is a group of free milling gold lodes that are well worthy of attention. This is a continuation of the Gilpin gold belt, but the mines are just over the line in Clear Creek county. As a rule these veins are not large, but are unusually rich in gold, with occasional bunches and pockets of ore that pay handsomely. There has been a revival of mining there since the Specie Payment was proved up in 1876–7, and now many men are obtaining snug revenues or a large per cent. on moneys and labor invested. A number of mines are regularly paying several hundred dollars monthly, or fifteen per cent. of their rated valuation. The Specie Payment, Champion, Trio, German, Racket, Clarissa, Sunshine, Gold Cloud, and Emerson are the most actively worked. The first nearly supplies the Sunshine twenty-five stamp mill at Idaho, and the others are the main feeders of the Tucker thirty-two stamp mill in Russell Gulch, Gilpin county.

The Specie Payment was discovered in 1875, and purchased the following year by parties from Troy, New York. It is said to have paid nearly all of the time since opened, and to look as well as ever. It intersects Bellevue Mountain near its summit, cutting down through it at a pitch or incline of about forty-five degrees. The vein has generally ranged from eighteen to forty inches thick, and does not bear a close resemblance to most Gilpin gold-bearing ores. White quartz is obtained occasionally, flecked and spotted with gold. The stamp mill averages a return of from $80 to $100 per cord, but returns of twenty and twenty-seven ounces have been made. A mill of fifteen stamps was built at Idaho Springs in 1877, and enlarged to twenty-five in 1878. The mine is extensively opened by an adit or tunnel over 350 feet long, driven on the vein toward the peak of the mountain, with shafts and levels connecting below. The first workings were in the ground above, and most of the ore has been removed for quite a distance. The mine has been yielding from $25,000 to $27,000 per annum.

The Trio mine, near the Champion, was purchased by Frederick C. Hardy, of New York, in 1878. Previous to that time it had yielded extremely rich ore—some of it containing several hundred dollars per cord. Owing to the slope of the mountain and the wet character of the mine a tunnel was driven into the lode from the bed of Virginia Cañon and then continued on the vein. This required months of time, and has been rewarded by the development of a rich body of ore below the old workings, and by the draining of the mine. When a distance of one thousand feet horizontally has been attained the depth below the crest of the mountain will be nearly 700 feet. The Champion was discovered in the spring of 1878, by Edward Williams and others, and was soon after purchased by Thomas I. Richman, the present mayor of Central, and some Chicago parties. It has given some remarkably rich milling ore—from twenty to thirty ounces, or from $300 to $480 per cord. The average mill returns are about seven ounces, $110 a cord, or $16 a ton. The ore sold to the smelter brings from $100 to $125 a ton. Two shafts have attained depths of 150 feet or more, and several levels are being carried forward. The vein matter is from one to four feet wide. The mine has paid a handsome profit ever since discovered. Eight men are employed, and 150 to 250 tons of mill ore mined monthly.

The German has yielded some $25,000 altogether, and the recent lessees report rich ore and large profits. A handsome vein of smelting ore is visible in the two shafts, varying from four to twenty inches wide, and flanked by ore that mills from $8 to $16 per ton. The Sunshine is another paying property. It has been supplying more or less mill ore for a year. The Clarissa employs some twenty men, and has been supplying from five to fifteen mill stamps. The richer mineral carries considerable silver and copper as well as gold. A strike is reported in the Patton lode down Virginia Cañon, and the Nonpareil and Fairmount, near Idaho, are attracting some attention, The latter is an old mine, and is sending rich quartz to the Sunshine quartz mill. The other supplies smelting ore—and so does the Monarch.

Southeasterly from this group of gold lodes is the parallel silver belt referred to before. Here are a number of mines that are paying all the way from good wages to several hundred dollars per month, according to size of vein and amount of development. The most actively worked lodes are the Tropic, Victor, Santa Fe, Queen, Kangaroo, Metropolitan, Telephone, Argo, and Cincinnati. The Seaton and Victor or flat vein cross one another and have yielded large amounts of silver, especially at the point of junction. More ore was coming out of that spot at one time than from the whole of this part of the county. The Veto has been extensively developed and quite profitable. The Crystal and the Franklin lodes have been famous properties. The Cascade lode, which has yielded some rich silver ore, is in Cascade district, near the headwaters of Chicago Creek, and the Edgar, near Fall River, is quite productive.

The Tropic mine, located between Idaho Springs and Central City, furnishes an example of silver veins of reliable and profitable character. It has been opened but a short time, and vigorous work has been prosecuted less than a year, yet but very few Clear Creek veins can show as large ore reserves, or as great possibilities of gross and net products. The lode has been opened for a length of 500 feet, and a depth of 200, and a rich vein of ore has been penetrated in every section of the mine. With the exception of one small piece of ground worked out near the surface, the ore reserves extend through this explored ground with no serious break or interruption.

The Tropic is a remarkably continuous true fissure vein, in granite and spar formation, and has a northeasterly and southwesterly direction, pitching towards the north. It varies in width from one to four feet. In this is the ore vein, which shows few lean spots, and carries from four to thirty inches of solid ore wherever entered. There is some material that requires concentration, but the general run of the ore is from 100 to 200 ounces of silver, $2 to $12 in gold, and from one to seven per cent. of copper. The average selling price of the ore is about $100 per ton. The average yield of all ground excavated has been $90 a fathom. The mine is advantageously situated, but a mile and a half of down grade teaming, at an outlay of two dollars per ton, being required to reach the railway station at Idaho Springs. Thence to the smelting works railway transportation is only three dollars a ton. The ground in the mine is soft and easily worked, but requires no timbering in the levels, and expenses are correspondingly light.

Enough ore has been sold from the shaft and levels to pay for the cost of driving them ; and it takes a good mine to do that. As the mine is now opened, the cost of mining the reserves will not be more than twenty-five per cent. of the receipts after stoping fairly begins. The present yield is reported at six or seven thousand dollars monthly, but if stopers enough were set at work nearly thirty thousand dollars could probably be taken out in a month's time. Before the present reserves can be worked out, as much more ground can be developed ahead of immediate requirements.

The character of the vein is galena, zinc-blende, gray copper and iron pyrites. Experts who have recently visited this mine state there are three thousand fathoms of unworked ground above the line of the lower workings, which developments and ore sales very conclusively prove to contain about thirty thousand tons of ore, worth from two hundred to three hundred thousand dollars, and that an average yield of $29.75 per foot was obtained in sinking and drifting. The statements above make a very fine showing for this promising mine, which has but recently come to the front, but which is very sure to pay large and frequent dividends hereafter.

South Clear Creek and its branches, including Chicago Creek, have been mined for gold every summer since 1859, and have probably yielded three quarters of a million in gold dust. Creek mining has been carried on there throughout the year by means of shafts, drifts, and tunnels, and occasionally by partially diverting the channels of the streams. There is one tunnel over nine hundred feet long extending into the bank and hill-side adjoining the creek, and just above Idaho numerous shafts have been sunk and long drifts extended through auriferous gravel. There are a number of creek and bar mines above and below Idaho that clear from one to several thousand dollars every season. There are hydraulic pumps, and other appliances along these streams.

The bullion product of the mines near Idaho Springs outside of the Hukill mine was not very large for years prior to 1877. The annual product has recently approached $200,000. The present year is likely to turn out half a million, and 1880 will probably double that amount. That part of Clear Creek county within a radius of five miles of Idaho Springs may give a greater tonnage of smelting ores during the next year than the Georgetown district, and about half as large a bullion product.

CHAPTER XV.

CLEAR CREEK COUNTY MINES—RED ELEPHANT MOUNTAIN AND ITS
SILVER VEINS—THE FAMOUS WHITE, BOULDER NEST, AND FREE
AMERICA—COLUMBIAN MOUNTAIN—THE JOE REYNOLDS AND
OTHER VEINS—THE EMPIRE GOLD DISTRICT.

Red Elephant Mountain is six miles northeast of Georgetown and about eight miles from Idaho Springs. It rises abruptly on the north side of South Clear Creek Valley. Although the Young America silver lode was located there long ago, no conception of the hidden wealth of the mountain was entertained by the old-time Georgetown miners or travelers. A veteran prospector named D. E. Dulany lived in that locality, and the presence of rich float ore among the slide and granite led him to hunt for silver veins long after less persistent men would have abandoned all hopes of success. He was finally so fortunate as to strike a lode of extraordinary richness, which he called the Free America or Purchase. Reports of mill runs quickly brought in an army of prospectors from Georgetown and Central. Dulany soon sold to General J. I. Gilbert and W. H. Moore for $25,000, and the latter sold to Joseph Reynolds, of Chicago. Other discoveries were made, the town of Lawson was built, and the next summer the Colorado Central railway was extended from Floyd Hill to Georgetown, passing close by Red Elephant, and within a half mile of its mines. Since then the district has been a very prosperous one.

The Free America was paying handsomely in the following spring and summer. When the location was made there had not been work enough done to determine the course of the vein, and the consequence was that only a part of it was secured. The remainder fell to the Free America Extension on the east, and the Boulder Nest on the west. The White, an equally important discovery, unites with the Boulder Nest, or is the same vein.

The Free America has five levels from the main shaft, the lower one just started being 430 feet below the surface. There is a small vein of solid ore in the lower workings, and there were large pockets and ore-bodies at various places from the surface down. A cross cut driven on the second level for a distance of thirty-six feet encountered no walls. The latest work done showed an increase of ore, indicating as good a body near by as in the upper levels. The yield of the Free America is said to have been $100,000 in 1877, and the receipts for ore sales about $60,000 in 1878.

Few mines in the country can show as fine a record for production and profit as the Boulder Nest in the twenty months since work fairly began upon it. Dubois Tooker, Walter Clark and A. Fellows leased a portion of it for one year, and began work in May, 1877. They did not get their shaft down to ore until some months later. Up to January, 1878, and mainly in three months, the actual smelter's yield was $116,133, currency value, or nearly $110,000, coin. This came from 718½ tons of ore, averaging $137.50, and 391 tons that averaged 37½ ounces of silver per ton—the last sold at concentrating works.

In six months ending April 30, 1878, the Tooker leased ground yielded 2,192 tons of ore that sold for $125,151. The average amount received per ton for all ore, high and low grades, was $57.60. The expenses averaged about thirty per cent. of the receipts. The receipts for the month of December were $35,721, and for March $31,376, and the expenses of the latter month were $9,376. Up to May 1, 1878, the lessees cleared about $72,000. The owners' royalty was about $27,000.

The actual yield of silver of the Boulder Nest mine for the year 1878 must have exceeded $230,000, for the receipts from sales of ore were $157,000. The receipts from time of discovery to December 1, 1878, were $214,376.17. The mine may have yielded $400,000 worth of silver to date.

The entire mine averages about 250 ounces of silver per ton for first class, from 100 to 150 for second, and from 30 to 40 ounces for third class. The latter is the most plentiful. So far only the eastern part of the lode has paid.

The White lode enters the Boulder Nest location and lode from the southeast. It has a breadth between granite walls of from twenty-two to twenty-six feet, with varying seams and bodies of ore, but extensive enough wherever opened to insure a heavy production. Several shafts have been sunk and an adit driven, and what is especially noticeable is the length of ore vein, as proved by these explorations in a distance of 1,500 feet. While much very profitable ground has been developed, but little has been worked out, thus leaving all the greater possibilities for present production.

Shafts are being sunk and connecting levels extended, and an adit 520 feet long has been driven in on the vein, the last 80 feet in rich ore. This gains a great deal of depth as it enters the mountain, and leaves a large amount of stoping ground above. By the time this adit has reached the Boulder Nest location, the breast of it will be hundreds of feet below the surface. Ore is being raised from three shafts, but the westernmost, called the Stevens, shows the best. Eighteen miners are at work there, and the ore vein is from eight to thirty inches thick in shaft, tents and stopes. In two weeks of June the Phillips lease, further east, gave four men 11¼ tons selling for $3,869 and yielding $6,100—2½ tons, containing $2,670.

The White was operated but a short time after discovery before litigation set in and work was enjoined. Last fall matters were amicably settled, and mining began again. For some time the monthly yield has been from $8,000 to $13,000, and the profits from $4,000 to $6,000 per month. The total yield has exceeded $100,000, mainly obtained in the past eight months, and in work of development. This is a splendid showing for what might be termed a commencement. The recent report of a well known expert estimates the future profits of this mine at ten thousand dollars a month. White ore averages from $80 to $350 per ton.

The Free America Extension has yielded very rich ore in the main shaft sunk, but the owners, Messrs. Weston, Moore and Gilbert, have been so busily engaged in mining near by and in localities all over the county, that development has not been pushed rapidly. In sinking 140 feet and drifting 40 feet, $28,000 were obtained. Two men mined ore in one day that yielded $1,000.

Recently Messrs. Moore and Weston have organized the Red Elephant Consolidated Mining Company on the 3,000 feet of the White, and the 1,500 feet of the Free America Extension—all patented ground. This embraces the larger part of the two main veins of the mountain. The capital stock of the company is a million and a half, in ten dollar shares, and the incorporators are

Clark Bell, ex-Senator A. McDonald, John H. Weston, Augustus Healy, William H. Moore, and J. W. Bigelow.

The White, Boulder Nest, and Free America have pretty much the same characteristics and grades of ore. The pitch of the veins is northward. The direction of the White is northwesterly and southeasterly, and that of the others—one vein—is north seventy degrees east, magnetic. The inclosing rock is granite.

These lodes, including four locations, but only two veins, which unite as above stated, have yielded over $700,000 altogether, of which the Boulder Nest gave probably $400,000. The yield of the Free America and Boulder Nest combined, in seventeen months ending March 1, 1879, was $508,980, currency, or an average of 144⅜ tons of ore and $29,940 monthly. The average cost of mining and getting each ton of ore on the cars at Lawson is given at $28. The average yield per month of the Free America, for the same seventeen months, is given at 31⅘ tons, averaging 150 ounces of silver per ton. There are some other lodes on Red Elephant, among which the Dexter and Lulu have been producing ore.

Some mining had been done on Columbian Mountain, but no great activity was displayed there until late in 1877. This activity resulted from the discovery of rich silver ore among many veins. The snows of winter stopped work for a time, but for over a year there has been quite an important mining camp. The more important lodes include the Joe Reynolds, Tom Moore, Hugo, Dictator, Oshkosh, La Crosse, Wall Street, Terrible, Gen. Gilbert, Nil Desperandum, Live Yankee, Native American, Russell, Monarch, Ophir, Baltic, Celtic, and Homestake. Gen. Gilbert and W. H. Moore were among the first in the district after the excitement began, and the Joe Reynolds is owned for 4,500 feet by Reynolds and Gilbert. It is a small but rich vein, and a little more developed than the similar Moore and Hugo veins. The Dictator lode is above the Highland Chief and is nearly on the crest of Columbian Mountain. It is owned by Colonel W. H. Doe, who was one of the early owners and operators on the famous Gunnell of Gilpin county, and who, after disposing of his interest there in 1864, resided in Wisconsin up to 1877. Like other miners and operators of the early days, who left Colorado with a fortune, he has drifted back again to the State that offers greater opportunities for making money than any other. Fortune still seems to favor him, for he is said to have

17

a very rich vein on this mountain. He began to develop it in 1878, and has been selling ore that yielded various amounts, of which the best was 687 ounces of silver per ton. The Wall Street is an old lode. It yielded nearly $30,000 one year. A lot of ore lately sold from the Glendower lode brought $454 per ton for fourth class, $942 for third class, and at the rate of $1,023 and $2,824 for small quantities of high grades.

South and west of Columbian Mountain are Anglo-Saxon and Griffith Mountains, the latter rising directly east of Georgetown and opposite Republican. On Anglo-Saxon Mountain is the lode of the same name that has produced ore yielding at the rate of from one to twenty thousand dollars per ton. It caused a great deal of attention in 1867, and paid something ten years later. The vein is small. The Saxon Extension, Pickwick, and Summit are yielding very rich mineral. The Magnet and Sequel have shown very rich pockets. The first had yielded $50,000 in eight years to 1875, and a large amount since.

Empire is located on the northern branch of South Clear Creek, about two miles above where the stream forks, and was built up by the gold-digging of the adjoining mountains in 1862–3. The out-croppings of the Great Equator, Conqueror, Tenth Legion, Rosecrans, and Silver Mountain lodes were extremely rich and productive, and sluicing and stamp-milling was extensively carried on, until the whole surface of the mountains had been washed over, torn up, and scarred with the operations of the gold-hunters. Judge H. C. Cowles, Russell, Majors & Co., Charles Martin, Dr. Carlton, J. S. Jones, S. F. Nuckolls and others, were the leading placer and lode miners of those days. It is said that a million dollars in gold was obtained there in a few years' time. For the past twelve years the amount of work done has been limited and the yield has been small; the district seems to be on the gain however. The Tenth Legion has produced a great deal of money, but some capital is needed to get it into condition to yield as it once did, and, first of all, the claims should be consolidated. The Knickerbocker Company of New York owns a small part of the lode and a twenty-stamp mill on the main stream at Empire. For two years David Ball has been making money from his Pioneer free gold lode. He built a sixteen-stamp mill in 1877, which the mine keeps supplied. He also owns and works a placer, and F. M. Taylor & Co. are operating another with hydraulics. A dozen gold lodes are worked.

CHAPTER XVI.

CLEAR CREEK COUNTY MINES—THE GEORGETOWN SILVER DISTRICT—
REPUBLICAN AND DEMOCRAT MOUNTAINS —WHAT HAS BEEN DONE
THERE—THE PELICAN-DIVES SILVER BONANZA—A MONSTER LODE
AND A MINT OF MONEY—STORY OF A GREAT MINING CONTEST—
THE PAY-ROCK, BAXTER, SNOWDRIFT, SILVER PLUME, AND OTHER
MINES.

Between the two forks of South Clear Creek, and extending southward toward Georgetown and westward toward the Continental
Divide, is a spur of the latter. The northern portion of this is
known under the names of Douglas, Columbia, and Colfax mountains,
whose mineral developments are not extensive. Still further south
is Democrat Mountain, overlooking the lower part of Georgetown.
Here are several lodes and groups of veins, some of them noticeable
for the high percentage of silver they carry. Among the principal ones worked at present are the W. B. Astor, Fred. Rogers,
Junction, Lucky Hesperus, Little Emma, and Polar Star, the latter
on a small scale. It is claimed that the ores of some of these lodes
can be treated by raw amalgamation. The entire mountain must
have yielded nearly a million in silver.

The W. B. Astor lode is situated near the summit of Democrat
Mountain. It had been worked to a depth of nearly or quite three
hundred feet in 1868. Its production was quite large for a time, but
work was afterwards suspended. It is again operated extensively.
The total yield is said to have been between sixty and one hundred
thousand dollars. There is one tunnel, 860 feet long. The Matilda
Fletcher has yielded over ten thousand dollars. Little mining
was done on Democrat in the years 1870-72.

In 1874 W. H. Moore sold some properties of this mountain to
Nebraska men, and about that time such rich developments were
made that a great prospecting excitement ensued. The results were
some valuable discoveries, fortunes for a few and good revenues for
many. The main vein and point where the ore-body seemed to
centre was the Junction-Galie lode; but the Fred Rogers, uniting

with the same, was nearly as productive, and there were numbers of parallel and crossing veins, spurs, and feeders between the granite formation that were exceedingly renumerative. Black sulphuret ore was mined from all of these, yielding from five to twelve hundred ounces of silver per ton. The Little Emma doubled those figures. There was a nest of veins in the gangue rock where the granite walls were from forty to sixty feet apart. The Lucky Hesperus yielded a great deal of money, and is doing so still. The Rogers has yielded over $200,000, currency value, mainly since 1874, and the entire Junction group of veins something like $600,000. Water from the snows of this timbered region is very troublesome, and has stopped or impeded work, and caused considerable tunneling. At the main producing point these lodes have been worked to depths of from four to five hundred feet.

The Junction is one of the oldest locations on Democrat Mountain, having been discovered in 1867, and application made for patent in 1873. There are two surface locations patented; the Junction, 800 feet, and the Galie, 1,590 feet in length; the Junction patent being wholly west of the discovery, and the Galie, 90 feet west and 1,500 feet east of its discovery shaft. But little work was done on the property prior to 1874, when systematic developments were commenced. The developments consist of three main openings; lower adit, 1,000 feet long; upper adit, 700 feet long, and the whim shaft, 200 feet deep, that is connected with the upper adit at a point 530 feet from its mouth. The work at present going forward is at the upper adit, where three parties of lessees are at work, and driving the lower tunnel and cross-cutting for the south wall of the vein. A cross-cut has been driven 35 feet in crevice matter, which is enough to show the lode to be one of the mammoth fissure veins. So far the mine has only been worked for the solid ore veins, and no attention has been given to the large bodies of concentrating ore that are exposed at various points in the mine, which can be made valuable only by the aid of machinery to dress them, but with a concentrating mill conveniently located would be of considerable value. The dump at the upper adit is estimated to contain an average of thirty ounces per ton.

Further west are the Silver Cloud and Queen of the West. The latter paid largely at one time, and yielded $60,000 altogether, but is now idle. A tunnel, already several hundred feet long, is being driven for drainage and working purposes for the Silver Cloud; this lode yielded about $40,000, currency value, in 1876, '7, '8.

The Polar Star mine was for a long time one of the most productive lodes on Democrat Mountain; its total product to date is reported at $160,000, currency value. The lode was discovered in 1872, and several thousand feet of shafts and tunnels have been driven. The owners state that 314 tons of ore had an average value of $213.22 per ton, and 200 tons an average of $173.75, and that the yield of 1874 was $25,766; that of 1876 was $23.263, and that of 1877 was $15,000. Only a small part of the property is worked at present.

Republican Mountain has probably produced more money than any other around Georgetown. It rises almost perpendicularly from the streets of that city, and likewise from those of Silver Plume, some two miles to the northwest, and extends from Democrat to Sherman mountains. Near its western extremity is the great Pelican-Dives group of lodes, whose aggregate production for seven or eight years mounts up into the millions. The principal lodes worked on this mountain at present are the Pelican, Dives, Dunkirk, Baxter, Pay Rock, Vulcan, Elm City, Silver Cloud, Edward Everett, Morning Star, Red Bird, Lebanon Tunnel Lode Number Five, and several veins intersected by the Diamond Tunnel, and owned by the tunnel company.

On this same mountain are other lodes that have been productive at times, such as the James Guthrie, Ben Hardin, Elijah Hise and White, located by John T. Harris in the days of the first silver excitement, and the Corry City, Loretta, South America, and Caledonia. Still more noted are the Snowdrift and Silver Plume, that yielded largely five and ten years ago.

The Pelican and Dives, until recently the most famous of Colorado silver mines, are located on the southern slope, and near the western end of Republican Mountain. The vein outcroppings are about seven hundred feet above, and in full view of Silver Plume, which dates its birth from the opening of these great ore deposits. The lodes were discovered in 1868, but for two years Streeter and McCunniff did not think the Pelican worth recording. The Dives produced little until 1871.

That same year the McCunniff brothers started to do a little work on the Pelican, with no expectation of finding anything very valuable. They were astonished at the size and richness of the vein that

steadily developed with their labor.   Nothing like it had previously
been encountered in the district, taking the great quantity of ore
into consideration, notwithstanding the fact that a Terrible, Equator, and Brown had been developed.   In a few short months up to
November, 1871, the coin value of the ore sold had amounted to

SILVER PLUME AND THE DIVES-PELICAN GROUP OF MINES.

$121,172.28.   The vein or series of veins were found to be of great
size, and no such thing as a wall on one side.

Then began the great war and almost endless litigation between the
Dives and Pelican.   As the yield of both mines grew larger and larger

the conflict became something like a battle of giants, in which the services of a small army of fighting men, leasers, and guards were secured, along with nearly all of the leading lawyers of the State, and some from the Pacific Slope. Suits and counter suits, injunctions and counter injunctions, followed each other in rapid succession, and much of the enormous revenues that came out of the mines went to the lawyers or were divided among supernumeraries and lessees. The latter, on account of the risks taken, mined only on very liberal terms for themselves. Some of them made fortunes ; for the vein was from one to seventeen feet wide, and worth from $40 to $800 a ton.

In 1874 the richest spot of ground held by the Dives or Perdue Company was enjoined. Before that the Pelican men had been attaching the ore for a time, until the others evaded attachment by disposing of it on Sundays. This was done for several successive weeks, and on the last Sabbath before the injunction came it is claimed that 65,000 worth of ore went out of the Dives mine. The lessees of the richest piece of ground cleared $42,000 that week.

At last the upper part of the great bonanzas had been mainly worked out, the owners had become exhausted with the long and costly struggle, and the lawyers and outsiders having reaped most of the harvest that should have gone into the owners' pockets, the latter concluded to sign a truce, "take a breathing spell," and suspend hostilities for a time. But the yield from that time forward was much smaller than before. Jacob Sneider, of the Pelican, had been killed by a lessee of a part of the Dives. McMurdy died, one or two of the Pelican owners were involved so as to be unable to escape from financial difficulties, and the result is that some of them have been sold out at sheriff's sale, and Hamill and others are securing interests in the property. The owners of both mines have combined in recent years to effect a consolidation and sale. One of the grandest mining operations in the country would be the natural result of the consummation of such a project. Even last year, when but a small force of leasers were at work, each mine is said to have yielded $60,000. Concentrations from one mine in one month brought $11,000. More work is going on in the Pelican now than for a year or two past. These mines have been opened by tunnels, shafts, and levels to a depth of from six to seven hundred feet, the Diamond Tunnel intersecting the Dives.

The receipts for ore and bullion sold from these two mines for six

years up to 1878, is reported as follows, previous and subsequent
products not included :

PELICAN MINE.

	Receipts.	Expenses.	Profits.
Jan. 1, 1872, to Jan. 1, 1877....	$902,905	$331,122	$571,783
1877.........................	114,471	34,098	80,373
Total.................	$1,017,376	$365.220	$652,156

DIVES AND PERDUE Co.

	Receipts.	Expenses.	Profits.
Jan. 1, 1872, to Jan. 1, 1877....	$676,377	$185,600	$490,777
1877.........................	97,500	42,500	55,000
Total Dives............	$773,877	$228,100	$545,777

Total Pelican and Dives yield....................$1,791,253
Add to this yield of both mines previous to 1872, and for the
    past year and a half, estimated at $170,000

Total receipts would be $1,961,253

The probable excess of contents of ore, over what was paid
    for it, should add $650,000 to the above, making total
    silver product in eight years.........................$2,611,253

Of this sum the Pelican probably yielded $1,400,000, and the
Dives the remainder. Most of the owners' share went to pay
lawyers, guards, sheriffs, etc. W. A. Hamill is now manager of the
Perdue and East Dives. Such is the record of two great silver
mines.

The Dunkirk is thought to be the east extension of the Dives. Its
shaft is 750 feet east of the Dives discovery shaft. It is owned and
was patented by the Herman Silver Mining Company, of which the
late John A. Dix was president. Charles H. Morris began work
here in 1870, and two years later organized the above-named company. He has since been its superintendent, and has shown a
persistency in developing this property under discouraging circumstances that is worthy of the reward that reports say he is now
meeting with in the lower west workings. The vein was developed
with shafts and levels, and steam-hoisting works secured to facilitate
operations, but no ore of any amount was found until last spring.
At that time a splendid body of ore was met with in the 410 level

west of the shaft, which has been milling hundreds of dollars per ton.
This is thought to be the extension of the old Dives ore body. It
looks as if the seventy thousand dollars expended on the property
would soon be regained, and more with it.

The Diamond Tunnel was started near the mouth of Cherokee
Gulch in 1872. It has since penetrated Republican Mountain about
1,600 feet, crossing some of the best veins of the district. Among
these are the Eagle Bird, Baxter, Dives, and others. The Baxter is
intersected 660 feet from the mouth of the tunnel, and 365 feet
below the surface. The mine is drained, and most of its workings
furnished with an ore outlet. Eight hundred feet in, Number Seven
vein is cut, and 1,136 feet in the Dives vein is intersected. Several
other veins have been passed, and are worked and owned by the company. The revenues from its own and other mines are said to render
the enterprise quite profitable. The tunnel is being driven forward
steadily.

The Pay Rock is one of the leading mines of this mountain, and
ranks next to the Pelican and Dives in the amount of silver produced. The mine comprises beside the three regular veins of the
Pay Rock lode, the Hopewell lode; all parallel with one another and
with the adjacent veins of the Pelican-Dives group; and a cross vein
called the Silver Point. The former have the same course as the
mountain at this point, nearly east and west. For drainage purposes, and to avoid as much of the steep ascent of the mountain as
possible, the mine has been opened by a series of intersecting tunnels,
driven one after another as new ground was required. These tunnels
pass through the veins and gangue of the Pay Rock veins and terminate with the Hopewell. These veins are from twenty to fifty feet apart.
The Pay Rock tunnel reaches the Hopewell at a distance of 250 feet,
and the Silver Bank tunnel, 86 feet deeper, requires a length of 376
feet to reach the same point. There are still deeper workings than
this, and the veins have been operated for depths of several hundred
feet below where they outcrop on the surface. A pump and steam
hoister are used. Levels extend hundreds of feet east and west,
showing continuous veins nearly all of the way. The quantity of
ore is variable, expanding and contracting at intervals, but the
quality is above the average of the district. The ore mined yields
from forty to eight hundred dollars per ton, and large quantities have
yielded from two to five hundred. Many miners have made large

and small sums of money in sections of the mine leased to them, although a high royalty was often charged. For several years the working force has ranged from forty-five to sixty-five men. Had the mine been opened by a deep tunnel from the valley below, much more rapid progress could have been made in opening it. The Pay Rock was discovered in 1872, and has yielded not far from $400,000, coin value. Its product in 1878 was about $60,000. The owners are T. W. Ellis, P. Ellis, J. A. Fairbanks, and Gray & Noyes.

The Baxter is an extremely rich and profitable lode, a short distance below the Dives and above the town of Silver Plume. It is usually worked by from thirty to fifty employees and leasers, and its annual yield has been not far from sixty thousand dollars for several years. The total yield of the mine is estimated at over three hundred thousand dollars. A large part of the ore yields from three to five hundred dollars per ton, and smaller quantities have milled from that up to ten and fifteen hundred dollars.

The Elm City is a small but very rich vein, some of the ore selling for over $1,000 a ton. The Snowdrift gave its largest yield in 1870-71, when silver to the amount of $96,316.80, currency value, was obtained. The Silver Plume has been a large producer.

The Lebanon Tunnel is owned by a company of the same name, and has been driven into Republican Mountain some nine hundred feet; the location is between Silver Plume and Georgetown, and the objective point the belt of lodes that includes the Hardin, Guthrie, White, and others. So far, eight lodes have been intersected, several of which are valuable, and one called Tunnel Lode Number Five has paid steadily for years. The Prentice and Hardin lodes, owned by the same company, have been worked from the surface. Beside the creek, and opposite the mouth of the tunnel, is a concentrating and sampling mill. The depth that will be attained on many of the lodes of this mountain is from one to two thousand feet; J. G. Pohle is general manager of this enterprise.

CHAPTER XVII.

CLEAR CREEK COUNTY MINES—SHERMAN, BROWN, McCLELLAN, AND
LEAVENWORTH MOUNTAINS—THE DUNDERBERG-TERRIBLE GROUP
OF MINES—MILLIONS IN SILVER—THE EQUATOR AND COLORADO
CENTRAL GROUP—MINING IN CLOUD LAND—THE STEVENS AND
BAKER—SOME LONG TUNNELS.

Sherman Mountain is immediately west of Republican. In reality
this is all one continuous range, in whcih ravines of no great depth
serve as boundaries. Cherokee Gulch lies between the mountains
just mentioned, and further west Brown Gulch is the dividing line of
Sherman and Brown Mountains. All of these elevations are very
abrupt and rugged and contain many nearly perpendicular silver-
bearing veins whose course is almost parallel with the creek and
valley below.

But few localities contain as much mineral wealth as Sherman
Mountain. Here are a large number of famous veins, of which the
Dunderberg, East Terrible, Sub-Treasury, Backbone, Mendota, Cap
Wells, Eagle Bird, Mammoth, Glasgow, Corry City, and a few others,
are actively worked. Not long ago work was temporarily sus-
pended on such noted and once-productive lodes as the Frostburg,
Phœnix, Coldstream, Cashier, Silver Cloud, and Cascade. The Mam-
moth and Glasgow have been worked steadily for many years.

The Phœnix and Coldstream lode or lodes are situated on the
eastern portion of Sherman Mountain, approaching and underlying
Cherokee Gulch. They began to pay in 1871, and litigation and
bitter contests, in which one or two men lost their lives, were carried
on by the owners of the respective properties for several years. The
total yield of both mines must have exceeded $300,000. Mill runs
gave from one to sixteen hundred ounces of silver. The Coldstream
was at first called the Maine. It yielded in the first eight months
of work $64,100, at a cost of little over $14,000. The ore vein is
argentiferous galena, containing more or less gray copper, ruby silver,
iron and copper pyrites.

Twelve years ago the Burleigh Tunnel enterprise was inaugurated under the auspices of the inventor of the Burleigh drill. The design was to penetrate Sherman Mountain and furnish an ore and drainage outlet for lodes outcropping one or two thousand feet above, and to explore for blind lodes. Work fairly began in 1868, and has been prosecuted at intervals down to the present year. It is now the longest tunnel in the State, having been driven forward over 2,300 feet. Several veins have been intersected, including the Rider, I. Phillips, and New Era. The latter yielded ore in paying quantities that carried from 60 to 70 per cent. of lead and a low value in silver. Colonel Ivers Phillips, an old Massachusetts railroad man, is general manager of this tunnel enterprise.

The Dunderberg, East Terrible, Sub-Treasury, Silver Chain, Muldoon, and Elephant, embracing 7,900 feet of mineral veins, were recently purchased by the Dunderberg Mining Company, organized in New York, with a capital stock of a million and a half in ten dollar shares. The East Terrible is that part of the Terrible lode that was not sold to the English company in 1870. It extends from the main shaft in Brown Gulch, used by both properties, eastward in Sherman Mountain to where the Dunderberg begins. The latter is the same vein further east, the location including 3,000 feet. The Sub-Treasury, supposed to be on the same vein, is still further east. This has occasionally shown sixty ounce galena ore for a width of two feet. It is said that $300,000 has been paid for East Terrible ore. The first class averaged about $500 a ton, and the second class $150.

No work of any importance was done on the Dunderberg until 1877. In December of that year George Tyler and Mr. Antoine, lessees, struck a very rich body of mineral, similar to that of the Terrible. The mine was soon after the most productive and profitable in the mountains, and has paid largely up to the present time. It appears that in a little over four months, to April, 1878, there were sold 474¾ tons, bringing $112,528.97, at an average price of $237 per ton. Four hundred and fourteen fathoms were extracted, with a net yield of $297 per fathom, and the average yield of one foot of drift, six feet high, was $49.50.

Hayes, Tyler & Co. received $255,000 for ore sold in 1878, and the total receipts from the time this ore-body was discovered to March 1, 1879, a period of a little over fourteen months, were

$308,468. The parties state that the actual cost of mining and getting the ore to market was but twenty-one per cent. of that sum. The Dunderberg has one of the best and richest veins ever opened in the Rocky Mountains. Last year it gave a larger aggregate and proportionate profit than anything in northern Colorado. Sometimes rich mineral widens out into pockets two feet broad. Several adits, shafts, levels, and stopes have been worked, and the lowest points reached are from two hundred and forty to three hundred feet below the surface.

The Terrible-Dunderberg fissure pierces the granite nearly vertically, with a course east of north and west of south. It has a crevice of from four to six feet, carrying a vein from one to eight inches wide, that averages from two to five hundred ounces of silver per ton. This vein carries argentiferous galena, gray copper, and sulphides of silver, and the gangue that makes up the remainder of the crevice is porphyry and quartz. A vein of this character has been traced pretty continuously for a distance of two thousand feet in Brown and Sherman mountains.

Brown Mountain has been one of the leading producers in the county ever since silver mining became prominent. The more prominent lodes are the Terrible, Silver Ore, Brown, Chelsea Beach, and others belonging to the Colorado United Mining Company, together with the Duncan, Hercules-Roe-Seven-Thirty, Shiveley, Owasco, Brick Pomeroy, Atlantic, and some others, all actively worked.

Previous to September, 1870, the Terrible lode had yielded $270,000, coin value. The product of 1872 was $168,625 from sales of ore, and the actual yield of 1874 was $203,000. Up to the close of 1876 the Silver Ore is said to have yielded $140,000. The latter and the English company property must have yielded a round million from time of discovery up to the close of 1877. The yield of these and of the East Terrible to the present time is estimated at $1,500,-000. The Colorado United Mining Company have been turning out from one hundred to one hundred and fifty thousand dollars per annum from its Terrible and Hamill and Chaffee group of mines.

The underground workings of many of the company lodes are very extensive. Work is progressing in both the Silver Ore and Terrible shafts—the lower workings of the latter being 650 feet deep, and of the former 500, and 170 feet deeper than the Union Tunnel. This part of the property, called the West Terrible, gives employment

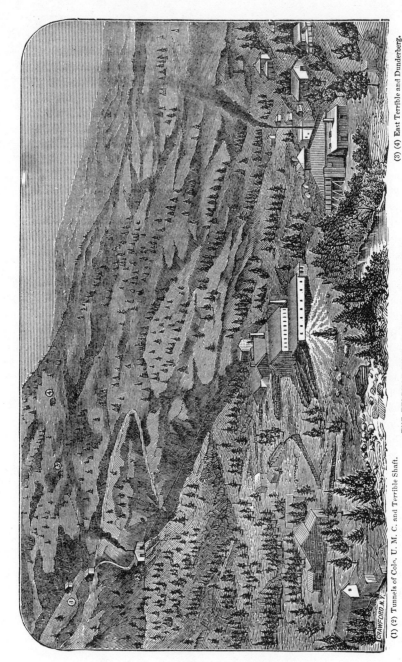

CRAWFORD.N.Y.

(1) (2) Tunnels of Colo. U. M. C. and Terrible Shaft.　(3) (4) East Terrible and Dunderberg.

THE TERRIBLE-DUNDERBERG GROUP OF MINES.

to over one hundred men. Lessees and employees of the company elsewhere foot up as many more. The Union tunnel is 570 feet long to the Terrible lode, and the Silver Ore tunnel is 900 feet long.

At the foot of the mountain are the old Brown Reducing Works, no longer used for smelting, and the concentrating mill, where the low grade ores are rendered available. This mill concentrates about twenty tons of ore daily, that averages about $17 a ton. Twelve tons are concentrated down to one composed of one-third galena, milling at the rate of 250 ounces, and two-thirds zinc-blende, milling at the rate of 125 ounces of silver per ton.

The Hercules, Roe, and Seven Thirty lodes, all crossing or nearly parallel veins at a point in Brown Gulch, are owned by a Denver company. They have been traced for long distances into either mountain, and pierced with a cross-cut tunnel and many levels, winzes, and shafts. Work is being prosecuted steadily, and the owners report the property quite profitable. The total yield from the beginning approaches $230,000. There are no less than ten leasing parties in various parts of this great property, and a fair amount of ore is in sight. The receipts for ore sold in May, 1879, were $2,466, and the ore taken out of different places gave the following yields per ton: 318 ounces of silver, 283 ounces, 163 ounces, 175 ounces, and 600 in one place and 300 in two others.

The Shiveley lode has produced nearly or quite $60,000. It was purchased by the Equitable Mining Company not long ago. The Duncan, Atlantic, and Pacific are all rich veins. On Hanna Mountain the Silver Cloud and Specie are worked.

Kelso Mountain is close beside Irwin's Peak, and opposite the circling McClellan ridge, with a valley and fork of South Clear Creek intervening. Richard Irwin, John Baker, and Fletcher Kelso prospected here in the summer of 1865, after having left the swarm of silver hunters that had congregated on McClellan mountain. They were so fortunate as to find a great vein that paid largely, sold for big figures, nearly broke up a company, and afterwards made money for lessees. The lode took the name of Baker, the mountain on which it was located that of Kelso, and a neighboring peak that has but few equals in height in the country, was named after Irwin. Some other discoveries were made in this section. In recent years the Brooklyn, since known as the Diamond

Joe, has yielded a great deal of rich ore, and is said to be quite remunerative.

Eastward from the solitudes of Gray's Peak extends the long elevated ridge known as McClellan Mountain. The side sloping towards Argentine Pass and Creek is smooth and grass-clad, but that facing Irwin and Kelso is as rugged and perpendicular as it well can be. Amid these granite cliffs of McClellan, far above timber line and nearly 12,000 feet above sea level, is the famous Stevens Mine. The sight of this, perched as it is a thousand feet above the valley in a seemingly inaccessible position, causes the Gray's Peak tourist to wonder how it was ever discovered and how it is worked. Closer inspection shows a tramway fastened to the mountain side and leading to the cabins and tunnels that appear above. One would think the dauntless prospector who found this lode must have come over by way of the southern slope, descending from the summit, or else have discovered "float ore" and "blossom" at the base of the mountain, and thereafter "lit" upon the vein in some unaccountable manner.

The Stevens has been worked pretty steadily for nearly twelve years. Long ago a kind of aerial tramway and ropeway had been built for transportation. In 1877, a substantial tramway was constructed to replace one partially demolished. This is 1,050 feet long, and has a superstructure resting on trestle-work high enough to prevent snow accumulations from blockading the ascending and descending cars. Beside this is a hand-rail and in its bed-timbers are cleats, to enable the miners to ascend and descend. Among the savage rocks at the upper terminus is the mouth of the tunnel and an ore house, with apparatus for operating the "tram," and for miners' and storage quarters. From this cars descend with four or five tons of ore on a trip, and return laden with provisions, powder, steel, charcoal, timbers, and lumber. From the ore house down on the edge of the valley wagons convey the ore to Georgetown during the summer months, and sleds are used at other times to Bakerville.

The main outlet to the mine is a tunnel which intersects the vein 320 feet from daylight and 500 feet below the mountain side directly overhead. This was driven the entire distance through frozen frosted rock—the same in winter or summer.

The Stevens ores carry a moderate amount of silver, and from fifty to seventy per cent. of lead. The quantity of ore and economical

plan of operations make up for the remote and unfavorable locality
of the mine. The annual yield is estimated at eighty thousand
dollars, more or less. On the southerly slope of McClellan are those
old discoveries, the Belmont and the International. Both have
turned out much silver.

GREEN LAKE, NEAR GEORGETOWN—ELEVATION 10,000 FEET.

Leavenworth mountain extends eastward and southward from
McClellan for a distance of several miles, and breaks off suddenly
at the head of the valley of Georgetown. This has been one of the
richest and most productive localities around the "Silver Queen."

Here is a cluster of celebrated lodes that have added largely to the county's product, and most of them have made fortunes, or a good deal of ready money, for those connected with them. The Colorado Central, Equator, Kirtley, Ocean Wave, O. K., Argentine, Steamboat, Gilpin, Alpha, Gates, S. J. Tilden, Ni Wott, and some others, are all actively worked and all said to be paying. On the southern slope of this mountain is one of the most important groups of lodes in the State, and below is the village of Silver Dale.

Among the early operators here was General F. J. Marshall, who has ever been one of the leading miners and ore shippers of the district. He developed a number of lodes, such as the Compass and Square, Robinson, Reynolds, and others, and started the Marshall and other tunnels, designed to pierce the mountain through to its northerly slope and discover and work the many veins of this belt. The results have been so satisfactory that an immense amount of ore and silver have been produced. The operations of General Marshall and of the Marshall Tunnel Company have led to many important discoveries and to a yield of nearly half a million in bullion. A half dozen lodes are now worked in this combination. The underground excavations embrace over 7,000 feet of workings. The Marshall Tunnel is 1,300 feet long, and 9,382 feet above the sea, and the upper tunnels are from 350 feet to 500 feet long. A score of shafts, and cross-cuts have been driven and long levels extended therefrom, at a cost of $160,000, and nearly half as much more for the extraction of $160,000 worth of ore. This does not include the returns of several lodes worked by the same manager.

In 1872 many men were making money by collecting and selling the float ore in the "slide" of Leavenworth Mountain. This led to much prospecting and to W. P. Lynn's discovery of the famous vein called the Colorado Central. Weaver, Shepard and others secured a lease of this, and all made fortunes in a year or two. The ore sometimes milled up in the thousands, and portions of it were so rich in lead and silver that it would not pulverize under the stamps. Marshall, Martine & Hall paid these lessees $68,918.23 for ore in 1873 alone. Up to 1876 the vein had yielded receipts to the amount of $150,000, and had been opened to a depth of 200 feet.

About the close of 1876 some leasers, engaged in driving a cross-cut from some of the interior tunnel properties, discovered one of the richest veins of ore ever developed. This was named the S. J.

Tilden, and yielded $100,000 in 1877, the first year of production. Some of the ore brought from four to six thousand dollars a ton, and the average for a long time was about twelve hundred. The discoverers paid a royalty amounting to one-third of the gross receipts. The vein was less productive in 1878, but is again improving.

The Equator is a wonderfully large and rich vein, but has not been worked as steadily or extensively as its value warrants. This was the leading producer of Clear Creek county for a time in 1868. Up to 1869 the yield was $68,600. The ore sold at from one to five hundred dollars a ton. The main shaft was carried down some 400 feet, but for reasons best known to its Chicago and Colorado owners, mining was not continued for years after 1870 except by tributors. In 1878 work began on an extensive scale, and one of the best ore bodies ever mined in the country was developed. There was a seam of ruby silver ore several inches thick, that is said to have yielded from one to five thousand dollars per ton, while the main portion of the mineral ran in the hundreds. It is reported that the lessee of this ground took out $40,000 in one month.

The Kirtley has been one of the prominent mines of the district ever since its discovery in 1877. Some years ago several Georgetown men began to drive a tunnel in Leavenworth Mountain for purposes of development and discovery. The Gates lode helped to repay the outlay, but it was not until the Kirtley was intersected that the enterprise became a very remunerative one. The vein has often been four feet wide, but is quite varied as regards value of contents. There are streaks and bunches of very rich ore, larger amounts of low grade material, and considerable gangue. The profits and products are believed to have been large and uniform. What the yield has been only the owners know—possibly a hundred thousand, and perhaps a great deal more or less. Ten inches of two and three hundred ounce ore were lately reported.

Geneva District is situated high up in the Continental Divide, near the point of union of Clear Creek, Park and Summit counties. As the outlets of the great Revenue, Leviathan, Star and other tunnels and mines are mainly in Summit county, the district will be noticed in a succeeding chapter.

CHAPTER XVIII.

LEADVILLE—CALIFORNIA GULCH AND ITS EARLY HISTORY—DISCOVERY
OF CARBONATES—THE SILVER AND LEAD BONANZAS—THE
FOUNDING AND GROWTH OF THE MAGIC CITY—THE ERA OF
GOLD AND THE DAYS OF CARBONATES— LUCK IN LEADVILLE—
THE DAYS OF 'FORTY-NINE REPEATED IN 'SEVENTY-NINE.

Late in the spring of 1860 a band of Gilpin county gold hunters
crossed the Park range of mountains and entered a heavily timbered
ravine, which they called California Gulch. They panned the surface dirt for gold and found it rich beyond expectation. The
reports that spread abroad brought in a continuous stream of prospectors, and the locality was soon alive with men. The original
discoverers secured two hundred feet up and down the stream, and
those who came after were allowed one hundred feet, until the
gulch was pre-empted for 33,000 feet, or nearly its entire length.

There was almost a continuous street bordering the stream, and
skirting the bases of the hills, but there were two points that were
centres of trade and traffic. One of these was at the place where
the hills break away towards the present site of Leadville, and since
called Old Oro. A few of the log structures of 1860 are still
standing as landmarks of the olden times. The other business
point, the Oro of to-day, was two and a half miles further up
the gulch. The last has continued to be a place of more or less
importance up to the present time, partly on account of the subsequent discovery of the Printer Boy and other gold veins.

Parts of the gulch were fabulously rich, but the water supply
was limited. This was used over and over again by each successive
claim owner, and by the time it reached the lower part of the
district was of the consistency of liquid mud. The sluice-box,
"long tom," and "rocker" were all used, and although difficulty was experienced in handling the dirt, the returns have seldom
been equaled in any country. Some claims yielded over a thousand dollars a day, and one firm is said to have taken out one
hundred thousand dollars in sixty days.

Before the summer was over more than five thousand men had assembled there, and the camp was the most productive and prosperous in the mountains. The usual miners' laws were in force, and the locality had much the same characteristics of other early mining settlements. There was the usual quota of gambling-houses, dance-houses, and saloons, and when night came many a miner lost the rich earnings of the day among them. Reckless and improvident, but few of the lucky ones saved the money they had made. Some lost it in subsequent investments at the East, and some squandered it in carousals or played it away almost as fast as they took it in. The camp saw its best days in 1861.

The working season was quite limited, for the elevation was very great and the location near timber line. The winters were long and lingered far into spring, and little work could be done outside of the summer months and September and a part of October. Every year when the deep snows " came to stay," most of the miners would betake themselves to milder climes, like Denver or the States, returning again with the approach of summer. Gold dust was the universal medium of exchange, and as fast as obtained would be deposited in a buckskin pouch or bag of some kind. In every store or saloon stood a pair of scales for weighing. When a miner bought a sack of flour or a glass of whiskey he handed his dust to the man behind the counter, who weighed out the required amount and handed back the remainder. The gold as it came from the sluices, passed at a valuation of about $18 an ounce. Some claims yielded an ounce or two daily to each man at work, and one pan of dirt, about the size of an ordinary milk pan, yielded five ounces of gold.

So matters continued for several years, until the most accessible ground had been worked over and the gold production had greatly declined. During this time the ever-restless spirits, so plentiful in such places, were moving on to newer diggings, and by 1866 almost the entire population had taken its departure.

The most reliable data at hand indicates a yield of a million a summer to begin with, and of a total yield of nearly four millions, coin value, up to the close of 1865. Some claim that three millions will cover the output. Production subsequent to 1866 was light; it had dropped to $60,000 in 1869, and to $20,000 in 1876.

The amount mentioned for the earlier years was all that conserva-

TWIN LAKES.

tive men believed was produced, although some enterprising reporters of the present time are doubling up the original estimates every few months, and in a way that may soon result in a total greater than the entire production of Colorado.

The camp was "pretty dead," as the "old-timers" would say, in 1868, when the development of the Printer Boy lode began. This was so remunerative that quite an excitement sprang up, much prospecting was done, and several gold veins located. The Printer Boy was the only very profitable mine worked; this showed an immense body of soft quartz that was very rich in gold. It was not long until a twenty-five-stamp mill was erected, and the Philadelphia company that was operating this and the great mine ought to have made a great deal of money. Up to 1875 the yield had exceeded a quarter of a million from work carried on about half of the time during six years. Previous to these gold lode discoveries in California Gulch, some profitable mining of a similar character had been inaugurated some seventeen miles distant, and near Granite; this began in 1866, and continued for two or three years before the surface pockets were exhausted so as to cause a suspension of work.

In the years succeeding 1871 some attempts at ore treatment were made at Granite, and a few discoveries were made thirty miles north, near the headwaters of the Tennessee fork of the Arkansas. One of these, called the Homestake, was of great size, and was rich in lead but poor in silver. Its promising character, and the result of ore shipments to the Golden Smelting Works, with the known presence of silver-lead veins among the hills east of the Arkansas, led to the building of a smelter near the junction of California Gulch and the Arkansas river. The place was called Malta, and the Malta smelting works fired up and did some business in the fall of 1876, and then remained idle until partly built over a year and a half later.

In 1874, W. H. Stevens, a wealthy Michigan and Colorado miner, came over from Park county, in company with A. B. Wood, and began to construct a twelve-mile ditch for the California Gulch placer claims that they had purchased. The plan was to bring in a sufficient water supply to permit of hydraulic mining and the cheap handling of the unworked gravel banks that bordered the stream. The headwaters of the Arkansas were the source of supply, and several summers were required to complete this great enterprise of the organization known as the Oro Ditch and Fluming Company. The first full season's work was put in on the placers in the summer of 1878.

Experience proves that, although these Colorado mountains have been annually overrun by restless hordes of prospectors, who have brought to light some marvelous revelations, the mineral wealth that underlies them has been but indefinitely comprehended. California Gulch had been occupied for a decade and a half, and had been worked over until millions of gold had been extracted, and yet close by an apparently exhaustless treasury of the valuable metals had lain embedded, unknown and untouched, until within the past two or three years.

During all the time that gulch mining had been going on in California district, the miners had suffered much inconvenience by reason of the great weight of the boulders they were obliged to move over and over in the creek. None of them knew, or stopped to investigate, the character of this heavy dirt they were obliged to handle. Messrs. Stevens and Wood found it to be carbonate of lead, carrying silver, but did not make their discovery known until they were in a fair way to secure government titles to nine claims. These were taken up lengthways along what they considered the crest or apex of the lodes, and each comprised 1,500 feet by 300, or thereabouts. The territory crossed California Gulch and extended high up on the hills. The name of the principal locations commencing at the south were, the Dome, Rock, Stone, Lime, Bull's Eye, and Iron. The ore was first found in place in the Rock claim, where it was over ten feet thick. It was rich in lead, but carried only a small amount of silver. A Mr. Durham claimed to have discovered carbonates prior to this, in sinking a shaft on the Oro La Plata lode.

For several years Maurice Hayes was conducting an assay office at Oro, and he and his brother were mining and prospecting extensively. They made some of the earliest carbonate of lead locations in the district, and were firm believers in the ultimate development of good mines outside of those then opened. As to who were the original discoverers or first locaters of carbonates the writer does not pretend to decide.

The first strike that was considered exceptionally good was that made by the Gallagher brothers, on the same hill as the Iron, but

CHESTNUT STREET, LEADVILLE.

nearer Stray Horse Gulch. But even here they were well-nigh discouraged before carbonates rich and plentiful enough were found to insure a profit. This claim was called the Camp Bird, and in the same fall and winter (1876–7) the Adelaide, Pine, and Charleston were " staked."

For quite a time previous to 1877 A. R. Meyer had been purchasing ores in Park and Lake counties for the St. Louis Smelting and Refining Company with headquarters at Alma. In April of that year the prospective production of the Rock, Camp Bird, and other claims, led him to establish sampling works on the present site of Leadville. A month later the Saint Louis Smelting Company began to erect a smelter, and had a blast furnace in operation in October. To insure an ore supply a contract was made with Stevens and Wood to furnish one thousand tons of ore from the Rock Mine. Before that had been entirely delivered such development had taken place, and so many discoveries had been made, that the only difficulty was in handling what was brought to both sampling and smelting works. The latter were called the Harrison Reduction Works, after the president of the company, Edwin F. Harrison.

Late in June, 1877, Charles Mater came up from Granite and started the first building on the original town site of Leadville, and opened out a stock of groceries. Several cabins were completed before Mater began to sell goods. In the meantime splendid mines were beginning to be developed in the neighboring hills, and settlers were slowly drifting in from the older camps of the State. H. A. W. Tabor, who had conducted a small store for many years up the gulch at Oro, brought a stock of goods to Leadville in this same summer of 1877.

About this time A. B. Wood sold his interest in the nine claims before mentioned to L. Z. Leiter, of the great Chicago dry goods firm of Field, Leiter & Co., for $40,000. The true value of the Iron lode was then unknown, and the low grade Rock mine was considered the best of the lot. The purchaser would hardly sell for a million to-day. In the fall of 1877, the former claim began to be worked extensively, and proved to be of immense value. The Camp Bird had been counted the best mine, but was then distanced by the Iron, which came to the front, and, more than any other property, gave the district its first great fame. It maintained the lead up to the time of the Fryer Hill developments in the latter half of 1878.

In the fall of 1877 several hundred men were in the district—most of them prospecting or sinking prospecting shafts, but the amount of mining done was considerable. The ore shipments were steadily increasing in volume, and a vast amount of low grade mineral was mined for which no market was afforded. It was becoming more and more evident that the mineral wealth of California district was of immense extent. Mines were being developed on every hand, notwithstanding the fact that it was necessary to team ore one hundred and twenty miles to the plains, and then send by rail nearly a thousand miles further to Saint Louis, or nearly as far to Omaha. Shipments to the latter place were made by Berdell & Witherill, who had established a sampling mill in the district late in 1877. To meet the growing demands of travel, Spottswood & McClellan extended their Denver and South Park stage lines to Leadville, and several ore transportation and freight lines were established between that point and the railway termini. The best paying mines at that time were the Iron, Camp Bird, Carbonate, and Long and Derry.

The population of Leadville increased steadily during that winter and spring, and a weekly newspaper, school, and two churches were established. In March, 1878, the first important transfer of mining property was made. Members of the St. Louis Smelting Company, having become aware of the value and quantity of ore in the Camp Bird claim, through purchases at their smelters, bought that and the adjoining Pine, Keystone, and Charleston claims for $225,000. Those who sold had been poor, hard-working men previous to the time when their mine began to produce so heavily.

The fame of the carbonate district had spread far and wide before the summer of 1878, and a tide of immigration was started that has since continued with ever-increasing momentum. Several discoveries already made were wonderfully rich and productive, but the developments that have given Leadville its grand pre-eminence over any other section in the world at the present time were those on Fryer Hill. Claims opened that same season were sufficiently explored in the ensuing fall to give pretty extensive indications of their immense extent and value. From that time the future of the district was assured and destiny beckoned in the direction of Leadville.

At first the town obtained its increase from older Colorado settlements, but more distant sections were drawn upon before the season was over. Each succeeding week saw the volume of immigration grow larger and larger, and every evening witnessed the arrival of new comers by stage, by freight teams, on horseback, and on foot. Friends or acquaintances who had not met for years found themselves together again in the new and fast-growing metropolis of the carbonate belt. There were gold-hunters who had left Colorado years agone for the newer territories; there were men who had been

THE BANK OF LEADVILLE.

rich and poor by turns, but were still as hopeful and ambitious as when life was new; there were men of every profession and calling; and every state and section were drawn upon to help swell the population of Leadville.

Many mines were already paying, and whenever mineral was struck in a new locality men were on hand ready to take it off of the finder's hands at liberal figures. New streets were built up in a single week and sleeping accommodations were ever at a premium.

This was Leadville before it grew to assume metropolitan proportions.

Visitors from abroad were at first distrustful of the camp's future, but would, ere long, catch the enthusiasm that pervaded the entire population, and be among the loudest to sound the praises and wonders of the magic city of Carbonateland. The district's growth was greatly accelerated, and its fame still further enhanced, by the wonderful developments and production of the Fryer Hill mines in the summer and fall of 1878. These ore deposits were so rich and plentiful and so easily mined that they surpassed anything previously discovered in the State, and, as far as mineral was concerned, in any other state or territory outside of the Comstock bonanzas. Meantime the Iron, Argentine, and other great mines, kept on producing as heavily as ever, and every month saw fresh additions to the many paying mines.

Winter came, but brought no cessation of the ever-augmenting caravan headed for the new land of promise. No matter how distant the land or locality, all roads seemed to lead to Leadville. Railways were started in that direction, roads were blocked with long lines of freight and immigrant teams, stage lines trebled their carrying capacity, and yet travel increased faster than accommodations could be afforded. A dozen saw-mills were turning out lumber night and day, and still could not half meet the demands made upon them for building purposes. Men who had made fortunes from working or selling their mines turned about and bought up prospects, or newly developed properties, at what would have seemed fabulous prices in former times. The streets and entire camp has been one whirl of excitement, and each successive month only added to the animation that pervaded all industries and every branch of trade. Men who had never before had a dollar ahead of actual necessities found themselves rolling in wealth, and the possessors of bank accounts far beyond what they had ever dared to dream of. The reports of prizes drawn by the few and of opportunities afforded the many were the magnetic influences that attracted less fortunate mortals from abroad. The snows and suffering attending a trip over mountain ranges had no terrors to those who had caught the " Leadville fever " and feared to lose their chances for a fortune by delay. One hundred a day was the average number of arrivals much of the time from January to June.

Mining has not been the only money making business. Fortunes have been made in real estate, and the several successive advances in the values of town lots were sources of heavy gains to many a property holder and speculator. Building sites that could be purchased for $25 in the summer of 1878, were selling for several thousands in the succeeding winter, and a single week has seen real estate quadruple in value. Chestnut street has been the business thoroughfare, but Harrison avenue bids fair to take the lead hereafter. Land

VIEW IN HARRISON AVENUE, LEADVILLE.

is held at from one hundred to over two hundred and fifty dollars per foot of front on these streets.

Every trade and calling proved a source of revenue for a time, and the merchant, lumber man, mechanic or professional man, had all the business they could attend to. One avocation helped another, and all helped the freighter. The transportation to and from the railway termini was something wonderful, even as connected with this wonderful locality. The Colorado Springs freight lines alone had two thousand animals engaged in the business, and yet lacked men and mules to such a degree as to be partially blockaded the entire winter and spring. Notwithstanding the fact that at the present time there are more goods and labor than are needed, Leadville continues its unprecedented growth; but while it is the same "roaring camp" as before, it is fast assuming the metropolitan airs that its size and the enterprising character of its people entitle it to possess. The church, free school, and press are all well represented, there being several of the former and three daily newspapers. Business houses, large and small, are there by the hundred, and there are nearly a hundred licensed saloons and a dozen gambling-houses in full blast night and day.

The result of all this increase of population and prodigious mining production and profit is to make Leadville the liveliest town the world can show to-day. The activity in building and in all branches of trade due to the above condition of things, and the vast amount of shaft prospecting, added to regular mining operations, all aid in giving work and opportunities to the new comers. The overplus of population that had accumulated before the disappearance of the spring snows is much less manifest at the present time, for with the summer, thousands moved out to explore the broad expanse of mountain that awaited the coming of the prospector.

The town is a marvel of activity, begotten of circumstances, surroundings, and great natural wealth and prosperity. Difficult as it is to make one's way along the main thoroughfares by day, it is still more so just before and after nightfall. Leadville by lamp-light fairly "booms" with excitement and life. The miners then drift into town in swarms; a dozen bands are drumming up audiences for the theatres and variety shows, scores of saloons and numerous gambling-houses are in full blast, and the entire scene gives the town and place the appearance of one grand holiday. Many of the places referred to do a tremendous business, for those who make money easy generally spend it quickly, and life in such places tends to prodigality. Thus those who come on business or pleasure, or to stay, are all bent on seeing what there is to see, regardless of expense, and with as little delay as possible. Such a condition of affairs helps to distribute money among all classes and callings.

Nearly every business or professional man, clerk, saloon-keeper, mechanic, or mill employee in Leadville is engaged in mining or prospecting. This is usually done by furnishing what is called a grub stake—consisting of supplies, the necessaries of life or wages to men who will sink a shaft, while the backer of the enterprise continues to follow his own calling. In this way a large number of men are afforded employment, and many has been the paying mine or sale of property resulting therefrom. Numerous instances

ON TO LEADVILLE—FREIGHT TRAIN ASCENDING UTE PASS.

can be related of men who came to the camp poor, and in a few months retired with a fortune. Others stay to win additional wealth, and have been almost universally successful, for money in this place, combined with experience and good judgment, has worked wonders.

Leadville's population was less than 1,500 in June, 1878, and double that in the succeeding fall. A census taken in January, 1879, showed 5,040 residents, beside half as many more just outside of the town limits. Since then the place has grown beyond all precedent, and the most moderate estimates of the present population of the carbonate metropolis range from twelve to fifteen thousand. Next fall it may be twenty thousand, with half as many more in the surrounding country.

Notwithstanding the haste with which the place has been built, there are scores of pretentious frame structures in Leadville, and a few elegant brick edifices, some completed and others under way, such as the Catholic cathedral and the banks. Among the live daily newspapers the Chronicle has few equals in the West for ability and enterprise. Leadville was badly off for hotels for a time. At length the Grand was built, and then the Clarendon, ranking among the first in the State. The city is supplied with first-class waterworks, and will be illuminated with gas within a very few weeks. A street railway is being constructed.

The Bank of Leadville was established in the fall of 1878, and moved into its present handsome quarters in February; H. A. W. Tabor is president, and George R. Fisher cashier. The First National Bank was started in the spring of 1878 (when the town was new), as the Lake County Bank; J. W. Zoïlars, cashier. The Miners' Exchange Bank was founded in the spring of 1878; George W. Trimble is cashier. The Merchants and Mechanics' Bank was established in 1879. The amounts of deposits and of exchange bought and sold in these institutions is remarkably large.

The Post Office is a wonder in itself, and does a larger local business than any other between Kansas City and San Francisco. One month ago the daily business was about $1,000 for sales of stamps, 8,000 letters received and 6,000 forwarded, and the average value of money orders forwarded $20,000 a week. The business increases about 40 per cent. each month. Long files of men can be seen at any time for twelve hours of the day awaiting their turn at the four general deliveries. Postmaster A. A. Smith employs thirteen clerks, and the entire force is overworked. The Leadville telegraph office does a correspondingly large business.

The climate cannot be called a severe one, and the mortality is not as heavy as reported. Although the population was largely made up of adventurers from all quarters, a good degree of order was maintained, and very little crime prevailed previous to the whole-sale immigration from the East and distant states and territories. As it is, the place is little worse than other cities. Leadville is most favorably located on a nearly level plain, at the western base of the rounded carbonate hills. The country was originally densely timbered, and most of it is so still. On either side distant mountain ranges rise far above timber line. Fifteen miles westward are Massive and Elbert, and beyond are Grizzly, Twin Peaks, Harvard, and Princeton. The views from the Iron or Long and Derry mines are at once lovely and inspiring. Extending along the entire western horizon is the grand-est range of mountains on the continent, and before them is the broad and level valley of the Arkansas. Of the many desirable pleasure resorts Twin Lakes take the lead. These connecting bodies of fresh water at the base of the Sierras are unsurpassed for beauty or attractiveness of surroundings. Sail boats, excellent trout fishing, and good hotels are afforded there, and all at a distance of only seventeen miles from Leadville, over a smooth and level roadway.

Apprehensions that Leadville will overstock the world's silver and lead market are groundless. The increase of silver will hardly make up for the falling off in the Nevada Comstock's production, and the increase of lead but offset the losses in some other states. If Leadville district should smelt or ship 90,000 tons of ore in 1878, there is no probability of its lead product exceeding 17,000 tons, which, at a valuation of $80 a ton, would give a total of $1,360,000. The district's silver yield may aggregate ten or fifteen millions.

The predictions that the Leadville mines will soon be exhausted, and that the prosperity of the camp is short-lived, are made only by those who have not considered all sides of the situation. There is no reason why a body of ore inclining slightly below the horizontal should not be as continuous as a vertical vein. The ease and rapidity with which the ore is mined is so much in favor of the mines, for everyone is desirous of making money in the shortest possible time. Better than all this, continual and rapid enlargement of the ore-producing area by numberless discoveries, make up many times over for any exhaustion of ground in the older locations. Better still are the seemingly endless layers or stratas of ore one below another. So there is no immediate prospect of the decline of Leadville, but, on the contrary, a continual increase in wealth and production.

CHAPTER XIX.

LEADVILLE MINES—THE CARBONATE BELT, ITS FORMATION AND CHARACTERISTICS— GOLD AND SILVER YIELD—RAPID INCREASE IN THE BULLION AND ORE PRODUCT—SMELTING AND SAMPLING WORKS—PROSPECTS AND POSSIBILITIES OF THE DISTRICT.

The Arkansas river flows in a southerly direction for some distance from its sources among the lofty Sierras. The valley that incloses it is bordered by the great Continental Divide on the west, whose peaks for a hundred miles average over 14,000 feet high, and the almost equally elevated Mosquito or Park range on the east. Both of these mountain systems unite near Mount Lincoln and the head of the easterly fork of the Arkansas. Below the bald and barren crest of the Mosquito range are what might be termed its foot hills, sloping westward to the Arkansas valley. Among these heavily timbered hills is the famous carbonate belt, and through it California, Stray Horse, Evans, and Iowa gulches lead westward down to the main stream. The Mosquito or Park range separates the Arkansas valley from that great natural basin of the "Rockies" called South Park. Leadville is on an inclined plain, sloping west and at the base of the carbonate hills, 10,025 or 10,200 feet above the sea.

The course of the carbonate zone or belt is north and south, and the general dip of the ore is eastward and from twelve to twenty-five degrees downward from the horizontal; but there are numerous faults and displacements, as with the overlying porphyritic trachyte and underlying limestone. Above the porphyry may be more or less "drift," and below is the limestone formation, quartzites, crystalline schists, and granite, tilting downward one below the other, but occasionally pushed out of place.

The direction of the ore deposits is often changed from the ordinary incline to the vertical, or to wave-like depressions and elevations corresponding to those of the limestone. The depressions contain most of the richer ore when it is in ordinary or thin layers. The underground workings are often like so many irregular steps and landings, making the construction of a regular incline finally necessary for large production and advantageous operations in the mines. The limestone forms the foot wall, on which the contact deposits have been made, and the porphyry the hanging wall. In places the porphyry is found under and beside the ore for short distances.

The veins or deposits so far opened have varied in thickness from the thinnest kind of a seam to several feet. There are claims that show ten feet of mineral, and a few have ore bodies twenty and thirty feet thick. The quantity of the valuable metals contained varies greatly, and, unlike most other districts, the largest deposits are as likely to be among the richest as any other way. Most of the ore is so soft as to require no blasting—the pick and shovel being sufficient to remove it.

It has been said that Leadville district defies all previously developed rules regarding mineral in place or in deposit. Mineral is found by sinking shafts, and not by the outcrop, as in mineral veins elsewhere. The objective point is the contact of the porphyry and limestone, for between those formations the mineral is almost universally encountered, if found at all. Below the porphyry is the iron, which is a sort of cap-rock to the ore, and is called the contact. Below this, if no ore is found, and otherwise beneath the ore, usually occurs the blue limestone, in undulations like a disturbed sea. If no ore is visible at such locations, the miner drifts on the contact to the right or left, or in any direction, with the hope of finding less barren localities beyond. Rich ore bodies have been found by drifting when none were manifest at the bottoms of shafts.

It will be seen that this prospecting for ore by "sinking" is attended with a great deal of uncertainty, and this uncertainty not only pertains to the ultimate results, but also to the depth necessary to go before anything definite can be ascertained. In some places the contact has been found at depths of thirty or forty feet, and in others it was more than two hundred feet below the surface.

It is generally conceded that four distinct stratifications, veins or mineral layers, have been developed in the Leadville carbonate district; that these stratifications extend in a northerly and southerly direction, and dip eastward into the mountains at an angle of from fifteen to twenty-five degrees below the horizontal.

The ore yields from a few ounces of silver per ton in some locali-

THE MEYER SAMPLING WORKS AND HARRISON SMELTER.

ties to fifty, one hundred, or two hundred in another. Bunches of one and two thousand dollar ore have been found, but they are not extensive. The proportion of lead is almost as variable, ranging all the way from a very few per cent. up to seventy. Ore rich in silver is more likely to be rich in lead than the reverse. Many claims have been opened that are too poor to work, and others contain bordering bodies of rich and poor ore. The average contents of the ores handled for many months by the ore buyers and shippers were from $100 to $170 in silver, and from 20 to 40 per cent. of lead. This was since the Fryer Hill mines began to produce so largely. Their output raised the average value per ton of the total yield of the district. But while these figures represent the ore shipments, they were far above the yield of ores treated in most of the smelters. In some of these five tons of ore usually resulted in one of lead bullion, carrying 250 ounces of silver, indicating that 20 per cent. of the ore was lead, and that it carried 50 ounces of silver per ton before smelting. Ore that contains 100 ounces of silver and 25 per cent. lead would have a silver valuation of about $113, and a lead valuation of about $17. This refers to the value of the ultimate bullion product, not to the selling or buying price of the ore. Much vein matter is left in the mines or on the dumps that is too poor to handle. This carries silver and lead in varying quantities from $50 down to $5 per ton. Some carbonate mines yield gold in small amounts.

There are carbonates of lead, with some galena, various oxides of iron and manganese, and small amounts of chloride of silver. There are what are called "hard carbonates" and "soft carbonates." Some of the latter have the appearance of moist sand, or the material that railroad grades are made of. Some are gray and others stained red or black with oxide of iron or manganese. The hard carbonates are of different colors, but generally have a variegated gray appearance. The oxides of iron are rarely as rich as the heavy lead carbonates. Leadville district is noted for qualities always desirable, but seldom found combined, such as rich mineral in enormous quantities, easily and cheaply mined, and capable of being reduced at a small expense. These are the causes of the pre-eminence of some of the leading mines over most others that the world can show.

So rapid has been the development and increase of production of the carbonate belt that no idea of the present and future yield can be obtained from that of the past. New strikes are constantly being made, and the steadily growing outputs of older mines are often rivaled by those of newer claims. The following shows the past yield of Lake county. Nearly all of this came from this same California district.

PRODUCT OF LAKE COUNTY 1860 TO 1879.

Gold, 14 years—		Gold, silver and lead—	
1860-1873, inclusive...	$6,400,000	1876	$85,200 00
1874, gold and silver..	145,000	1877	555,330 00
1875, gold and silver..	113,000	1878	3,152,925 44
Total.....................		$10,451,455 44	

The product of 1879 will probably exceed this total of nineteen years. The figures for the years prior to 1874 are estimated.

The yield of Lake county in the valuable metals has been $6,856,146 in gold, $3,074,984.44 in silver, and $520,324.73 in lead. These figures include a small production in Lake county, principally in the Granite district.

The product of 1877, principally obtained in the last six months of the year, was $414,930 in silver, $76,400 in lead, and $55,000 in gold. Over 3,700 tons of ore were shipped away or smelted at Leadville, and a larger quantity remained on the dumps of the mines. The product of that year came from the following sources:

	Tons.	
Silver lead ores shipped away, mainly to St. Louis..	3,300	$467,500
Silver ores smelted into bullion at Leadville.........	350	17,310
Silver ores smelted or shipped from Alpine district..	50	5,520
Gold dust from California Gulch..................		20,000
Gold dust from Cash Creek.......................		30,000
Gold from other sources.........................		5,000
Total.............................	3,700	$545,330

The product of 1878 was as follows:

Value in different metals—		Form of shipment—	
Silver	$2,591,054 71	Bullion	$686,422 39
Lead	443,924 73	Ore shipped........	2,366,503 05
Gold.............	117,946 00	Gold dust....	100,000 00
Total	$3,152,925 44	Total.........	$3,152,925 44

The tonnage of ore was 21,746, turning out 5,549½ tons of lead. The amounts of ore handled, and the values of bullion and ore shipped by the various smelters and sampling works, were as follows :

BULLION.

NAME OF WORKS.	Tons of Ore Treated	VALUE OF SILVER.	VALUE OF LEAD.	VALUE OF GOLD.	TOTAL VALUE OF BULLION.
Harrison Reduction Works	2,166	$185,984 09	$72,930 60	$12,946	$271,860 69
Grant Smelter.........	1,600	130,487 50	26,170 00	......	156,657 50
Berdell & Witherell.......	440	113,929 00	25,200 00	......	139,129 00
Malta Works..............	1,200	61,600 00	24,500 00	......	86,100 00
Adlaide..................	500	14,785 20	12,950 00	5,000	32,735 20
Total........	5,906	$506,785 79	$161,750 60	$17,946	$686,482 39

ORE SHIPMENTS.

NAME OF SAMPLING WORKS.	Tons of Ore.	VALUE OF SILVER CONTENTS.	VALUE OF LEAD.	TOTAL.
A. R. Meyer.........	8,781	$1,027,025 39	$135,534 00	$1,162,559 39
Eddy & James................	4,031	647,781 70	82,250 00	730,081 70
Berdell & Witherell............	2,778	384,461 83	64,400 13	448,861 96
Other shipments..............	240	25,000 00	....	25,000 00
Totals............ ...	15,840	$2,084,268 92	$282,174 13	$2,366,503 05

These figures do not include ore on hand at the close of the year. Meyer handled 10,454 tons in the year, Eddy & James had 800 tons in hand on the 31st of December, and the Harrison works one or two thousand tons.

The production of gold dust was $65,000 from California Gulch, and $35,000 from Cash Creek, the Arkansas, and other localities. Of the former the Oro Ditch & Fluming Company took out $31,000, Wells, on the Stevens & Leiter claim, about $12,000 ; and Thomas Starr and others $21,000. Of the county's gold product the Lake County Bank (now First National) shipped $59,750.

The Grant Smelter was erected by J. and J. B. Grant, and is situated in the lower portion of the city of Leadville. The first furnace was fired up October 1, 1878, and continued work without interruption. In three months the following excellent run had been made : 1,600 tons of ore treated, giving 370 tons of lead bullion, averaging 325 ounces of silver per ton ; value of product, $156,657.50 ; value of ore on hand over $100,000. The ore handled was generally as rich as the high grade shipping ores. On the first day of January a second furnace was fired up, and the month's product footed up $132,000. So great were the demands upon the place that two more furnaces were added, one after another, in the spring, since when the output has been correspondingly larger and greater than that of most other works. Unlike many similar establishments, no furnace troubles were met with, or interruptions of any kind. The plant consists of crushers, rolls, four blast furnaces (some thirty-three inches across the tuyerre, and others thirty-nine or forty), and Baker blowers. The four furnaces handle from eighty-five to ninety-five tons of ore daily, and turn out from twenty to thirty tons of lead or base bullion. J. B. Grant has superintended the works from the beginning. Hereafter they will handle the entire Little Pittsburg Company's ore product, which will necessitate the addition of four more furnaces.

The ores of this district are treated by smelting without roasting, nature having obviated the necessity of the latter. The method is like that long in use in Missouri, Utah, and other lead producing regions, and there is no particular difference in Leadville smelters.

The ores are smelted in what are called "water-jacket" furnaces. These are constructed of iron, generally circular in shape, about six feet in diameter, lined with fire clay internally, and rest on a cement and clay foundation.

Charges of ore and coke or charcoal are shoveled in from a floor above that where the bullion is discharged—the furnaces being up-rights and extending upward through the building, with outlets for fumes and smoke above. The proper mixture of ores and the requisite proportions of fuel are important points to success, and the more refractory the ores the greater is the care necessary to avoid disaster, such as chilling the furnace and other troubles.

Weighing the ores is one means of determining their character. Into these furnaces are fed the charges, consisting, as before stated, of the proper proportions of ore, coke, charcoal, and slag, the latter the refuse from previous charges. The molten mass separates itself according to its specific gravity—the lead with its silver contents settling in the lead well at one side and near the bottom of the furnace, from which the bullion is dipped into iron moulds, where it cools into bars of about 100 pounds weight. Each furnace turns out from 60 to 100 of these bars or from 6,000 to 10,000 pounds daily, each ton of bullion carrying about $400 worth of silver. The water-jacket furnace is prevented from succumbing to the terrible heat by the continual circulation of water between the inner and outer plates that compose it.

The directors and sub-directors of such works as these, as well as the ore mixers, hold very responsible places, for ignorance, inattention, or lack of skill, is likely to throw everything out of gear, chill the furnace, and stop operations for an indefinite period. The feeder is obliged to exercise equal care and judgment, and is subject to that great evil of smelting, getting "leaded" or poisoned by lead fumes. A melter and other employees are required below, where the lead bullion is taken from one outlet and the refuse or iron slag from another.

A furnace is run night and day from one month's end to another; to allow it to cool down would entail a heavy expense in drilling out the mass of iron and slag that would have to be removed—and in fact would stop business completely. The fuels used are charcoal and coke, the former bought from the adjoining forests at sixteen cents a bushel, and the latter shipped by rail and wagon train from Trinidad and El Moro, over 200 miles away, and costing from $28 to $35 a ton. The price was $68 for a time during the freight blockade of last spring, but will drop to reasonable figures on the advent of the railway.

Over sixty men are employed at present at the Grant Smelter, and fuel and labor each cost over $300 daily. Equal quantities of coke and coal are generally used, although the high price of freight last spring excluded coke for a time. To smelt each ton of ore something like forty bushels, or five hundred and sixty pounds of charcoal, worth $6.40, are required, along with about six hundred and sixty pounds of coke, worth $10 or more. In blockade times, coke was from $60 to $70 per ton. These works contain a fifty horse-power engine, two tubular boilers, and the usual crushing and drying apparatus.

THE GRANT SMELTER — LEADVILLE.

The business of the Grant Smelter, in the first quarter of 1879, with two furnaces at work, was as follows:

| | MONTHS. | | | TOTALS. |
	JANUARY.	FEBRUARY.	MARCH.	
Tons of ore treated.....	1,000	860	1,000	2,860
Tons of Lead bullion...........	291	280	288	859
Average Silver per ton of bullion, ounces.................	343	315	376	......
Ounces of Silver...............	99,813	88,200	108,288	296,301
Value of Lead and Silver.......	$130,164 30	$116,620 00	$139,276 80	$386,061 10

The Harrison Reduction Works were the first in operation at Leadville. They fired up for the first time about the first of October, 1877, with one furnace. Another was added in the summer of 1878; also a roasting furnace. In one year, 3,097 tons and 1,139 pounds of ore were treated, turning out 1,479 tons and 169 pounds of lead, 134,895 ounces of silver, and 497 ounces of gold, with a total value of $229,424.25. In the year 1878 the lead bullion product was 1,041 tons, that of silver was 164,168 ounces, and that of gold worth $12,946; total value of all metals, $266,460.69. The business for the first four weeks of January, 1879, was the reduction of 841 tons and 1,100 pounds of ore into 222 tons of lead; value of silver, $75,657.50; value of lead, $17,760; total, $93,417.50. The ores are generally of much higher grades than in 1877-8. Over 1,500 tons of ore were on hand ready for treatment. Beside charcoal, a little over 293 tons of coke were used in smelting 841 tons of ore.

A. R. Meyer put up the first sampling and ore buying works in the carbonate district as soon as the season of 1877 opened. The establishment of this mill to a great extent caused the town to be built on the present site. Since that year the works of A. R. Meyer & Co. have been enlarged until they are four times their original size. They handle from fifty to sixty tons of ore daily, and have done an immense business for the past fifteen months—more than any other one ore shipping concern in the State. Their business in 1877 was not far from $400,000 worth of ore bought and shipped. In 1878, 10,454

EDDY & JAMES' SAMPLING WORKS, LEADVILLE.

tons of ore were sampled and purchased, whose total value was nearly $1,400,000. A portion of this went to the Harrison smelters. The value of that shipped to St. Louis aggregated not far from $1,002,951.60 in silver, and $135,534 in lead. The purchases and shipments of the first quarter of 1879 were proportionately much larger, and allowing the low average of 100 ounces of silver to each ton of of ore, and 25 per cent. lead, the following total is attained:

	Tons of Ore.	Value of Silver.	Value of Lead.	Total Value.
January........	$1,433\frac{109}{2000}$	$157,630	$25,760	$183,390
February................	$2,160\frac{13}{2000}$	237,600	37,800	275,400
March...................	$2,108\frac{919}{2000}$	231,885	36,800	268,775
Totals	$5,701\frac{1041}{2000}$	$627,115	$100,450	$727,565

The works are supplied with steam engines, boilers, crushers, rolls, sampling machinery, and all necessary appliances. The average amount of ore on hand must be worth several hundred thousand dollars.

Eddy & James completed and started up their sampling works at Leadville on the third day of July, 1878. They did an extensive business from the beginning, and their fine mill was soon crowded to its utmost capacity. Up to December 31, a period of less than six months, they had done the enormous business of sampling and buying and shipping 4,031 tons and 298 pounds of ore, containing a total value of $730,031.70. Of this $647,781.70 was silver and $82,250 lead. They also had over 800 tons of ore on hand. Their shipments were mainly to Mather & Giest's smelter at Pueblo, the Omaha Smelting Works, and a smaller amount to Golden.

In January the business of these works was 1,600 tons of ore sampled, bought, and shipped, containing about $308,400; value of silver, $270,320; of lead, $38,080. The ore handled averaged about 155 ounces of silver per ton, and 34 per cent. of lead.

The capacity of the mill is fifty tons daily, and that is the usual amount of ore handled. The plant of machinery comprises a thirty-horse-power engine, tubular boiler, Dodge crusher, Cornish rolls, and drying floors, screens, and other necessary apparatus.

Gillespie, Ballou & Co. began to ship ores last spring.

Names of Works.	No. of Stacks.	Estimated Capacity in Tons of Ore.
Harrison.............................	2	25
Grant................................	4	75
Malta................................	2	35
Adlaide........	1	15
Berdell & Witherell La Plata Co........	3	75
Germania............................	.	100
Iowa................................	2	35
Garbutt.............................	2	35
Saint Joseph	2	35
Little Chief......	1	20
Total..		445

Total capacity of sampling, mills and smelters, 570 tons daily.

A little over five months of 1879 gave the following product— partly ore blockade times. Many discoveries have since been made.

Ores Shipped.	Tons Ore.	Yield.
A. R. Meyer & Co., January 1 to May 10....	8,244	$1,092,200
Eddy & James...........................	7,500	1,000,000
Total.............................	15,744	$2,092,290

BULLION.	TONS ORE.	TONS BULLION.	VALUE.
Grant Smelter to May 15...........	5,500	1,280	$694,202 80
Harrison Smelter to May 1........	2,549	560¼	500,000 00
Malta Smelter to May 15..........	5,510	625	254,090 00
Berdell & Witherell, five months, estimated...................	4,000	1,000	400,000 00
Total........	17,559	3,460¼	$1,848,292 80

Miners' wages are usually three dollars a day. Mechanics generally get more, and some laborers less. The contract price for sinking and timbering shafts, 4 feet by 7, has usually ranged from five to six dollars per foot of depth. Where water is plentiful the cost is greater. The character of the ground also makes some difference.

CHAPTER XX.

LEADVILLE MINES THE IRON, CARBONATE, AND PENDERY GROUPS—
VAST EXTENT OF MINERAL BEDS—THE DISCOVERY OF THE PEN-
DERY—THE LEADVILLE, CRESCENT, MORNING STAR, SHAMROCK,
WASHBURN, AND OTHER MINES—THE IRON BELT AND THE IRON
MINE—ITS IMMENSE RESOURCES AND LARGE PRODUCTION—THE
ALPS AND LONG AND DERRY ZONE AND MINES—ON THE EDGE
OF TIMBER LINE—TWO MILES ABOVE THE SEA.

As a beginning must be made somewhere in the description of the
mines of the carbonate belt, it may be as well to start on those
nearest Leadville. As it happens, the mines nearest town are the
ones in which the latest important discoveries were made. The developments in the Pendery claim are very important, since they show
the existence of another ore strata or vein at a lower and more
westerly location than was known before, making the fourth belt or
zone so far opened. The shaft which revealed this ore body was
sunk to a depth of one hundred and ninety feet under very doubtful
and discouraging circumstances, and few believed it would result in
anything but loss to the owners. The size and value of the vein are
rewards sufficient for the nerve and energy displayed in finding it.
Further evidence is thus furnished of the vast extent of the partially
developed Leadville mining region. Ore is sold in large quantities,
worth from $130 to $400 a ton. There is reason to believe this will
continue one of the important producers of the camp. The Washburn is some 300 feet north of the Pendery mine, and between
that and the Crescent, and appears to carry about the same value,
characteristics, and size. This discovery, like its neighbor, was
developed by sinking a prospecting shaft for a long distance through
the wash and porphyritic formation. Ore was found just after the
strike in the Pendery. These developments have caused great
activity all along the lower slope of the hill facing Leadville, and
near the Harrison Reduction Works, and shafts are being sunk in
all directions. The Washburn shaft is 235 feet deep—the last 12

feet sunk partly through decomposed porphyry and partly in mineral and iron. The quantity of ore increases as drifting progresses. Specimen assays go over 1,000 ounces, and the ore sold is above the general average. The Pendery produces ore containing from 80 to 500 ounces of silver and only 6 per cent. of lead.

The Shamrock adjoins the celebrated Carbonate mine on the southeast. Its United States government patent carries a title to a plot of ground 1,500 by 300 feet. On the same belt, and but a short distance away, are the Yankee Doodle, Crescent, and Morning Star, all of which have been very productive. Beneath is the Pendery strata, which depth may reach.

IN THE INCLINE.

The Shamrock was formerly owned by Thomas Wells, an old placer miner of California Gulch. He sold one-half of it to the Leadville Company, and subsequently the Shamrock Company organized and purchased the mine, but the Leadville still owns one-half of the capital stock. Wells had sunk a shaft 100 feet deep, and took out some ore that sold as high as $750 a ton. Recently a joint incline or shaft has been driven on the line of the Carbonate and Shamrock claims, and, at latest advices, was passing along a vein two and a half feet thick, from which ore has been sold which brought $238 a ton. A steam-engine and hoisting apparatus have just been set in operation. This discovery not only shows that the Shamrock will make a great mine but also increases the value of the Leadville property, as it indicates that the ore-body continues over 500 feet from the former claim to the main Leadville workings, through previously unexplored ground. Recent explorations north and south show this same zone of ore to be much more extensive than was at first believed. The last advices say $600 worth of ore was taken out in a single day.

The Shamrock Mining Company was incorporated May 7, 1879, under the laws of New York, with headquarters at 57 Broadway.

The capital stock embraces 200,000 shares at ten dollars each, or on a basis of a capitalization of $2,000,000. The trustees are John P. Jones, J. B. Chaffee, S. B. Elkins, Robert Sewell, E. B. Dorsey, A. W. Gill, and Vanderbilt Allen, with J. S. Lockwood, secretary.

What is now known as the Leadville mine was discovered and located as the Carbonate claim or lode on the 25th day of June, 1877. The first ore was sold in August of that year. The deposit entered by the shaft and levels proved to be wonderfully rich—much more so on the entire ore-body than in other claims previously opened. The owners were Nelson Hallock and Captain A. Cooper, who had been operating a saw-mill in the district. Their mine proved vastly more remunerative than their former business, for up to April, 1878, a period of eight months, they had sold 363 tons of ore at an average price of $131 per ton, or $47,644 altogether. Only seven men had been employed, and it cost them but $7,200 to get this ore out and to market, leaving a profit of $40,444. The actual assay value of this ore was about $210 a ton or $71,466 altogether. From April to July, 1878, 200 tons of ore were sold for $36,704.63, with a total expense of $3,212.55, leaving the still more remarkable profit of $33,492.08. The average price paid per ton was $182.61. The total receipts of the mine for the first eleven months worked were $81,136.08, and the profits $70,723.53—the largest proportionate profit for so long a period that had ever been reported in this country up to that time. These returns do not include a large amount of low grade ore that was not shipped, but which would pay a profit. The actual yield of the mine had been $120,405.

The average yield for the first 310 feet of workings was $151 per foot of advance, and for the next 218 feet $218 per foot of advance. Among the sales of ore three tons assayed 662 ounces of silver, and sold for $1,951; another lot sold at the rate of $462.60, and another $361.60. The first-class ores averaged from 275 to over 600 ounces of silver and from 35 to 55 per cent. of lead, and what were sold in the second and third classes carried from 100 to 250 ounces of silver, and from 8 to 25 per cent. lead. These figures were taken from the books of Hallock & Cooper. Up to that time the mine had been worked without system, the ore-body having been followed wherever it dipped, dropped, or inclined.

In order to facilitate operations and permit of extensive work, a new incline was started from the surface. This was of large size, of regular course, and contains two tracks. The still newer Carbonate-Shamrock incline 500 feet west shows the same ore-body.

In January, 1879, the mine was sold to an association of New York and Colorado men, who organized the Leadville Mining Company, and the property has since been known as the Leadville mine. The sales of ore up to that time footed up $150,000.

The mine has yielded over $300,000 worth of silver and lead to date, the receipts for May being $36,000. Dividends aggregating $20,000 are paid every month or semi-monthly. The stock is capitalized at $2,000,000, with a par value of $10 to a share. A. W. Gill is president of the company, Robert Sewall, vice-president, and John S. Lockwood, secretary.

The vein is usually from one to five feet thick—occasionally more or less—and may average two feet. There are said to be from seven to nine feet in a ton of ore. The average yield has been much above $100 per ton and $100 per yard, or $940 per fathom, with a cost of $15 per yard, or $150 per fathom, for breaking and hoisting ore, timbering, track-laying, ore-sorting, and all other outlays. It costs $16 per foot of advance on the main incline, and $60 a fathom to drift. The incline has penetrated the hill for hundreds of feet, with many levels leading therefrom north and south. The ore and ground is cut into blocks for stoping by means of drifts. As it was impossible to drive levels and inclines of uniform grade and keep on the ore-body, these are driven at a lower average elevation, and the ore is broken above and dropped down into the cars in the levels.

The Little Alice, Prospect, Peora, Joe Wilson, and D. H. Moffat are situated on Carbonate Hill, in the immediate vicinity of the Carbonate, Shamrock, and Little Giant mines. The first two adjoin the Shamrock, and the same contact vein has been found in them. This is about two feet in thickness and averages about 70 ounces of silver to the ton. There is a shaft 103 feet deep on the Peora, and shafts have reached a depth of 40 feet on the D. H. Moffat and Joe Wilson. These claims were lately consolidated in one management, are controlled by one of the strongest companies yet organized, and are considered among the most promising of the Carbonate Hill group. So far but little work has been done on them, but what has been done gives assurance of their great value and of their being

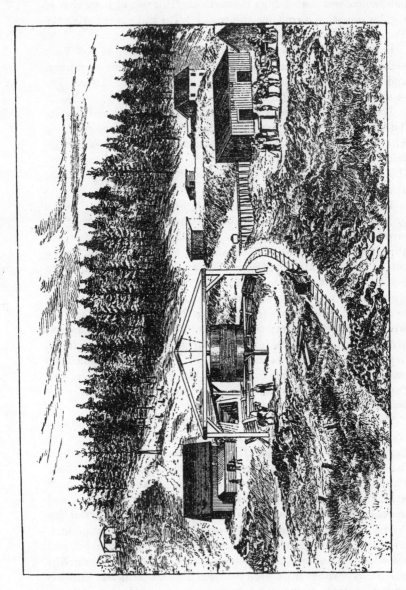

THE LEADVILLE MINE.

underlaid with the continuation of the adjoining Carbonate and
Shamrock bonanza. The new owners are pushing the work of
development as fast as possible. When extensively opened there is
every probability that this property will be one of the great bullion
producers of the district.

In this vicinity are the Weldon, Rough and Ready, Bonus, and
Coddigan. The Little Giant is above the Carbonate mine. In
sinking 190 feet on the Rough and Ready claim several layers of low
grade mineral were penetrated. The Ætna and Gem of the
Mountains are located on this same part of the hill.

The Crescent mine is next east of the Yankee Doodle and on this
hill ranks next to the Carbonate in past production. It was located
in 1877, and some time after became the property of the Meyer M.
and E. Co. It was yielding very rich ore during the year 1878,
when the sales netted $40,000. Considerable time was consumed in
sinking a new shaft and in driving a large double track incline and
other developments. This incline is over 400 feet long with eight
diverging levels, comprising 4,000 linear feet of workings, all
of which greatly facilitate operations. A. R. Meyer is general
manager. The working force of the Crescent has ranged from 25 to
50 men. It is said that $100,000 has been taken out this year. The
ore is known to extend over a broad area, is generally from one to
six feet thick, and returns an average of 125 ounces of silver per ton
and from 50 to 60 per cent. of lead.

The Catalpa and Evening Star mines are north of the Crescent.

The Consolidated Morning Star and Waterloo mines are still further north of the Leadville mine, and have recently become famous
by reason of the size and value of the mineral body developed. The
surface area of these claims is 1,500 feet east and west by 502 north
and south. Near the western border of the claims the apex or top
of the vein material is but five or six feet from the surface. Further up the hill it took seventy feet of sinking to find it and a
level on the vein reaches a point over 160 feet below the surface. The
new and main shaft is 250 feet down to the drift and the sump makes
it ten feet deeper. It is one of the best in the country, while the entire
mine, under the direction of J. W. Watson, has been opened in the
most systematic manner. The shaft is four feet by eight inside the
timbers, with platforms of two-inch plank ten feet one above another
and ladders between. The last two items cost at the rate of $2 per

foot of depth, and sinking and drifting $10 per foot; a total of
$4,000 for the entire work.   The bottom of the shaft is 650 feet lower
than the surface of the upper end of the claim, and levels and cross
levels extend easterly to and on the dip of the vein. Streaks of ore
had been found in the older workings and some very rich chlorides
in small quantities.

The ore-body now worked was entered in a depression in the main
incline east of the shaft. At first there was ore carrying from 10 to
100 ounces of silver and 51 per cent. lead, with patches of galena
carrying 70 per cent. of lead.   There was the usual porphyry above
the limestone, with some of the latter converted into iron oxide by
past action of water, and perhaps other causes—the black iron being
poor in silver. As the ore deposit was penetrated to the eastward it
increased greatly in value, and several feet of carbonates, mainly of fair
grade, were reported as continuing without interruption. This is the
condition of the mine at last accounts. Hundreds of tons of rich
ore are sold monthly. Steam hoisting machinery was substituted
for horse power in the spring, which can hoist forty tons of ore daily.
The head of the drift shows saleable sand and hard carbonates nine
feet thick. Among the owners is ex-Governor John L. Routt. North
of these claims are the Henriette and other locations.

The hill next east of Carbonate Hill, and extending from California Gulch northward to near the head of Stray Horse Gulch, contains what is often termed the famous Iron mine zone or belt. On
the slope rising from the first-named gulch, nearly two miles above
Leadville, and a short distance from Oro, are the Lime, Bull's Eye,
Smuggler, and other claims. Not far from the centre, and on the
western slope of the hill, is the great Iron mine, and east of it such
properties as the Argentine and Adlaide.

The Iron mine has been considered by miners and experts as the
typical carbonate deposit, perhaps the most regular in form and
continuous in extent of any in the district. There are larger bodies
of ore elsewhere, but none more uniform. It was the first to be
systematically opened and developed, and although operations have
been seriously interrupted by contests with adjoining claimants,
its workings are perhaps more extensive than those of any other
mine.   The amount of mineral explored and in reserve is very great,
and is partly of very high average grade. More than a year ago
experts estimated the amount of ore in sight at a valuation of over

half a million, and the quantity must have been doubled by subsequent explorations. Some estimates are much higher.

The main entrance and outlet to the mine is a great "incline," which has been driven easterly down into the hill, and as near as possible along the course of the ore-body for a distance of 475 feet. This inclined shaft descends one foot to every three or four feet of advance, is substantially timbered, and is underlaid with a double iron track. Up this track cars convey the ore product from the various levels to daylight and the ore buildings and platforms.

Stations are cut at intervals of one hundred feet, from which levels lead north and south. These levels are hundreds of feet in length, and altogether aggregate several thousands of feet. Some of them follow the dip, depressions, and windings of the deposits pretty closely, and all show ore of either high or low grade. One drift passes a hundred feet through carbonates of a gray complexion and largely composed of three hundred ounce mineral. Another follows the pitch of the contact waves for over four hundred feet, crossing other openings diagonally, and others are driven for shorter distances at right angles one with another in opening up ground and great blocks of ore.

Above rests the chalky porphyry, jointed in crystalline forms, with no fragments of lime intermixed, as in many other claims, and below is the solid unbroken limestone foot-wall, with a uniform general dip eastward in a series of undulations, slopes, and steps. In one place there is a solid mass of galena and there are streaks and patches of chlorides and of galena scattered in nearly all parts of the mine. The deeply tinged iron is often of low grade, but there are hard carbonates in immense quantities, as well as those of softer character.

The average width of the ore is not far from three or four feet, but varies from six inches to ten feet. The yield varies greatly. Large quantities of ore have been sold at from $100 to $300 per ton, but there is much poorer material that is not marketed. The average of high and low grades may be not far from 60 ounces of silver and of high grades alone 130 ounces.

The mine began to produce in August, 1877, and up to the succeeding June $70,000 had been cleared. The ore sold is said to have smelted $150,000 worth of silver and lead. Since then the production has not been pushed and has been greatly retarded by contests with another mine. The yield in 1878 is believed to have exceeded $200,000, and quite an amount of ore was raised from the locality penetrated by the Williams shaft from the hillside above. It is said that 800 tons of ore have been sold from the mine that averaged 221 ounces of silver and 54 per cent. lead. The working force has generally ranged from 60 to 100 men.

The owners of the Iron mine, W. H. Stevens and L. Z. Leiter, have had a long and protracted contest with the owners of the Law claim on the hillside just above them. The Iron location embraces a surface location 1,500 feet along the outcrop or apex of the vein or ledge, by 300 feet wide, up and down the hill.

Last fall, a man named Williams went up the hill beyond the Iron side lines and sunk a shaft to strike the contact—which was done at a depth of 200 feet below the surface, and 75 feet west of the end of the Iron incline. He then barricaded the latter at that point, and by force of arms held the interior workings against the Stevens and Leiter miners. During the winter, it is said, a force of old Georgetown miners were engaged to hire to the Williams party as guards, and they turned the barricaded workings back into possession of Stevens. Before and afterwards, the mine was heavily guarded, and internally somewhat resembled a magazine.

Meantime the case was up before the courts, the Iron owners claiming they could follow their ore vein wherever it led to, and the other side asserting that there was no vein in the true sense of that term, but only a deposit, which could not be followed beyond side lines. The second trial of this case occurred very recently, and was decided in favor of Stevens and Leiter of the Iron mine. This will probably stop all trouble, and will enable the property to be worked so as to insure an enormous product.

The Smuggler is in one of the best localities on Iron Hill, bearing near the Iron mine. George T. Clark developed a very large body of ore in it, some of which has milled $50 per ton in gold, $10 to $50 in silver, and 70 per cent. in lead.

The Belle of Colorado is the next claim east of the Iron. It is owned by Joseph Pierce and H. A. W. Tabor. Ore was found at a depth of 190 feet, and the claim is favorably located for a large production and valuation.

The Double Decker is famous for the production of carbonates carrying a great deal of gold as well as silver and lead. An idea of the proportions of the two metals may be had from the fact that several tons of ore averaged $200 in silver and $155 in gold. Another lot went still higher, and from one to two hundred dollars per ton is not an unusual yield. The Agazziz, Dunderberg, and Loveland are all in this vicinity.

The Breese Iron mine attracted a great deal of attention a few months ago. Its ore had been purchased by the smelters mainly for the iron it contained—being valuable for fluxing with other ores in smelting. At last it was found that much of this ore carried considerable silver and some gold. After that $22 a ton was paid for it at the mine, instead of $6. One hundred tons can be mined daily, at a cost of fifty cents a ton, and there are from 20 to 30 feet of it on four claims.

The Cleora mine of W. J. McDermith & Co. is near the Iron mine and the Lauwalla, both of which show immense quantities of ore. The Cleora is 250 feet deep.

The Highland Chief and Highland Mary have been consolidated. Here is another bonanza. In one shaft the ore is said to be 14 feet thick, and at another 21 feet thick, carrying from 50 to 200 ounces in silver, from 35 per cent. to 60 per cent. in lead, and containing but very little waste rock mixed in it. The present product is 20 to 40 tons daily. During the past few months these claims have shown themselves to be among the most valuable in the district.

The Argentine mine comprises five claims, known as the Camp Bird, Charleston, Keystone, Pine, and Young America. The Camp Bird claim was located by three brothers, Patrick, Charles, and John Gallagher. The surface ground had gradually washed away and left the carbonates outcropping. The Gallagher brothers did not have a very profitable time at first. One and then all of them were so discouraged with trying to get a living out of their lode that they were about to abandon it altogether when a final improvement in the ore was noticeable. In 1877, it began to pay handsomely, especially after the completion of the Harrison smelter. The brothers squandered their earnings, but finally the mine made money faster than they could spend it. Then they sold to members of the Saint Louis Smelting and Refining Company for $225,000, and one went to Paris, and the others to different parts of America. All seemed bent on getting rid of their money as fast as possible. The mine had yielded nearly $150,000 up to that time, and some

$80,000 had been paid for the ore. The workings displayed no skill or system, but had been "gophered" in any way to strip the mine of ore in the easiest possible manner.

It took Messrs. Loker and Kleinfelter several months to open the mine in a workmanlike manner, but it was finally done. The yield has generally ranged from five to twenty tons of ore daily, selling for from $40 to $80 a ton. Here the system of mining is by a tunnel connecting the mines, which are on a slope above its mouth. The tunnel runs into the hill, horizontally, 800 feet, and will be continued to 2,000 feet. Much of the vein lies above the tunnel, and the ore is brought from the levels in the vein to shafts at various distances along the tunnel, and dumped into chutes that conduct it into cars on a tramway in the tunnel. About 3,000 feet of drifts have been opened in the Pine, Camp Bird, and Charleston. The mines are not worked to their full capacity, as the owners, like other mining companies, are waiting for railroad facilities, which will greatly reduce freight charges, not only on ores shipped, but on all the materials used in smelting here. The high-grade ores from the Argentine are sent to the works in St. Louis, and the low grades are smelted in Leadville. The usual position of the silver-bearing ore is under a layer of porphyry rock and above a layer of limestone, but in the Argentine some silver-bearing iron has been found under the limestone, yielding fifty ounces of the precious metal to the ton.

The Adlaide mine adjoins the Argentine. It was purchased over a year ago by eastern parties, and is owned by the Argentine Company. In this organization are J. R. Magruder, the general manager, ex-Governor Henry D. Cooke, of Washington, and others. Smelting works were erected at the mines. The ore body is large, but of low grade. The average in 1878 was from 9 to 12 ounces in silver per ton of ore, and from 60 to 70 per cent. of lead with some gold.

The Small Hopes Mining Company was organized in the spring of 1878 by Denver men, among them J. F. Sanders, George T. Clark, William Parker, C. Bell, and others. The property includes fine contiguous claims in Stray Horse Gulch, called the Robert Emmet, Result, Ranchero, Amanda H. and Forest. A large amount of ore of various grades has been produced.

There is a belt of gold-bearing lodes near Oro and the head of California Gulch, of which the Printer Boy has been the most famous and productive. Great activity is displayed in that section at present, and many veins are worked that had been idle for years. These veins are located in quartzite, and are nearly vertical.

The Printer Boy was discovered in 1868 by Charles Mullen, who eight years after found the Smuggler lode in Boulder county. The Printer Boy began to produce largely in 1869, and soon proved to be wonderfully rich. A Philadelphia company purchased it and erected a twenty-five stamp quartz mill in the gulch at Oro. About $60,000 were taken out in the first year of actual work. There was an immense body of soft quartz that gave a yield of several hundred thousand dollars in the course of a few years, although the property was idle portions of the time. The mine is again worked.

The Tiger is one of the main lodes of this section. It is systematically worked by D. Bauman & Co., who are said to derive a good profit therefrom. Among other mines are the Mike, Yellow Jacket, Oro La Plata, Miner's Hope, Maria and Lower Printer Boy.

The Pilot was famous and productive years ago, when it ranked next to the Printer Boy. It is now worked by Joseph Watson, who is opening it with a tunnel. The vein is large and small at various points, with occasional rich pockets.

The Long and Derry mine is on the elevated divide between Iowa and Empire gulches, south of the head of California Gulch, and four miles southeast of Leadville. Its elevation is about 11,000 feet above sea-level, or near timber line. It comprises the Porphyry, J. D. Dana, Faint Hope, and three other claims—forty-five acres of surface ground altogether.

Jacob Long and his brother came to California Gulch in 1860, and have been pretty much all over Colorado. For sixteen long years they prospected and mined with unvarying ill-fortune. Of the typical prospecting class, they were often ragged and generally without money, but ever hopeful and persevering. In September, in company with a Mr. Derry, they made the discovery of the above named locations, which are known as the Long and Derry mine. It was a prize worth toiling years to secure ; but they could have had it years before if they had known anything about carbonates. Little work was done until 1877, and shipments could not be made regularly at all seasons until a road to Leadville was constructed early in 1878. This cost from six to eight thousand dollars, all obtained from the early profits of the mine.

The number of men employed has varied, but has averaged about

eleven. Drifts and shafts to the extent of nearly 2,000 feet have
been run in various directions and places. The amount of mineral
in gross taken from the mine up to June, 1878, was 738 tons and 116
pounds, yielding 209 tons and 412 pounds of lead, and a total value
of silver and lead of $98,840. From these figures it will be seen
that the yield of silver per ton has been very nearly $134. There
has been no system or skill displayed in mining, and much dead
work has been done. These figures of the product of ore and the
value of it are taken from the books of the company, and are compiled from the mill runs made at the several mills where mineral has
been sold.

On the south, and immediately adjoining the Long and Derry mine,
the "Himmala" mine has struck a good body of paying mineral of
unusual richness. On the north a very small amount of work has
developed most favorable indications.

There is a large amount of low grade ore on the dump, and
plentiful reserves in and near some of the shafts and drifts. The
vein contains galena, chlorides and other varieties, and there have
been seams of ore assaying from five hundred to two thousand dollars
per ton. This is one of the leading mines and was one of the early
prominent ones.

On this same hill is the Doris lode, in which a rich ore-body was
found in April. The mineral deposit seems to be regular and of a
generally uniform character, and mill runs show a yield of from one
hundred to four hundred dollars per ton. The ore is much like
that of the neighboring Long and Derry.

The De Merry mine is located on the south slope of the divide
between California and Iowa gulches. The ore is found in bluish
lime below the contact, and is rich in lead; but generally runs low
in silver.

The Ready Cash is above the Long and Derry mine, and is owned
by Tucker and Houks. Ore of various grades is sold. The ore
has a width of eighteen inches and less—some of it very rich—and
carries chlorides and sulphides of silver and native gold.

South Evans, six miles east of Leadville, and near the snowy
range, is a very prosperous mining camp. Many good mines have
been developed there within eight months. Among them, the Alps
is very prominent. The Ashtabula shows five feet of seventy-five
ounce ore at a depth of sixty-one feet. In the Little Ella the car-

bonates are thirteen feet thick, and a great deal of ore containing over $135 a ton is mined. Among other mines near by are the Little Rische, Forest City, Lulu, Nevada, Adriatic, Ajax, Little Edenburg, North American, Fairview, and Dauntless. The Idaho and Highland Mary mines are very valuable and productive. The Black Prince is one of the best claims, and the Red Warrior has seven feet of ore at a depth of thirty feet below the surface.

The Alps is counted as the representative mine of the upper stratification—the most easterly of the four mineral zones or belts of the carbonate region. It is located near the south fork of South Evans Gulch, between Bross and Bald mountains, and above timber line, almost on the slope of the Mosquito range. The Long and Derry mine, further south and just below timber line, is probably on the same belt. The Alps ledge, embracing claims one, two, three, and four, is of mammoth size. The outcropping is from 20 to 22 feet thick. The ore contains from 15 to 450 ounces of silver to the ton with from 60 to 70 per cent. of lead. The quantity of gray carbonates is very great. Smith and Miller and George K. Sabin are owners. A large force of men are at work.

The Dyer mine is close into the Park range and several miles east of Leadville. It has been worked more or less for two years. In the winter time it can only be approached on snow shoes. It is not a carbonate mine, but appears to be a silver bearing deposit, like those of Mount Bross and Lincoln in the same range. It has yielded much ore, worth from $100 to $1,000.

Adlaide City is beautifully located among the hills and in a park near the Adlaide mine and some two miles east of Leadville. It contains a population of over one thousand. There is almost one continuous town, extending along Stray Horse Gulch, between Leadville proper and Adlaide.

The Highland Chief is claimed to possess the grandest bonanza yet developed. This has been recently opened as far as this great body of carbonates is concerned and the indications are good for millions. Below the carbonates of varying values in gold and silver is another layer of ore, carrying gold. Wire and free gold is said to be found there; and there appears to be no end to the wealth of this Highland Chief. The location is several miles east of Leadville, in the timber above Adlaide and Park cities.

FRYER HILL.

CHAPTER XXI.

LEADVILLE MINES—THE CARBONATE BONANZAS OF FRYER HILL—THE
GREAT TREASURE VAULT OF THE TIMES, AND HOW IT WAS DEVEL-
OPED—THE LITTLE PITTSBURG AND NEW DISCOVERY—MILLIONS
OF SILVER—THE LITTLE CHIEF, CARBONIFEROUS, DUNCAN, VUL-
TURE, AMIE, AND OTHER MINES—THE STRIKE IN THE ROBERT
E. LEE—THE RICHEST SPOT YET DEVELOPED.

While the Leadville mining camp was excited over the Iron, Camp
Bird, and Carbonate mines, George H. Fryer sunk a shaft on a hill
north of Stray Horse Gulch. He found low grade carbonates on
the 4th day of April, 1878, and called his claim the New Discovery.
This was the beginning of what has since become the best part of the
best paying mine in America at the present time.

A month later, August Rische and George T. Hook began to sink
a shaft on the same hill. They had no money to obtain supplies
or tools for a prospecting campaign, and H. A. W. Tabor, one of
Leadville's merchants, furnished them what they needed for a one-
third interest in whatever they might discover. It cost about
seventeen dollars to outfit the party.

It happened that the ore strata was unusually near the surface at
that point, and so it did not take long to reach it. The first wagon-
load of ore proved to be quite valuable, and netted the owners two
or three hundred dollars. As Rische and Hook continued their
drift from the shaft, the ore body grew larger, until it was several
feet thick, and the discoverers were then sure they had "struck a
fortune." After each sale of ore a few days' recreation would be in-
dulged in, but a force of men were engaged in June, and work was
then pushed more rapidly. The location was called the Little
Pittsburg, after Hook's old home in Pennsylvania, and this was the
starting of the prefix "Little," since so fashionable in carbonate
mining nomenclature. At this time the Union claim, further east,
had been located and a deep shaft sunk, and as soon as the news of

the Little Pittsburg ore sales spread abroad, there was a general rush to this previously almost unknown part of the district.

In the latter half of July, 1878, the Little Pittsburg and New Discovery were each yielding seventy-five tons of ore per week. That from the former milled from ninety to over two hundred ounces of silver per ton, but Fryer ore did not average much if any over fifty ounces per ton. It was quite profitable at that figure however. The locality was called Fryer Hill in honor of the first discoverer, and by that name will ever be famous as the richest silver depository the world could show in the year 1879, and probably for many years later. During the summer men were sinking shafts on all parts of the hill, and ore was successively found in the Little Chief, Winnemuck Carboniferous, and Chrysolite claims.

The Little Pittsburg was paying thousands of dollars per week in August, and in September was the leading producer of the district. In the latter month Hook accepted the offer of his partners, Tabor and Rische, and received $98,000 down in cash for his one-third interest in the mine. The buyers cleared the purchase money in three weeks thereafter.

A shaft was started on a claim, called the Winnemuck, before Rische and Hook came on the hill. They found ore at a depth of only twenty-six feet, and in locating the Little Pittsburg took in the then barren Winnemuck shaft. Before that time Dr. C. F. Bissell, A. H. Foss, George W. Trimble and A. V. Hunter had purchased most of the Winnemuck, and subsequently owned all of it. They did not "strike mineral" until the shaft was 150 feet deep, and then they had from ten to thirty feet of it. Tabor and Rische claimed it, and so matters stood near the end of September, when Bissell and partners went over to the other side of the Little Pittsburg and bought out Borden's half interest in the New Discovery for $40,000. They had cleared that and much more in a few weeks' work in the Winnemuck. This purchase was a serious flank movement, as the older title of the New Discovery might eventually take in the Little Pittsburg, if the ore strata was decided to be a regular vein. Before the Winnemuck men could secure Fryer's interest, Senator Jerome B. Chaffee bought it for $50,000. The New Discovery was not then thought to be worth $90,000 so much for its contents as for its position and older title.

Before Chaffee left the camp Tabor and Rische, fearing that the

THE LITTLE PITTSBURG CONS. MINES.

older title of the New Discovery might imperil their claim to the
Little Pittsburg, took it off of his hands at $125,000. The mines
kept on improving faster than ever, and Chaffee and Moffat, becoming confident and enthusiastic over the mines and the district,
bought Rische's entire interest for $262,500, and thus became half
owners with Tabor in these claims and the Dives.

On the 18th day of November these claim owners organized
the Little Pittsburg Consolidated Mining Company. This included
the New Discovery, Little Pittsburg, Dives, and Winnemuck, the
owners of the latter coming in on a basis of twenty-seven hun-
dredths of the entire property and profits. Joseph C. Wilson was
then placed in charge of the consolidated mines as general manager
and superintendent, and work was inaugurated on a much larger
and more systematic scale than previously. Up to this time the
receipts for ore sales on the Little Pittsburg aggregated the handsome total of $375,000, and the actual yield much more—all in a
few short months, and before the mine was fairly opened. The
New Discovery receipts were less than $100,000. The Winnemuck's
ore sales netted $153,000, with a clear profit to the owners of
$112,000, within forty-nine days from the first ore shipment.

Several shafts were then sunk on the New Discovery and Little
Pittsburg, shaft-houses and hoisting whims were put up, and a huge
mine building erected on the last-named claim. It took time to get
the property in satisfactory working condition; after that the product was heavier than had ever been known in mines east of Nevada.

This was largely due to the enormous bonanza penetrated by the
new shafts and levels of the New Discovery. The claim that had
previously been somewhat in the background, now came to the front
and took the lead. The new underground workings penetrated an
ore-body of vast extent. This, including the high grade carbonates
and low grade iron ore, had a thickness at nearly all points explored
by levels of from six to twenty-five feet. Within the past few
months, this wonderful bonanza shows a width in places of thirty
feet. The uneven limestone foot wall has not been reached in much
of the ground and there the ore extends still deeper. In a long
level or cross cut there has been opened this summer a body of gray
carbonates that bring $100 per ton, of an average thickness of 15 feet.
The Little Pittsburg has shown from 7 to 15 feet of ore and more in
nearly all parts of the explored ground. There was much the same

DOWN IN THE NEW DISCOVERY BONANZA—UNDERGROUND WORKINGS.

showing in the adjoining Winnemuck. In these claims some stoping was done by the former management and owners, but almost insignificant as compared with unexplored ground. With such resources to draw upon, it did not take long to clear the Rische purchase.

The company developments long ago proved that this was not a limited bunch of ore, but an enormous bonanza with millions in it. The same great deposit was found to extend into the Little Chief, Carboniferous, Chrysolite, and Vulture claims, and more recently far to the eastward in the Duncan, R. E. Lee, and others. What is remarkable is that the New Discovery production and much of that of other claims has come almost entirely from development work, driving levels, etc. Stoping would greatly enlarge the output.

When the great ore bodies were being opened last fall and winter, it became evident that horse power was too "slow" for even these short shafts of from forty to eighty feet. Accordingly, four steam engines were procured and set at work in the spring. Levels were driven forward so as to leave great blocks of mineral standing.

The enormous size of the ore deposits called for a different style of timbering from that in general use, and the Comstock square set system was adopted for supporting the walls and roofs of the underground excavations. These sets consist of upright hewn logs or of sawed timbers from a foot and a half to two feet thick, and from seven to eight feet high, fastened securely by similar but shorter cross timbers above and below, as shown in engravings. In the thicker portions of these great ore deposits, three or four sets of these timbers are required one above the other.

The company books show the cost to obtain the first $539,269 of receipts, beside the low grade ore, was $93,665.25 for mining, hauling, timbering, and assaying, and $14,693.98 for buildings, engines, machinery, horses, tools, and permanent improvements. It is evident that since the advance in market prices paid for ore that ten per cent. of the receipts, or nine dollars a ton, will pay all mining, timbering, and hauling expenses.

The tabulated statements compiled from books of the old owners and of the company succeeding them, to April 18, 1879, show the tonnage, receipts, and assay value of ore sold, but not of all produced. There were over 873 tons of ore unsettled for at the smelters, and about 15,000 tons of low grade ore on the mine dumps that will sell for ten or twenty dollars a ton. This brings the actual output to July to $3,500,000. The figures for time subsequent to April, 1878, are partly based on previous operations.

The map of the little Pittsburg properties shows the amount of ground excavated in the spring. Subsequent work has enlarged these excavations probably one-third. In April, when nearly two million dollars' worth of silver and lead had been obtained from ore that brought the owners over $1,000,000, only two and one tenth per cent. of the entire area of over twenty acres had been worked out, or exhausted of pay. While it is not expected that all of this property is underlaid with ore, there are no evidences of the bonanza giving out near the present producing shafts. The production of the mines appears as follows:

FROM DISCOVERY TO NOVEMBER 18, 1878.	ESTIMATED TONNAGE.	RECEIPTS TO OWNERS FOR ORE SOLD.	SMELTERS' YIELD OF ORE SOLD, ESTIMATED.
Little Pittsburg......................	4,000	$375,000 00	$600,000 00
New Discovery.......................	1,000	60,000 00	100,000 00
Winnemuck..........................	2,000	153,000 00	200,000 00
Total.....................	7,000	$588,000 00	$900,000 00

FROM NOVEMBER 18, 1878, TO APRIL 18, 1879.	TONNAGE OF ORE SOLD.	RECEIPTS TO OWNERS.	ACTUAL YIELD OF ORE SOLD OR ASSAY.
Little Pittsburg......................	$3,109\frac{1144}{2000}$	$171,647 32	....
New Discovery.......................	$4,313\frac{1535}{2000}$	294,731 43	....
Winnemuck..........................	$384\frac{500}{2000}$	18,605 85	....
Total.....................	$7,807\frac{1179}{2000}$	$484,984 60	$1,078,586 00

FROM APRIL 18 TO JULY 1, 1879.	TONNAGE.	RECEIPTS.	ESTIMATED ACTUAL YIELD TO SMELTERS.
Consolidated Mines.................	7,900	$480,748 00	$1,106,000 00
Grand Total...............	25,007	$1,553,732 60	$3,084,586 00

The actual average contents of the ore sold in five months, to April 18, 1878, as proved by smelting and sample assays, was 111 40-100 ounces of silver per ton, and 22 47-100 per cent. lead. This gives the aggregate yield $1,078,586 that appears in the third column above. The ore continues as valuable as ever, but to be on the safe side, the actual yield after April 18 is rated a little lower, $140 a ton.

The average price at which all ore was sold, in five months to April 18, was $62.12. Reduction of expenses, freights and smelting gives better prices now. The company receipts per ton are now 30 or 40 per cent. more than formerly.

The receipts from sales of ore in May were $149,796.39, from less than 2,500 tons of ore.

A contract has just been made with the Grant Smelter for treating the entire ore product, by which the company can save $22,500 monthly.

The company has paid seven consecutive monthly dividends of $100,000 each, or 50 cents monthly to each share—the last, July 7. It is expected that the monthly dividends will be increased to $150,000 in October and to $200,000 in January.

In June, 1879, several mining experts made a thorough examination of these mines. Professor R. W. Raymond estimated that the high grade ores alone would sell to the smelters for $2,000,000. The New Discovery, where opened 300 feet long by 100 wide by levels and cross cuts is allowed 13,000 tons, $1,100,000—9 cubic feet to a ton of ore; in ground more recently explored by a long cross cut, 4,000 tons, $400,000—gray carbonate ore; Little Pittsburg, $350,000, and Winnemuck, $50,000. Estimated receipts for low grade ore on the dumps, $100,000. This does not include the contents of any unexplored ground. The assay value of the ground opened must approach $4,000,000. It seems as if there was no possibility of the ore-body giving out before many millions have been netted to the company, for fresh ore reserves are constantly being opened.

The Little Pittsburg Company employs something like 200 men. Wages are $3 per day, and some hands receive 30 cents an hour. The number of hours that constitute a day vary with different work from eight to twelve hours. There is a foreman to each shaft, and one to each shift or force of workmen; also an assistant mining

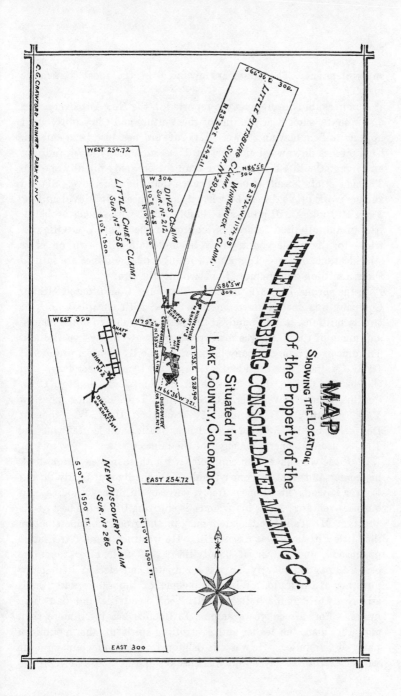

MAP

SHOWING THE LOCATION,

Of the Property of the

LITTLE PITTSBURG CONSOLIDATED MINING CO.

Situated in

LAKE COUNTY, COLORADO.

C.G. CRAWFORD PRINTER PARK PL. N.Y.

superintendent. The mines are operated in the most systematic manner.

A remarkable development is reported in the New Discovery. In a new shaft, sunk near the line of the Vulture and Chrysolite, what appears to be a new and lower strata of ore has just been entered. This pitches downward and eastward in such a way as to indicate an average depth 125 feet greater than the ore body already opened. The new strata is said to be richer even than the one above. Should further work prove this to be what it now appears, it is evident that Fryer Hill mines will possess a double value, with strong probabilities of an unlimited future production for the whole Leadville district—for the whole country may be underlaid with two or more stratifications of ore. The other workings of the mines are said to show a million dollars more than two months ago.

In the spring of 1879 the Little Pittsburg Consolidated Mining Company was incorporated in New York, with a capital stock of twenty millions, in two hundred thousand one hundred dollar shares, and much of the stock was readily taken up at twenty-five dollars. The officers of the company include Jerome B. Chaffee, president; D. H. Moffat, vice-president; George C. Lyman, secretary, and Charles C. Dodge, J. D. Smith, A. J. Dam, J. T. Soutter, C. L. Perkins, Henry Havemeyer, D. S. Draper, I. C. Babcock of New York, Senator W. H. Barnum of Connecticut, H. A. W. Tabor of Denver, James H. Chase of Providence, Chaffee and Moffat, trustees. J. C. Wilson is general manager of the mines.

Of those who have been connected with these mines Hook took his money and went to Pennsylvania. Rische lives at Leadville and Denver, spends his money freely, invests in mines, houses and business ventures, helps his friends, is enjoying life to the best of his ability. Mr. Tabor had made money in the grocery business before the Little Pittsburg was discovered. He was then county treasurer, postmaster, and mayor of Leadville. Last fall, after the mine began to pay extensively, he was nominated and elected lieutenant-governor of Colorado. With his income of thousands daily, he is still ready to "go his bottom dollar" on Leadville and San Juan mines. For fifteen years Jerome B. Chaffee has been, more than any other man, the leader and controlling spirit of the republican party of Colorado. He was a legislator from Gilpin county in the earlier territorial days, and was speaker of the house of representatives at Denver. In 1865–6, after he had made a fortune on the Bobtail mine, he was chosen United States Senator, but the State was not admitted at that time. He was delegate to Congress from 1871 to 1875, and became United States Senator when Colorado became a State, retiring last March. D. H. Moffat, although much younger, has been equally prominent in financial operations. Since 1865 he has been cashier of the First National Bank of Denver, of which Mr. Chaffee is president, and has been connected with the latter in many mining operations. He is treasurer of three railways leading from Denver, and has held important territorial and state offices. Dr. C. F. Bissell, a prominent citizen of Central long ago, and later of Colorado Springs, now resides in New York. J. C. Wilson resigned the office of internal revenue collector of Colorado, to take charge of these great mines. He was president of the convention that framed the state constitution.

The Little Chief mine is bounded by the Little Pittsburg on the east and the New Discovery and Carboniferous on the west. It is owned by a Chicago company, including J. V. Farwell, G. H. Holt, Wirt Dexter, Mr. Partridge, and others. G. H. Holt is general manager, George K. Sabin mining superintendent, and Charles Hill assistant superintendent. When the purchase was made the underground workings were in poor condition and unsafe in one locality. The new management, after some outlay and expense, placed the mine in excellent shape, and opened it with several fine shafts, supplied with double cages and cars. Spacious buildings were erected, and three engines, boilers and sets of steam hoisting machinery and a smelter were put up and set at work. The yield last winter, when work was uninterrupted, was twenty tons or more of one hundred dollar ore daily, but the new developments should increase the product two or three-fold.

The ore bodies opened last winter were of tremendous proportions, rivaling the best on the hill. There are long drifts driven ten feet wide and twenty-two feet high in ore that brings $100 per ton, and the same pay material extends between or on either side. The yield is said to have been very great since the improvements spoken of above were completed. There was one locality where the ore is nearly or quite 30 feet thick. Work goes on with steam machinery through three shafts, and the profits are said to be very great. From 65 to 90 men have been employed.

20

The contact is from 30 to 100 feet below the surface.   One shaft has a depth of 115 feet.   From shaft number one the vein dips downward in nearly every direction, but mainly to the east and west, a porphyry "horse" serving as the base down whose sides the ore body inclines. Here are black sand carbonates averaging $150 a ton, and so soft that nothing but a pick is required to pull them down.

The Little Chief claim was located by four hard-working men, Peter Finnerty, Richard and Patrick Dillon, and John Taylor. Soon after Tabor and partners, and Fryer began to take out ore rapidly, these men "struck" carbonates, and in a few months had more money than they knew what to do with.   They received about $100,000 for ore, and in December last sold to J. V. Farwell and associates of Chicago for $300,000.   Since then all but Finnerty have been traveling.   He is mining on other Leadville claims. Both of the great Chicago dry goods firms are now interested in Leadville mines.

The mines of John Borden, H. A. W. Tabor and Marshall Field extend from the Little Chief northwesterly and westerly down Fryer Hill, and comprise a portion of the bonanza ground already described.   These mines were opened in the fall and winter of 1878. When the Little Pittsburg harvest was fairly rolling in, Mr. Tabor began to buy up all the claims around him that could be had at reasonable figures, and where there were probabilities of future production.   There was no outcrop and no blossom-rock to indicate what was beneath the ground, and it required considerable "nerve" and confidence to pay ten, twenty, or fifty thousand dollars at a time for undeveloped and unknown ground.   That Tabor's judgment was correct, the subsequent enormous profits of this ground have proved, but few would have made those investments a year ago. The claims referred to are the Carboniferous, Chrysolite, Little Eva, and a part of the Vulture, Colorado Chief and Fairview.   Probably Mr. Field has as valuable an interest in these mines as his partner in the Chicago dry goods business has in the Iron.   The profits since November have been from $20,000 to $40,000 monthly.

The Carboniferous was the first developed of these properties. The underground workings of the mine and of the Little Chief open into one another, and the same body of ore, from 22 to' 30 feet thick in one locality, is found there.   The same square sets of timbers are in use as in adjacent claims.   This mine was opened under the direction of P. J. Folsom. It was necessary to sink to a depth of 115 feet below the surface in order to reach the limestone formation. There were usually five feet of hard carbonates and the remainder of the vein material has been what are called sand carbonates. In the first five months of work 2,890 tons of ore were mined, hoisted, and sold. The yield ranged from 35 to 570 ounces of silver per ton. Much of the ore sold at $100 per ton, more or less.

The Chrysolite adjoins the Carboniferous on the west, is owned by the same firm, and has much the same quantity and quality of ore. The main shaft is over 100 feet deep. The yield of this claim in two or three months, to January 1, was about $50,000. The ore carries over 20 per cent. of lead.

Shafts had been sunk but no ore found in the Vulture and adjacent claims up to late in the fall of 1878. The prospecting had been done on the wrong slope of the hill. D. Bowman, an experienced lead miner of Missouri, believed from the lay of the ground that ore would be found on the northern slope. The first shaft in that locality, at a depth of 47 feet, developed one of the best paying ore bodies in the district. Tabor, Borden & Co. soon bought a two-thirds interest in the Vulture. The ore was from 15 to 18 feet thick. Much of it yielded from 80 to 200 ounces of silver per ton, and from 30 to 70 per cent. of lead. At one time nine-tenths of the mineral mined was rich enough to sell to smelters. The mine is said to pay as well as ever.

The Triangle was the name given to a small spot of ground of triangular shape adjoining the Vulture and Little Eva, which had been overlooked at first and was not included in the surveys of adjoining claims. It was from thirty-five to sixty feet long on a side, and included only 2,200 square feet of surface ground. It was underlaid with the same Fryer Hill bonanza. This produced ore that sold for $38,000 in two or three months. During the winter a part interest sold for $16,000. Its total yield is reported at $58,000, and the cost less than $6,000. Its shaft is now used for the profitable Little Eva claim.

Not far away was another fragment of unclaimed land, about sixty feet long and from one to six feet wide. This was called the Sliver. Some miners made money by sinking a shaft sixty feet and taking out the ore from the narrow strip of ground.

On this same Fryer Hill are the Buckeye, O. K., Pandora, Muldoon, and Hope claims.

The Amie is parallel with and on the eastern side of the Little
Pittsburg. The locations were originally surveyed about the same
time. Scattering seams of mineral were found at intervals all the
way down three shafts, but they were not drifted on, and were not
generally large enough to pay. The owners knew their claim was
too near rich deposits to be generally barren, and so another shaft
was sunk further north. This struck the desired carbonate layer—
one hundred and forty feet deep—rich enough and extensive enough
to insure fortunes for the owners. The ore was penetrated in June,
and in two or three weeks twenty thousand dollars are said to have
been cleared from sales of ore taken out. The ore body is four
feet thick, and the average value very high. Over the mine are
shaft houses and engines, boilers, and whims for hoisting. The
Amie was owned and developed by A. P. Hereford and G. K. Harten-
stein, lawyers of Leadville, but was recently sold to Senator P. B.
Plumb, of Kansas, and associates.

The Climax mine is on Fryer Hill, east of the Amie, and west of
the Duncan. It is owned by Berdell, Witherell, and others, and is
superintended by Paul S. Ross. This mine is opened by three
shafts and many levels. Shaft number one is down two hundred
and twenty-two feet, and the bottom is in iron. Shaft number two
is one hundred and ninety feet deep, and cut an eighteen inch strata
of carbonates one hundred and twenty feet deep, and then passed
through layers of porphyry and lime. The third shaft is one hundred and forty feet deep. Quite a large amount of ore has been
mined, and some of the better classes turned out from $800 to
$1,000 a ton. Only portions of the workings have shown pay
material, but there are undoubtedly large ore bodies not far away.

The Duncan is on the eastern portion of Fryer Hill, and, like some
of its neighbors, is remarkable for the extent and value of its ore
bodies. These were not encountered in large quantities for quite a
while, but perseverance finally led the way to fortune. The ore
mills from forty to five hundred ounces of silver to the ton. The
claim is 1,360 feet long by 300 broad. The depth to the ore-body
of eight feet is one hundred and twelve feet.

The Matchless mine is partly between the Duncan, Robert E. Lee,
and Union, the same rich body of ore extending into all of these
claims. At a depth of one hundred feet the shaft entered a body of
iron running sixty ounces per ton. Valuable sand carbonates were

found in drifting southeast. A drift following the foot wall of silicate of lime with galena, carrying sixty ounces of silver, finally entered into ore of better average grade. The mineral has lately been rich and plentiful outside of small amounts of chlorides. The strata is similar to that of the Little Pittsburg.

TIMBER SETS IN THE BONANZA MINES.

The Robert E. Lee is the latest wonder of this wonderful district. A bonanza of surpassing richness has been discovered there this summer. The ore is from ten to twelve feet thick, and said to yield from $200 to $400 a ton, being the highest average grade of any in the district. This property was claimed by a party of Colorado Springs men, and by Henry and E. O. Wolcott and others. The former obtained possession of the mine and held it by force of arms, and the latter got out an injunction to stop work, and this was the way matters stood early in July, when Jerome B. Chaffee and others stepped in and purchased it for $240,000, all claimants getting portions of the money. Trouble among the old owners was all that caused them to dispose of it at that figure, as it is asserted that the purchase-money can be taken out of the mine in a month or two. This is a continuation of the same Little Pittsburg and Duncan ore-body, but it is richer here than elsewhere. The purchasers of the Robert E. Lee are Jerome B. Chaffee, D. H. Moffat, Senator J. P. Jones, of Nevada, Congressman S. B. Elkins, of New Mexico, and Delmonico of New York city.

Placer mining is again becoming an important industry in California Gulch. Many years ago the bed of the stream, comprising the richest diggings, was worked in a primitive way. Lack of water prevented the vast amount of outlying ground from being handled. Within a few years water has been brought in from streams miles away by means of ditches and flumes. This water supply permits of the use of hydraulics, which washes down huge quantities of gravel and bank so speedily and cheaply that heavy profits are obtainable from ground carrying but a small amount of gold. The most important enterprise of the kind is that of the Oro Ditch and Fluming Company, managed by W. H. Stevens. The claims are at Leadville, and several Little Giant hydraulics are used. The claims of Thomas Starr and of Stevens and Leiter are worked in the same way.

The growing wealth and capacity of the district is shown in the fact that more than a dozen claims were developed " into pay " for the first time during the spring months of 1879, while several others that had previously displayed but little mineral have since been producing regularly. Some of these possess ore bodies of immense size and value. The properties referred to are the Robert E. Lee, Duncan, Joe Bates, Highland Mary, Morning Star, Henrietta, Pendery, Washburn, Wild Cat, Shamrock, Little Sliver, California, Great Hope, Silver Wave, Cleora, Baron de Basco, Breese Iron, Highland Chief, Alps, Ashtabula, and Black Prince. It is no wonder that an enthusiastic news correspondent calls Leadville " the marvelous city set in a sea of silver."

CHAPTER XXII.

CUSTER COUNTY MINES—SILVER CLIFF AND ROSITA—CHLORIDES AND
MIXED GOLD AND SILVER ORES—BASSICK'S WONDERFUL FIND—
A HILL FULL OF MINERAL—A CLIFF OF SILVER ORES—THE
RACINE BOY BONANZA—THE PLATA VERDE, JOHN BULL, DOMINGO,
AND IRON MOUNTAIN—THE WORK OF VOLCANIC AGENCIES—THE
POCAHONTAS-HUMBOLDT TRUE FISSURE.

Custer county extends from the Sangre de Cristo Mountains easterly
to the borders of the plains and the foot hills of Fremont county.
It was set off from the latter by act of the legislature in 1876.
Within its limits are the Wet Mountains and the valley of the same
name. The mineral wealth of the district has recently been found
to be far more varied, novel, and extensive than was supposed, and
the pastoral and farming resources are by no means insignificant.
On the north and east is Fremont county, and on the east and south
is Huerfano, both excellant farm and stock regions, and both possessing coal measures of great extent and superior quality.

The three pioneer prospectors and miners were Irwin, Robinson,
and Pringle, who discovered the Senator lode in the fall of 1872.
They named the settlement Rosita—the Spanish for "a little rose."
It has since grown to be a pretty town of twelve hundred people,
and the centre of a valuable mining district. The location is a
beautiful one, surrounded as it is by dome-shaped hills, smooth and
grass-clad on the sides facing Wet Mountain valley and the great
Sangre de Christo range and covered with pines on the reverse.

In 1874 the Pocahontas-Humboldt and other lodes began to produce and have since yielded not far from $600,000 in silver. In
1877 the wonderful Maine or Bassick mine began to turn out its gold
and silver ore, and a year later the Silver Cliff excitement sprung
up. This arose from the discovery of a veritable bonanza in the
way of chloride silver ores, called the Racine Boy, and of other
lodes of great importance. The year 1879 opened very favorably
for the district.

The production of Custer county mines has been as follows, over a million being in silver:

1874, and previously.	$40,000 00	1877	$354,081 34
1875	294,827 58	1878	452,500 50
1876	351,121 06		
	Total		$1,392,529 98

The Humboldt lode was discovered in April, 1874. The following month the Pocahontas and Southeast Leviathan, and Leavenworth were located to the northwest of it, and the Virginia on the southeast. Subsequent explorations proved these to be all on one vein of great length and uniformity, and rich in silver. The enclosing formation is trachytic, bordering on the granite of the hills and ridges to the northward. The lode extends across the head of the valley in which Rosita is built. The Pocahontas and Humboldt did not produce largely until 1875-6. During the last year and a half poor ground has been encountered, and the old owners of the former suspended work. The Pocahontas, Powhattan and Pawnee lodes were recently purchased by California men of the Silver Cliff Company who will develop and operate them extensively. The Pocahontas and Humboldt each have 1,385 feet on the vein, the Virginia 1,500, and the Leviathan, Leavenworth and others foot up over 3,500 feet additional, or a mile and a half on one vein.

Up to the end of 1877 the Pocahontas mine yielded 2,543 tons of ore, containing $279,353.02, and selling for $167,523.33. Of this 564½ tons averaged 36.8 ounces of silver per ton, and 1,979 averaged 98.7 ounces, or $127.61. It cost $190,375 for buildings, machinery, and to mine, hoist, and open up ground; but a large portion of this was for the first two items, which are good for years to come. The cost of sinking the shaft is given at $20 per foot of depth; of driving levels, $5 to $5.50; adits, $7. When George C. Munson operated the mine in 1878 he drove a level 112 feet, at $5.50 per foot.

The Humboldt became the property of the Humboldt Silver Mining Company in October, 1875, 1,900 feet of the vein being included. The vein of paying ore has varied from four inches to four feet in width. The main shaft is 540 feet deep. Three levels have been driven at intervals of 100 feet westward to the Pocahontas ground and eastward nearly or quite the same distance. A cross-cut, starting 400 feet down the shaft, was driven nearly 200 feet at right angles from the vein to explore ground, into which ore-feeders were found to branch off in sinking the shaft. This cross-cut passes through a kind of conglomerate cement, with occasional ore seams, and has cost six dollars per foot of advance. The cost of sinking the main shaft five feet by twelve was from eight to thirty dollars per foot. It costs to break rock in the levels, four feet by seven, from four to six dollars per foot. Stoping costs two dollars for every foot of advance six feet high and two feet wide. The hoisting machinery is of the best description, and includes a fifty horse-power engine. The explored ground has been mostly exhausted for a depth of 300 feet. A. Thornton is general superintendent.

The Virginia has been owned by a company of the same name since April, 1876. Its main shaft is 355 feet deep and there are 700 feet of levels and 465 square fathoms of stoping. The hoisting and pumping machinery is first-class. The Leviathan has a shaft 171 feet deep and several short levels.

The Humboldt and Virginia companies built the Pennsylvania reduction works in 1876. They contain 10 stamps for crushing, 2 revolving cylinders for roasting, 6 amalgamating pans, 2 agitators and vats for leaching with copper. Five men are required by day and four by night. Daily capacity 9 to 10 tons of Humboldt ore.

R. Neilson Clark, M. E., who has operated the Virginia and other mines, compiled a pamphlet on the Pocahontas-Humboldt vein, from which the following statement of the workings and yield of the four mines to 1878 is taken, with product of that year added. The values are currency, with gold ranging from 115 to 100.

	Shafting.	Drifting.	Adits and Tunnels.	Stoped.	Shipped.	Currency Value.	Mill Returns.	Average per Sq. Fathom.	Average per Ton.
	Feet.	Feet.	Feet.	Sq. Fath.	Tons.				
Southeast Leviathan	171	190	....	....	50	$4,300 00	$2,100 00	....	$86
Pocahontas	690	1,946	460	2,300	2,559	323,477 51	171,247 91	$138	124
Humboldt..	1,490	2,200	....	3,100	2,105	275,604 15	132,145 06	73	107
Virginia....	510	700	140	465	179	18,547 85	9,821 20	40	103
	2,861	5,036	600	5,865	4,893	$621,929 51	$315,314 17	....	...

The vein, with an average trend of north 50° west, conforms to the part of the range in which it occurs. Its hanging wall is remarkably regular and smooth; the foot-wall is less regular, and often swells from the hanging wall. Many insist that the vein is at least twenty-five feet thick; they assume that a parallel streak occurring on the foot-wall side is part of the vein, and that all the rock between is fissure matter. I question the correctness of this view, for in most places both walls of this one pay streak are identical in all respects, except perhaps smoothness and hardness. The gangue is a soft clay, easily mined as a gouge, occurring usually towards the foot-wall; it is undoubtedly decomposed trachyte, usually showing the characteristic color, etc., of that portion of the wall against which it lies. The pay-streak usually lies against the hanging wall, often separated from it by a clay selvage. It is always accompanied with heavy spar (remarkably free from rhomb-spar), and galena is also found. Generically the ore is a barytic-tetrahedrite; copper and iron pyrites are common, together with stephanite and the like. The more valuable specimens are the antimonial compounds of silver. The vein pitches strongly to the southeast."

The Leavenworth is the westernmost portion of the same vein, and has much the same characteristics as the Pocahontas. The main shaft, 140 feet deep, and levels extending therefrom, yielded 150 tons of ore, that brought $10,000 in fifteen months ending March, 1879. The mine was opening up finely at last accounts. There are several cross veins. One of these yields ore similar to the main vein—or from two to three hundred dollars per ton. The owners are Paul Gerkie & Co. The Pioneer and Chieftain cross the Leavenworth.

A number of tunnels have been driven into the hills of Rosita district. The Custer County Tunnel Company has pushed one of these into Robinson Hill over 300 feet. W. A. Offenbacher, Charles Baker, and other Custer county men, are the officers and stockholders of the enterprise. Pockets and bodies of ore yielding from 300 to 400 ounces of silver per ton have often been found on the surface of this hill, which led to the opinion that a great ore-body existed somewhere in the vicinity. Last May a valuable vein was intersected by this tunnel. There is said to be three feet of 40-ounce ore, but parts of the vein yield from $100 to $400 a ton.

The Michigan Tunnel Company have driven a prospecting tunnel

THE MAINE OR BASSICK MINE.

into Tyndall Hill, adjoining the Bassick Hill, some 400 feet. The Minnesota tunnel has penetrated Robinson Hill over 300 feet.

The Benjamin Franklin lode was discovered on a hill near the Bassick in July, 1877, and is owned by Thurman, Prescott, Maxwell & Co., who purchased it early in 1878. In less than a year they sold seventy tons of ore for $9,940. A level is being driven at a depth of 200 feet in the main shaft which is a little deeper. The crevice is large and the ore is found in pockets of from a few hundred pounds to ten or fifteen tons. The ore of the first sixty feet was carbonates, below that galena and zinc-blende, and copper pyrites and gray copper have lately been plentiful, with black sulphurets and some very rich ore. Mill returns from 80 to 175 ounces.

Among veins that have paid are the Chieftain, Lucille, Victoria, Polonia, Hector, Tecumseh, Triumph, Twenty-six, Plymouth and others. Forty tons of ore from the Victoria sold in a portion of 1878, yielded 1,680 ounces of silver. Richard Irwin operates the Golden Eagle gold lode in Hardscrabble district.

Among those who settled at Rosita while the Pocahontas and Humboldt mines were at the height of their production was Mr. E. C. Bassick. He had been pretty much all over the world and had once made a fortune in the Australian gold mines, but had subsequently lost it. In the summer of 1877 he was engaged in tunneling Tyndall Hill, something over two miles north of Rosita. In passing to and from his work he had often noticed float or blossom rock of a peculiar appearance scattered along a neighboring hillside. He finally had some of this assayed, and the result caused him to take some of the surface material to the reduction-works. This brought thirty dollars, and as the ground proved more profitable than that of the tunnel, he continued to sink in his new prospect hole, which he called the Maine, after his native state. He soon after sent a lot of eight or ten tons of ore to the mill, and, to his astonishment, received over $12,000 therefor. This unexpected good fortune was all the more acceptable to one who had experienced many and long-continued reverses.

From that time forward the immense value of the discovery seemed assured, and subsequent developments have made its wealth more and more apparent. Month after month saw an increase in production, and the owner was raised from poverty to affluence in a very short space of time.

The character and appearance of the mineral and formation were so different from anything previously known in Colorado that prospectors had overlooked or passed by this hill as worthless. It remained for Mr. Bassick to unlock the treasure-vault that has few equals anywhere. From the time of the first sale of ore he kept steadily at the work of development. Near the surface a nest of boulders coated and mixed with chlorodized mineral was encountered, supposed to be a huge mineralized chimney nearly perpendicular in direction. Decomposed material was found to extend downward about one hundred and fifty feet, with a yield of from one hundred to over one thousand dollars per ton, and the same boulder formation. Below, the crevice is less decomposed and oxidized. The great quantity and superior quality of the ore enabled the owner to reap a very respectable fortune

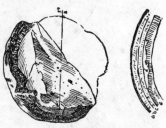

BOULDER AND SHELL.

monthly. A rich ore body was drifted on at a depth of sixty feet, which was followed southward seventy feet, where sinking was again resorted to. Finally, the old shaft was driven downward on an incline so as to connect with the other, and then continued below. Levels and a stope were started in two or three localities. The shaft is wider in one direction than in the other. It varies in size from sixteen to twenty-four feet, and near the bottom is about thirty feet wide, with mineralized ground all around it.

The mine was wonderfully productive and profitable. Some of the records of ore sales are supposed to have been lost, but those at hand show that $423,608.20 were received for ore sold to smelters within twelve months after the first shipment. Nearly all of this was the product of a single shaft, the excavations leading from that being small. With freight and smelter's charges added to the above the amount of the actual yield would certainly reach $508,329.84. The ore was hauled in wagons out of the mountains to the railway, and then taken partly to Black Hawk and partly to Omaha. The average yield of the ore shipped was not far from $225 per ton. While the above was being mined and sold an immense amount of poorer material was raised and piled near the ore house, ready for treatment when works should be erected close by. Ore sold from this heap has brought about $36 per ton, indicating an assay value of over $61. The dump is also valuable. It is said to contain an average

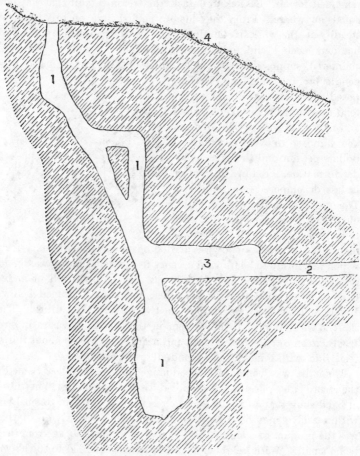

1 Shaft, 215 feet deep. 2 Tunnel, 400 feet long. 3 Engine Chamber. 4 Surface of the Hill.

THE MAINE MINE.

of $20 per ton in gold, and $5 or more in silver. All of this would indicate the total contents of the output of twelve months to approach something like three quarters of a million. The average value per fathom of the ground excavated boulders and all, is found to be $1,475.98 per fathom, or not far from $113 per ton.

The shaft had now reached a depth of 215 feet, and steam hoisting power was needed in place of horse power. The property had been worked mainly in a single shaft, because there was thought for a long time to be only a large chimney of pay material. The later investigations indicated that this ore-body and boulder nest extended all through the centre of the hill. A tunnel was driven from the base of the hill which intersected the shaft 165 feet deep

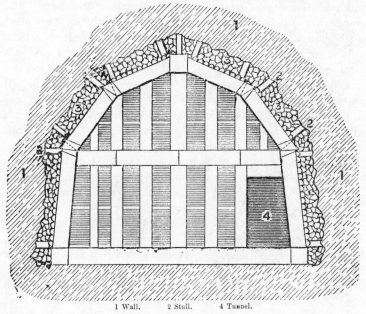

1 Wall. 2 Stull. 4 Tunnel.

THE GREAT UNDERGROUND ENGINE CHAMBER OF THE MAINE MINE.

and 375 feet from the tunnel's mouth. It was deemed best to place the steam-hoisting machinery in an excavation at the junction of the shaft and tunnel. The underground chamber, containing the machinery, is sixty feet long by twenty-seven wide and is larger than first intended, because the crevice matter was found to be much wider than expected.

The roof and sides of this immense excavation are supported by timber work of the most solid and substantial character. It was

planned and completed by the superintendent of the mine, George C.
Munson. It is safe to say that no finer underground timbering can
be shown anywhere than this. Here are located the engine, boiler,
and hoisting machinery, and from here an iron smoke-stack extends
to the surface.

Production has been small of late, owing to the delay in excavating and placing the machinery; otherwise the total production
might have doubled. Another shaft, started seventy feet away
from the old one, has reached a depth of not far from sixty feet
and levels have been started in three directions therefrom. The
ore was found to be as rich and abundant as elsewhere. Two other
shafts show well, and one of them appears to have developed a well-
defined north wall to the lode. Another shaft has been started at a
considerable distance east. All of this development goes to show
that the ore-body has an east and west direction, and that it will
prove to be a regular vein instead of a chimney or blow-out, as was
at first believed. As depth is gained and cross-cuts are driven this
will undoubtedly be more fully demonstrated. Past developments
indicate the lode or ledge to be 120 feet wide.

The formation of this section is trachyte, with granite to the northward. There appears to be a grand porphyry dike extending east

and west, but it may be more
properly termed trachyte. The
boulders and pebbles in the great
ore channel of the Maine are of
the same material, and carry more
or less mineral. They are cemented together with porphyry and
other material, and coated over
with mineral, and the entire filling
is very rich in gold and silver as

MASS OF MINERALIZED BOULDERS.

well as copper, the latter increasing as depth is gained. From
sixty to seventy per cent. of the value obtained is in gold, and ten
per cent. or more of the ore is copper. Down to the water-line, or
a depth of 150 feet or more, the boulders have a film or coating of
rich mineral, varying in thickness from a knife blade to half an inch.
Below that depth the ore is more in the shape of shells. While the
boulders are mineralized, the filling between them carries chlorides,
iron and copper pyrites, gray copper, tellurides, sylvanite, galena,

zinc, carbonates, talc, native silver, and free gold. In fact, this hill comprises a strange conglomeration of nearly all kinds of mineral, and in quantity seemingly almost without end. To obtain the large production noted above, only from seven to nine underground miners have usually been employed, and about twice as many men beside in sorting ore and on surface work. The future yield is likely to so far surpass that of the past that there may be no comparison between the two. It appears to be a veritable bonanza, whose equal in value has rarely been found in the history of mining. Owing to negotiations pending for the purchase of the Maine, and to preparations in the chamber of the tunnel, work and production have not been pushed for some months. The new shaft makes about the same showing that the old one did, proving that this is something more than the chimney that was at first supposed. Now that the mine is reported sold, on the basis of a million and a half, very extensive operations will be inaugurated.

Silver Cliff is a new mining district, organized and settled within the past year. It is on the eastern slope of Wet Mountain Valley, and is mainly smooth prairie land, with occasional dome-shaped hills. It is seven miles west of Rosita, about the same distance east of the base of the Sangre de Christo range, and thirty miles south or southwest of Cañon City and the railway. Wet Mountain valley had long been known as a fine stock-growing country, but few believed it possessed mineral resources of value.

Near Round Mountain a long sloping hill rises from the plain, but comes to an abrupt termination at one end. This was known as "the Cliff," and around it cattle had been grazing for years. A miner named Edwards passed along that way in the spring of 1878, and carelessly broke a piece of rock from the face of the cliff. With no expectation of its being rich in the precious metals, he had it assayed, and to his surprise it gave a return of 27 ounces of silver per ton. As that kind of silver ore would not pay expenses of treatment at smelting works, he paid no more attention to the place.

The next summer Edwards and a man named Powell mined among the hills toward Rosita. After working until August without making a dollar, it occurred to Edwards that the low grade assay of the "Cliff" rock was better than what they were getting. Acting on the suggestion of his partner, these men "broke camp" and moved over to the Cliff. The first assay they ordered went $1,700. This was good enough to tie to, and, taking a third party named Spoffard "in with them," they began work. They gave the locality the name of Silver Cliff, but kept their discovery a secret in order to be sure of a title and of more lodes in the future. It was not long, however, before the sight of some big bright silver buttons of theirs in a Rosita assay office caused a miner to follow up the clew until he discovered the owners and their mine. The Plata Verde and other claims were then located, and the reports of rich horn silver mines once noised abroad brought in scores of miners. Soon after the fame of the district attracted men from all parts of the State. The cattle were displaced from their old herding grounds by herds of men, busy and wild in their search for wealth, and the locality became a veritable staked plain.

Among the early comers to the camp was J. W. Bailey, an old Pacific Slope and Black Hills mining operator and mill man. He purchased a large interest in the Racine Boy claims in August, and built the first house on the present site of Silver Cliff in September. Before the snows of November came a populous town was there, with stores, saloons, gambling-houses, and as great a medley of men of every class and description as one would wish to see. Specimens of horn silver were picked from the ashes or lava of the cliff that assayed ten and twenty thousand dollars, and chlorides in immense quantities were found in the Racine Boy, Plata Verde, and Horn Silver claims; and this is the way that the Racine Boy mine and the town of Silver Cliff, now so famous, came to be located. Very soon after the discovery, and until the recent sale, this mine was owned by J. W. Bailey, who had nearly a half interest, and J. T. Beck, R. Curtis, and the original discoverer, Edwards.

An unusually severe winter acted as a serious drawback to prospecting and surface mining, but it was not long until the camp was again prosperous and progressive. Chloride of silver ores were something new for Colorado, and Bailey, who had handled them extensively on the Pacific slope, saw there was an extensive field of operations awaiting their treatment. Other discoveries were made in the winter and spring months, including galena and other deposits, and Custer County will hereafter take an important place among the bullion producing counties of the State.

The first car load of ore from the Racine Boy and Silver Cliff mines was sent to Omaha in September. Pending negotiations for the mine in the fall, and while the snows of December and January obstructed operations, work was not pushed extensively, yet the following production was made up to last spring.

Cañon City Works bought 259 tons ore, containing....... $25,097
Cañon City Works bought 75 tons ore, containing....... 4,500
B. & C. Works and others bought 183 tons ore, containing.. 22,121
Silver Cliff Sampling Works bought 191 tons ore, containing 18,356

$70,074

Other shipments of ore are said to have brought the total yield of the mine up to $100,000, outside of vast quantities of mineral on hand.

The Racine Boy is worked by a tunnel 200 feet long, and by shafts and open cuts. One of the latter is sixty feet long by forty wide, and is thirty feet deep, with a shaft in the centre. It resembles a large quarry, and from this the main exported production of the mine came. This is located just above the edge of the cliff, which is sixty feet high. It cost but $10,000 to mine ore from this cut that sold for over $50,000; most of it yielded over $100 a ton, and one lot of eight tons sold for $5,800. This ore was teamed 30 miles to Cañon, at a cost of from $8 to $10 a ton, and then sent to Denver by rail, at a further cost of $4 a ton; it was then sold for the usual schedule price for refractory ores, which allow for a smelter's charge of from $35 to $50 per ton.

Shipments and ore sales were finally discontinued, because it was useless to pay from $50 to $65 for freight and smelting when a raw amalgamation mill could be operated at the mine at a cost of four or five dollars a ton. The reason there is no mill of this description in Colorado is because chlorodized silver ores were not plentiful previous to the late discoveries at Silver Cliff, and consequently there was no call for one; all silver ores previously mined required more costly and complicated methods of treatment. These Silver Cliff veins are of a combination barren of base minerals, and hence possess free milling ores. For some time, ore has been treated at the Pennsylvania reduction works at Rosita by the raw amalgamation process referred to, the roasting cylinders of the mill not being used; the cost per ton has been $4.80; eighty per cent. of the silver was saved, and the bullion is 900 fine.

Besides quantities of ore rich in silver and carrying smaller amounts of gold, there are several thousand tons of low grade ore broken at the various workings of the mine or laying on the dumps. Mill runs and numerous assays show this to contain from $20 to $40 per ton—too poor to ship or sell to the smelters, but like the free milling gold ores of Gilpin county, endless quantities of these free milling silver ores can be made extremely profitable by treatment in the manner proposed. A tunnel 200 feet long, and several shafts and cuts, indicate the lode to be vertical in direction and two or three hundred feet wide; it has also been traced for several hundred feet in length along its course. If only a fraction of this is ore of the lower grade, it will be seen that the available wealth of the mine is enormous, and that it can be estimated by millions without going far below the tunnel level. The owners believe they can turn out thousands of tons monthly, and that the yield will be several times the cost of mining and milling. Miner's wages are $2.50 a day. It costs less than a dollar a ton to mine the ore.

Dr. G. C. Munson, superintendent of the Bassick mine, and a gentleman who has had great experience in mining and reducing, ore, estimates that Silver Cliff ore can be mined and reduced at a cost of less than $5 per ton at the mine. Other experts and mining men who have examined the rock estimate the cost of milling and reducing at from four to seven dollars per ton; the latter being the very highest figure.

The company that has recently purchased the property will soon have a forty-stamp mill in operation. These stamps will be run at the rate of over ninety drops a minute, and will each crush two tons of rock every twenty-four hours. Amalgamation will be effected in pans.

The Racine Boy and Silver Cliff mines, embracing 1,500 feet in length by 450 feet in width of surface ground, were recently purchased by Pacific Coast and New York men, who organized the Silver Cliff Mining Company thereon. The capital stock is ten millions, in two hundred thousand fifty-dollar shares, and there is a paid up working capital of one hundred thousand dollars. The officers of the company are James R. Keene, president; James H. Banker, vice-president; I. Wormser, treasurer, and the same and Senator J. P. Jones, Jacob Lorillard, R. L. Cutting, George L. Rives, J. S. Moore, and J. W. Gashwiler, directors.

QUARRYING CHLORIDES FROM THE RACINE BOY MINE.

The vein is considered by the best informed experts to be a true fissure. Recent developments show an obsidian dike to be the east wall, with a clay seam and trachyte strata between the quartz and porphyry of the vein, and there is a similar dike parallel to other lodes further north. The clay seam is perpendicular, and obsidian dikes are always so. The famous Ontario mine of Utah was bought largely on the strength of a bordering formation of that kind. The "slickenside" on the face of the Cliff proves an upheaval and disproves the overflow theory of some who saw the locality before late developments.

The surface ore shows considerable trachyte and porphyry mixed with silica; but this is considered the natural result of an upheaval near so hot a neighbor as the obsidian dike. The porphyry or trachytic formation in which these mines are formed is about two miles wide, traversing the granite country northwest and southeast for a distance of fifteen or twenty miles. The Rosita mines and the Maine are in the same belt, and so are the Plata Verde, Horn Silver, and Domingo, or John Bull. In some sections copper ores are visible; in others, lead, in very large quantities. In the Maine is tellurium, while gold and silver are found from one end of the belt to the other.

The Western mine, close by the Racine Boy, is turning out ore in large quantities. Amalgamating and reducing mills will soon be in operation at Silver Cliff. Dillingham & Co. are rebuilding their ore sampling and shipping mill that was burned last spring.

The Plata Verde is situated well up on Round Mountain, and has from discovery ranked next to the Racine Boy. It is another enormous vein or deposit, and carries rich chlorides, horn silver, as well as low grade mineral. It has been worked by open cuts, and paying rock has been quarried from the mountain side in very large quantities. What the yield has been is not generally known, but if worked to the greatest advantage would be very large. This mine needs a stamp and amalgamating mill near by, and is likely to have one at an early day. The lack of cheap milling facilities alone has prevented the owners from getting out one hundred tons of ore daily. The ore mined so far has averaged sixty dollars. A lot of six tons, sent to Denver, yielded two hundred and sixty ounces of silver to the ton, and forty-three tons taken from the mine without sorting gave sixty ounces per ton. Chlorides and manganese are the prevailing characteristics. W. J. Robinson, cne of the pioneers of Rosita, discovered and located the Plata Verde on the second day of September, 1878. The Lone Mountain and other claims adjoin it.

The Horn Silver mine is located near the base of Round Mountain. It has a large body of low grade material, but rich ore has lately been found. Forty men are at work, and the production is good. The King of the Valley and Gray Eagle, owned by the Buckeye Company, are opened by several shafts, over one of which is a small steam-engine and hoisting works. The Ula company are mining and prospecting extensively.

The Iron Mountain lode is said to be of great value, and somewhat resembles the Maine. It was discovered last spring and is a fissure in a kind of black porphyritic trachyte, filled with common yellow gangue, intermixed with boulders of agatized quartz, which yield as high as 140 ounces of silver to the ton and a little gold. The mine is a mile and a half from the Maine.

The Dirigo mine, near the Bassick and Benjamin Franklin, has lately developed a wonderful mineral deposit somewhat resembling that of the former. It carries galena, sulphurets, gray copper, and pyrites of iron. Trachytic boulders are found of all sizes. Some of the pay material carries two or three hundred ounces of silver, and some gold.

Among the most remarkable developments of even this remarkable belt of country are those of the Domingo and John Bull mines, about three or four miles northeast of Silver Cliff. This is apparently one immense deposit with two locations so close together that contests, litigation, and injunctions have been the order of the day almost from the time of discovery, last February. These locations contain a huge gold and silver bearing boulder deposit, similar in some respects to the Maine mine, but mainly carrying galena silver ore. The Domingo employs 50 men.

There are extensive iron deposits on Grape Creek near the borders of Custer and Fremont counties. These are of the magnetic species, containing about 65 per cent. of pure iron. The main drawback arises from the presence of platinum in the ore, which causes difficulty in smelting. For a long period, eight tons of this ore have been shipped to the Mather and Geist smelting works at Pueblo. The outcrop covers about 320 acres of hills and valleys.

CHAPTER XXIII.

SUMMIT COUNTY AND ITS MINES OF SILVER AND GOLD—THE LAND
BEYOND THE SNOWY RANGE—PAYING PLACERS OF 1860—ANNALS
OF THE GOLD HUNTERS—SOME BIG PLACER OPERATIONS OF THE
PRESENT TIME—BLUE RIVER, SNAKE RIVER, AND TEN MILE—
SUMMIT COUNTY'S YIELD OF GOLD, SILVER AND LEAD—THE EAGLE
—GUNNISON, ROUTT AND GRAND COUNTIES—THE NEW MINES.

Summit County extends from the crest of the Snowy Range westward to Utah, and lies entirely on the Pacific slope of the mountains.
Clear Creek and Park counties bound it on the east, Grand and
Routt on the north, and Lake and Gunnison on the south. It embraces a large amount of country adapted to farming and pastoral
purposes and is rich in silver lodes and gold placers. The yield of
the latter has been very great and that of the lode veins will evidently be immense in the near future. In the western portion are
coal measures of excellent quality.

Summit is a county of immense extent. It is larger than Delaware and Rhode Island combined, and has an area equal to that of
Connecticut. Its scenery is grand and magnificent. Mountain
ranges border and intersect it in almost all directions, and among
them are noble rivers, and hundreds of sparkling streams and dashing waterfalls. Vast forests of pine and spruce extend up the
mountain sides, and here and there are broad valleys green as emerald
and watered by the purest streams.

The first silver lode opened in Colorado was the Coaley in Summit County. Its discovery came about in this way : Some gulch
miners from the Blue River or Georgia Gulch were hunting for deer
in 1861, and getting out of bullets manufactured a few from the
outcroppings of what they called a lead vein. A year or two later
they were in Nevada, and found that the silver-bearing galena ores
of that section very much resembled the material which had supplied them with bullets in the Colorado mountains. They wrote to
an old friend in Empire and advised him to go over and locate the

lode. After some delay he did so, but never made a fortune from it. Yet it led to a great silver excitement and to the development of the Georgetown silver district.

That great natural barrier, the Snowy Range, has acted as a serious drawback to Summit County's progress and advancement. The heavy snows blockaded the entire region from the outside world in the winter season and the difficulty of crossing mountains from twelve to thirteen thousand feet high caused freighting and traveling to be slow and very expensive. Matters have assumed a different shape during the past few months. New wagon roads have been built at much lower elevations and on better grades, furnishing connection with Georgetown and Leadville. Railways are also projected and surveyed to both of these points. An extension of the Colorado Central Railroad is likely to be built through this county within a year. The leading towns of Summit are Kokomo, Carbonateville, and Summit City in the Ten Mile section—all founded within a few months—Montezuma and Saints John in the Snake river region, and Breckenridge in the Blue river placer country.

There are several important mining districts, old and new, that are attracting much attention. Of these the gold placers or alluvial deposits of the Blue and Swan rivers and their tributaries are the oldest. Extending north from these among the mountains is a belt of veins carrying silver and lead. The Snake river region contains both argentiferous galena and sulphuret and copper-bearing veins. There are some very rich veins in the vicinity of Montezuma, Saints John, Peru, Geneva, and Hall Valley—all located on the main range or some of its spurs. Near the headwaters of the Blue carbonates have lately been found.

The great excitement, however, at the present time is over the Ten Mile district. This locality has become famous during the past seven or eight months. Rich galena veins have been opened in the mountains west of Ten Mile River, and several thousand men have assembled there. The indications are good for one of the leading silver districts of the State. Further west valuable mineral discoveries are reported in the Eagle River region, but these were made this season, and of course sufficient time has not yet elapsed for their development. The fame of Ten Mile has brought in people enough to prospect the county very extensively, and there is no doubt but that its mineral wealth is of the first order.

21

The yield of Summit county mines from first to last was some-what as follows, the earlier years being estimated :

Gold from placers, 1860 to 1870.......	$5,500,000		$5,000,000
" " 1870.............	100,000		
" " 1871.............	70,C00		
" " 1872.............	60,000		
" " 1873.............	101,000		
Silver and lead, 1869 to 1874.........	200,000		531,000
Gold from placers, 1874.............	76,408		
Silver and lead, 1874.............	50,000		126,408
Gold from placers, 1875.............	72,413		
Silver, 1875.............	50,000		152,413
Gold from placers, 1876.............	150,000		
Silver and lead, 1876.............	200,000		350,000
Gold from placers, 1877.............	150,000		
Silver and lead, 1877.............	40,000		190,000
Gold from placers, 1878.............	165,774		
Silver and lead, 1878.............	155,000		320,774

Total..................................... $7,041,195

Total gold, $6,320,195 ; silver, $595,000 ; lead, $100,000.

In the early years of Colorado mining, the tributaries of the Blue River were among the most productive in the country. Mining fairly began in 1860, and for several summers the yield of gold in Georgia, French, and Humbug gulches, the Blue and Gold Run, was very great ; there was a score of other localities, such as Illinois, McNulty, etc., but those named above were the most famous. It is claimed that a million a season was taken out at first, the years 1860–61 being the best; after that, many diggings had been more or less exhausted. The yield was very large, however, for years, and mining has been carried on there every summer since the first discoveries ; the great placer enterprises that have lately been inaugurated promise to give a much more reliable and nearly as great an annual yield as when Georgia Gulch ranked next to California Gulch in the yield of the yellow metal. Many are the Aladdin-like tales of fortunes made in that locality in the days of 1860–61, when men made from twenty to a hundred dollars a day.

The yield of the placer and gulch mines of the Blue River and tributaries in 1877 was as follows, some of the claims and localities being estimated:

Blue River—J. Bemrose, $3,500; L. Gorham, $800; A. McLeod, $2,000; Fuller & Krom, $10,000; H. Zingling, $800; A. Stahl, $1,000; J. E. Rankin, $1,500; R. Adams, $1,500; Nolan & Kromer, $3,500; G. Mumford, $1,000; T. Clague, $300; J. Izzard, $4,600; D. Schriven, $4,800; J. Bisly, $450; McMahon, $200.

Gold Run—L. S. Peabody, $8,500; S. Walker, $3,500.

Swan River—J. M. Riland, $3,000; A. Delaney, $500; D. Stogsdill, $8,000; Fuller Placer Co., $32,000; P. Iveson, $1,500; North Swan miners, $800.

French Gulch—Stillson Patch, $3,500; Badger Co., $3,000; Calvin Clark, $15,000; Ebert & Co., $8,000.

Ten Mile—Follett, L. S. Ballou and Tucker, $2,500; and miners of McNulty Gulch, $7,500.

Total yield of placer gold for the county, $150,000 in coin value. The expense of getting out this amount, exclusive of permanent improvements, is estimated at only 40 per cent. of the gross yield, leaving 60 per cent. of receipts as net gain. The average yield per cubic yard of placer ground was given at the handsome figure of 25 cents, while that of Izzard's claim was $1.45 per cubic yard.

The gold placer yield of 1878 was still larger and approximated as follows on the various streams and gulches. Some of these returns are exact and others are estimated:

Total, $165,774.

Blue River—J. B. Bemrose, $3,000; L. H. Gorham, $300; A. D. McLeod, $1,000; Fuller & Krom, $6,000; J. D. Rankin, in Corkscrew Gulch, $1,000; the Klack diggings, $500.

Blue Tributaries—Lomax Gulch—Ellis Stahl, $1,500; Picket & Downing, $1,000. Iowa Gulch—Adams & Engle, $2,600; Boston & Colorado P. M. Company, $500. Izzardville—A. Alexander, $6,000. Salt Lick Gulch—R. Schriven, $4,000. Ryan Gulch—Roby & Silverthorn, $800. Maryland Gulch—Blaisley & Albett, $1,000. Soda Gulch, $300; Yuba Dam, Nolan & Kroner, $3,000; other gulches, $5,000.

Swan River Tributaries—Gold Run—L. C. Barnard, $1,550; D. Peabody, $8,000; Silas Walker, $3,000; Barrett & Co., $1,000.

HYDRAULIC MINING, FRENCH GULCH.

Delaware Flats—Andy Delaine, $500. Galena Gulch—D. Stogsdill, $6,000. Brown Gulch—J. Cyphart, $1,000.

Bed of the Swan—Isaac Williams, $500; Eckhart & Co., $500.

Fuller Placer Company, including Georgia and other gulches, $36,000.

French Gulch—H. Farncomb, $8,000; T. Murphy, $500; George Clark, $20,000; Calvin Clark, $5,424; J. Sisler, $1,000; L. S. Ballou, $20,000; Goodman Steele, J. J. Cobb, etc., $500.

Illinois Gulch—Fuller Placer Company, $4,000.

Ten Mile River—Follett, $1,000. McNulty Gulch—McNasser & Brandon, $5,000. All others, $3,000.

The two great placer operations of the county are conducted by the Fuller Placer Company and by L. S. Ballou. Their extensive lands have been brought into condition to produce largely, and hydraulics, flumes, and all necessary appliances are in use. There are three requisites to successful placer mining—valuable ground, sufficient water, and sufficient "fall" or "dump." No matter how much gold the ground contains, it cannot be extracted without water.

The Fuller Placer Company, possessing the most extensive appliances, and probably the most placer land of any one company east of California, possesses all of these requirements. But water has been procured only at an outlay of a great deal of labor and money, and of no little display of engineering abilities. The water supply was totally inadequate, and the necessary quantity could not be obtained without constructing long ditches and flumes, and in some places by carrying the latter at great elevations over ravines and along rugged mountain sides. The placer lands were partially divided among many owners, and it took years to purchase and consolidate the vast amount of property now owned and controlled.

There was a vast tract of country known to be auriferous for which there seemed to be no possibility of obtaining water. At length it was found that a pass in the main Continental Divide or watershed of the continent, 11,811 feet above sea level, was lower than a lake on the eastern slope, located among and fed by the eternal snows. The manager, with the eye of a true engineer, saw that this lake on the Atlantic slope could be made available for the Fuller placers on the Pacific side of the range by the construction of many miles of ditch and flume. There were noble forests of pine at hand, and a saw-mill was soon set at work manufacturing the timber required

for the great flume. At length the work was completed, and the
waters turned from their natural course around Georgia Pass to
eventually mingle with the waters of the Pacific.

The Fuller Placer Company's property embraces 3,000 acres of
"pay gravel" patented and pre-empted, besides 30,000 acres controlled by its water. This land is on the western slope of the Rocky
Mountains, around the headwaters of the Swan River, and some of
the tributaries of the Blue, which is a tributary of the Grand. The

THE LONG FLUME.

property is classed as
the Mayo and Georgia
divisions. On this
property are from
twenty to thirty miles
of flume and ditch, a
score of buildings for
the accommodation
of workmen, and for
a year's supplies.
There is also a steam
saw-mill, many hy-
draulics, tools, imple-
ments, and appliances
for working the
mines.

These placers are
worked about five and
a-half months every
year —that being the
length of the warm
season available for
placer mining. Last
year the gold product was reported at $42,000, and the expenses
at $15,000. The yield of 1879, the present summer and fall, may
reach $100,000, as everything is now in first-class condition. Six
Little Giant hydraulics are at work in different gulches. There are
altogether about 34,000,000 cubic yards of pay gravel, said to be
capable of yielding at a low estimate twenty-five cents per cubic
yard, indicating the total contents to exceed $8,000,000. The
ground worked in American Gulch last season yielded one dollar

per cubic yard. M. J. Cole is superintendent of this great enterprise, and Col. T. H. Fuller, president and treasurer.

The Mayo property embraces claims in Mayo, Negro, Dry, Boston, Pacific, and Illinois gulches, and Sargent and Page patches, and situated about two miles from Breckenridge. Its improvements consist of Mayo Ditch, six miles long, conveying water from Indiana Creek to all the mining claims of Mayo property, with a capacity of 600 inches of water. There is also a new ditch, 5,775 feet in length, to convey the excess of water in the spring season. There are two reservoirs in Illinois Gulch, with capacity of 500,000 gallons each, two in Mayo, one of 300,000 gallons capacity, and one of 600,000, the latter new and built last fall at head of Mayo, commanding a large amount of territory, and one reservoir in Negro, 100,000 gallons capacity. In these gulches are 1,200 feet of bed rock flume, riffled the whole distance, and 1,200 feet of iron pipe and one Little Giant hydraulic.

The Georgia property embraces many gulches, patches, and claims. The improvements consist of the Swan River and Georgia Gulch Mining, Ditching and Fluming Company, now belonging to Fuller Placer Mining Company, is 14 miles long, 48 inches on bottom and 70 on top, capacity 2,500 inches; also American Ditch, 6½ miles long, with a capacity of 400 inches; Flume Extension Ditch, 3,465 feet long, 600 inches capacity, side ditches, 2,227½ feet; 5,445 feeding ditches to the great flume; ½ interest in the Pollard Ditch, 2 miles long, 400 inches capacity, and the Stevens Flume, 8 miles long, 200 inches capacity; Mount Guyot Flume, 2 miles long, crossing Divide at Georgia Pass, 400 inches capacity, the only place on this continent where the waters of the Atlantic are diverted to the Pacific slope. On this property are 2,000 feet of bed-rock flume, riffled the whole distance ; also 5,000 feet of iron pipe laid in the different gulches, and 2,000 feet of extra pipe on hand, and six Little Giants in different gulches.

On the same tract of land the Fuller Company owns many valuable lode veins, which, since the approach of the railway to Hall Valley and Fairplay, can be worked to advantage, and which may be still more profitable if the Colorado Central railway is extended as contemplated. Two of these lodes carry from $10 to $170 in silver, from $5 to $10 in gold, and from 24 to 68 per cent. in lead. Others contain gold in varying amounts up to as much as $120 per ton. These are all of a great size and are more or less opened by shafts. Among them are the Emmet, Washington, Pacific, Uncle Sam, Etta, Bunker Hill, Bay State, Independence, and Summit 1, 2, and 3.

Where Geneva and Hall valleys slope eastward, and Montezuma valley dips in the opposite direction, the bald and barren crest of the snowy range is ribbed with silver veins, and extensive mining enterprises are going forward. Some veins extend from the summit down either slope, and are, consequently, partly in Summit county and partly in Clear Creek or Park. Others are wholly in the first or last named section. Geneva district includes many of these, Hall Valley district others, and Montezuma district the remainder. There is a mining camp in a park near the head of Geneva Creek, on the Atlantic or eastern slope, and there is a Geneva settlement in both Park and Clear Creek counties. Most of the mining in that vicinity is done on the Summit county slope. The ores in this cluster are argentiferous galena, gray copper, iron pyrites, zinc blende, and bismide, and carry ruby, brittle, and native silver. The argentiferous bismuth ores are very rich in silver, but are not usually very plentiful. Most lodes of this section carry some gold. Here are the Revenue-Star, the Gilman, United States Treasury, Baltic, Celtic, and others. On Teller and Glacier mountains are the Radical, Chatauqua, Erie, Star of the West, and the mines of the Boston Mining Company. Most mines of this section are worked on the Summit county slope.

These lodes are from 11,000 to 13,000 feet above sea level. Below them the mountain slopes are covered with magnificent forests of pine. During the winter season it is impossible to approach or leave some of the more elevated mines, except on snow-shoes, and a season's supplies are taken in before the snows of the later autumn settle down on peak and valley. Securely housed, in warm and comfortable quarters, the miners continue to tunnel, drift, and blast, regardless of storms without. Several years ago huge avalanches of snow rolled down the mountain sides and swept the buildings and some of the men of the Whale and Champion mines to destruction. Steps have since been taken so that no such disaster will occur again at those localities.

The Revenue Mineral Company has driven the Britannic Tunnel easterly into the range over 1,025 feet, at an elevation of 11,900 feet above sea level. Fourteen lodes have been intersected, of which the paying ones are the Celtic, cut 454 feet from the tunnel's mouth, the Baltic, 674 feet, and the Revenue, 888 feet. From the tunnel, levels have been driven to the right and left along the veins, and shafts, winzes and stopes opened. At the intersection of the Baltic, which is the most extensively developed, a chamber has been excavated, and an engine and machinery planted. That vein has from four to twenty-four inches of ore, worth $170 a ton, mainly gray copper and iron pyrites. The Celtic averages $90 a ton, and carries gray copper, zinc, and some galena. The Revenue has a gray copper vein of similar size to the Baltic, containing from $175 to $200 per ton. Last winter this company constructed a crushing and sampling mill and reduction works for handling its ore, in Geneva Park. A good wagon road had previously been built some ten miles down to Grant, on the Denver and South Park Railway. Captain Sparks is general manager, and A. H. Stockdale superintendent. Forty or fifty men are employed at the mines, and a smaller number at the mills. The Star is a continuation of the Revenue vein in Clear Creek county.

The Leviathan Tunnel Company has driven a tunnel over 800 feet into the same mountain, and nearly a quarter of a mile distant. It has intersected the Green and Blue lodes—both productive of silver, gold, and bismuth, to amounts of from $200 to $1,200 a ton—and will eventually intersect the Congress, Revenue, and U. S. Treasury lodes. The Herman, Belle East, and Belle West, on Glacier Mountain, comprise 4,500 feet on one vein, and are opened by many adits and shafts. The Cashier and Champion mines each comprise half of three parallel veins. They have been producing from fifteen to thirty thousand dollars per annum—the ore averaging about $250 a ton. The Champion is owned by Major E. S. Platt & Co., who have been developing it to the best possible advantage. Both properties are profitable and valuable.

The Montezuma Silver Mining Company is conducting one of the great enterprises of this section. It was organized last year by Eastern men, who had purchased eleven lodes on Glacier and Teller mountains of Senator H. M. Teller and others. The property comprises 11,500 linear feet of veins, divided among the Chatauqua, Danube, Sciota, Itasca, Little Emma, No Name, General Teller, Dunkirk, Erie, Radical, and Radical Junior. Two tunnels are being driven, with machine drills and air compressor, towards the Chatauqua lode. One of them is some five hundred and fifty feet long, and may cut the lode 500 feet deep in August, and under the discovery shaft, which is 200 feet deep. A steam engine and boiler are located at the mouth of the main tunnel. Shafts have been opened on the Teller, Eric, and Radical. A tunnel intersects the latter 277 feet in, from which a drift extends 300 feet. The company has a saw-mill, and recently erected a concentrating mill. This, as well as the mine, is stocked with the most approved machinery. The company has several mill sites, and an abundance of timber and water. The Chatauqua, Radical, Erie, and Teller, the only lodes that have been developed much, are large, and most of them continuous and regular. The ore is mainly galena and gray copper. Ore from a four and a half foot vein in the Chatauqua shaft has yielded $118 a ton, and lots of a few hundred pounds have gone at the rate of over $700 per ton. Specimens are obtained assaying in the thousands. The shaft and levels of the Radical mine average sixty ounces of silver and sixty per cent. lead. Much of the ore product is dressed at the concentrating works. Last year the company built a wagon road of easy grade over Hand-cart Pass to Webster, on the D. & S. P. Railway, twelve miles distant. The route of the proposed extension of the Colorado Central passes through this property, which is about twenty miles distant from Georgetown. General Craig is general manager and George Teal superintendent. The property is being opened as rapidly as possible, and bids fair to be very productive.

The Star of the West is on Teller Mountain, about 1,200 feet north of the Radical lode, and is well developed and productive. It carries more bismuth than any other vein ; silver to the amount of over $200 a ton, and generally more gold than silver. Copper, iron, and lead are also ingredients of the ore. The North Star is on Collier Mountain, and is rich in lead and silver. There are many other lodes in this section that are valuable.

Sts. John is the headquarters and settlement of the Boston Mining Company, which has been operating there for ten or twelve years, and has expended large sums in smelting and other works, mills, machinery, tunnel work, and mining. A splendid tunnel has been driven in Glacier Mountain some 1,500 feet, which has intersected eight veins carrying silver, lead, zinc, and gray copper. One of these is very valuable. Many hundred tons of ore were mined during the past year, and concentrated and smelted at the company works. The Hall Valley Smelting Works have been leased for seven years, and a large product may result from this year's mining operations. From sixty to one hundred men are employed in the mines and works, and in teaming, timber cutting, charcoal burning, etc. Colonel W. L. Candler is at the head of this enterprise, and Captain Ware is mining superintendent. Over 2,000 tons of ore have been mined in some of the years that work has gone on.

Further south the veins of the same mineral belt are poorer in silver and richer in lead. Around the head of Swan river and of French Gulch are numerous galena veins, and here a small smelter was established and set at work in 1874. In the fall of 1878, G. K. Gooding started up the works for the Lincoln City Silver Company, treating ores from the Cincinnati and other veins. The ore handled averaged 63 per cent. lead, and from $12 to $25 in silver. It being demonstrated that money could be made at the business, the works were enlarged, and are said to turn out at present about 8 tons of lead (carrying silver) every twenty-four hours.

The great mineral wealth of Summit county is further shown by the recent valuable carbonate discoveries near Breckenridge. In that locality are deposits and true fissures, many of which are of great size and value, but the majority average 25 ounces in silver per ton, and 45 per cent. lead. Some are pronounced genuine carbonates. Samuel Mishler, one of the original owners of the Caribou mine, and Hal Sayr made the first discoveries of this locality, and among them the only very rich contact deposit. Ore has been smelted from that which yielded as high as 321 and 333 ounces of silver per ton, and assays of over $1,500 were obtained. The average of the mass of ore runs 45 ounces of silver, and 55 per cent. of lead. Surface ore from another claim assays from a few hundred up to $2,500. These carbonate mines are said to show as well according to development as those around Leadville.

The Snake River mining region comprises Peru and Montezuma districts, and lies on the western slope of the Rocky Mountains. Its elevation is from nine to thirteen thousand feet above sea level, and its distance from Georgetown and Ten Mile is from twelve to twenty miles. Gray's Peak and other mountains of great height overlook and partly inclose it, and with its magnificent forests and grassy vales present a landscape grand and picturesque in the extreme. Snake River enters the Blue from the east at nearly the same point where Ten Mile comes in from the south. East of the Montezuma section are the Geneva district mines, located on the crest of the Continental Divide, and on the line of Clear Creek and Summit. The Tariff lode is located on and outcrops a thousand feet above the base of Cooper Mountain. The distance to Georgetown is about fifteen miles and to Montezuma five. The old Argentine Pass road is close by, and the new Georgetown and Leadville stage road, *via* Loveland Pass, is less than a mile distant. Over this the Colorado Central railway extension may be built next season.

The Tariff is considered one of the best lodes in this section, and so good a showing has rarely been made on such limited developments. The fact that it has paid so well, notwithstanding distance and difficulties of transportation to an ore market, and when worked to great disadvantage, are evidences of its value. The width between walls is from three to fifteen feet. A rich vein of solid ore has been opened in the various workings that is usually from four to twelve inches wide and occasionally more, flanked by more or less scattered mineral. The average width of the ore in the main level is from six to eight inches. Two shafts have been sunk, one of which shows eighteen inches of scattered mineral in the bottom, while the other in the same part has a three inch vein of ruby silver, and of course extremely rich. The deepest level is 180 feet below the surface. In this part of the mine is ore assaying 3,400 ounces. The average value per ton of all ore shipped to Georgetown, is-$270. The first class ore averaged 445 ounces, the second class 230, and the third class 109.

The vein is continuous, carries rich ruby silver, gray copper and brittle silver, with argentiferous galena and copper and iron pyrites, and is free from zinc. The inclosing rock is soft, easily broken, and solid enough to stand without timbers. The surrounding country is covered with forest. It is proposed to intersect the lode at a depth of 300 feet with a tunnel 400 feet long, which in its course will cut the large and strong Mississippi vein. Very little stoping has been done in the mine and the quantity of ore exposed is quite large. Heretofore ore was transported to Georgetown on the backs of pack animals, but the new road will permit of its being hauled there at much less expense. With the completion of a railway the ore can be handled still more cheaply, as the mine is near the line of travel. Work was suspended while the estate of a

1 Robinson Cons. Mines.   2 Grand Union Mine.   3 Wheel of Fortune Mine.   4 Sheep Mtn.   5 Elk Mtn.   6 Jack Mtn.   7 Red Mtn.   8 McNulty Mtn.   9 Kokomo.   10 Carbonateville.

TEN MILE.

deceased owner was being settled, but it has lately been purchased by Eastern men, who are working it systematically and to the best advantage.

The Ten Mile District comprises the converging slopes of two parallel ranges of mountains and the intervening valley of Ten Mile Creek. The upper and settled portion of this valley is a mile wide and 11,000 feet above sea level. The westerly range, containing most of the mines, is from 1,000 to 1,500 feet higher, is called the Godey range, and further north is divided by the Grand River. On the east Ten Mile range has several peaks from 13,500 to 14,200 feet high. The creek was called Ten Mile because it was supposed to be ten miles long, but it is in reality seventeen miles in length. The two ranges bordering Ten Mile valley extend northward from the main divide on either side of a depression called Arkansas Pass. This is fourteen miles north of Leadville, and from it, waters flow towards either ocean. About two miles further west the Eagle River starts from Tennessee Pass.

McNulty Gulch empties into Ten Mile Creek near its source and the site of the new town of Carbonateville. It gave its main gold product in 1860, '1, '2, but is still worked by Colonel James McNassar, and turns out from four to seven thousand dollars a summer. Its total yield from 1860 is estimated by old miners at nearly $350,000. Further down Ten Mile are the Follett placer diggings.

This region had been prospected by several different parties, but no high grade ore was found in quantity. In the summer of 1878, George B. Robinson, a leading Leadville merchant, outfitted an old prospector named Charles Jones, and the Seventy-eight, Smuggler, and other mines of the Robinson group were found, and subsequently the Wheel of Fortune and Grand Union. Then people began to move over that way, and to stake off claims sometimes on top of the snow in mid-winter. Leadville and Ten Mile have afforded a rich harvest for surveyors.

In this elevated region snow falls deep and often, and there is usually five or six feet of it on the ground from January to late in April, but nothing could stop the fever-heat of excitement that set in with the present year. Men kept coming in over routes that were terrible to think of ; trees were felled, cabins built, tents pitched on top of the snow, and prospecting carried on irrespective of the difficulties in the way. The lack of surface indications were made

up for by a superabundance of faith. The miner would seek for
unclaimed ground, clear away the snow from a chosen locality, and
then commence to sink in search of deposit or vein. This hazardous style of prospecting was occasionally successful, and a few good
strikes were reported on Sheep, Elk, and Jack Mountains, all of
which greatly advertised the fame of Ten Mile. Town sites were
staked off for a distance of six miles down the valley, and the dull
roar of the miner's blast or the echo of the woodman's axe could be
heard all day long among the stately forests of pine.

The embryo cities of Kokomo, Summit, or Ten Mile, and Carbonateville presented a strange medley of log cabins, tents, and primitive habitations, and the prices of town lots compared in altitude
with the places in which they were located. There were from thirty
to fifty arrivals daily all through the spring, when the melting
snows made the imperfect roads almost impassable. With the
opening of summer Kokomo claimed a population of 1,500, and had
an organized city government, a bank, hotels, stores, saloons, saw-
mills, and the telegraph, where there was not a single settler a few
months before. A newspaper and several smelters are now on the
way there, or already in camp. There are over 3,000 people in the
entire district. Smelting works and a home market for the mining
product is the great necessity.

The Robinson consolidated mines embrace the following locations, mostly of 10.33 acres of surface ground: Seventy-eight,
Little Giant, Big Giant, Undine, Smuggler, Pirate, Checkmate,
Rhone, Ten Mile, G. B. R., and one or two others. They were
discovered or staked in the order they appear from July 16, 1878, to
January 5, 1879, and later. William E. Musgrove, the general manager
for the owner, is developing the entire property with shafts, drifts,
and levels, and has some forty men at work. This is considered
the great mine of this section, and is good enough to give any
district fame and reputation abroad.

The Seventy-eight, Undine, and Smuggler all show the same
large, high grade body of mineral—there being one great incline
vein, pitching thirty degrees below the horizontal, and extending some
distance below nd nearly parallel with the surface of the mountain side. An inc.. ne level has been extended across these and other
locations along the vein, which shows a continuous body of mineral
for the entire distance. Drifts driven at right angles with this

incline show an equally continuous ore-body. The thickness of this vein is from two to eight feet, averaging four feet, and most of it composed of ore containing from $100 to $250 a ton. The second class material assays seventy ounces of silver more or less, and is kept on hand for the smelter soon to be operated for the mine. Last winter and spring, ore was transported over terrible roads, ten miles on runners and seven in wagons, to Leadville.

The only ore removed from the mine is that broken in drifting, and there are said to be hundreds of thousands in sight. Explorations indicate that much of the surface of the great mountain side is underlaid with this immense vein, which is seemingly inexhaustible. When supplied with a smelter the entire property can undoubtedly yield many thousand dollars daily, with a large per cent. of profit. This mine caused the building of the settlement known as Ten Mile, or Summit.

The ore carries galena, zinc blende, iron pyrites, and specular iron. Average lots of ore sold yielded as follows: 260 ounces of silver per ton and 27 per cent. lead; 250 ounces of silver and 50 per cent. lead; several lots 118 to 145 ounces of silver and 20 to 30 per cent. lead, and others at another purchasing point—yielded from 95 to 194 ounces of silver and 15 to 20 per cent. of lead. Very little ore was shipped that contained less than $120 a ton. Ore was first found in the Undine, nine feet below the surface. The formation of this part of the mountain is an indefinite amount of red sandstone, about four feet of shale, thirty feet or less of micaceous sandstone, lime, mineral, crystal lime, and sandstone formation of unknown thickness. In places where this structure maintained the usual depth the ore is forty or fifty feet below the surface.

The Wheel of Fortune mine is located on the summit of Sheep Mountain, overlooking the valleys of Ten Mile and Eagle. It embraces four claims—the Wheel of Fortune, Star of the West, Spare Ground, and Highland Mary. Jacob Hecht discovered mineral nine feet from the surface in the summer of 1878. In time an immense body of ore was opened and daily shipments were made to Leadville last winter and spring. The first 300 feet of drifts were excavated in an unbroken body of mineral and crevice averaging six feet thick, and vast quantities of pay material have since been developed. Twelve feet of crevice was reported at one place, and some have considered the whole as one grand deposit. The first class ore has generally yielded from 80 to 125 ounces of silver per ton, and much of it carries considerable lead. The mineral carries galena and sulphurets, and all the way from a few ounces up to over 200 per ton. Over 500 tons of ore are reported on the dump good enough to smelt. Recently George T. Clark and William Parker have been operating the property.

On the same mountain the Carbonate Company of Col. N. B. Lord, L. S. Ballou, Gage, and others has been sinking a dozen shafts, some of which are reported to show mineral in large amounts. Among other mines are the Black Dragon and Invincible, Big Horn, Baby Mine, Little Fortune, Hidden Treasure, Tip Top, Rattler, Gray Eagle; Idalie, Ballarat, Annie Lisle; Roderick Dhu Ruby, Silver Tip, and Paris.

On the main range is the Grand Union or Lennon mine, one of the first found and most valuable of the district. This is twelve feet wide, with ore carrying from a few ounces in silver up to two hundred. Some very high assays are obtained, and one sack of ore was sold at the rate of fifty cents a pound.

The Iron lode, near the Robinson, is a valuable galena vein, with the top ore converted into carbonates by decomposition a little more extensively than in most neighboring mines. There are many locations well up on the southeast face of this mountain, near the edge of timber line. Among them the Idalie, owned by Robert Emmet, has a vein yielding from eight to three hundred and eleven ounces of silver per ton. During the winter the Silver Tip was discovered by sinking a shaft at random on unclaimed ground. It showed eight feet of ore, carrying from twenty to one hundred ounces of silver per ton, and was very soon sold to a Mr. Hamilton, of St. Louis, for $10,000.

North of Sheep Mountain, and in the same Godey range, are Elk and Jack mountains. Near the mouth of Kokomo Gulch is the town of Kokomo. On Elk Mountain are the White Quail, Climax, Mountain lode, Silver Chain, Elk, and Governor Gilpin, the latter yielding ore worth from sixty to one hundred and forty dollars a ton. Two lodes were found in the town of Kokomo by men while excavating for cellars. One carries galena worth from two hundred dollars down to low figures, and the other copper pyrites. On Jack Mountain is the Rising Sun and Racen lodes. The Frank lode, on Ford Mountain, carries sixty per cent. lead and ninety ounces, more or less, of silver. On the eastern or Ten-mile range the Colorado Springs Company have large amounts of ore.

The Eagle River starts from the vicinity of Tennessee Pass, west of the head of Ten Mile, and flows northwesterly between the Godey and a more westerly range of Mountains into the Grand. It is the newest mining district of the almost unexplored regions of western Colorado. The mountains that enclose it are said to contain many silver veins, some of them assaying from one to eleven hundred ounces. Many prospectors went in there this summer, and in a beautiful park the embryo metropolis Eagle City has been located. West of the head-waters of the Eagle is the Mountain of the Holy Cross, whose eastern face always shows vast beds of snow, which have the form of a cross This snow fills two mammoth ravines. The height of the cross is about 1,500 feet and the arms are each about 700 feet long. The climate of the Eagle river country, and of that beyond, is fine. The river valleys form excellent grazing lands, and lower portions are adapted to farming. The country is full of wild game, and the streams abound in fish.

GRAND COUNTY.

Grand county includes the Middle and North Parks and the slopes of bordering mountains, together with the Rabbit Ear range. Some silver veins have been discovered in the latter, but are generally of low grade. It is claimed that carbonates have been discovered in both parks, but this does not seem to be authenticated. Placer mining is carried on at Willow Creek in Middle Park, and in several localities in North Park, and good returns are reported.

ROUTT COUNTY.

Routt county is the northwestern division of the State. It is composed of mountain ranges and spurs, divided by rivers and bordering valleys well adapted to grazing, and sometimes to farming. There are extensive placer lands on the headwaters of the Snake and Elk rivers, which are operated by several companies and individuals. The principal of these is the International Company of Chicago, near Hanne's Peak, which has been making preparations for work on a large scale for several summers, and is now in shape to push matters. This tract of land is supplied with great flumes and ditches, miles in length, and with hydraulics, which command an immense amount of paying gravel. About $10,000 was taken

ISLAND OR SPECTRE MONUMENT—WESTERN COLORADO.

out last season in a few weeks' time. The Elk river ditch and flume is 17 miles long, and two other ditches combined are 6½ miles long. Three giant hydraulics are used, one with 1,300 feet of iron pipe and

SUMMIT OF ITALIAN MOUNTAIN.

another with 500 feet. A bed rock flume is being run. In drifting and washing a dike of porphyry and 170 feet of slate has been passed through. There are over 1,000 acres of gravel land, from **40** to 60 men are employed, and probably $60,000 will be obtained this year. Wages are $2.75 a day. In this section of country are Steamboat Springs and Hayden.

GUNNISON COUNTY.

Gunnison county is probably the largest in the State, and embraces more than 10,000 square miles of territory. North of it is Summit county ; Lake and Chaffee bound it on the east, the San Juan region on the south, and Utah on the west. Noble rivers and countless streams flow from and between its mountains, and there is considerable good grazing and tillable land outside of the Indian reservation. Gunnison got its name from the main river of that section, whose massive cañons are among the wonders of the world, and the river was so called from Lieut. Gunnison of the regular army, who was killed by Indians in that locality many years ago.

This until recently unknown land beyond the great Sawatch range, or Continental Divide, has been the scene of a great mining excitement in this eventful year of 1879. Rumors of discoveries of carbonates had been circulated the fall before, and the distance of the locality was enough to fascinate the adventurous prospector, even if there was no great evidence of mineral wealth. The rush that set in there late in the spring from Leadville compared with the wildest previous stampedes. To reach the headwaters of the Gunnison, it was necessary to cross a lofty range of mountains where the passes were filled with gigantic snow-banks. In one place an immense deposit of snow was tunneled and cut through in order to reach the desired land of promise ahead of those who would come with the summer.

Conflicting reports have come from the new districts of Taylor River, Ohio Creek, Tin Cup, Crested Butte, the Elk Mountains, and other localities, as is always the case with new mining sections, but one thing is evident, mineral veins have been found. How rich or important they will prove remains to be seen. Hundreds of men who have gone there are exploring, several settlements have been made, and Virginia City, Hillerton, and Gothic City are struggling for pre-eminence. A newspaper has already found its way there. The town of Gunnison is the county seat, and has a smelter. The latest reports indicate that valuable silver discoveries have been made.

CHAPTER XXIV.

PARK COUNTY —GENERAL FORMATION—GOLD LODES AND PLACERS—
THE SILVER BELT OF THE MOSQUITO RANGE—MOUNTS LINCOLN
AND BROSS—MINING ABOVE THE CLOUDS—ETERNAL FROST AND
SNOW—THE MOOSE, DOLLY VARDEN, SACRAMENTO, AND OTHERS—
THE HIGHEST MINE IN NORTH AMERICA—THE BULLION PRODUCT
—THE PLACERS OF THE PLATTE—THE RAILWAY.

Park county occupies the South Park region and portions of the surrounding ranges of mountains. It is east of Lake and Summit counties, and west of the Snowy Range, south of Jefferson and Clear Creek counties, and west of the Pike's Peak section. The elevation of the park, which embraces nearly 1,000 square miles, is 9,000 to 10,000 feet above sea level. The outlaying mountains rise some thousands of feet higher. The Mosquito range includes Mount Lincoln, with an elevation of 14,297 feet above sea level, and in a spur of the range to the northward are Mounts Evans and Rosalie, 14,330 and 14,340 respectively. The climate is cool but pleasant in summer, but the winters are long and severe.

This region is rich in gold and silver. The placers have yielded largely and are again doing so, but in a less degree. Up to the time of the silver discoveries in 1871 the gold lodes and placers had produced $2,500,000, principally obtained prior to 1866. The silver deposits are however of vastly greater value and extent. They did not produce much until 1873, but have yielded over $3,000,000.

The argentiferous riches of the Mosquito range are found in limestone and sometimes porphyry formations—a different condition from that existing among the northern mining districts of Colorado. Instead of true fissure veins, deposits, chambers and pockets of mineral are found often between two formations. These deposits carry galena, gray copper, zinc blende, and a quartz gangue, when located in the higher sandstone, and galena, gray copper and silver glance, and usually a heavy spar gangue in the higher limestone of Mount Lincoln. Far above timber line and vegetation, from

twelve to fourteen thousand feet above sea level, mining is successfully conducted in winter and summer.

The production of Park county, estimating the yield of the first
thirteen years at two and a half millions of gold, was as follows:

1859–71 inclusive..	$2,500,000 00	1875	$716,258 62
1872	250,000 00	1876	550,044 84
1873	459,000 00	1877	616,459 32
1874	596,392 00	1878*	426,698 00

Total to 1879.................................$6,114,852 78

Total gold, $3,050,200; silver, $3,014,652.78; copper, $36,500;
lead, $13,500.

The first silver mine that attracted attention was the Moose in
1871. The fall of that year saw a small army of prospectors on
Mounts Bross and Lincoln, and when the snows disappeared in the
following summer this was the great centre of excitement. The
villages of Alma and Dudleyville grew from the development of
these silver mines, and smelting works were soon in operation at
both places.

The active ore-treating works of Park county embrace the Moose
chlorodizing-amalgamating establishment at Dudleyville, a stamp
mill at Montgomery, and dressing works at Alma; there are sampling
mills, such as Kendrick's, for the Golden works, and others. The
Boston and Colorado Smelting Company do not smelt ores at Alma
now, but buy, sample, and ship to Argo. Grose's wet concentrating
works, built at Alma in 1876, dress 10 tons of ore daily. A quartz
mill in the same building is running on ores from the Satisfaction,
Phillips, and other lodes.

The Park mineral belt is about 35 miles long, and perhaps 14
wide. The following silver lodes of the Mosquito Range have been
worked in recent years, some steadily and others at intervals: Sacramento, Moose, Dolly Varden, Russia, Ford, Security, Hiawatha,
London, Lone Star, Guinea Pig, Ten-Forty, Silver Lake, North
Star, Ocean Wave, D. H. Hill, Spring Cat, Danville, Buckskin,
Mono, Hidden Treasure, Forest Queen, Keystone, Badger, Occi-

* Exclusive of this a large amount of ore awaited shipment at the close of the
year at the B. & C. branch smelting works, which discontinued work early in the
fall. The valuation will appear in the product of 1879.

COLORADO.

dental, Lioness, Milwaukee, Danville (on Lincoln), Ford, Musk Ox, Buckeye, Mammoth (Mt. Lincoln), Schuyler, Kansas, Empress, Present Help, Gertrude, Hidden Treasure, Hunter, No End, Champaign, and Joe Chaffee; also, the Wheeler and other gold lodes near Montgomery, the Nova Zembla on Quandary Mountain, carrying gold and silver, and the Phillips, Orphan Boy, and other gold veins at Buckskin. Many other silver lodes have been worked.

The Moose has been the most productive mine in Park county. It was first opened in 1871, and yielded $21,768 in the first forty days. With the summer of 1872 mining was resumed and has been continued ever since. Dudley, Gill and McNab purchased the mine at an early date, and the Moose Mining Company was afterwards organized. The property consists of one hundred acres of surface ground, including twenty-one claims, mostly patented, and roasting and amalgamating works (with two furnaces) at Dudleyville. The capital stock is two millions, in ten dollar shares. The yield in 1872 was $105,000, and had exceeded $600,000 up to 1876. A company statement shows that the yield for the year ending March 31, 1877, was nearly 1,393 tons of ore, returning $164,425.62, with an assay coin value of $237,485; average assay of ore, 144 ounces; average price received $110.85. There were 650 tons of ore on hand. To get this 2,043 tons of ore, 6,898½ tons of rock were broken altogether, which included driving 2,122½ feet of levels or tunnels, and 333 fathoms of stopes. The Moose, like other mineral bodies of this section, is a series of deposits, some of them of great size. These are opened by tunnels, drifts, or stopes. From sixty to seventy men are usually employed, at $3 a day or by contract. The total yield of silver for less than eight years up to 1879 must have exceeded $1,150,000.

The Dolly Varden mine ranks next to the Moose in production and size of deposits, and often surpasses that mine in richness of ore. It was discovered in 1872, and has since then made a fortune for its owners, George W. Brunk and Assyria Hall, or the Hall and Brunk Silver Mining Company. The mine has paid from the time it was opened, and is remarkable for the large proportion of ore returning from three to seven hundred dollars a ton. The last reports from the mine show that the first-class ore averaged 624 ounces of silver per ton, the second class 313 ounces, and the third class 206 ounces.

The yield of the Dolly Varden in four years, up to June 27, 1878, was as follows :

YEAR.	TONS OF ORE SOLD.	PRODUCT IN OUNCES OF SILVER.	VALUE.
1874..........................	$159\frac{1190}{2000}$	15,061	$18,173 00
1875...........................	$233\frac{214}{2000}$	28,666	34,401 00
1876............	461	61,801	74,161 00
1877 (six months)..............	$66\frac{1886}{2000}$	Receipts.	19,070 96
1877–8 (fiscal year).............	$299\frac{1071}{2000}$	Receipts.	80,624 41
Total.................	1,219	....	$226,430 37

The figures given above for 1877 and the first half of 1878 are the receipts for the ore sold, and not its actual value. The ore probably yielded $45 a ton more than was paid for it, or $16,470 more than given above, bringing the total yield to June 27, 1878, up to $246,575.78. The total yield to August, 1879, probably exceeds $300,000. The profits on the first half of 1877 were $12,124.69 on $19,070.96 of receipts.

During the year ending June 27, 1878, the Dolly Varden ore sales returned $80,624, of which $63,164.02 were clear profit. Few mines can make such a showing. More ore has been turned out this year than ever before, the yield running five and six tons a day, which averaged 257 ounces of silver per ton one month, and nearly 300 another, for all classes combined. Twenty men have been worked, and from three to eight thousand dollars has been cleared monthly. The expenditures for the year ending June 27, 1878, went in the following ways: Labor, $11,005.67; supplies, $2,807.30; ore hauling, and packing, $1,147.96; hauling timber, wood, and supplies up to mine, $974.52; powder and fuse, $462.75; paid for lode and placer claims, $575; surveying, etc., $184.50; lumber, $241.69; assaying, $61.

Mount Lincoln, that great natural monument, named in honor of President Lincoln, lies north of Mount Bross and in the Mosquito or Park range, just south of its point of union with the Continental Divide. Its summit is 14,297 feet above sea level, being one of the

22

highest peaks in the country. The mountain is so situated regarding the various ranges and parks and valleys that the view is probably as fine as North America can afford. There are a large number of mines on Mount Lincoln, some of them paying handsomely. The ores are of lower average grade than on Mount Bross, but the Ford and Musk Ox have turned out very rich mineral. The ores carry galena, gray copper, sulphurets, brittle silver, and copper pyrites. The Russia has produced the most silver, and since it was well opened, early in 1876, it has yielded something like $50,000 per annum. The Danville, 1, 2, and 3, has been extensively and profitably worked for several years. The Gertrude, Mossvale, Present Help, and those mentioned above are on the north spur of Mount Lincoln. The Present Help is 14,200 feet above the level of the sea, and is the highest mine in North America. In Montgomery district are the Chicago, Wheeler, and Atlantic. The last two have yielded a great deal of free milling gold quartz.

In Buckskin Gulch the Ten Forty and other mines are worked. In Mosquito district is the Forest Queen, in which a tunnel is driven from which ore is shipped that has milled as follows, per ton : 158 ounces, 221 ounces, 489 ounces, 541 ounces, 651 ounces, 690 ounces. The Champaign is another valuable lode. The Joe Chaffee, carrying silver and gold, is said to be paying well. The London mine is in this district. The Kansas is one of the leading mines of this section. It shows large bodies of rich ore and pays good profits. Several mines are worked on Mount Bross besides the Moose, Dolly Varden, and Saddle, and others are idle.

The Phillips, in Buckskin, is the great gold lode of this section. This was discovered in 1862, and in a few short years produced something like $300,000. Stamp mills were running in full blast, and a lively town was in existence when the Phillips and Orphan Boy were yielding their thousands weekly. Some of the surface ore compared with the best in Gilpin County. When iron and copper pyrites were reached, work stopped, because the mill men of those days did not make a success of handling them. Some work has been done in recent times and preparations are now being made to operate the property on a large scale. About 1,200 feet of the lode was opened by shafts, open cuts, and levels, which showed the immense width between walls of from 25 to 40 feet. J. Q. A. Rollins owns a large part of the property.

The Orphan Boy is about a mile southwest, and is said to be on the same vein as the Phillips. In size, character, and past productiveness these lodes are much alike. J. W. Smith, of Denver, made his fortune here in 1862-3. The total yield of the Orphan Boy is reported at $250,000. Locations between this and the Phillips, claimed to be on the same vein, are now worked.

Hall Valley is in the northwest corner of Park county, and heads at the crest of the main range. The lower eight miles of the valley, including the steep mountain slopes on either side, are covered with splendid forests, and on the range itself are the great Whale and Leftwick silver mines. The Hall Valley Company operated these mines and expended large sums of money in building smelting works, a connecting tramway, and in other ways. The Whale is a large vein, and is said to be paying.

The Sacramento, near the head of Sacramento Gulch, and not far from Horseshoe Mountain, is one of the most valuable mines in the country. It was discovered in October, 1878, and the quantity and value of the ore and its supposed wealth in carbonates caused quite an excitement for a time. The ore bears some resemblance to those of both Leadville and Mount Bross mines, and the deposit resembles the Moose. An early shipment of 9½ tons sold for $1,346, and at the same time 5½ tons brought $303. The yield of the mine for March, 1879, is reported at the handsome figure of $39,000, and the cost of mining was very small. Toby, Dwelle, Le Duc, and others were the owners. No figures of recent production are at hand, but the great size of the horizontal mineral deposit of the various claims comprising the Sacramento mine, indicate an enormous production hereafter. Other claims have been located and opened near by.

The placers of the Platte are said to have yielded $1,750,000 altogether, mostly in a few years succeeding 1859. The early mining camps of Fairplay, Tarryall, and Hamilton have already been referred to in the historical narrative. Thayer's placer operations in the Platte at Fairplay are the most extensive in the county. The Fairplay placer property embraces five miles of ground along the stream with dams, and miles of ditches and flumes. Nearly a hundred Chinamen are employed under the head man, Lin Sou, in Thayer's leased ground, and under his management.

The Tarryall placer claim of Hall, Barrett & Rische has a very rich streak in an old channel of the stream lately discovered. The

twenty-five or thirty Chinamen working there are each making from
$10 to $20 dollars a day. Mills, Hodges & Co. have worked
a large placer claim on the Platte river at Alma. This has yielded
from $12,000 to $13,000 per annum, or some $65,000 altogether since
they took hold of it, and now pays better than ever.

In the southwestern portion of South Park are saline springs of
great strength and volume. Salt works were established there years
ago by the owner, J. Q. A. Rollins. Now that the railroad is in
the park, these works will have an opportunity to ship their product
to a market at living rates. Tests show these waters to contain
from 12 to 16 per cent. of salt and water.

Railway communication will work greatly to the advantage of
Park county. It is likely to reduce expenditures nearly one-third.
The Denver and South Park railway was completed to the vicinity
of Fairplay this summer, and is being extended on to Leadville.

CHAFFEE COUNTY.

Chaffee county was set off from Lake county last winter, taking
with it the old county seat, Granite. It embraces a large portion of
the upper Arkansas valley and is south of Lake county. Gulch and
placer mining is carried on in Cash Creek and along the Arkansas
River, and lode mining near Granite, and in the Sawatch range.
The oldest and best developed silver lodes are in Alpine district.
The Tilden lode on Boulder Mountain has been the most prominent
so far. It has a twenty inch vein, largely of ore, mining up in the
hundreds. With more extensive developments its production would
undoubtedly be very large. From ten to twenty men have usually
been at work, and quantities of ore have been shipped. In
Grizzly Cañon are the Deborah and Evening Star, Virginia, Lillie,
and Black Swan lodes, and the Lake View Chrysolite tunnels. The
Hortense mine is one of the leading properties, and is said to produce large amounts of rich ore. The Riggins, Murphy, and other
mines are worked steadily and are of recognized value. The Alpine
Silver Mining Company was recently organized in New York on a
number of lodes, some of which are producing ore as follows:
Yellow Jacket, 84 ounces of silver and 9 ounces of gold per ton;
Amna, 100 ounces of silver; extension of the Captain Jack, 333
ounces of silver, 106 of silver and 1½ of gold, 102 ounces silver;
Smuggler, 102 and 62; Grand Central, 145 of silver, 2½ of gold.
Several other mineral districts are being opened near Twin Lakes,
Cottonwood Creek, and South Arkansas.

CHAPTER XXV.

THE SAN JUAN REGION—RIO GRANDE AND HINSDALE COUNTIES—
AMONG THE GREAT SOUTHERN MINES—LAKE CITY AND SUMMIT
DISTRICTS—BULLION STATISTICS OF THE SAN JUAN COUNTRY—
NARRATIVE OF GENERAL AND INDIVIDUAL OPERATIONS.

The San Juan country or region embraces the southwestern portion of Colorado. Under this name are included the mountainous counties of Hinsdale, Rio Grande, San Juan, La Plata, Conejos and Ouray; and San Luis Park, with the counties of Saguache and Costilla, are often classed under the same head. Here is an area of some 15,000 square miles, or more territory than is included in any one of the States of New Jersey, New Hampshire, or Vermont, with Delaware thrown in. West of San Luis Park is one mass of mountains, thrown together in the most chaotic confusion.

These mountains contain thousands of silver veins, many of them of huge size, and some of great richness. There are also gold lodes and placers. The Rocky Mountain range extends to the westward in this region. The silver belt is from twenty to forty miles wide, and perhaps eighty miles long in an air line. The rugged and almost impassable character of the mountains and their vast extent, and the heavy snows and long winters, have acted as serious drawbacks to growth and development. There is probably more country standing on edge in this section than anywhere else beneath the sun. Until recently no work was prosecuted in the winter seasons, except on a very few mines and on tunnels. It took years to build roads to the most important points—trails or foot-paths being the only thing previously afforded. The approach of the railway and the completion of many smelting works are bringing the San Juan country forward.

After the expulsion of the Baker expedition of 1860 by the Indians, few white men ventured among the San Juan mountains, and it remained a "terra incognita" for many years. Adnah French is considered the pioneer. After him came Miles T. Johnson, who dis-

covered the Little Giant gold mine in 1870, and others. The outside world knew little of what these isolated prospectors were doing
until the Little Giant mine began to yield in 1872. When Major
Hamilton was operating it in 1873, a great contest for possession
arose. It yielded $22,000 in a few years.

MINERS' PACK TRAIN IN THE SAN JUAN MOUNTAINS.

Most of the San Juan region was formerly included in the county
of Conejos. After several mining districts had been located and
settled, the counties of La Plata, Rio Grande, and Hinsdale were
created, and afterwards those of San Juan and Ouray. As many of
the names of towns, rivers, and mountains in this section are of

Spanish origin, the pronunciation of some of them are given—the name appearing first and the pronunciation and definition immediately after:

Conejos, Kon-à-hos, rabbits.

Costilla, Kos-téel-ya or Cos-tée-ya, ribs.

Rio Grande, Re-o Gránd-a, grand river.

Hermosilla, Her-mos-èel-ya, beautiful.

Huerfano, Whár-fan-oh, orphan.

La Plata, Lah Plát-ah, the silver.

Saguache, Sa-wash.

San Juan, San Whón, Saint John.

San Miguel, San Me-géel, Saint Michael.

San Luis, San Lú-e, Saint Louis.

Santa Fe, San-ta Fa, Holy Faith.

Ouray, Yu-rá.

Ulé, Yu-lá.

Uncompahgre, Un-com-pàr-gra.

The San Juan region had produced, prior to 1879, as near as can be ascertained:

Silver	$823,561
Gold	416,000
Lead	115,000
Total	$1,354,561

The yield prior to 1876 had been about $102,000 in gold and $75,000 in silver. The subsequent product is given below. A portion of the yield credited to Lake City came from San Juan and Ouray mines, the ores being treated in Lake City.

1876.

San Juan County, Greene & Co. shipped lead bullion valued at	$106,000
Hinsdale County, Crooke & Co. shipped silver ore, bought and concentrated	40,000
Gulch, bar, and lode gold and other silver ores shipped, La Plata, etc	15,000
Rio Grande County, Summit mines, stamp mill gold	65,000
Gold ores shipped	30,000
Sangre de Cristo range stamp mill and gulch gold, and elsewhere	10,000
Total	$266,000

1877.

	TONS ORE.	TONS BULLION.	COIN VALUE.
Gold from Summit district, Rio Grande County.............................	6,000	....	$95,000
Gold from placers and veins elsewhere	....	...	10,000
Silver ore shipped from various districts.................................	....	....	15,000
Silver bars, Van Gieson, Hinsdale County..................	400	....	35,000
SILVER LEAD BULLION.			
Crook's Smelters, Hinsdale County...	1,500	300	54,415
Ocean Wave Smelter...........	250	120	24,057
Greene's Silverton Smelter. San Juan County	1,400	400	141,000
Smelter, Ouray County.......	30	....	3,000
Total...........	9,580	820	$377,472

1878.

Greene & Co.'s Smelter, Silverton, 350 tons bullion.....................$142,256 00
Lixiviation Works, Cement Creek, San Juan........................... 3,000 00
Animas Mining and Smelting Works, Niegold Concentrating Works, 100 tons, San Juan........... .... 15,000 00
Dacotah & San Juan Works, Animas Forks Conc. Works, San Juan....... 5,000 00
St. L. & S. J. Company, Ouray... 19,320 00
Windham Smelter, Ouray 11,430 00
Norfolk & Ouray Works, Ouray..... .... 8,000 00
Crooke Works, Lake City............... .... 93,208 00
Van Gieson Works, Lake City............................... .... 6,400 00
Ocean Wave Smelter, Lake City................................... 56,483 00
Summit district, gold, Rio Grande............................... 80,000 00
San Miguel & Sangre de Cristo placers................................ 9,000 00
Ores shipped elsewhere............... .... 85,000 00

Total............................ ....$534,089 00
Increase over 1877.......... .... 164,016 48

In the above is included a small amount of ore from the new silver mines of Spanish Peaks, 20 tons going in one shipment.

The lead yield, allowing the eastern price of $80 a ton, exceeded $20,000 prior to 1877. That year gave about $35,000 worth, and

1878 gave about $60,000 worth. Some of the figures given in the above tables are estimated.

RIO GRANDE COUNTY.

Rio Grande county is composed partly of plain and partly of mountain. Del Norte, the main town and county seat, is located on the Rio Grande where it leaves the mountains and enters the plains of San Luis Park. There are several mining districts, but the only one that has produced much is the gold-bearing portion of the Summit Mountains, which has yielded over $400,000 to date.

The richest gold district of Southern Colorado is that of South Mountain in the Summit Range, twenty-six miles south of Del Norte and nearly 12,000 feet above sea level. The great drawbacks are a severe climate, heavy snows, and the altitude—a divide of 13,000 feet must be crossed to reach Summit. The summers are short and the roads are almost impassable from snow or mud during most of the year. But the gold is there, and that has built a town and attracted miners, capitalists, and stamp mills.

In 1873 it began to be noised abroad that Peterson and Brandt had made a wonderful discovery in the far-off southern mountains, and the free gold quartz and nuggets they exhibited created no little excitement in Pueblo and Denver. In the short summers of 1874-5 hundreds of prospectors went there, and locations were made until the whole mountain was covered with pre-emptions—all in the endeavor to secure a piece, however small, of the precious ground. It appeared to be a vast mass of " float ore " or " slide," and for a time was considered one huge mountain of quartz. Subsequent developments show veins, and that it is not simply a deposit or a "blow out." The country rock is a kind of porphyry. The main lode or ledge runs diagonally across the mountain, south thirty degrees east, and numerous spurs and feeders put into it. The claims were generally located north and south—being made before the " slide " or float ore had been entered enough to determine the true course of the vein. The locations on it are those of the Little Annie, Odin, Golden Queen, and San Juan Consolidated companies.

As usual with prospectors, Peterson and Brandt had no money to build stamp-mills, although they had what appeared to be a mountain of " free gold" quartz. In 1874 they transported sacks of ore on the backs of mules down to Del Norte (there was no road then),

THE LITTLE ANNIE MINE.

and from there sent it by teams to Cañon and thence by rail to Golden, three hundred and fifty miles away. One lot of four tons sold for $1,660. As soon as the snows had disappeared in (June) 1875, a five-stamp mill was brought in, and soon after W. H. Van Gieson brought in a mill. After that the Crooke Brothers of New York secured a controlling interest in the Little Annie mine and put up a ten-stamp mill. A United States signal station was established here two or three years ago. Elevation, over 11,500 feet.

A very complete and elaborate report of C. E. Robins, treasurer of the Little Annie Company, shows that the mine had yielded gold retorts to the value of $164,641.54 up to September 1, 1878—taken out in less than two years of actual work subsequent to 1875. The above does not include ores shipped away. The production still keeps up, and probably has exceeded $300,000 from time of discovery to August, 1879. F. J. Peterson is superintendent. The Golden Queen mine has yielded quite an amount of gold.

The San Juan Consolidated Company has been managed by Judge Thomas M. Bowen. It embraces a large portion of the auriferous part of South Mountain, near the Little Annie, and has a thirty-stamp mill. This property embraces an enormous amount of low grade quartz, averaging $7 a ton, which the company are preparing to mine and mill.

HINSDALE COUNTY.

Hinsdale county is the most easterly of the important silver districts of San Juan. Its metropolis is Lake City, dating from 1874–5, located at the junction of Hensen Creek with the Lake Fork of the Gunnison. Here are two smelting works in operation—Crooke & Co. and the Ocean Wave — the Crooke concentrating works and a chlorination and lixiviation mill—the latter not run steadily. The location of the town is grand and beautiful and resembles that of Georgetown. There are numberless silver lodes in the lofty mountains that rise almost perpendicularly for a half mile or a mile on every side—many of them worked extensively.

Promising as were the numerous discoveries of the San Juan country in 1873–4–5, they were generally of no immediate benefit to their owners, on account of the distance from an ore market, wagon roads and railways. The region labored under peculiar disadvantages. It was made up of almost inaccessible mountain ranges, and

at that time was so remote from railways that capitalists and mill
men were not inclined to investigate its mineral wealth. The
pioneers who had been making discoveries of rich veins were too
poor to build works for the extraction of the precious metals, and
it cost too much to get ore to market to admit of attempting it,

LAKE CITY.

unless it was wonderfully rich and money was at hand to defray
shipping expenses.

This was the condition of affairs when the Crooke brothers—the
first eastern capitalists that showed their appreciation of the region

by putting their money into it—began to buy mines and erect mills. They were conducting a smelting business in New York city, and inspection and contact with its ores begat that confidence in its worth that subsequent experience has in no wise abated. The results of their investments in the Little Annie and Golden Queen mines and mills in the Summit Mountain gold district induced them to look further.

An investigation of the Lake City silver district caused them to erect a concentrating mill there. This separated the silver-bearing mineral from the gangue, or waste rock of the ore. The miner then had his value in one ton of concentrates instead of having it distributed among five or ten tons as before. This was an important item where it cost more to get ore to a market than it did to treat it after it reached there.

The Ute and Ulé mines were purchased late in 1876 and the new owners then erected quarters for workmen and shaft and ore houses for the mine. The next spring contracts were let for sinking shafts and running drifts, and for the construction of works for the treatment of the ore. The stack furnace was not completed till near the close of the season, but 2,000 tons of ore had been mined and concentrated, and the dressed ore sent to New York. It yielded a net profit of twelve dollars per ton. The smelting works were completed so that reduction, parting and refining began in July, 1878. Up to this time Crooke & Co. had expended over $400,000 on their mines, works, and other property of this locality.

The Ute mine is situated well up on a mountain, and the Ulé is located at the foot of the same. The patented surface ground of each is 1,500 feet long by 300 wide, and both are in Galena mining district near Lake City. Up to the time when these mines were purchased, the Ute mine had produced 250 tons of ore from a shaft thirty feet deep, and the Ulé 200 tons from a shaft twenty feet deep. The ore is galena and gray copper in the Ute vein, and is richer in the lower workings than near the surface. Beginning with 20 ounces of silver per ton, it has increased to from 40 to 90. The percentage of lead is about forty. In the mine are large and heavy masses of gray copper. There are three or four shafts connected by levels, embracing many hundreds of feet of workings altogether. The Ute has from 30 inches to 7 feet of vein matter, regular well defined walls, a northeast and southwest direction, and a northwest dip ;

THE CROOKE SMELTING AND CONCENTRATING WORKS NEAR LAKE CITY.

average yield of all ore reduced, 25 ounces of silver and from $3 to $5 per ton in gold and 40 per cent. of lead. Later returns raise the silver to 65 ounces a ton, and reduce the lead to 30 per cent.; 50 tons daily can probably be mined when steam hoisting works and pumps are used. The ore reserves are large.

The Ulé has the same direction and dip as the Ute. The ore is galena and gray copper, and carries from $5 to $10 in gold, from $30 to $550 in silver per ton, and forty per cent. lead. In shaft number one the vein is five feet wide, and in drift number two from thirty to sixty inches. It is proposed to run drift number two clear under the mountain and as far as the vein goes, and to cross by a tunnel 300 feet over to the Ute which would be cut at a depth of 1,000 feet. Both mines would then have drainage and an ore channel. About 400 tons of ore came from shaft number one in sinking.

The works and mill site have the finest water power in the State, and, owing to the location, one thousand horse power can be made available. The Crooke Mining and Smelting Company, owning these mines and works, is officered by president, John N. Goodwin, ex-governor of Arizona; vice-president, Thomas F. Mason; secretary and treasurer, W. Hart Smith; and the above and Lewis Crooke, E. J. Granger, William Spence, and S. W. Hill, trustees.

The Dolly Varden lode is on Hensen Creek, and carries a very rich vein, often four to ten inches. During the year 1878 considerable ore was sold that yielded from $225 to $1,100 a ton. It was sold last fall to ex-Governor Henry Cooke, of Washington, James L. Hill, Major Hurlbert, and J. R. Magruder, who are pushing work thereon. The George Washington lode has ore worth hundreds of dollars. Among other lodes of note are the Big Casino, Belle of the East, Belle of the West, Cora, East Boston, Little Chief.

The following tables will give an idea of the characteristics of Hinsdale county lodes. Such statements, however, do not always show the comparative size and value, as one lode may carry its ore in bunches, pockets, or short chimneys, while another is continuous vertically and horizontally, and consequently carries vastly more ore and money in the aggregate. More than this, the richest veins do not insure the largest products or profits; quantity of mineral plays an equally important part. Most figures for yields per ton on both Hinsdale and Ouray counties refers to ore after being assorted, and not just as it lays in the vein.

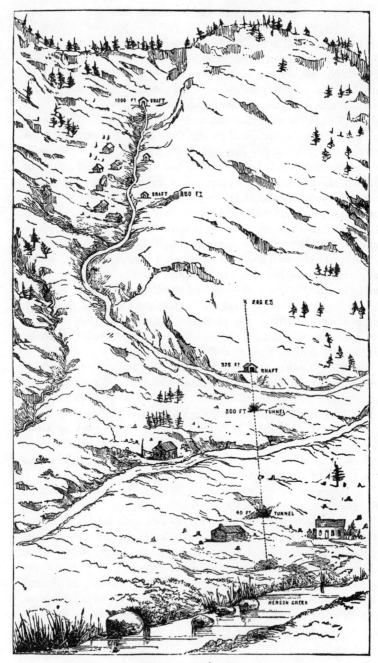

THE UTE AND ULÉ MINES.

HINSDALE COUNTY.—Some of the Leading Lodes.

Name of Lode.	Location.	Width.	Development.	Character.	Yield, Per Ton.	Owners.
Accidental	Galena District	Lode, 4 ft., pay, 10 in.	Well developed	Carb. of copper and sulph. of silver	Average of ore sold, 350 oz.	John F. Dodds. W. N. Ewing. T. J. Peter, et al.
American	Galena District	Lode, 7 ft., pay, vein, 5 to 10 in.	3 drifts, 20, 25, 30 ft. each	Gray copper and galena	100 to 600 oz. silver	J. George. J. N. Akers.
Belle of the East	Near Lake City	Lode, 4 ft., pay, 15 in.	Shaft, 100 ft., levels, 110 and 80 ft. each	Gray copper and galena		J. W. McFerran. L. Whipple. Wm. Peck.
Belle of the West	Near Lake City	Lode, 5 ft., pay, vein, 10 in.	4 shafts; drift, 585 ft.	Gray copper and galena	85 oz. silver	Samuel Wade. Otto Mears.
Belle of the West No. 2	Hotchkiss Mountain, Lake District.	Lode, 3 ft., vein, 15 in.	Drift, adit	Gray copper and galena	80 oz. silver	Jos. Chambers. Reilly & Co
Big Casino	Galena Gulch, Galena District.	Lode, 3 ft.	Shaft, 50 ft.; tunnel, 90 ft.	Gray copper and galena	65 oz. silver	J. J. Holbrook. W. T. Forrest.
Cresus	Capitol Mountain, Galena District.	Lode, 7 ft. wide, vein, 28 in.	Levels and shafts.	Gray copper, iron, and copper pyrites.	60 oz. silver	Mesler & Co
Dolly Varden	Copper Mountain, Galena District.	Lode, 4 ft. wide, vein, 10 in.	Shafts and levels.	Gray copper and copper pyrites.	$100 up to many thousands	Henry Cooke, J. L. Hill & Co.
Gray Copper	Alpine Creek, Lake District.	Lode, 5 ft., vein, 3 in. to 3 ft.	Tunnel, 25 ft., drift, 70 ft.	Tellurium, galena, and gray copper	200, oz. silver	G. Crummy. J. Williams. W. Richards. H. Musgrave.
Hidden Treasure	Ute Hill	Lode, 4 ft., vein, 18 in.	Tunnel, 340 ft.	Gray copper and galena		J. S. Hough.

HINSDALE COUNTY—Some of the Leading Lodes.

Name of Lode.	Location.	Width.	Development.	Character.	Yield, Per Ton.	Owners.
Hotchkiss	Lake fork of Gunnison, Lake District	Vein, 14 in.	Tunnel, 120 ft.; tunnel, 80 ft.	Gold, silver, tellurium and gray copper	400 oz. silver	F. C. Peck. M. S. Taylor. J. H. Shaw. George Wilson.
Melrose	Galena District	Lode, 4 ft., vein, 20 in.	Adit, 30 ft.	Galena and gray copper	400 oz. silver	Franklin & Co.
Ocean Wave and Extension	Red Rover Mountain, Galena District	Lode, 4 ft., vein, 2 ft.	4 tunnels, 60, 220, 300 and 420 ft. in length	Galena and gray copper	$50 to $200	Ocean Wave Mining and Smelting Company.
Plutarch	Hotchkiss Mountain, Lake District	Lode, 3 ft., vein, 18 in.	3 shafts, 100, 75 and 50 ft.; tunnel, 200 ft.	Gray copper and brittle silver	190 oz. silver	Nutting, Chambers & Co.
Ulé	Henson Creek	Vein, 30 in. to 5 ft.	Shafts and tunnels well opened	Galena and gray copper, silver, lead, and brittle gold	$30 to $550	Crooke & Co.
Ute	Galena District	30 in. to 7 ft.	Shafts and tunnels well opened	Galena and gray copper	$20 to $100	Crooke & Co.
Wave of the Ocean	Red Rover Mountain, Galena Dist.	Lode, 4 ft., vein, 2 ft.	Well opened with tunnels and shafts	Galena and gray copper	$50 to $200	Ocean Wave Mining and Smelting Company.

CHAPTER XXVI.

THE SAN JUAN REGION—MOUNTAINS RIBBED WITH SILVER VEINS—
SAN JUAN, OURAY, AND LA PLATA COUNTIES—SILVERTON AND
OTHER POINTS—THE PLACERS OF THE SAN MIGUEL—GOLD AND
SILVER MINING.

SAN JUAN COUNTY.

San Juan county is the best opened mineral section of southwestern
Colorado, and yet the continuous developments and discoveries that
are going on are evidences that the beginning only of its great natural
resources have been revealed; Silverton is the metropolis and
county seat, and is steadily growing in size and importance. The
lodes of this section are usually of great size, and are already numbered by thousands. Both high and low grade ores are found, according to character of veins. Many mines are worked, and a
number of great tunnel enterprises are going forward, such as the
Bonanza, Mineral Point, I. X. L., Susquehanna, and others. Greene
& Co. have the oldest smelting works in this part of the State; they
have been worked steadily every summer and fall. There are several
other reduction and one or two sets of concentrating works in
operation in the district. Ore and bullion yield of 1878 over $250,000.

This county is the point where several massive ranges of
mountains unite with the main one. Here a half dozen streams
have their sources, and here are such famous mineral districts as
Animas, and Eureka. Among the leading lodes are the North Star,
Terrible, Mountaineer, Philadelphia, and Pride of the West. Among
the enterprises going forward on Galena Mountain is the Roedel
Tunnel, owned by the Midland Mining Company. This is designed
to intersect at great depth the Begole, Roedel, and other lodes.

Poughkeepsie Gulch is a famous mining locality. It contains 250
lodes on which assessment work is done annually, and a large
number of lodes are worked steadily—five or ten paying handsomely. Here are the rich and productive Alaska, the Bonanza,
Alabama, Acapulco, Red Roger, and Saxon; also the Napoleon,

St. Joseph, Poughkeepsie, Gipsy King, Kentucky Giant, Bonanza. The Bonanza tunnel is in this locality.

The Aspen on Hazelton Mountain has produced more silver than any other mine in the San Juan country. It had been worked pretty steadily for four years to 1878; up to that time its yield was $165,-000. Its vein of ore has an average width of from 10 to 12 inches, and much of the ore returns 175 ounces, or nearly $200 a ton; the lode is regular and uniform, and can be depended on for a steady yield; it is owned by Reese, Mulholland, and five others, and is said to have been very profitable. Beside cross-cuts and tunnels there are hundreds of feet of levels and of stopes. The Victor is another great mine on this famous Hazelton Mountain. It has produced and paid handsomely. The Mammoth is also a prominent vein.

The Prospector lode is nearly on a line with and approaches the Aspen at one end, and has a similar vein. In the same locality the Susquehanna lode comes in at an acute angle. Up to the time when work closed on the latter, late in 1876, it had yielded $60,000. The Susquehanna vein averages from 8 to 10 inches of ore, and yielded $40,000 prior to 1879. George Ingersol & Co. are driving the Susquehanna tunnel to intersect the lodes of Hazelton Mountain. It is already nearly a quarter of a mile long, and its head is 1,500 feet below the surface.

Between the Animas River and Cunningham Gulch, and near the junction of those streams, silver-ribbed King Solomon Mountain rears its lofty summit. Of the numerous veins traceable for long distances on its face the North Star is apparently the mother lode. It will average forty feet wide, and this enormous mass of crevice-matter is composed of nearly vertical streaks of decomposed ferruginous quartz in contact with great seams and streaks of argentiferous mineral. It can be seen for a distance of two miles and has been traced for three miles. Some of the veins or seams of ore have a width in places of three feet of argentiferous galena, gray copper, and yellow sulphide of copper. The ore smelts readily, and yields from 40 to 500 ounces of silver per ton and a uniform per cent. of from 60 to 62 of lead. The direction is northeast and southwest and the dip 85 to 90 degrees northwest.

Not far away, and on the westerly side of the mountain, is the Royal Tiger lode, with about the same dip, cropping out for the whole length of the surface ground, and yielding similar ores. The

North Star extends 750 feet each way from the summit of the mountain, while its neighbor is further down the side. The ground of each is 1,500 feet long by 300 wide.

These mines belong to the North Star Mining and Smelting Company of New York, of which McPherson Le Moyne is president; John N. Goodwin, vice-president; and Lewis Crooke, secretary and treasurer, and those gentlemen and John J. Crooke, F. Farrell, E. J. Granger, and N. A. Boynton, trustees. Beside the lode property the corporation owns a part of a town site, and a mill site, on which sampling works, with crusher, rolls and sizing machinery, are to be erected. The ores will be delivered there from the mine by means of a tramway, and will be crushed, sized, and sampled ready for reduction.

The North Star has been worked in the openings 40 feet wide without finding walls. Over 325 tons of ore had been taken out up to the close of last season. Shafts, tunnels, and adits are being driven. The following shipments to the Crooke Smelting Works at Lake City, last September, show the character of ore produced and the number of ounces of silver per ton: 3,147 pounds of ore, 238 ounces per ton; 17,528 pounds, 136 ounces silver; 1,113 pounds, 436 ounces; 12,437 pounds, 314 ounces; 12 678 pounds, 176 ounces; 6,677 pounds, 291 ounces; 1,887 pounds, 298 ounces; 7,218 pounds of ore, 126 ounces. Smelting works will be erected when the Denver & Rio Grande railway extension reaches Silverton, for which money has been raised. The line of this road comes within two miles of the mines. They are between and but a few miles from Silverton and Howardsville, and from 12,000 to 13,000 feet above sea level.

The Graham Silver Mining Company, operating at and near Animas Forks, own fifteen mines. Among them the E Pluribus Unum has a twenty-inch pay vein. The company has expended $32,000 so far.

The Alaska is one of the great mines of this section. At depths of forty-five and fifty feet in the shaft it is reported that nearly six feet of ore were found—three feet of gray copper on the west wall and nearly two feet of like material on the other in an equal amount of quartz intervening. It is reported that twenty-five tons of ore, taken out and on the dump at one time, averaged $800 a ton, or $20,000 altogether. Now that the lode is beginning to be pretty well developed an immense product may be looked for.

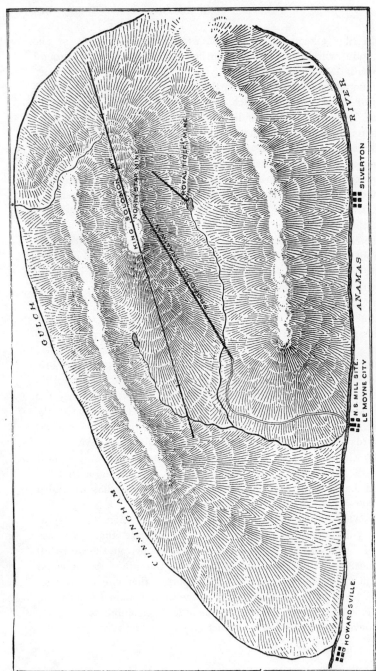

MAP OF THE NORTH STAR MINE AND KING SOLOMON MOUNTAIN.

The Alaska, Adelphi, Acapulco, Victory, Red Rover, and Saxon are all valuable true fissure veins near the headwaters of the

SILVER VEINS IN THE SAN JUAN MOUNTAINS.

Uncompahgre. Negotiations were pending for the sale of some of these lodes in Ohio, last spring, but the negotiators were afraid that the mines were not good enough, and so the sale dragged until Lieutenant-Governor Tabor, of Colorado, came along, stopped in Cleveland, and bought up the properties for $125,000 for himself and August Rische. Four men are said to have netted $20,000 from working in the Adelphi last winter. It shows two or three feet of gray copper in places, and some ore mills from $500 to $1,000.

The Mountain Queen is a galena vein of great size, but of rather low average grade—not so low, however, but that the mine is very profitable. The body of ore was five feet wide and under, yielding from thirty-five to seventy-five ounces of silver, and about sixty-five per cent. lead. Last year F. Beaudry operated the mine, working from thirty to forty men. He sold 1,100 tons, and 400 remained on hand at the close of the season. The assay value of the product must have exceeded $100,000. The workings then comprised a shaft 104 feet deep and a few short drifts. The five feet of ore was found on the hanging wall. There is said to be much ore in sight, and the mine's capacity for production is very great. The Prince of Wales lode, near the Mountain Queen, has a vein two and a half feet wide. Ore smelted yielded $170 a ton. It is owned by the San Juan Bullion Company.

OURAY COUNTY.

Ouray is on the Pacific slope of the range, and comprises the northwestern portion of the San Juan region. Like its neighbors, it is almost entirely composed of rugged and almost perpendicular mountains and deeply cut ravines and river gorges, among which it is generally an impossibility to build roads. The inaccessibility of the section has retarded rapid growth, but reduction works having at last been established, future advancement will be much more rapid. A railway has been projected, and may be built within two years, from Leadville or the Arkansas River through Marshall Pass. Heretofore it has cost $25 a ton to pack the ore on burros from the mines to Silverton, or to a wagon road, and as much more to get it to Denver or Pueblo. The unusual value of the mineral is all that enabled the miners to dispose of their products under such disadvantages. Last year the mines of Ouray county yielded $69,500, of which $15,000 worth of ore was kept on hand. Ouray is the main town and county seat.

The Norfolk and Ouray reduction works are supplied with ore

by the Begole " Mineral Farm," owned by the same company. Concentrating works were added this season to handle the low grade material from the same locality. The Windham Company smelter, with 20 tons daily capacity, started up not long ago with a large supply of ore on hand. One or two other works have been built, but the above, if operated steadily, will turn out a quarter of a million or more per annum.

The Begole "Mineral Farm" is one of the wonders of this part of the State. This is near the town of Ouray, and at about 800 feet greater elevation. It comprises forty acres of ground, being four claims 1,500 feet long by 300 wide, and was at first supposed to be a horizontal deposit of silver-bearing ore, but subsequent developments prove it to contain four mineral channels or lodes, from ten to twenty feet wide. One of these lodes has a streak of bright fine galena with heavy spar—the former carrying over 100 ounces of silver, and 40 per cent. of lead, and another streak of thirty-ounce galena with much antimony. Another lode has a very rich gray copper vein in a gangue of quartzite, and often milling from $400 to $700 a ton. A third lode carries sulphurets, and in places chlorides. This property was discovered and located in 1875, by Augustus Begole, an old Arizona miner, and by John Eckles. They had worked it in the summer seasons up to the fall of 1878, when they sold for $75,000 to the Norfolk and Ouray Reduction Company, who had built works at Ouray. Before that the principal work done was by quarrying or stripping the veins at and near the surface, and by sinking one or two short shafts. The new owners, having works near by, save enormous transportation and mill charges. They are mining large amounts of ore, concentrating the low grades and reducing the high grades and concentrates.

The Grand View mine is near Ouray and is extensively opened. The ore milled so far contains from $100 to $150 in gold, and from $10 to $20 in silver. The Trout and Fisherman vein, extending on either side of Cañon Creek vein, is in quartzite and mica schist, at a point where the sandstone caps over the quartzite. The Mother Cline, Prince Albert, Royal George, and other veins, are owned by Governor Pitkin and Sherman. The Pride of the West, J. V. Dexter, Smuggler, and Union are large veins.

Mount Sneffels district has no superior among the silver sections of Southern Colorado, and is daily growing in importance as its

WINTER AMONG THE MINES OF THE SAN JUAN MOUNTAINS.

great mineral wealth is developed.   It is located at and near Ouray.
Here are the famous and productive Virginius, Yankee Boy, and
Wheel of Fortune.   Among other leading veins are the Terrible,
Security, Hidden Treasure, Silver Queen, Bank of San Juan, Monon-
gahela, York State and its extension the Genesee, the Millionaire
and United States Depository, both on one vein, the Mark Twain and
Grand Trunk on one vein, Norma, Crusader and Nonesuch.   Quinn
and Richardson hold government titles for the following :
Pocahontas, Imogene, Buckeye Girl, Highland Chief, Highland
Lassie, Seven Thirty, Potosi, Circassian, Caribou and Chief Deposit.
The latter has an eighteen inch vein, and has shipped ore that mills
from 300 to 500 ounces of silver per ton, and some of still higher
grade.   Hundreds of other lodes have been located and many of
them are worked.   Most Mount Sneffels veins carry gray copper
plentifully, and ruby silver and silver glance often appear, and there
is some galena.

The Yankee Boy lode contains about three feet of spar, and
attached are gangue and pockets of mineral carrying ruby silver.
The spar can be concentrated to salable ore.   In 1878, the lowest
mill run gave 235 ounces of silver per ton, and the highest, 1,700
ounces, the rich ore usually being from six to eight inches wide.
During that year 225 tons of ore were mined, packed out of the
country, over the mountains, on the backs of burros, and sold for
$56,000.   Last winter two levels, 200 and 225 feet long, respectively,
had been driven, with a winze connecting.   A tunnel 155 feet long
cuts the lode 265 feet deep, from which new levels are being driven.
This mine was recently operated by F. Beaudry.   The Black
Diamond is another paying property.

The Virginius is considered as good a mine as there is in this
region, and has been very profitable.   Its yield is said to have been
from thirty to fifty thousand dollars per annum since work began two
or three years ago, with prospect of many times these figures when
properly developed.   From twelve to fifteen men have usually been
at work.   There are from 6 to 12 inches of either gray copper or
heavy galena zinc ores worth $300.

San Miguel (Me-géel) mining district occupies the mountains and
streams of a tract of country forty miles broad by some seventy miles
long, and located west of Ouray and Mount Sneffels.   Along the San
Miguel River and its forks and tributaries are extensive gravel de-

posits, rich in gold. These, after much preparatory work in the way of flumes, hydraulics, etc., are being worked on a large scale by many companies and firms. The adjoining mountains are seamed with numberless gold and silver veins, some newly discovered and others already productive.

The season of 1879 sees increased activity among the lode mines of the upper San Miguel, Turkey Creek, and Howard's Fork, and many are shipping rich ore to Ouray and Pueblo for treatment. The Pandora, a gold mine, is extensively worked by its owners, Lothian and Medley, who have opened a fine body of ore, worth $100 or more a ton, beside immense masses of low grade material. The Cimarron is another promising mine, showing specimens with wire gold on one side and brittle and wire silver on the other. Rich gold lodes have lately been found on Turkey Creek, between Howard's Fork and the upper San Miguel.

Howard's Fork mining district bids fair to rival Mount Sneffels in number and value of its mineral veins. It is further west than the latter. and more recently prospected. New discoveries are occurring frequently. Among exceedingly valuable mines are the Osceola, Alta, and Gold Chief.

Extensive preparations have been and are being made to open up the immense placer deposits of the San Miguel River. Experts from the gravel deposits of California, after examining these, report very highly upon them. Several large companies that secured ground last year are now at work with hydraulics. Beginning at the upper part of the stream, the Keystone Hydraulic Company, near the south fork of the river, has been putting in all the latest appliances for saving gold and for moving gravel on a grand scale. Its gravel bank has 150 feet of face—flume capacity, 3,000 inches—1,000 feet of pipe, and 300 feet of pressure, with a No. 5 "Giant" hydraulic —move 2,000 cubic yards per day. D. T. Thompson is president of the company. The Red Cross Company, about ten miles below, has interested eastern capitalists and is preparing to work extensively.

The Wheeler and Kimball property, adjoining the Red Cross, has very rich and extensive claims that are worked to their full capacity. This comprises 400 acres in which the pay gravel lays in bars ; average yield, fifty cents to the cubic yard ; width of bottom, from 350 to 2,500 feet. Wheeler and Kimball began to construct a

CAÑON OF THE UNCOMPAHGRE RIVER.

five-mile ditch to secure a water supply in the fall of 1877, and brought the water on the bar last fall, but not in time to wash much gravel. They are now running in full blast with hydraulics—600 feet of iron pipe under pressure of 200 feet fall. Water is brought from the head of Alder Creek, comes in 1,000 feet above the mines and runs down the solid sandstone on to the pay ground and gravel. In washing away the ground, marble boulders of variegated colors and iron and granite are uncovered.

The Keithly Company have built a great flume high up around the perpendicular walls of the mountains for a distance of over three miles, which carries 1,200 inches of water—use No. 5 Giant hydraulic, 200 feet pressure; have all the best appliances for work and several million yards of gravel to handle. This claim is ably managed by a Mr. Manly, an experienced placer miner from Dutch Flat, California. The Ware bar, owned by St. Louis men, will soon be in shape for work if not so already.

The "Montana Bar," owned by Greene & Co., of Keokuk, Iowa, a very large and rich deposit of gravel, is worked on a small scale by sending the gravel down a chute to the river where the sluices are located. Worked under such disadvantages it more than pays wages. Immediately below is a series of bars, extending several miles down the river, containing many millions of yards of pay gravel. Chief among them is the "Kansas City" claim, with several million yards of gravel, estimated from tests made to average $1 per yard. Such a property will not long remain without ditches and hydraulics. The product of San Miguel is usually what is known as "coarse gold," worth $17.50 per ounce, and the gravel deposits are all high bars, from 50 to 150 feet above the river.

Some idea of the value and extent of these grand deposits of an ancient river bed, from 50 to 150 feet above the present bed of the river, can be obtained from the fact that it costs from $25,000 to $100,000 to bring water upon them and to construct ditches and flumes. These immense deposits, like those of California, have been attracting the attention of capitalists, and it is safe to say that in a few years the yield of gold dust will be enormous.

Prospectors are making discoveries still further west in the Sierra La Sal and Rio Dolores sections. Succeeding tabulated statements will give a general but not accurate idea of some leading Ouray county lodes.

OURAY COUNTY—SOME OF THE LEADING LODES.

NAME OF LODE.	LOCATION.	WIDTH.	DEVELOPMENT.	CHARACTER.	YIELD, PER TON.	OWNERS.
Begole, Mineral Farm	Cañon Creek	....	2 shafts, 20 ft. each; 11 adits, 12 ft. each	Galena and gray copper	160 oz. silver	Norfolk & Ouray Mining Company.
Belle of the West	Yellow Mountain, Iron Springs District	Lode, 8 ft., vein, 3 ft.	Adit, shafts and drift	Galena and gray copper	150 oz. silver	J. L. Haines. M.C.McCormick.
Big Casino	Gold Run, Upper San Miguel District	Lode, 15 ft.	1 drift, 30 ft.	Gray copper and ruby silver	Rich in silver	W.A.Walker & Co.
Byron	Engineer Mountain, Uncompahgre District	Lode, 4 ft., vein, 10 in.	2 drifts, 40 ft. each	Galena	260 oz. silver	Chas. Thurmond.
Chief Deposit and Caribou	Buckeye Mount'n	Lode, 8 to 16 ft., vein, 3 to 8 ft.	2 tunnels, 7 open cuts	Galena, gray copper, sulphurets of iron and copper	200 to 1,500 oz. silver	F.G. & J.H.King. L. C. Kilham. D. D. Mallory.
Circassian	Old Stony Mountain	Lode, 12 ft., vein, 4 ft.	Tunnel	Galena, gray copper, brittle silver, iron and copperpyrites	Large in silver	F.G. & J.H.King. L. C. Kilham. D. D. Mallory.
Denver	Abraham Mountain, Uncompahgre District	Lode, 6 ft., vein, 1 ft.	Drift, 130 ft.	Gray copper, galena	100 oz. silver	M. W. Dresser. G. H. Smith.
Eclipse	Engineer Mountain, Uncompahgre District	Lode, 30 in., vein, 12 in.	Tunnel, 20 ft.	Galena, gray copper	500 oz. silver	M. P. Nutting. E. Brolaskie.
Fidelity	Mount Sneffels, Sneffels District	Lode, 30 in., vein, 6 in.	Tunnel, 30 ft.	Gray copper and galena	400 oz. silver	John Ray & Co.

OURAY COUNTY—SOME OF THE LEADING LODES.

Name of Lode.	Location.	Width.	Development.	Character.	Yield, Per Ton.	Owners.
Free Gold	Silver Mountain, Upper San Miguel District	Lode, 3 ft., vein, 5 in.	Shaft, 12 ft.; drift, 100 ft.	Free gold	22 oz. gold	W. B. Fonda. F. Gardner & Co.
Geneva	Silver Mountain, Iron Springs District	Lode, 4 ft., vein, 8 in.	Adit, 20 ft.; level, 50 ft.	Galena	100 oz. silver	Staatsburg Silver Mining Comp'y.
Gold Queen	Silver Mountain, Upper San Miguel District	Lode, 6 ft., vein, 6 in.	Shaft, 40 ft.; tunnel, 40 ft.; level, 150 ft.	Free gold	$1,200	B. B. Haddox. J. B. Laffoon. Munn Bros.
Grub Stake	Uncompahgre River	Lode, 5 ft., vein, 20 in.	2 drifts, 42 ft.	Copper, pyrites and galena	100 oz	M. W. Dresser. G. H. Smith.
Hidden Treasure	Imogene Basin, Mount Sneffels District	Lode, 5 ft., vein, 4 ft.	Drift, 125 ft.	Gray copper and galena	172 oz	Geo. A. Brantley. Robert W. Bell.
Highland Chief	Silver Creek, Mt. Sneffels District	Lode, 4 ft., vein, 6 to 18 in	Tunnel, 50 ft.	Gray copper and galena	40 to 800 oz	D. P. Quinn. A. W. Richardson.
Imogene	Buckeye Mountain, Mount Sneffels District	Lode, 4 ft., vein, 1 to 4 in	Tunnel, 108 ft.	Galena and gray copper, iron and copper pyrites	56 to 1,370 oz	F. G. & J. H. King. L. C. Kilham. D. D. Mallory.
Kentucky Giant	Abraham Mountain, Uncompahgre District	Lode, 12 ft., vein, 4 ft.	Shaft, 70 ft.; adits, 12 and 18 ft.	Brittle silver, iron pyrites	65 oz. silver	G. Purcells. J. A. White. P. Cusick.
Mineral Farm	Cañon Creek, Uncompahgre District	Lode, 3 ft., vein, 16 in.	Drift, 30 ft.	Iron pyrites, gray copper and galena	300 oz. silver	Norfolk & Ouray Mining Comp'y.

OURAY COUNTY—SOME OF THE LEADING LODES.

NAME OF LODE.	LOCATION.	WIDTH.	DEVELOPMENT.	CHARACTER.	YIELD, PER TON.	OWNERS.
Montezuma	Howard fork of San Miguel	Lode, 5 ft., vein, 8 in.	Shaft and level	Gray copper and galena	135 oz. silver	M. Rich. Harry Beattie. A. Y. Davis.
Mountain Ram	Engineer Mountain, Uncompahgre District	Lode, 10 ft., vein, 5 ft. in places	Adit, 30 ft.	Galena and gray copper	80 oz. silver	Chas. Josephs & Co
Norma	Imogene Basin, Mount Sneffels District	Lode, 12 ft., vein, 3 ft.	Tunnel, 100 ft.	Gray copper	100 to 160 oz. silv'r	W. Weston & Co.
Osceola	Silver Mountain, Iron Springs District	Lode, 4 ft., vein, 10 in.	Shaft, 50 ft.	Free gold	Very high grade	W. S. Fink. Mrs. M. Roberts.
Powhattan	Silver Mountain, Iron Springs District	Lode, 5 ft., vein, 20 in.	Drift, 125 ft.	Free gold	High grade	W. S. Fink. Mrs. M. Roberts.
San Juan	Yellow Mountain, Iron Springs District	Lode, 4 ft., vein, 18 in.	Drift, 160 ft.	Gray copper	$245	Joseph Cuenin. C. J. Rouech.
Silver King	Uncompahgre Creek, Uncompahgre District	Lode, 20 ft., vein, 3 ft.	Drift, 16 ft.	Galena and iron pyrites	90 oz. silver	W. & G. Mitchell.
Staatsburg	Silver Mountain, Iron Springs District	Lode, 15 ft., vein, 15 in.	Well developed	Sulphurets and galena	150 oz. silver	Staatsburg Silver Mining Comp'y.
U. S. Depository	Sneffels District	Vein, 28 in.	Drift and adits	Silver	High grade	John C. Waring.
Virginius	Mount Sneffels	12 in. of ore	Well opened	Galena-copper	300 oz. silver	C. C. Alvord.
Yankee Boy	Mount Sneffels	Vein, 20 in.	1,000 ft. workings	Silver	200 to 400 oz	Morrison & Co.

LA PLATA COUNTY.

La Plata county is the extreme southwestern division of Colorado, bordering on New Mexico and Utah, and touching the corner of Arizona. This section is rich in coal, possesses silver veins, gold placers, and many fine fertile valleys; farming and stock-growing are especially successful. The county is settling up rapidly; a railway is expected from the East, in which case La Plata would be the smelting depot of San Juan county mines.

The stock and agricultural resources and advantages of La Plata county and of its valleys along the San Juan River and tributaries have already been referred to in part third of this volume. The coal measures are deserving of especial mention, on account of their quality and enormous size. The area of coal land is estimated at over 600 square miles, and is cut or intersected by the Pinos, Florida, Animas, La Plata, and Mancos rivers, which flow southward into the San Juan. The thickness of the vein is reported at from 10 to 50 and 60 feet between floor and roof. There are two distinct beds of coal, separated only by four feet of iron shale. In some places the two beds are said to aggregate from 88 to 98 feet in thickness. Those who have tested this coal, pronounce it of a semi-bituminous character and of a better coking quality than any in the West except the Trinidad beds. In this same county are lodes carrying gold, silver, lead, copper, zinc, iron pyrites, tellurium, platina, etc.

In this extreme southwestern corner of Colorado, and far over among the mountains of the Pacific slope, are ancient ruins of towns and cities, built by an extinct race of people. These ruins are found at intervals over an area of 6,000 square miles, and are generally the remnants of stone structures. W. H. Holmes, in the Hayden Government Survey Reports, classes them under three heads: (1) Lowland or agricultural settlements, largely composed of rubble and adobe combined; (2) Cave dwellings; and (3) Cliff houses or fortresses. Those of the first class are on the low and fertile river bottoms; those of the second, near the agricultural lands, but built in low bluff faces, while the cliff houses are built high up in the inaccessible walls of cliffs and excavated therein. The latter must have been used only as a place of refuge and defense in times of war and invasion. Many of them are of massive character, and were built by a race totally distinct and far superior to the nomadic savages that occupied the country in more recent times.]

CHAPTER XXVII.

COAL—THE LIGNITES OF COLORADO—FACTS AND STATISTICS CONCERN-
ING THE COAL MINES AND THEIR PRODUCT—THE COKING COALS OF
TRINIDAD AND EL MORO—BOULDER, JEFFERSON AND FREMONT.

Colorado is rich in coal of a superior lignite quality: in some
sections, like the Trinidad district, the veins take up with the character of bituminous coals to such an extent that they are often
referred to as such. The coal-bearing lands embrace many thousand
square miles of the State's area; the bulk of these so far located extend along the plains east of the foot hills, from Weld county in the
north to the New Mexican line in the south. The coal lands of the
mountains and parks are also very extensive, but have been worked
but little, owing to their remoteness from railways and markets. The
veins of La Plata county and White River are of superior quality
and very extensive, those of North and South Park are excellent lignites, and those of the Gunnison are considered anthracite of a very
inferior quality to that of Pennsylvania. The coal mines of Boulder, Weld, and Jefferson counties, on the plains and borders of the
foot hills of northern Colorado, are very extensive and embrace many
mines ; there are other deposits near Colorado Springs. Coal Creek
or Fremont county, Walsenburg, and the Trinidad section contain
the best qualities of Colorado coal that are now mined extensively ;
the Trinidad coals are the only ones so far thoroughly tested that
coke well, and they are said to be equal to those of Connellsville,
Pennsylvania. The coking interests of El Moro and Trinidad are
growing steadily in importance, and the product finds a continually
increasing demand from the smelters of Leadville, Pueblo, San Juan
and elsewhere. After the advent of the Pacific railways in Colorado,
and the building of local roads, there was a heavy demand for
Colorado coal, which caused the opening of many veins, horizontal
and vertical; the production soon exceeded 100,000 tons per annum,
and as the demands of Denver and other towns increased, and the
coal began to be used extensively in Gilpin and Clear Creek mining

districts, the yield became much larger. In 1877 the product was about 160,000 tons, worth, probably, $600,000; in 1878, 200,630 tons were mined, worth some $800,000.

The tonnage of coal produced in Colorado for 1878 was as follows:

LOCALITY AND NAME OF MINE.	Tons of Coal Mined.	LOCALITY AND NAME OF MINE.	Tons of Coal Mined.
BOULDER COUNTY—		**JEFFERSON COUNTY—**	
Marshall............	13,965	Colorado Company..........	11,599
Welch......................	12,929	Pittsburg (Nichols).........	2,000
Star (Canfield).............	11,500	Rocky Mountain (E. Jones).	1,130
Boulder Valley.............	12,000	White Ash (Hall & Jones)..	2,500
Other Erie Mines, Dietz, etc.	18,000	Murphy.....................	800
Total.................	68,404	Total.................	17,229

	Tons
Total given above...	85,633
Weld and El Paso Counties.....	2,192
Huerfano County—Walsenburg	7,608
Fremont County—Coal Creek or Cañon.............................	73,137
Las Animas County—Trinidad, etc.................................	32,060
Total tonnage produced in 1878.............................	200,630

Two or three companies are engaged in manufacturing coke near Trinidad. The Trinidad Coal and Coke Company had increased its capacity to 36 ovens at the close of the year, and to 70 afterwards. In 1878 there were 6,042 tons of coke exported.

The most productive mine along the line of the Colorado Central Railway in northern Colorado is the Welch, which has been extensively opened within a year. Its product at last accounts, was 25 cars or 250 tons of coal daily. Some Colorado coal banks are vertical and others horizontal. They vary in thickness from six to fifteen feet. The Marshall is an immense vein of very good quality. The town of Erie is built among some of the leading coal banks, such as the Boulder Valley. The bed of the Coal creek mines near Cañon is about ten miles long by four wide. The product is unsurpassed if equaled for fuel purposes in the West. The mine contains over three miles of entry ways and drifts. Now that the D. & S. P. Railway has entered the South Park, the Lechner coal bank will have a ready market.

The Far Western Frontier

An Arno Press Collection

[Angel, Myron, editor]. **History of Nevada.** 1881.

Barnes, Demas. **From the Atlantic to the Pacific, Overland.** 1866.

Beadle, J[ohn] H[anson]. **The Undeveloped West; Or, Five Years in the Territories.** [1873].

Bidwell, John. **Echoes of the Past:** An Account of the First Emigrant Train to California. [1914].

Bowles, Samuel. **Our New West.** 1869.

Browne, J[ohn] Ross. **Adventures in the Apache Country.** 1871.

Browne, J[ohn] Ross. **Report of the Debates in the Convention of California, on the Formation of the State Constitution.** 1850.

Byers, W[illiam] N. and J[ohn] H. Kellom. **Hand Book to the Gold Fields of Nebraska and Kansas.** 1859.

Carvalho, S[olomon] N. **Incidents of Travel and Adventure in the Far West; with Col. Fremont's Last Expedition Across the Rocky Mountains.** 1857.

Clayton, William. **William Clayton's Journal.** 1921.

Cooke, P[hilip] St. G[eorge]. **Scenes and Adventures in the Army.** 1857.

Cornwallis, Kinahan. **The New El Dorado; Or, British Columbia.** 1858.

Davis, W[illiam] W. H. **El Gringo; Or, New Mexico and Her People.** 1857.

De Quille, Dan. (William Wright). **A History of the Comstock Silver Lode & Mines.** 1889.

Delano, A[lonzo]. **Life on the Plains and Among the Diggings;** Being Scenes and Adventures of an Overland Journey to California. 1854.

Ferguson, Charles D. **The Experiences of a Forty-niner in California.** (Originally published as *The Experiences of a Forty-niner During Thirty-four Years' Residence in California and Australia*). 1888.

Forbes, Alexander. **California:** A History of Upper and Lower California. 1839.

Fossett, Frank. **Colorado:** Its Gold and Silver Mines, Farms and Stock Ranges, and Health and Pleasure Resorts. 1879.

The Gold Mines of California: Two Guidebooks. 1973.

Gray, W[illiam] H[enry]. **A History of Oregon, 1792–1849.** 1870.

Green, Thomas J. **Journal of the Texian Expedition Against Mier.** 1845.

Henry, W[illiam] S[eaton]. **Campaign Sketches of the War with Mexico.** 1847.

[Hildreth, James]. **Dragoon Campaigns to the Rocky Mountains.** 1836.

Hines, Gustavus. **Oregon:** Its History, Condition and Prospects. 1851.

Holley, Mary Austin. **Texas:** Observations, Historical, Geographical and Descriptive. 1833.

Hollister, Ovando J[ames]. **The Mines of Colorado.** 1867.

Hughes, John T. **Doniphan's Expedition.** 1847.

Johnston, W[illiam] G. **Experiences of a Forty-niner.** 1892.

Jones, Anson. **Memoranda and Official Correspondence Relating to the Republic of Texas, Its History and Annexation.** 1859.

Kelly, William. **An Excursion to California Over the Prairie, Rocky Mountains, and Great Sierra Nevada.** 1851. 2 Volumes in 1.

Lee, D[aniel] and J[oseph] H. Frost. **Ten Years in Oregon.** 1844.

Macfie, Matthew. **Vancouver Island and British Columbia.** 1865.

Marsh, James B. **Four Years in the Rockies; Or, the Adventures of Isaac P. Rose.** 1884.

Mowry, Sylvester. **Arizona and Sonora:** The Geography, History, and Resources of the Silver Region of North America. 1864.

Mullan, John. **Miners and Travelers' Guide to Oregon, Washington, Idaho, Montana, Wyoming, and Colorado.** 1865.

Newell, C[hester]. **History of the Revolution in Texas.** 1838.

Parker, A[mos] A[ndrew]. **Trip to the West and Texas.** 1835.

Pattie, James O[hio]. **The Personal Narrative of James O. Pattie, of Kentucky.** 1831.

Rae, W[illiam] F[raser]. **Westward by Rail:** The New Route to the East. 1871.

Ryan, William Redmond. **Personal Adventures in Upper and Lower California, in 1848–9.** 1850/1851. 2 Volumes in 1.

Shaw, William. **Golden Dreams and Waking Realities:** Being the Adventures of a Gold-Seeker in California and the Pacific Islands. 1851.

Stuart, Granville. **Montana As It Is:** Being a General Description of its Resources. 1865.

Texas in 1840, Or the Emigrant's Guide to the New Republic. 1840.

Thornton, J. Quinn. **Oregon and California in 1848.** 1849. 2 Volumes in 1.

Upham, Samuel C. **Notes of a Voyage to California via Cape Horn, Together with Scenes in El Dorado, in the Years 1849–'50.** 1878.

Woods, Daniel B. **Sixteen Months at the Gold Diggings.** 1851.

Young, F[rank] G., editor. **The Correspondence and Journals of Captain Nathaniel J. Wyeth, 1831–6.** 1899.